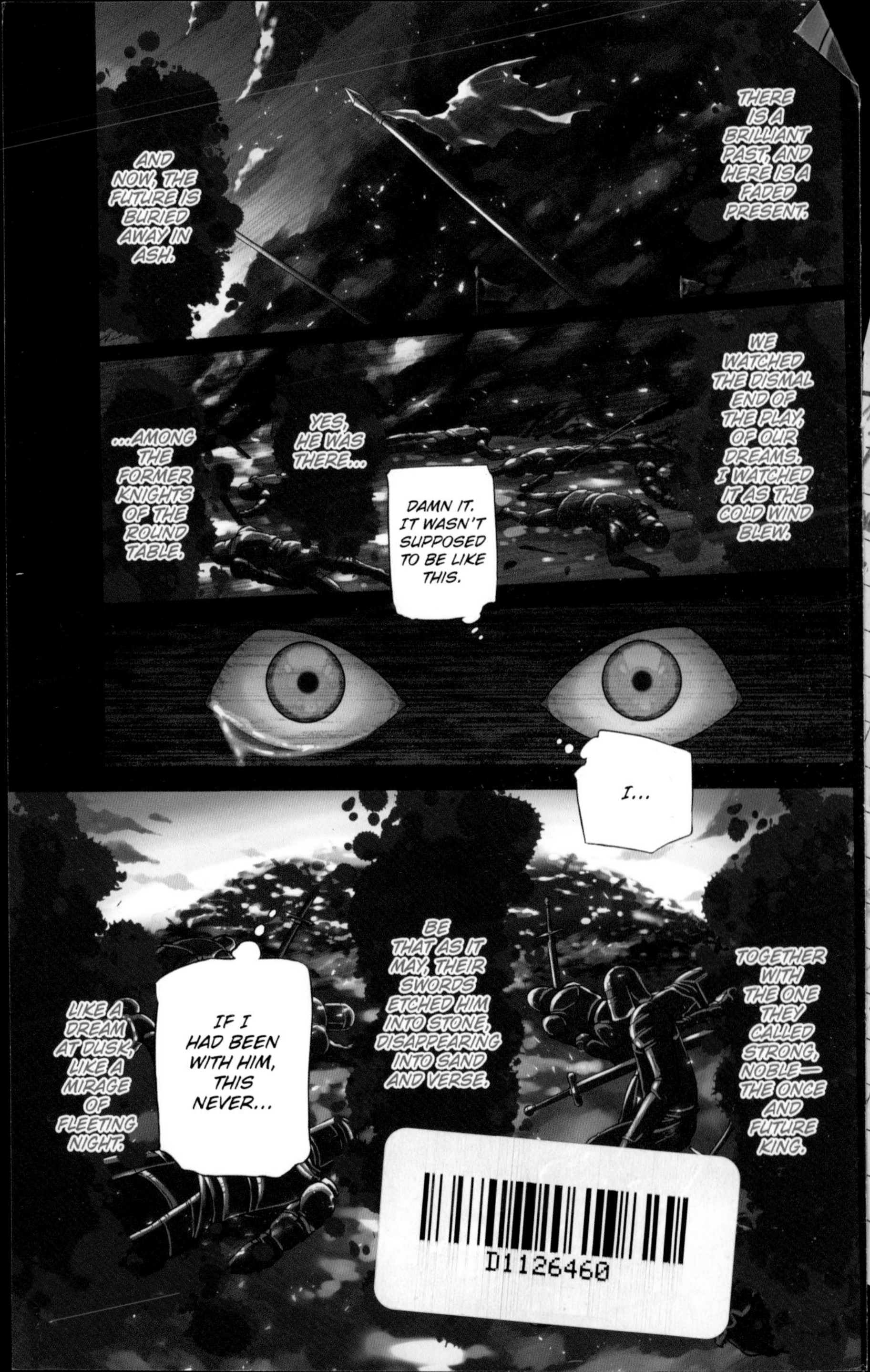
THERE IS A BRILLIANT PAST, AND HERE IS A FADED PRESENT.
AND NOW, THE FUTURE IS BURIED AWAY IN ASH.
WE WATCHED THE DISMAL END OF THE PLAY, OF OUR DREAMS. I WATCHED IT AS THE COLD WIND BLEW.
YES, HE WAS THERE...
...AMONG THE FORMER KNIGHTS OF THE ROUND TABLE.
DAMN IT. IT WASN'T SUPPOSED TO BE LIKE THIS.
I...
TOGETHER WITH THE ONE THEY CALLED STRONG, NOBLE—THE ONCE AND FUTURE KING.
BE THAT AS IT MAY, THEIR SWORDS ETCHED HIM INTO STONE, DISAPPEARING INTO SAND AND VERSE.
IF I HAD BEEN WITH HIM, THIS NEVER...
LIKE A DREAM AT DUSK, LIKE A MIRAGE OF FLEETING NIGHT.

1 CHAPTER ONE
Kings and Jacks and Jokers

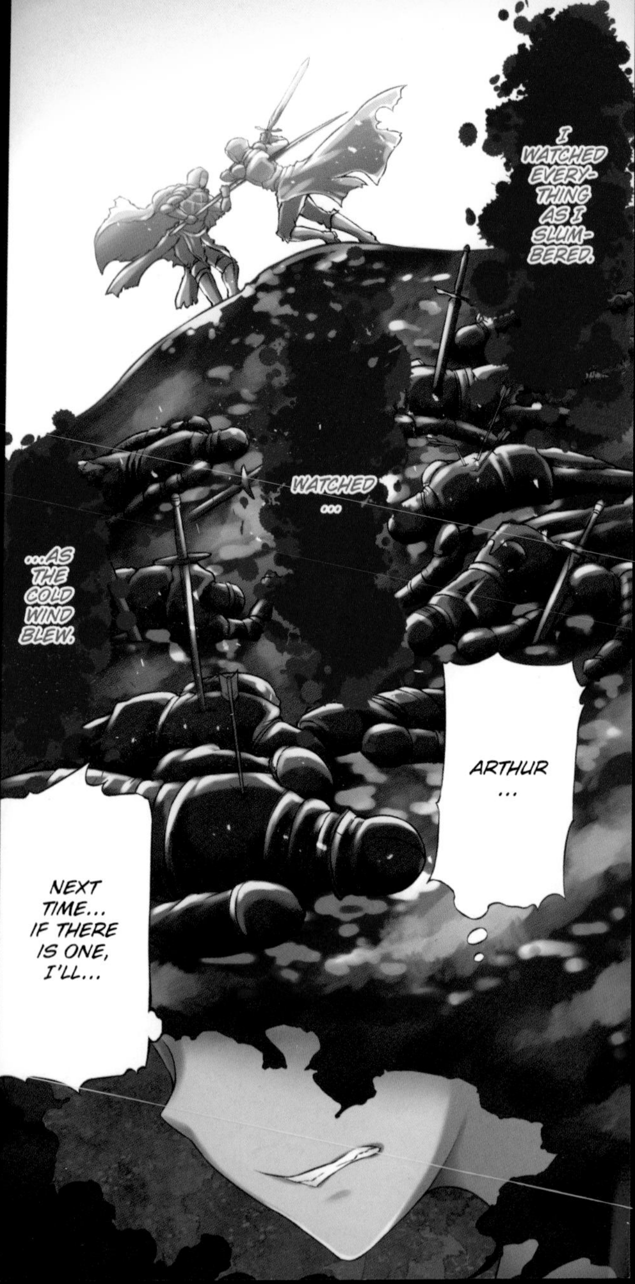
I WATCHED EVERY-THING AS I SLUM-BERED.
WATCHED ...
...AS THE COLD WIND BLEW.
ARTHUR ...
NEXT TIME... IF THERE IS ONE, I'LL...

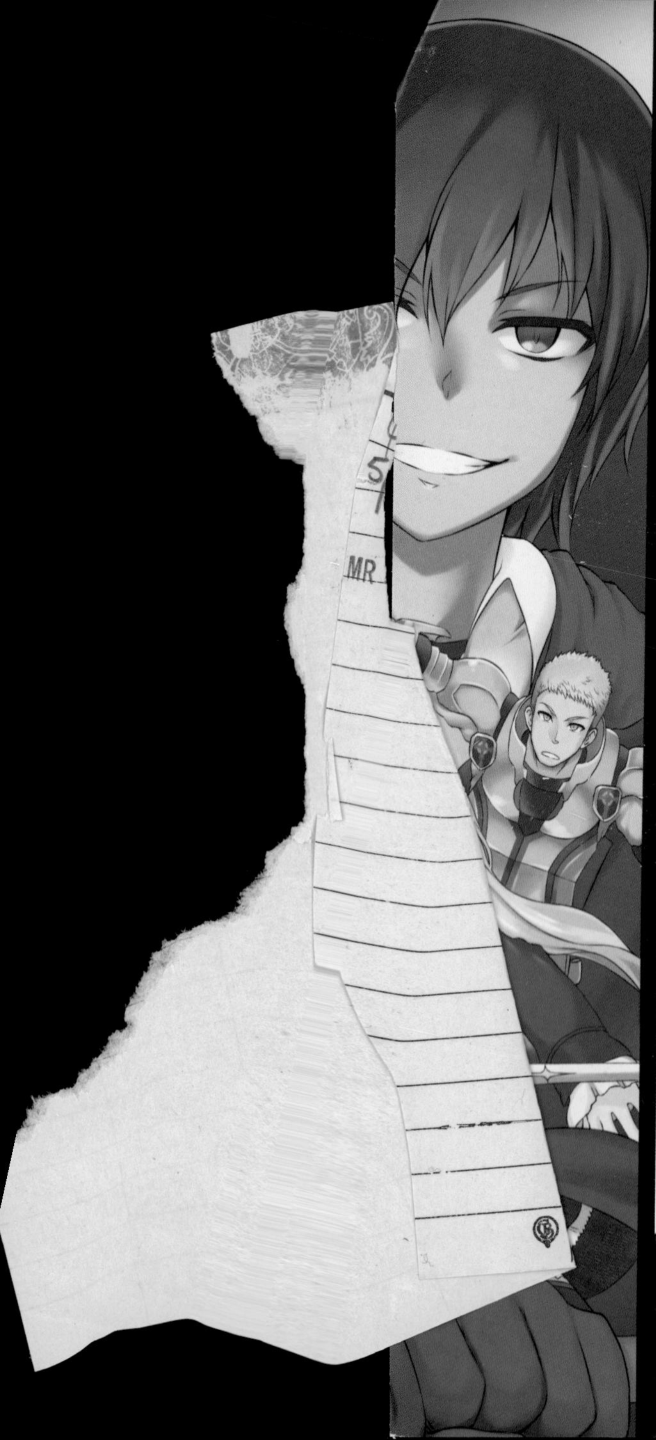

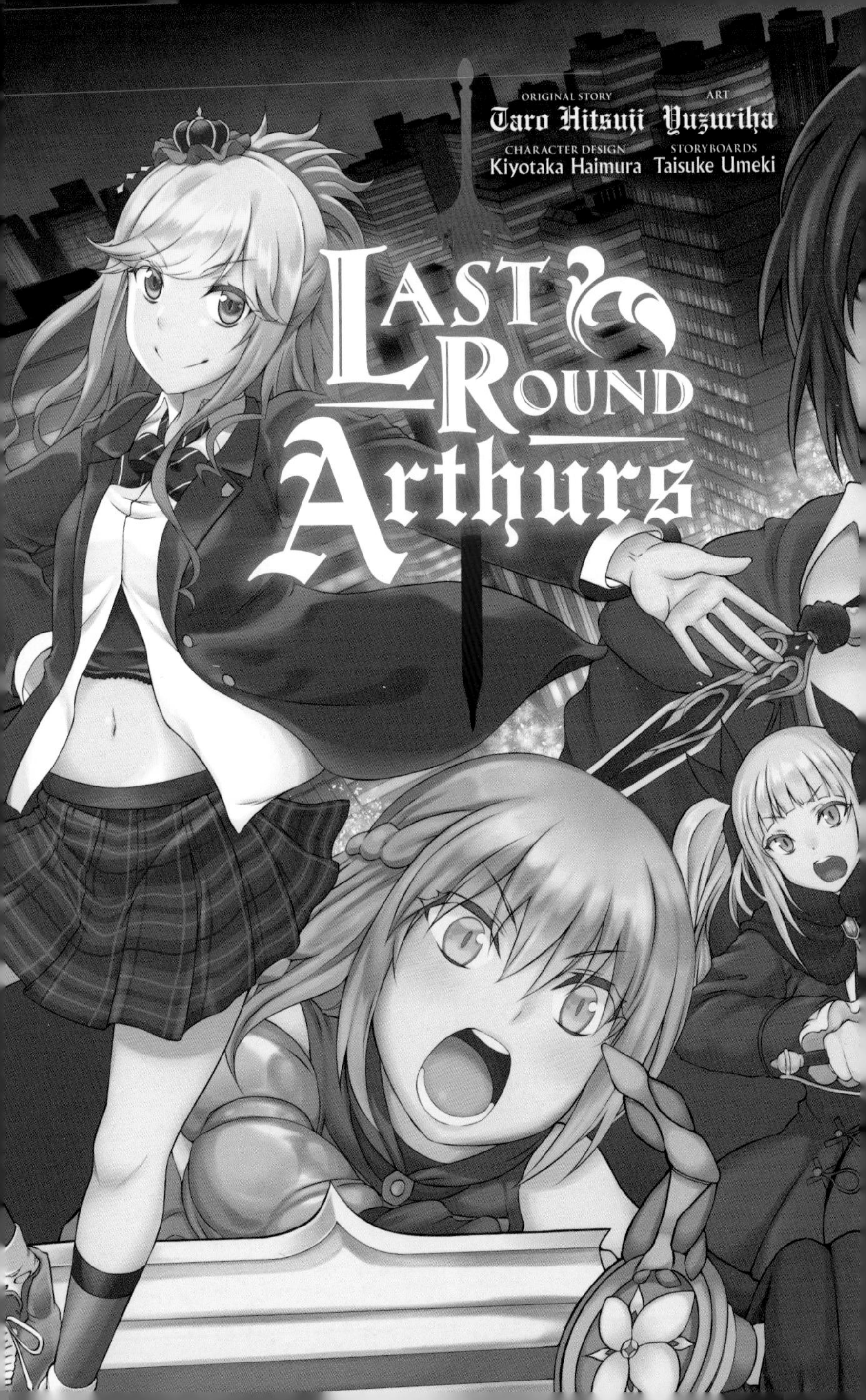
ORIGINAL STORY
Taro Hitsuji
ART
Yuzuriha
CHARACTER DESIGN
Kiyotaka Haimura
STORYBOARDS
Taisuke Umeki
LAST ROUND
Arthurs

— · —

CONTENTS

LAST ROUND ARTHURS

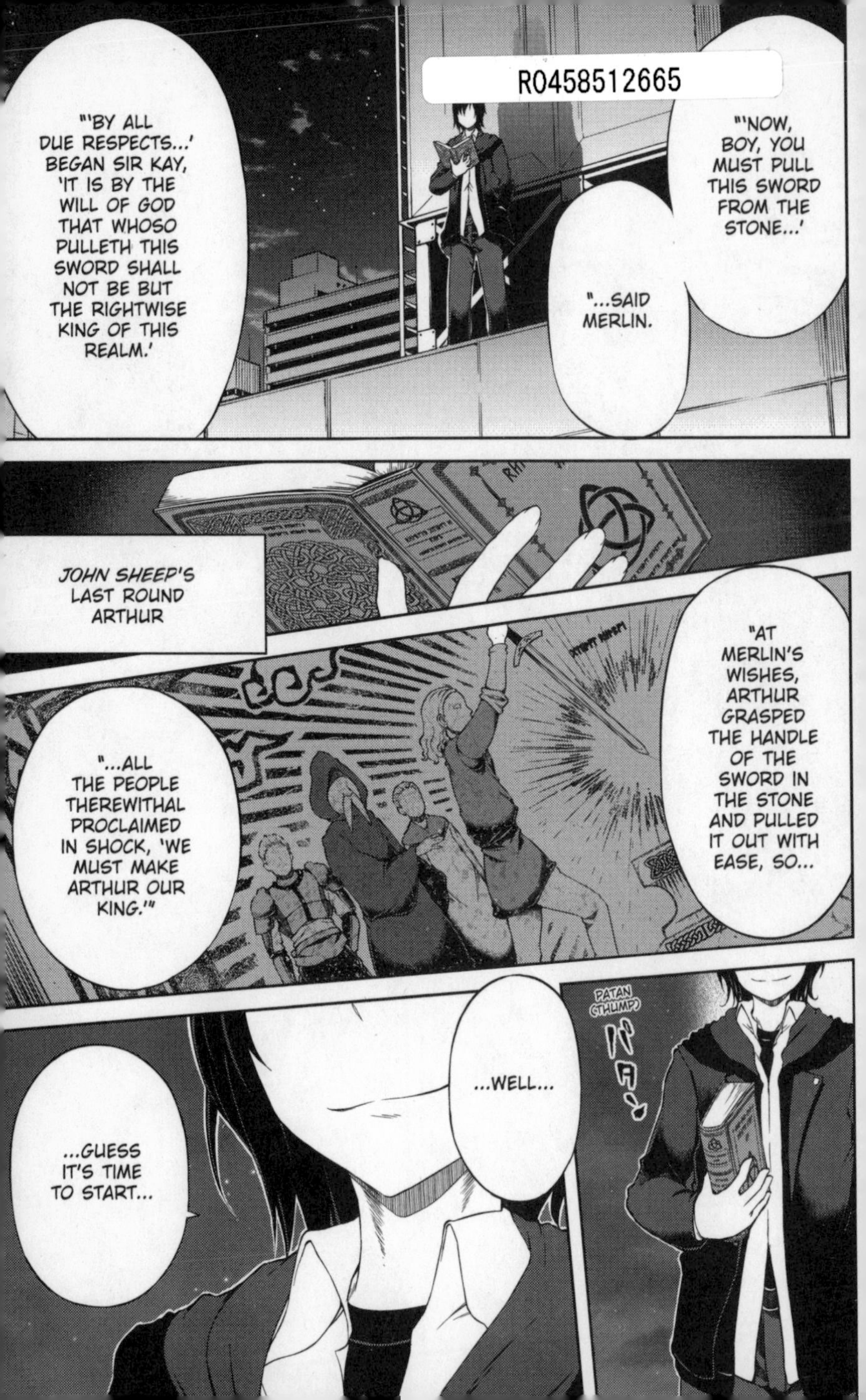
"'NOW, BOY, YOU MUST PULL THIS SWORD FROM THE STONE...'
"...SAID MERLIN.
"'BY ALL DUE RESPECTS...' BEGAN SIR KAY, 'IT IS BY THE WILL OF GOD THAT WHOSO PULLETH THIS SWORD SHALL NOT BE BUT THE RIGHTWISE KING OF THIS REALM.'
JOHN SHEEP'S LAST ROUND ARTHUR
"AT MERLIN'S WISHES, ARTHUR GRASPED THE HANDLE OF THE SWORD IN THE STONE AND PULLED IT OUT WITH EASE, SO...
"...ALL THE PEOPLE THEREWITHAL PROCLAIMED IN SHOCK, 'WE MUST MAKE ARTHUR OUR KING.'"
PATAN (THUMP)
...WELL...
...GUESS IT'S TIME TO START...

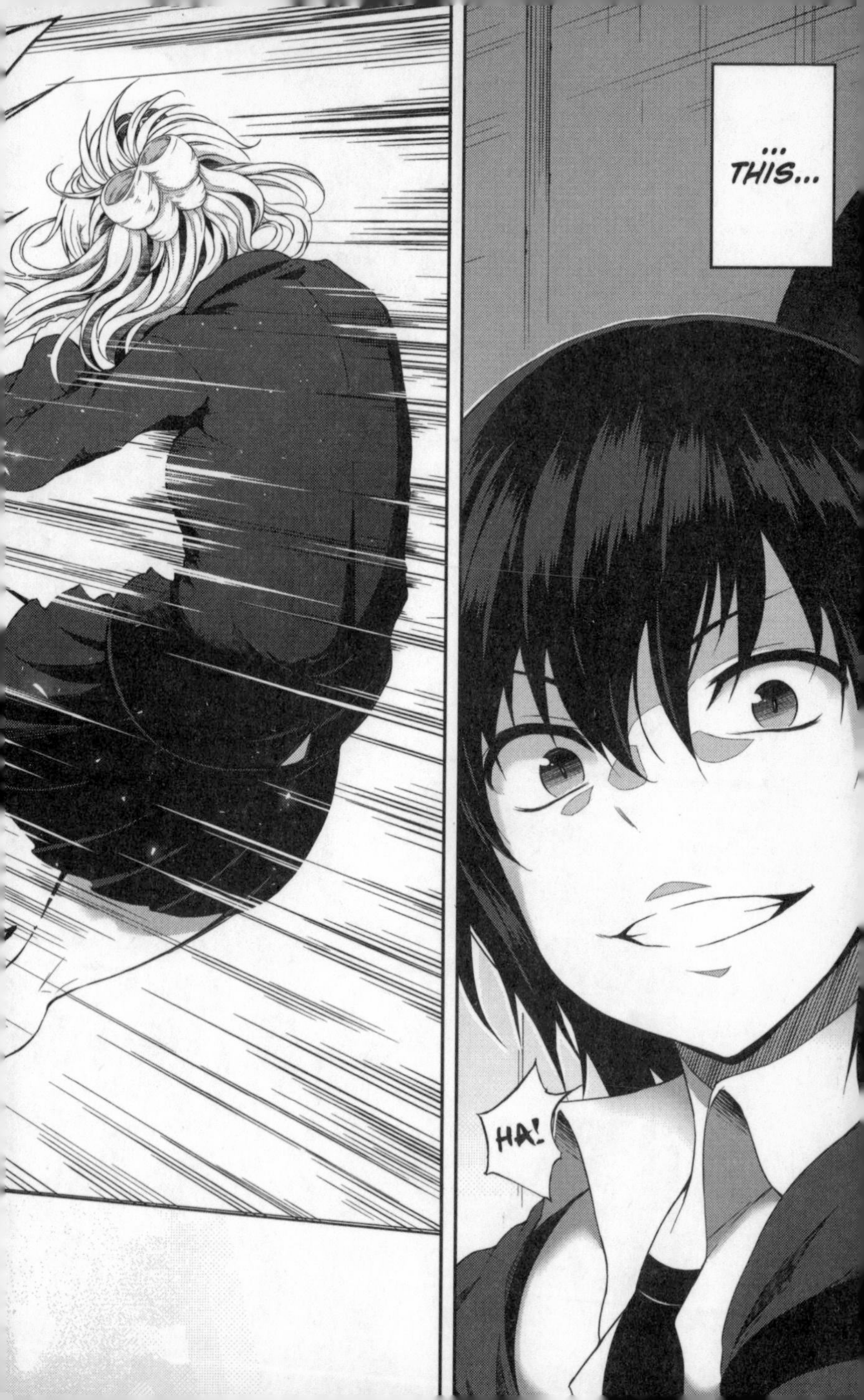
... THIS...
HA!

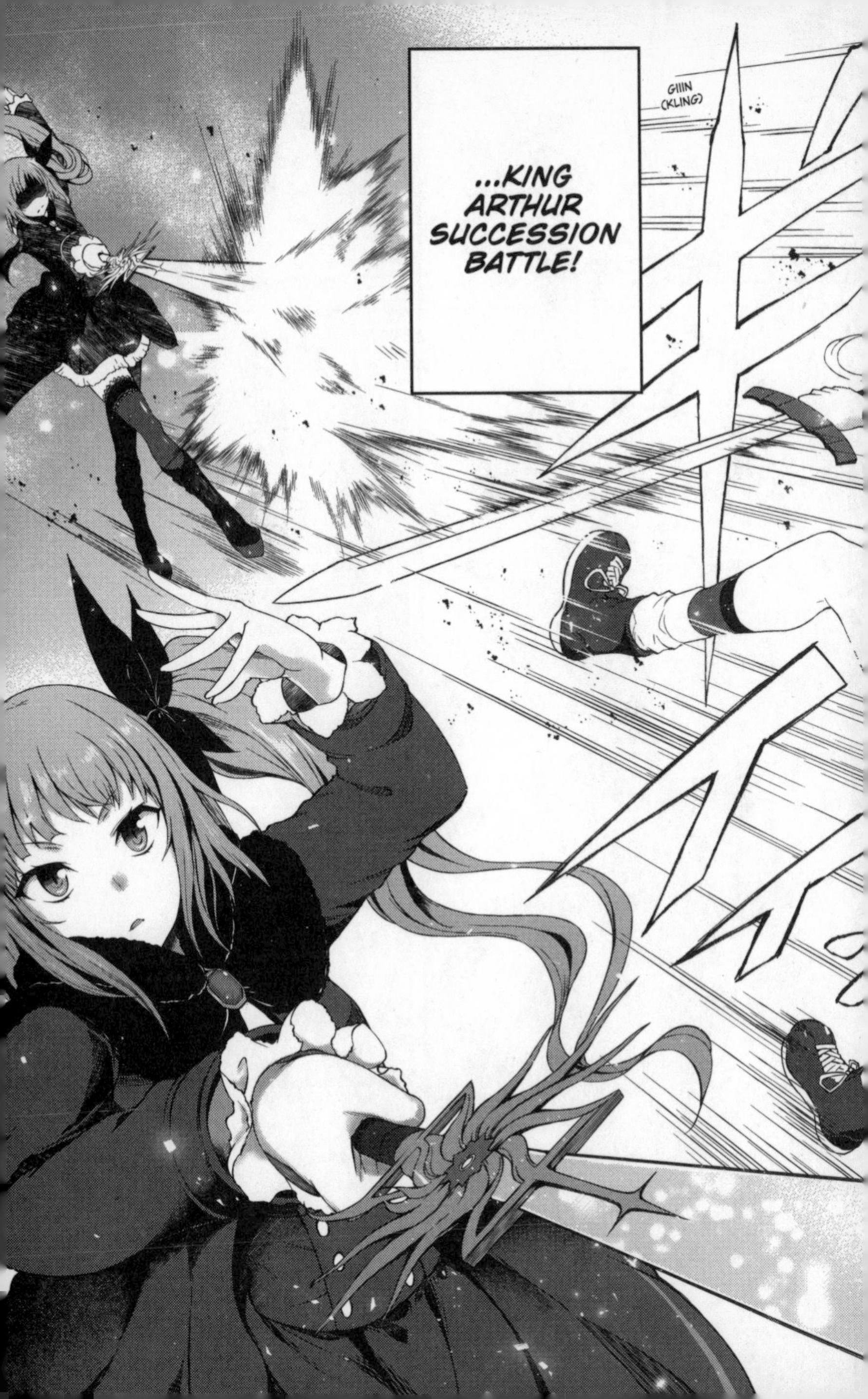
GIIIN
(KLING)
...KING
ARTHUR
SUCCESSION
BATTLE!

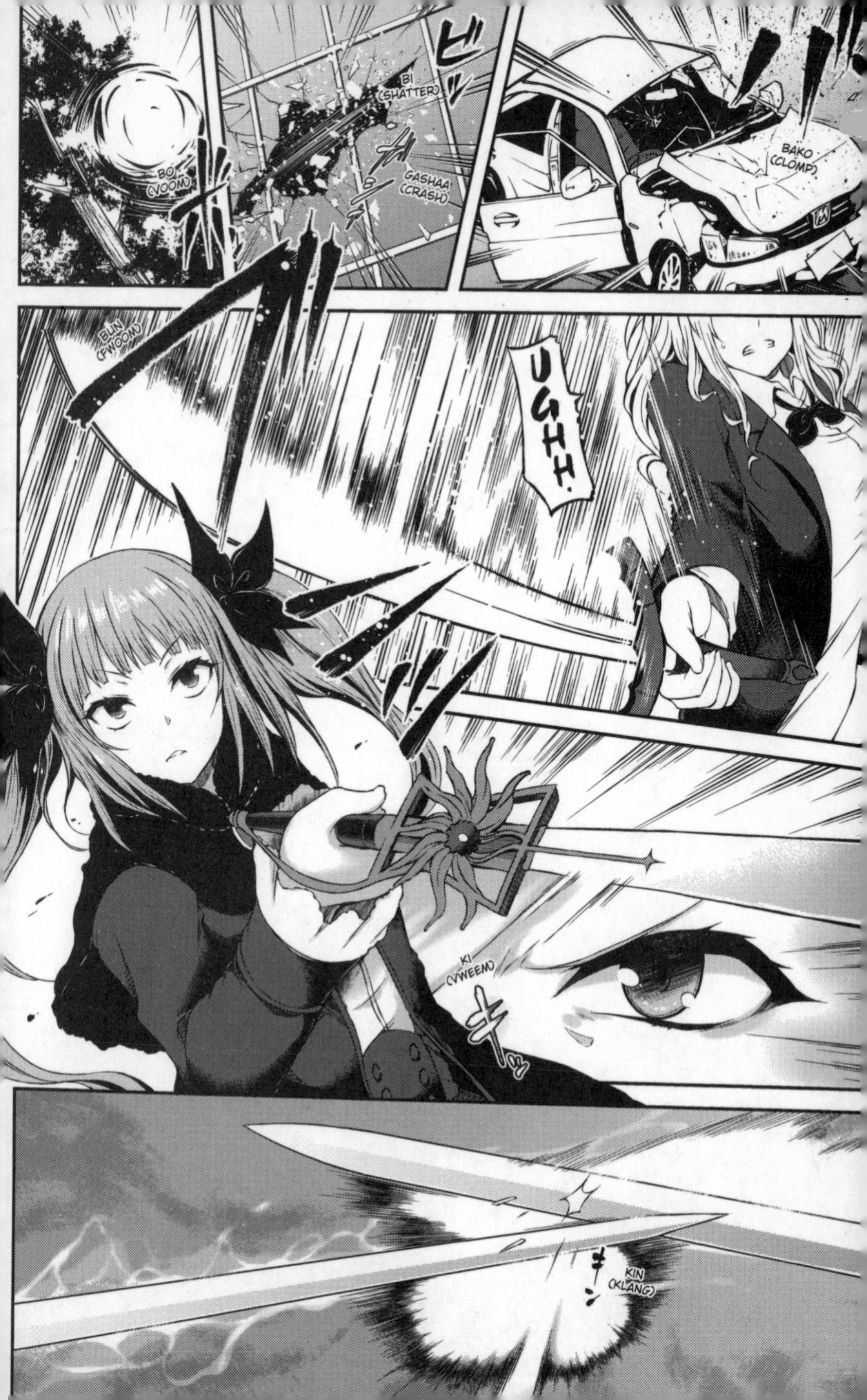
BAKO (CLOMP)
BI (SHATTER)
GASHAA! (CRASH)
BO (VOOM)
UGHH.
BUN (FWOOM)
KI (VWEEM)
KIN (KLANG)

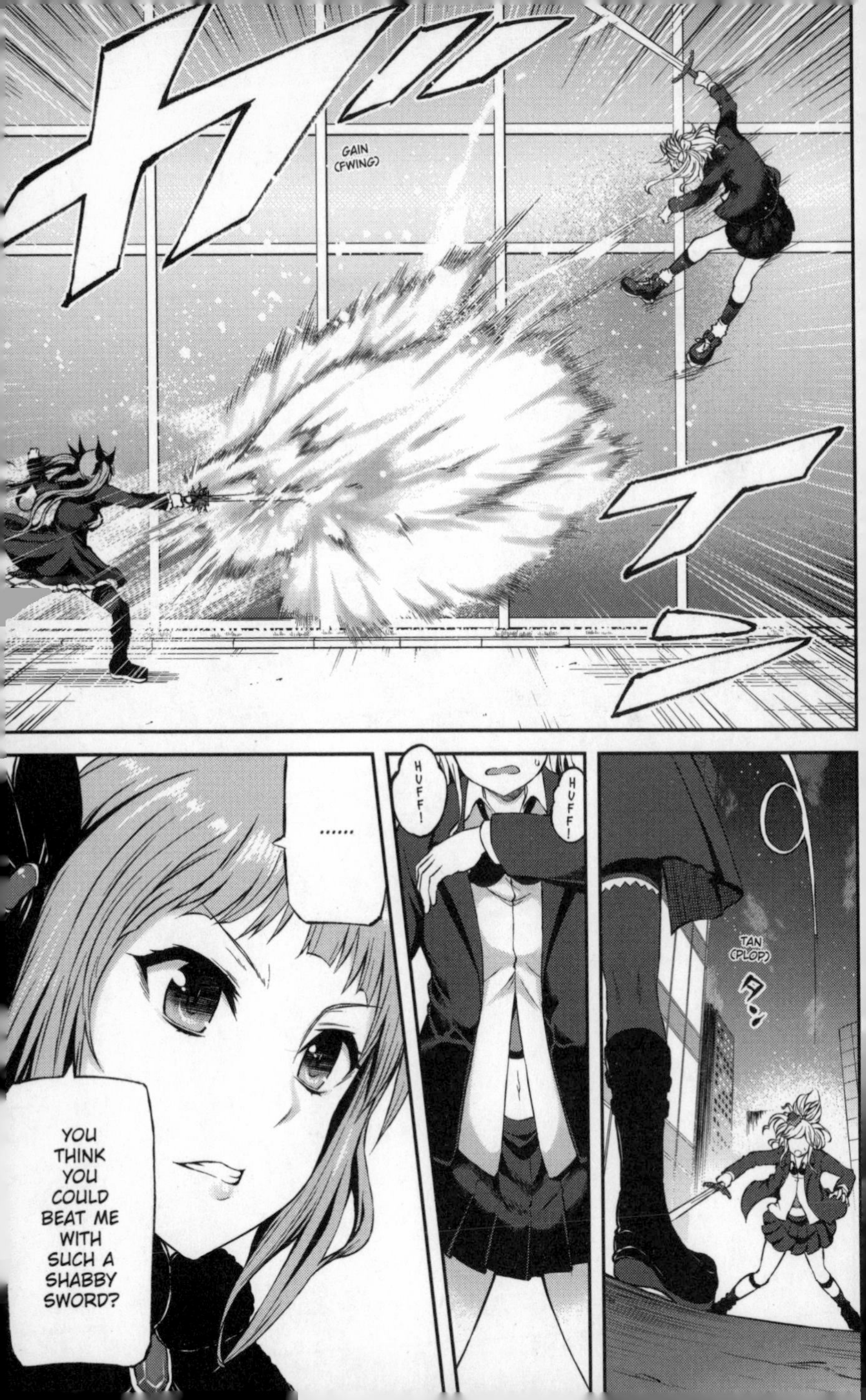
GAIN (FWING)
TAN (PLOP)
HUFF!
HUFF!
......
YOU THINK YOU COULD BEAT ME WITH SUCH A SHABBY SWORD?

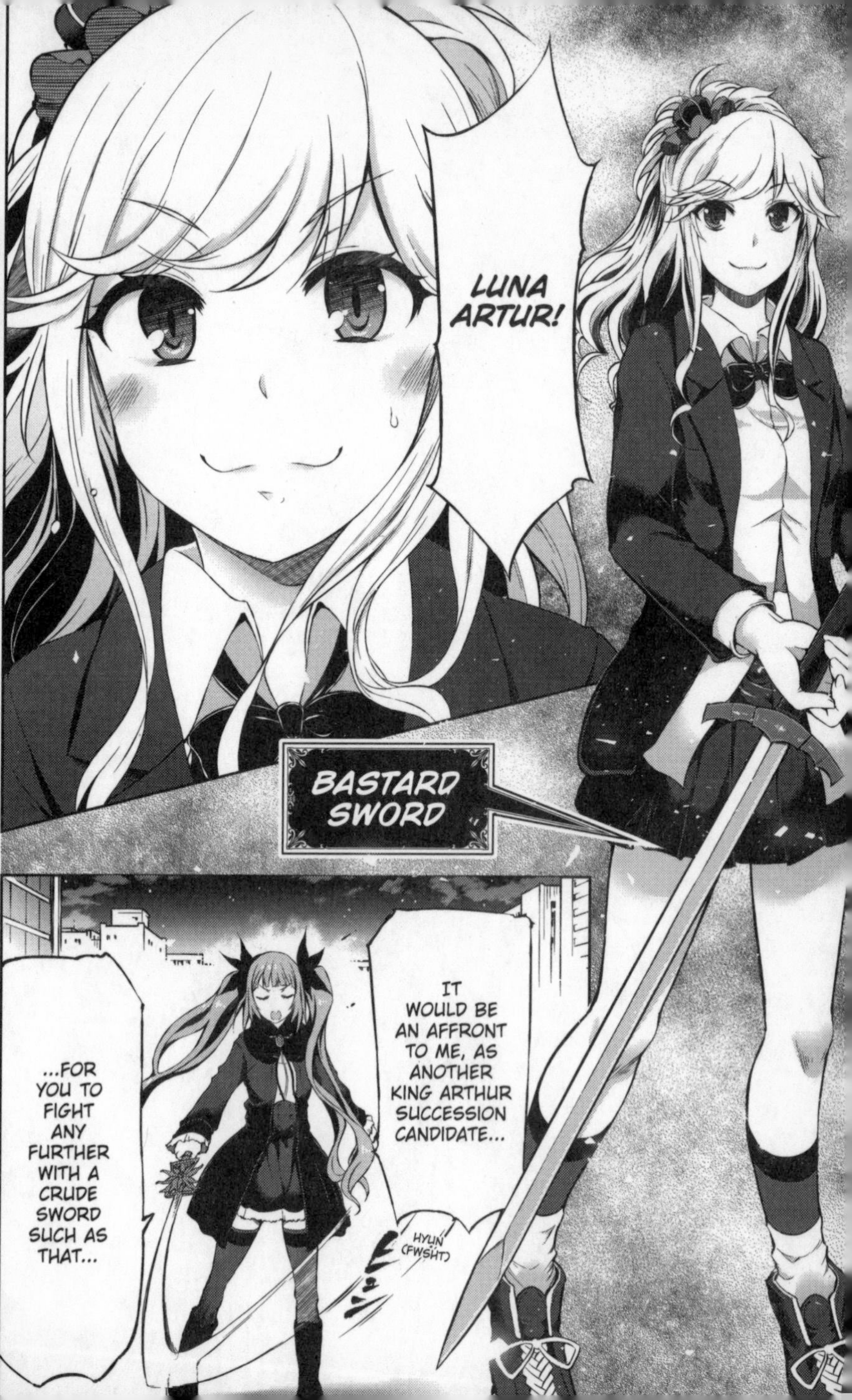
BASTARD SWORD
LUNA ARTUR!
IT WOULD BE AN AFFRONT TO ME, AS ANOTHER KING ARTHUR SUCCESSION CANDIDATE...
...FOR YOU TO FIGHT ANY FURTHER WITH A CRUDE SWORD SUCH AS THAT...
HYUN (FWSHT)

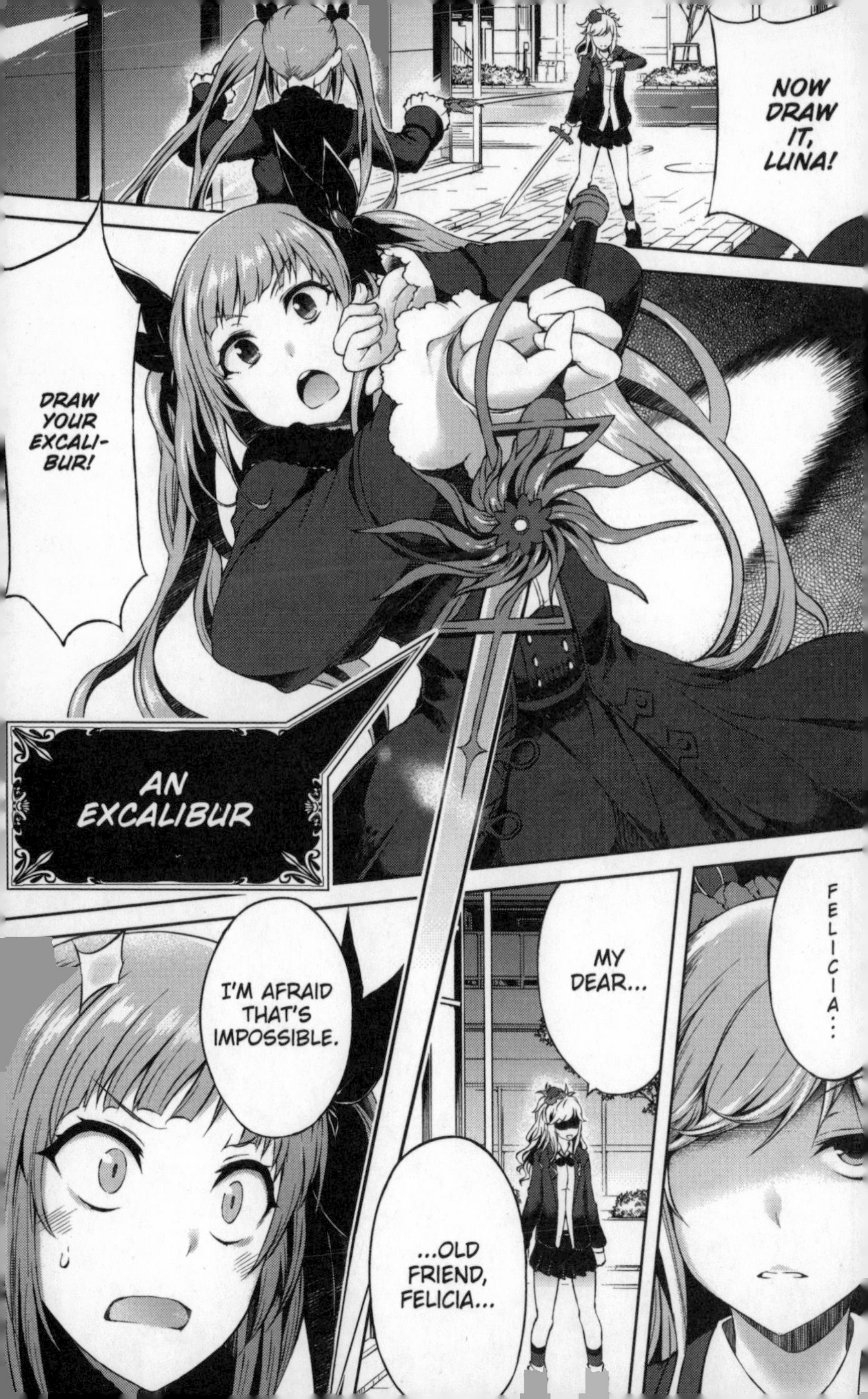
NOW DRAW IT, LUNA!
DRAW YOUR EXCALI-BUR!
AN EXCALIBUR
FELICIA...
MY DEAR...
...OLD FRIEND, FELICIA...
I'M AFRAID THAT'S IMPOSSIBLE.

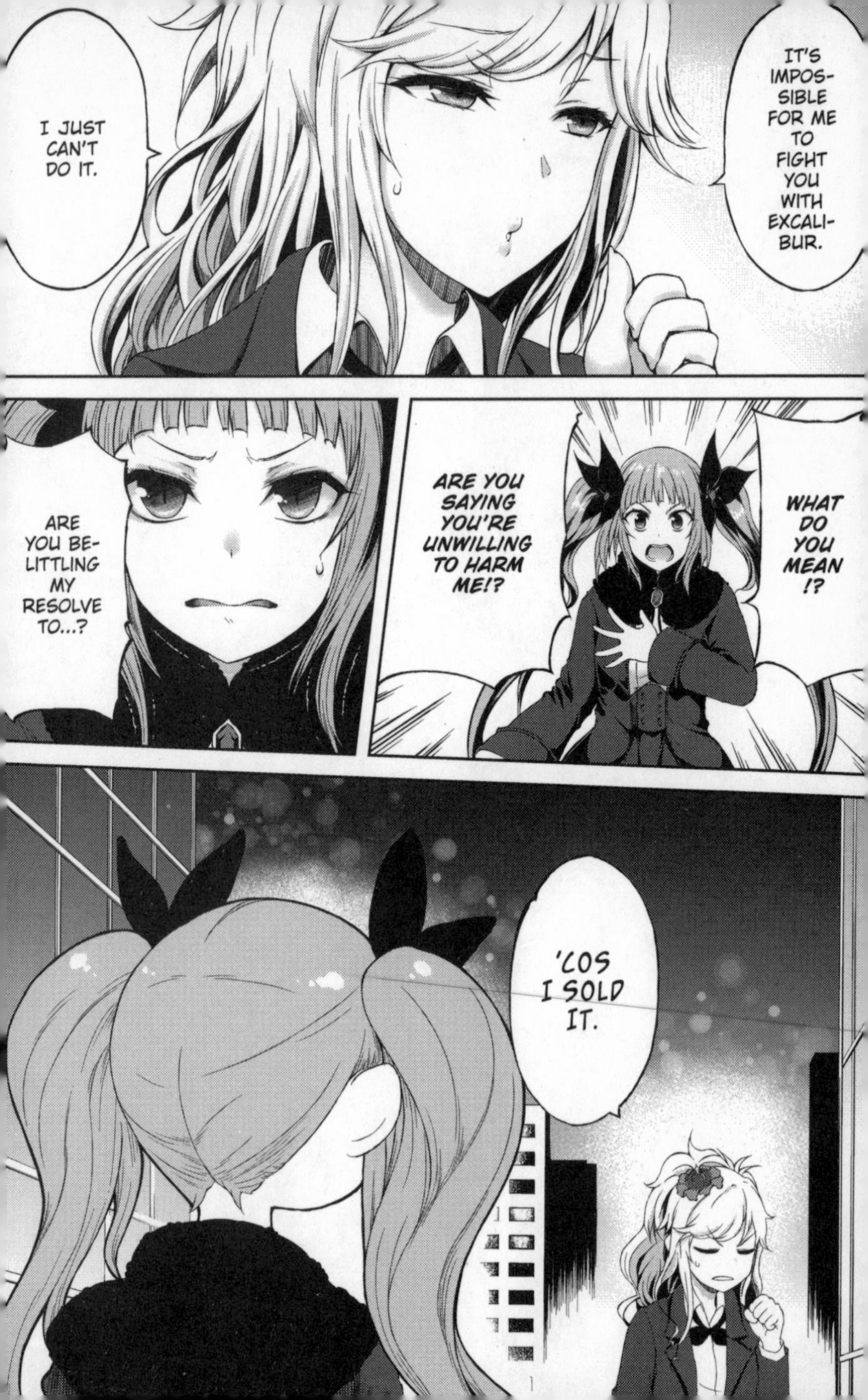
IT'S IMPOSSIBLE FOR ME TO FIGHT YOU WITH EXCALIBUR.
I JUST CAN'T DO IT.
WHAT DO YOU MEAN!?
ARE YOU SAYING YOU'RE UNWILLING TO HARM ME!?
ARE YOU BELITTLING MY RESOLVE TO...?
'COS I SOLD IT.

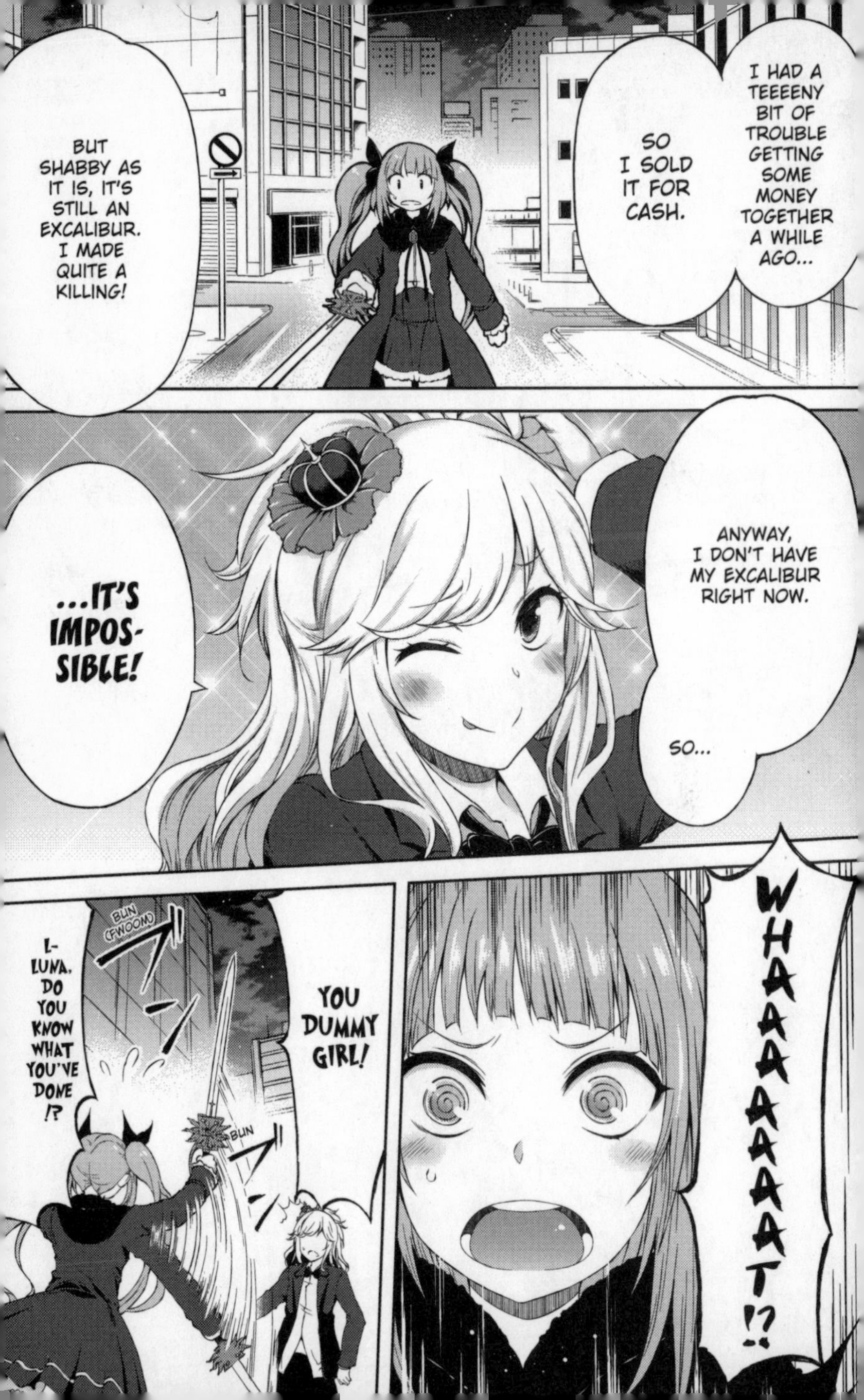
I HAD A TEEEENY BIT OF TROUBLE GETTING SOME MONEY TOGETHER A WHILE AGO...
SO I SOLD IT FOR CASH.
BUT SHABBY AS IT IS, IT'S STILL AN EXCALIBUR. I MADE QUITE A KILLING!
ANYWAY, I DON'T HAVE MY EXCALIBUR RIGHT NOW.
SO...
...IT'S IMPOSSIBLE!
WHAAAAAAAAT!?
YOU DUMMY GIRL!
BUN (FWOOM)
BUN
L-LUNA, DO YOU KNOW WHAT YOU'VE DONE!?

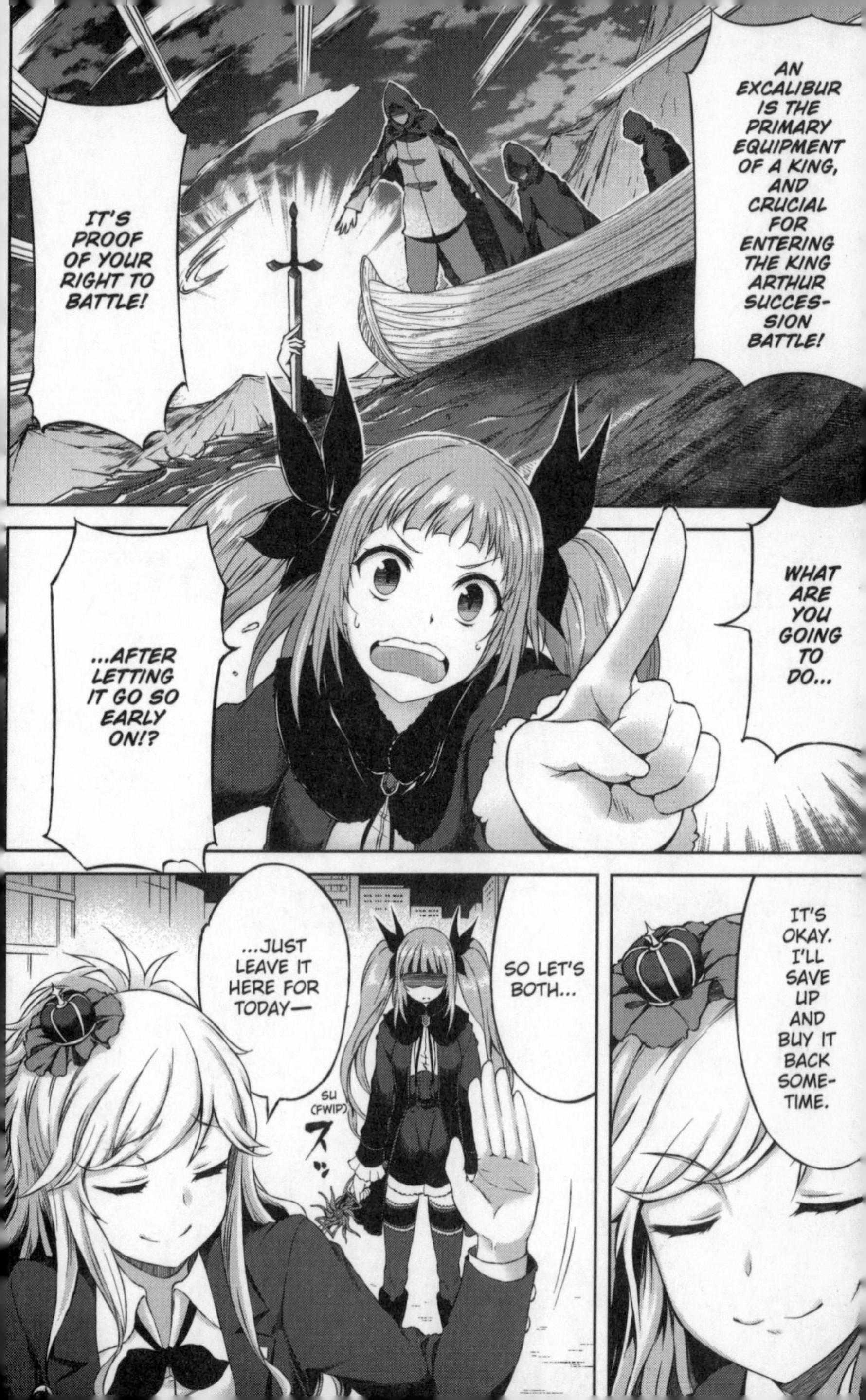
AN EXCALIBUR IS THE PRIMARY EQUIPMENT OF A KING, AND CRUCIAL FOR ENTERING THE KING ARTHUR SUCCES-SION BATTLE!
IT'S PROOF OF YOUR RIGHT TO BATTLE!
WHAT ARE YOU GOING TO DO...
...AFTER LETTING IT GO SO EARLY ON!?
IT'S OKAY. I'LL SAVE UP AND BUY IT BACK SOME-TIME.
SO LET'S BOTH...
...JUST LEAVE IT HERE FOR TODAY—
SU (FWIP)
ス

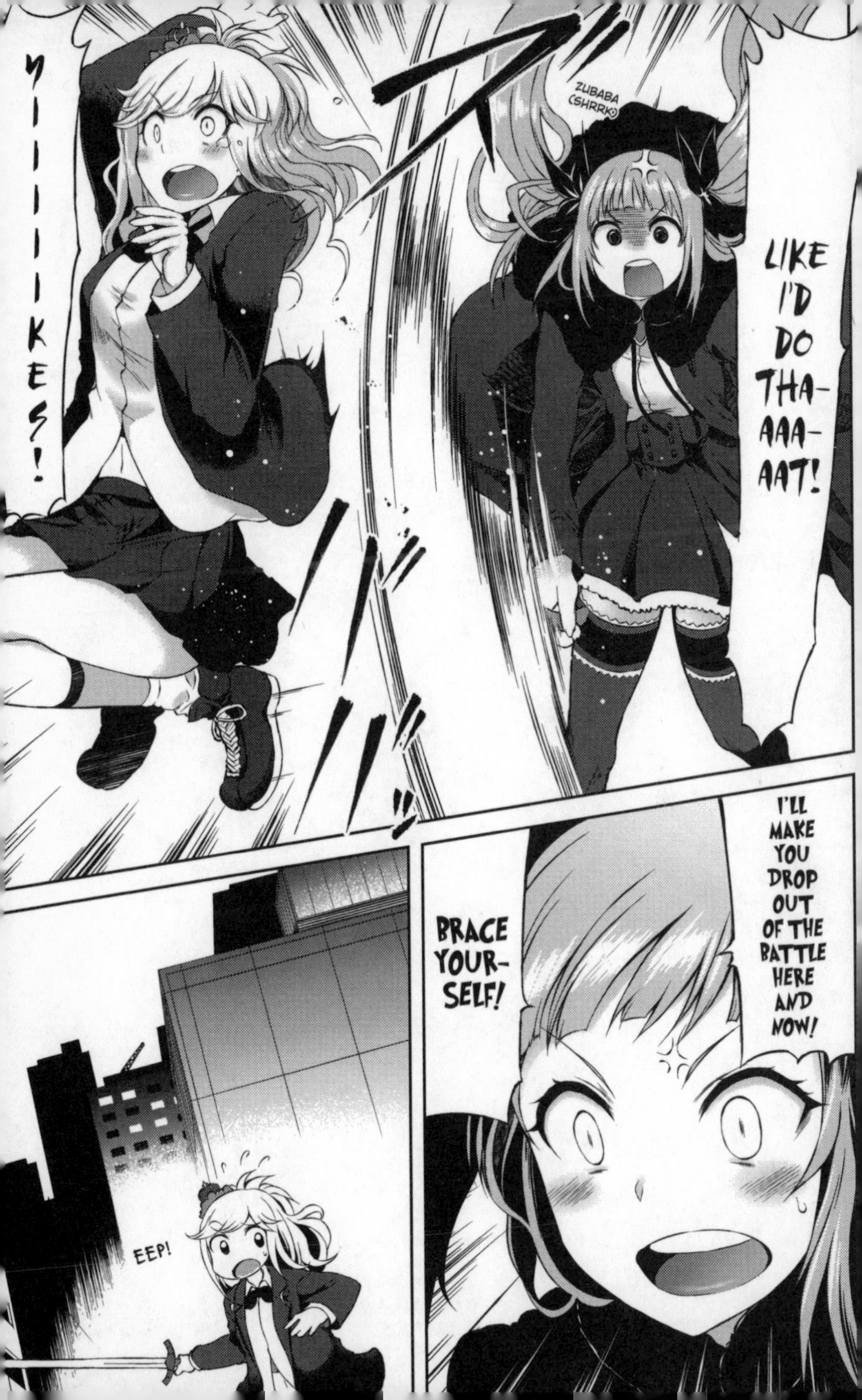
ZUBABA (SHRRK)
LIKE I'D DO THA-AAA-AAT!
YIIIIIKES!
I'LL MAKE YOU DROP OUT OF THE BATTLE HERE AND NOW!
BRACE YOUR-SELF!
EEP!

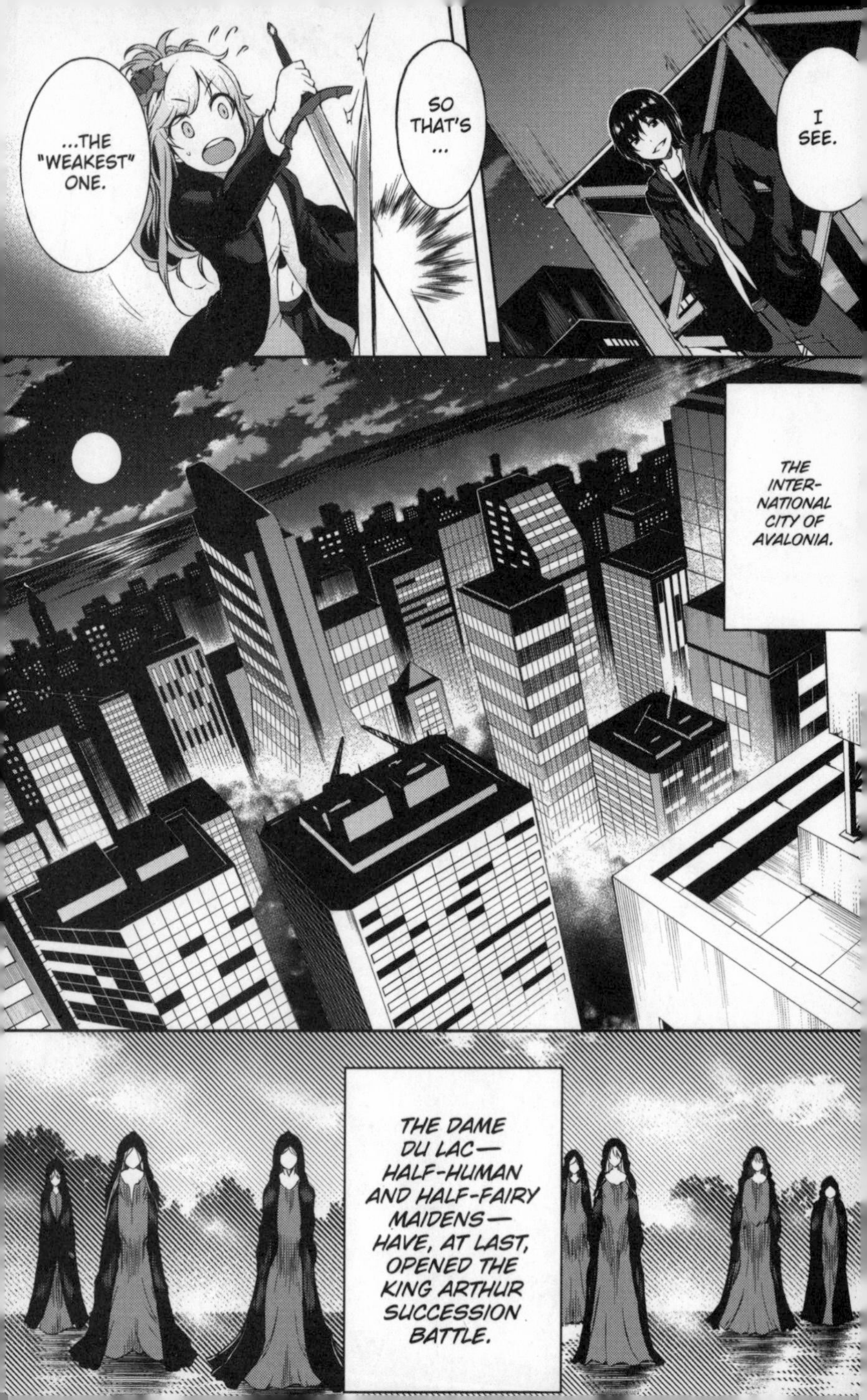
I SEE.
SO THAT'S ...
...THE "WEAKEST" ONE.
THE INTER-NATIONAL CITY OF AVALONIA.
THE DAME DU LAC—HALF-HUMAN AND HALF-FAIRY MAIDENS—HAVE, AT LAST, OPENED THE KING ARTHUR SUCCESSION BATTLE.

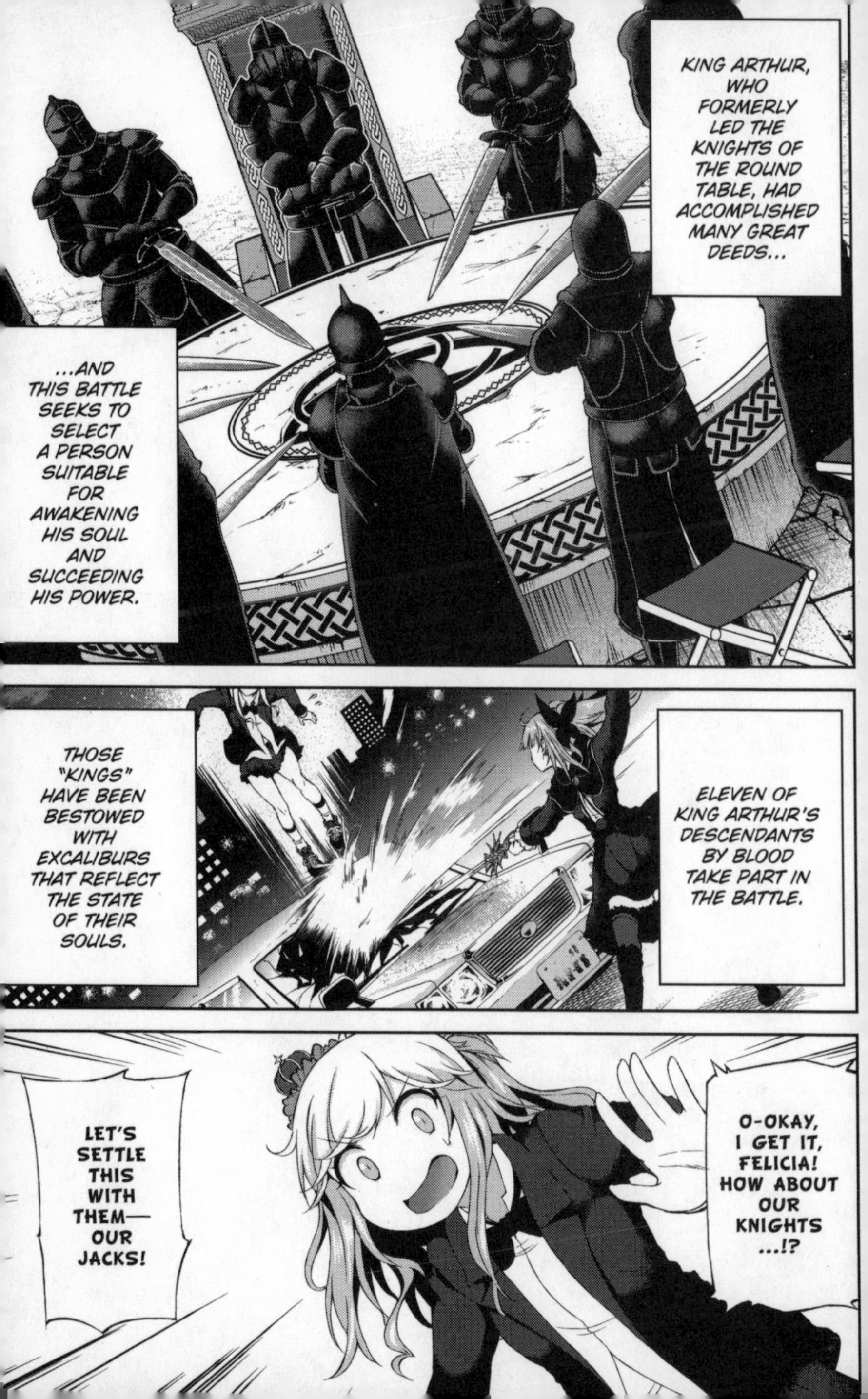
KING ARTHUR, WHO FORMERLY LED THE KNIGHTS OF THE ROUND TABLE, HAD ACCOMPLISHED MANY GREAT DEEDS...
...AND THIS BATTLE SEEKS TO SELECT A PERSON SUITABLE FOR AWAKENING HIS SOUL AND SUCCEEDING HIS POWER.
ELEVEN OF KING ARTHUR'S DESCENDANTS BY BLOOD TAKE PART IN THE BATTLE.
THOSE "KINGS" HAVE BEEN BESTOWED WITH EXCALIBURS THAT REFLECT THE STATE OF THEIR SOULS.
O-OKAY, I GET IT, FELICIA! HOW ABOUT OUR KNIGHTS ...!?
LET'S SETTLE THIS WITH THEM— OUR JACKS!

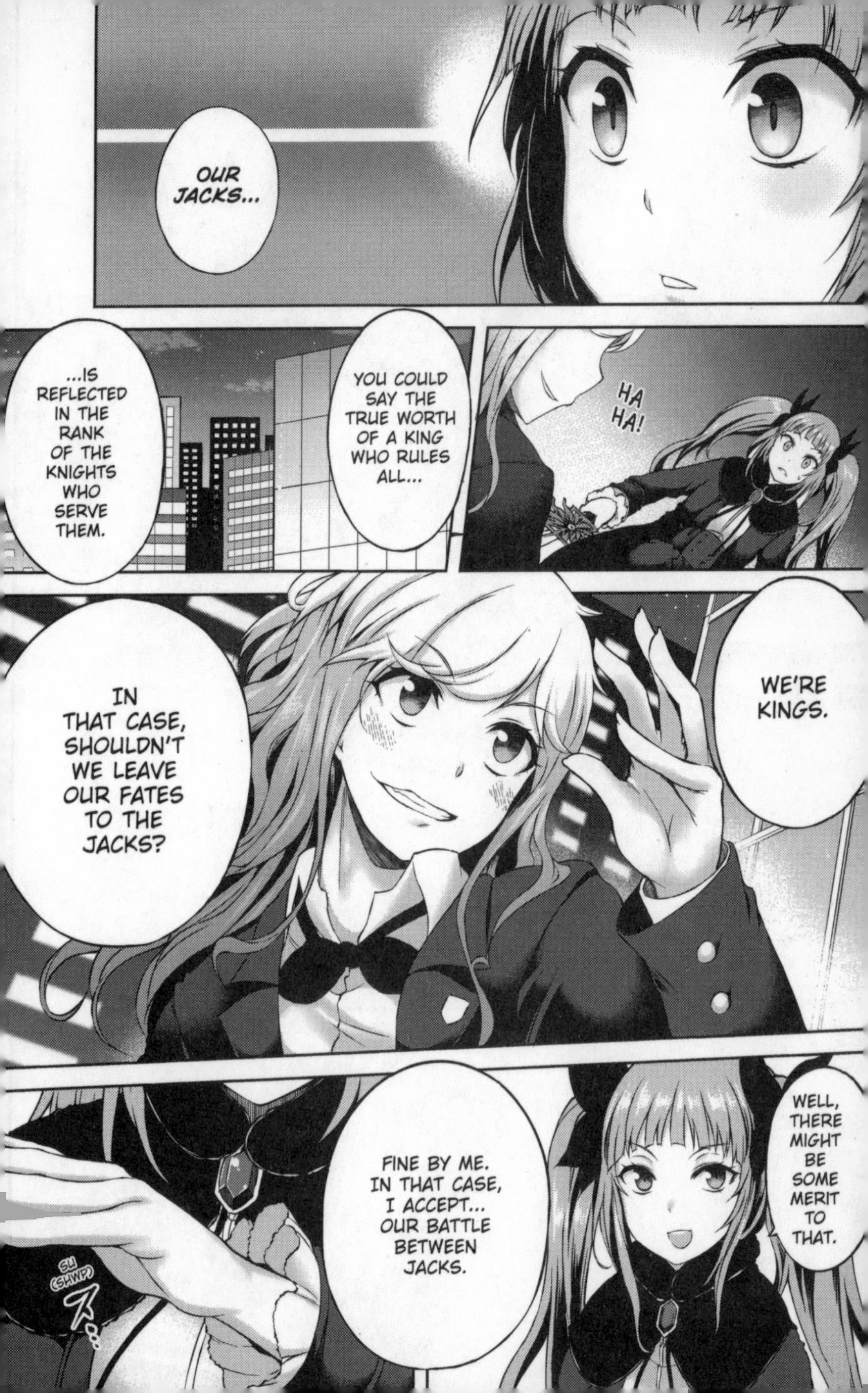
OUR JACKS...
HA HA!
YOU COULD SAY THE TRUE WORTH OF A KING WHO RULES ALL...
...IS REFLECTED IN THE RANK OF THE KNIGHTS WHO SERVE THEM.
WE'RE KINGS.
IN THAT CASE, SHOULDN'T WE LEAVE OUR FATES TO THE JACKS?
WELL, THERE MIGHT BE SOME MERIT TO THAT.
FINE BY ME. IN THAT CASE, I ACCEPT... OUR BATTLE BETWEEN JACKS.
SU (SHWP)

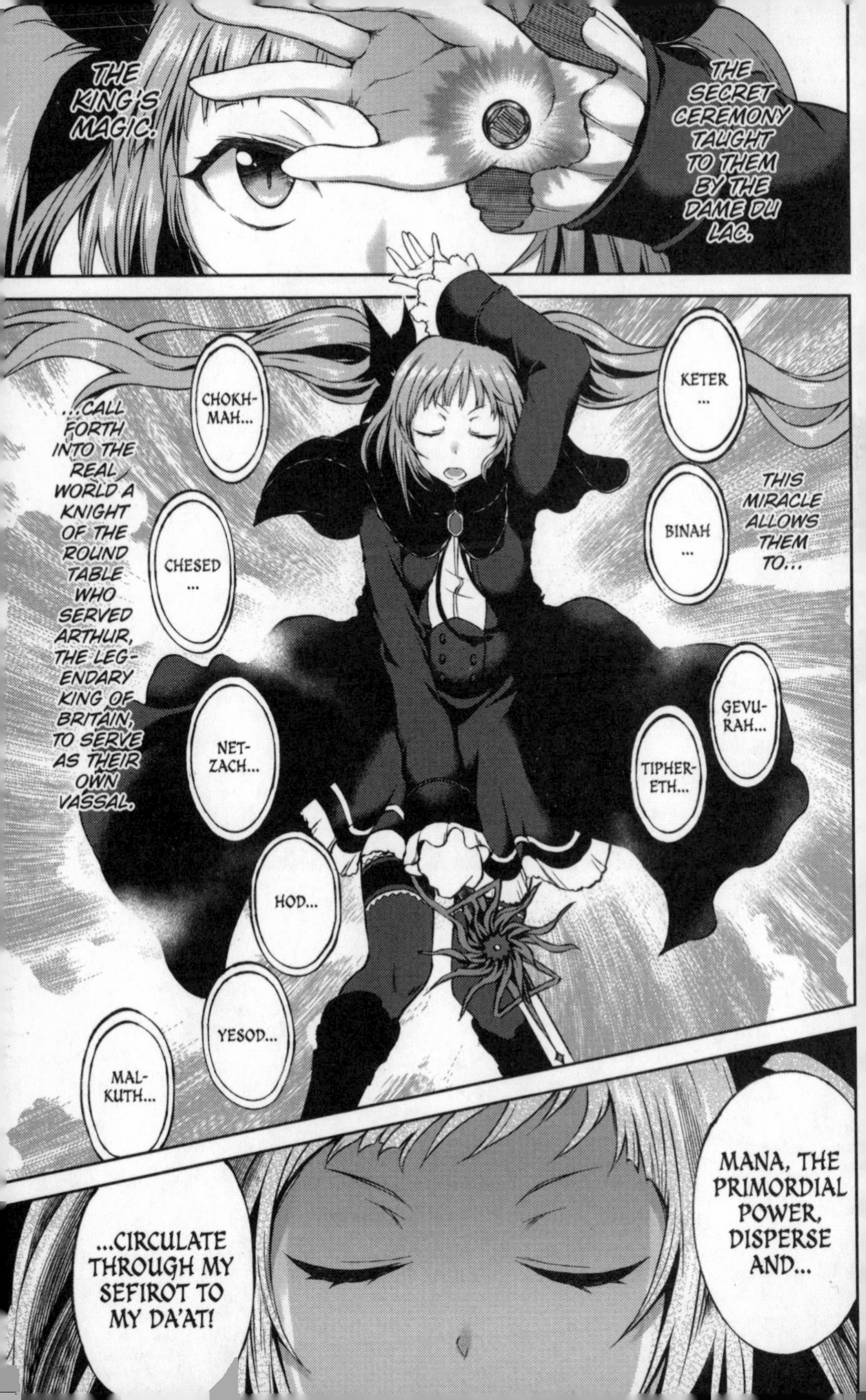
THE SECRET CEREMONY TAUGHT TO THEM BY THE DAME DU LAC.
THE KING'S MAGIC.
KETER...
THIS MIRACLE ALLOWS THEM TO...
CHOKH-MAH...
...CALL FORTH INTO THE REAL WORLD A KNIGHT OF THE ROUND TABLE WHO SERVED ARTHUR, THE LEG-ENDARY KING OF BRITAIN, TO SERVE AS THEIR OWN VASSAL.
BINAH...
CHESED...
GEVU-RAH...
TIPHER-ETH...
NET-ZACH...
HOD...
YESOD...
MAL-KUTH...
MANA, THE PRIMORDIAL POWER, DISPERSE AND...
...CIRCULATE THROUGH MY SEFIROT TO MY DA'AT!

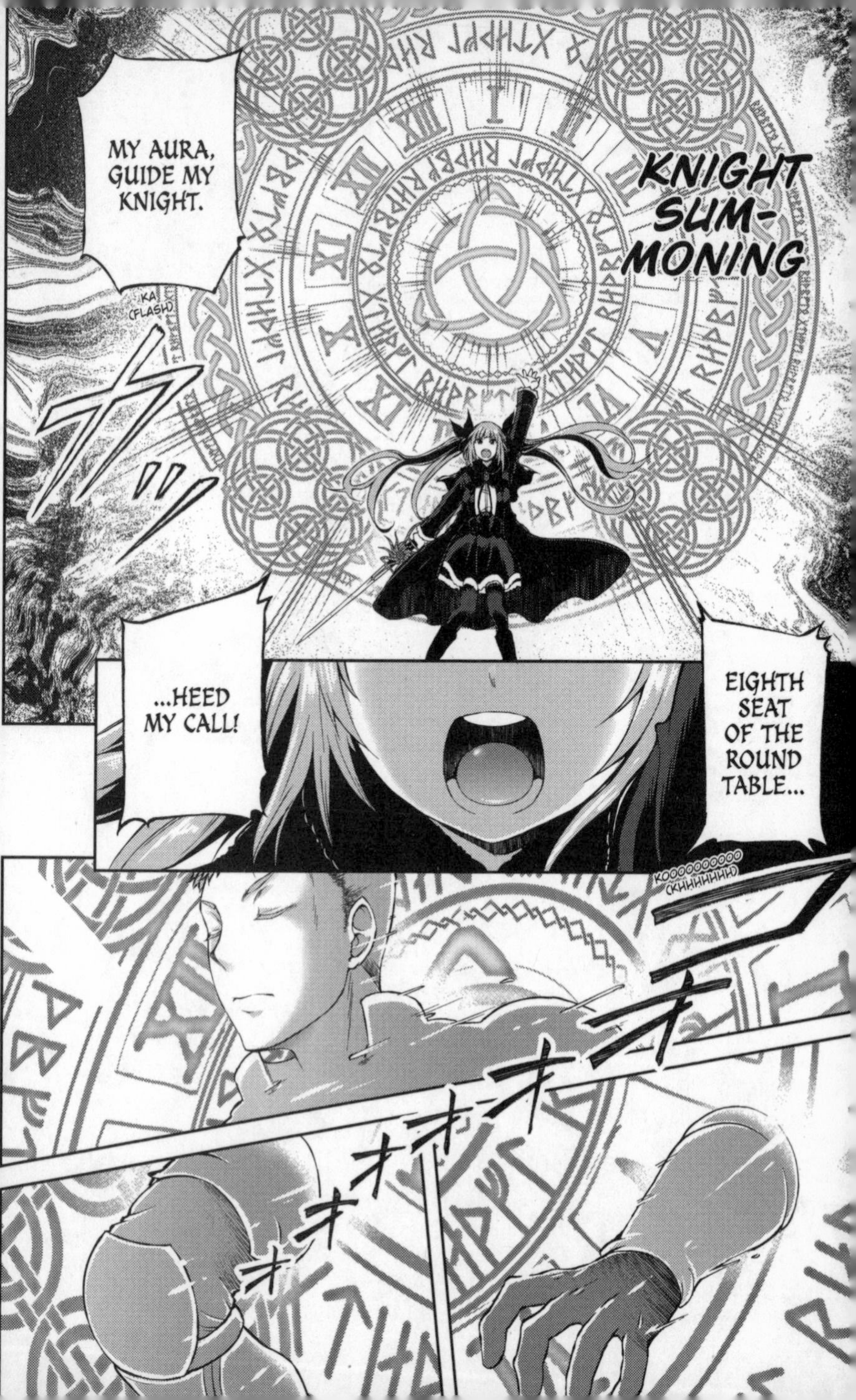
KNIGHT SUMMONING
MY AURA, GUIDE MY KNIGHT.
KA (FLASH)
EIGHTH SEAT OF THE ROUND TABLE...
...HEED MY CALL!
KOOOOOOOOOO (KHHHHHHHH)

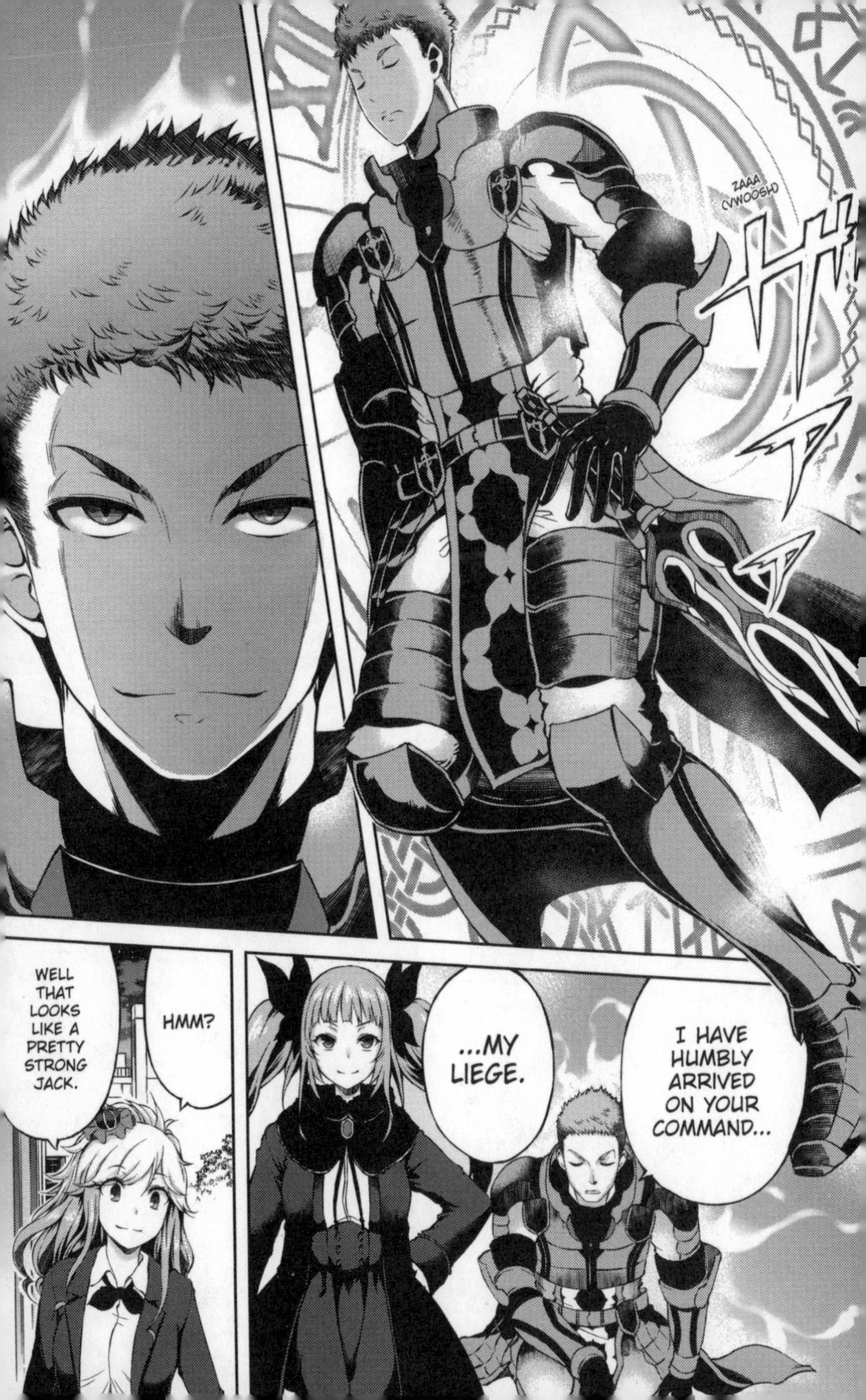
ZAAA (VWOOSH)
I HAVE HUMBLY ARRIVED ON YOUR COMMAND...
...MY LIEGE.
HMM?
WELL THAT LOOKS LIKE A PRETTY STRONG JACK.

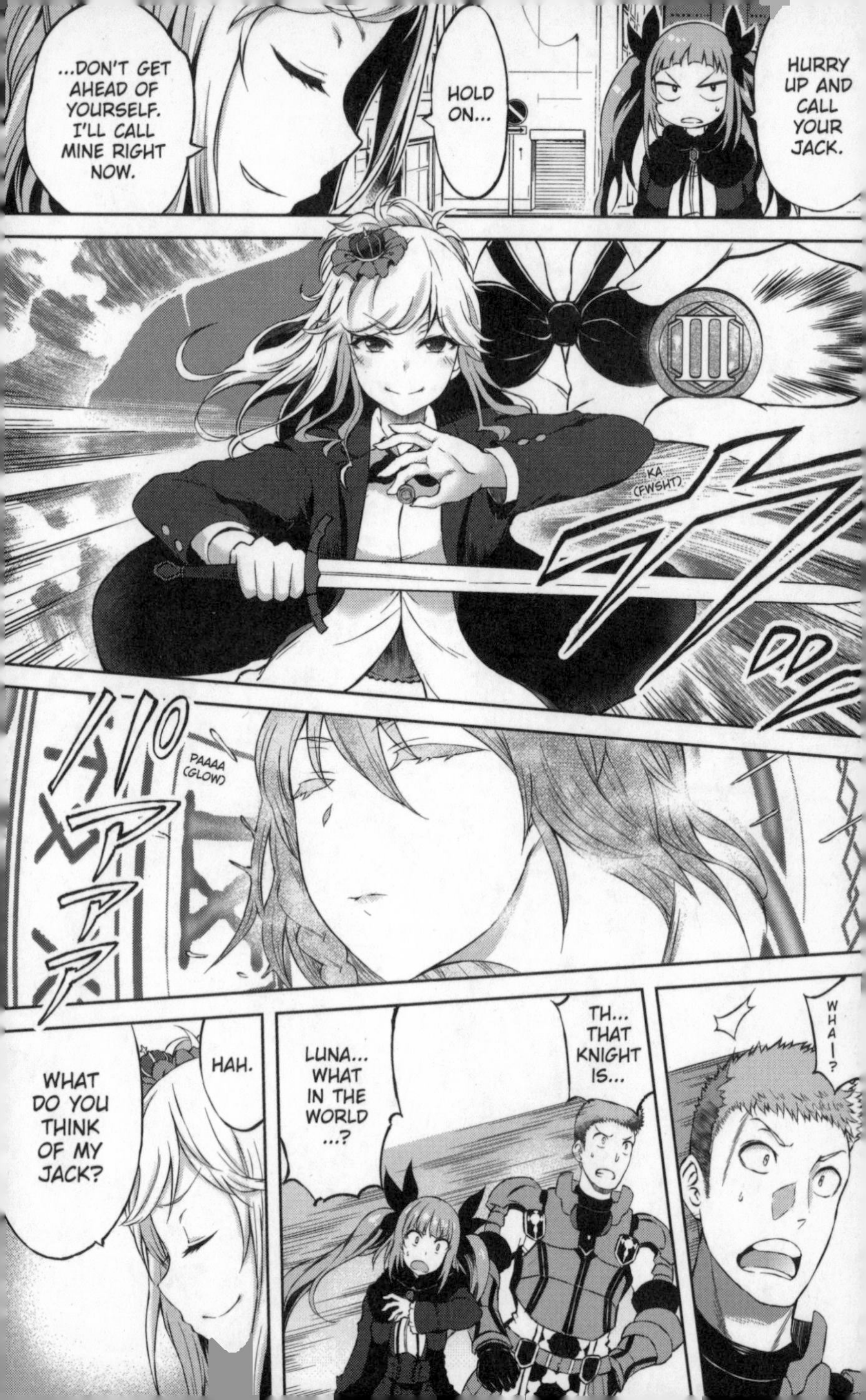
HURRY UP AND CALL YOUR JACK.
HOLD ON...
...DON'T GET AHEAD OF YOURSELF. I'LL CALL MINE RIGHT NOW.
KA (FWSHT)
PAAAA (GLOW)
WHA—?
TH... THAT KNIGHT IS...
LUNA... WHAT IN THE WORLD ...?
HAH.
WHAT DO YOU THINK OF MY JACK?

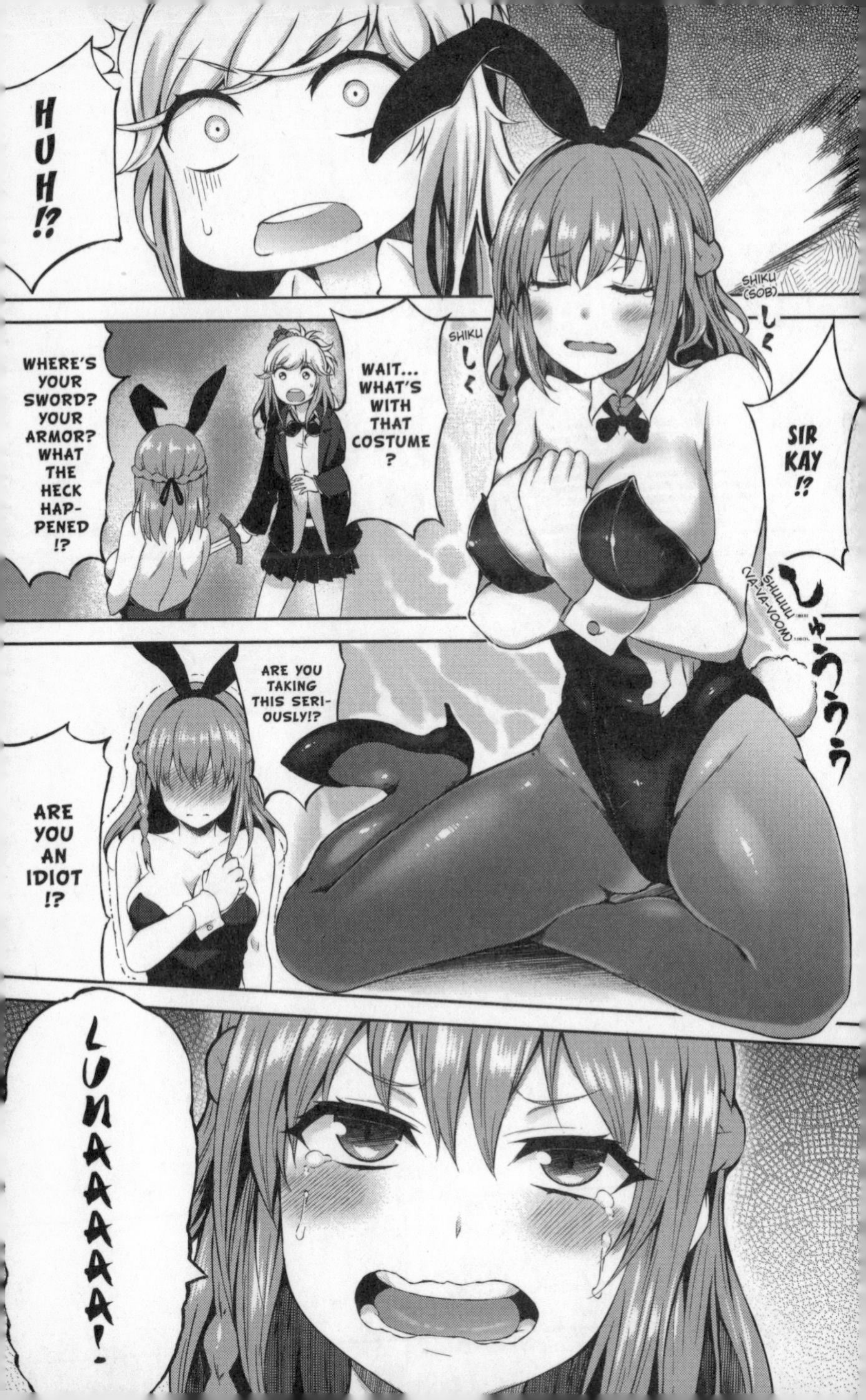
SHIKU (SOB)
しく
SHIKU
しく
SIR KAY !?
SHUUUUU (VA-VA-VOOM)
しゅううう
HUH!?
WAIT... WHAT'S WITH THAT COSTUME ?
WHERE'S YOUR SWORD? YOUR ARMOR? WHAT THE HECK HAP-PENED !?
ARE YOU TAKING THIS SERI-OUSLY!?
ARE YOU AN IDIOT !?
LUNAAAAAAA!

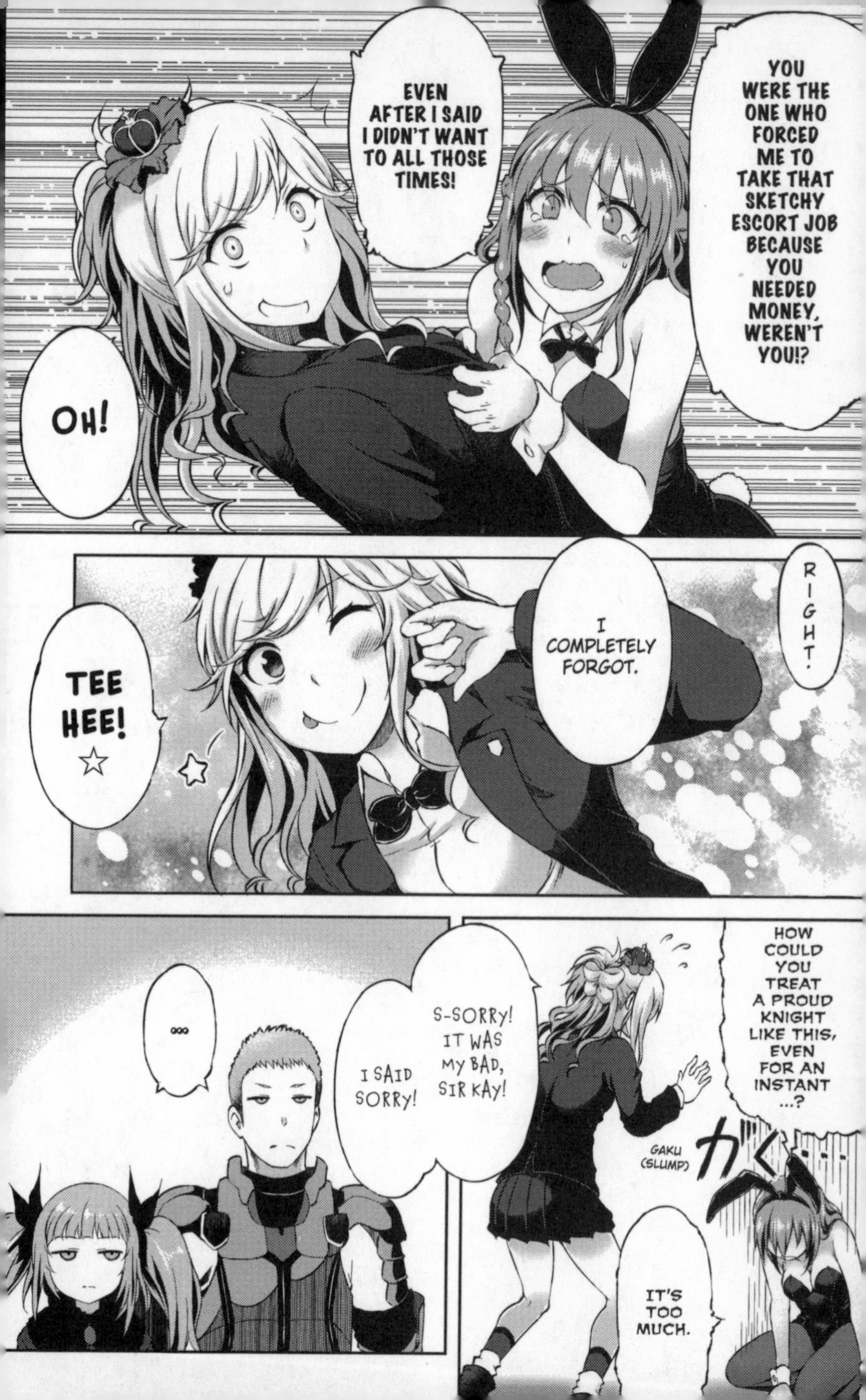
YOU WERE THE ONE WHO FORCED ME TO TAKE THAT SKETCHY ESCORT JOB BECAUSE YOU NEEDED MONEY, WEREN'T YOU!?
EVEN AFTER I SAID I DIDN'T WANT TO ALL THOSE TIMES!
OH!
RIGHT.
I COMPLETELY FORGOT.
TEE HEE! ☆
HOW COULD YOU TREAT A PROUD KNIGHT LIKE THIS, EVEN FOR AN INSTANT ...?
がく…
GAKU (SLUMP)
IT'S TOO MUCH.
S-SORRY! IT WAS MY BAD, SIR KAY!
I SAID SORRY!
...

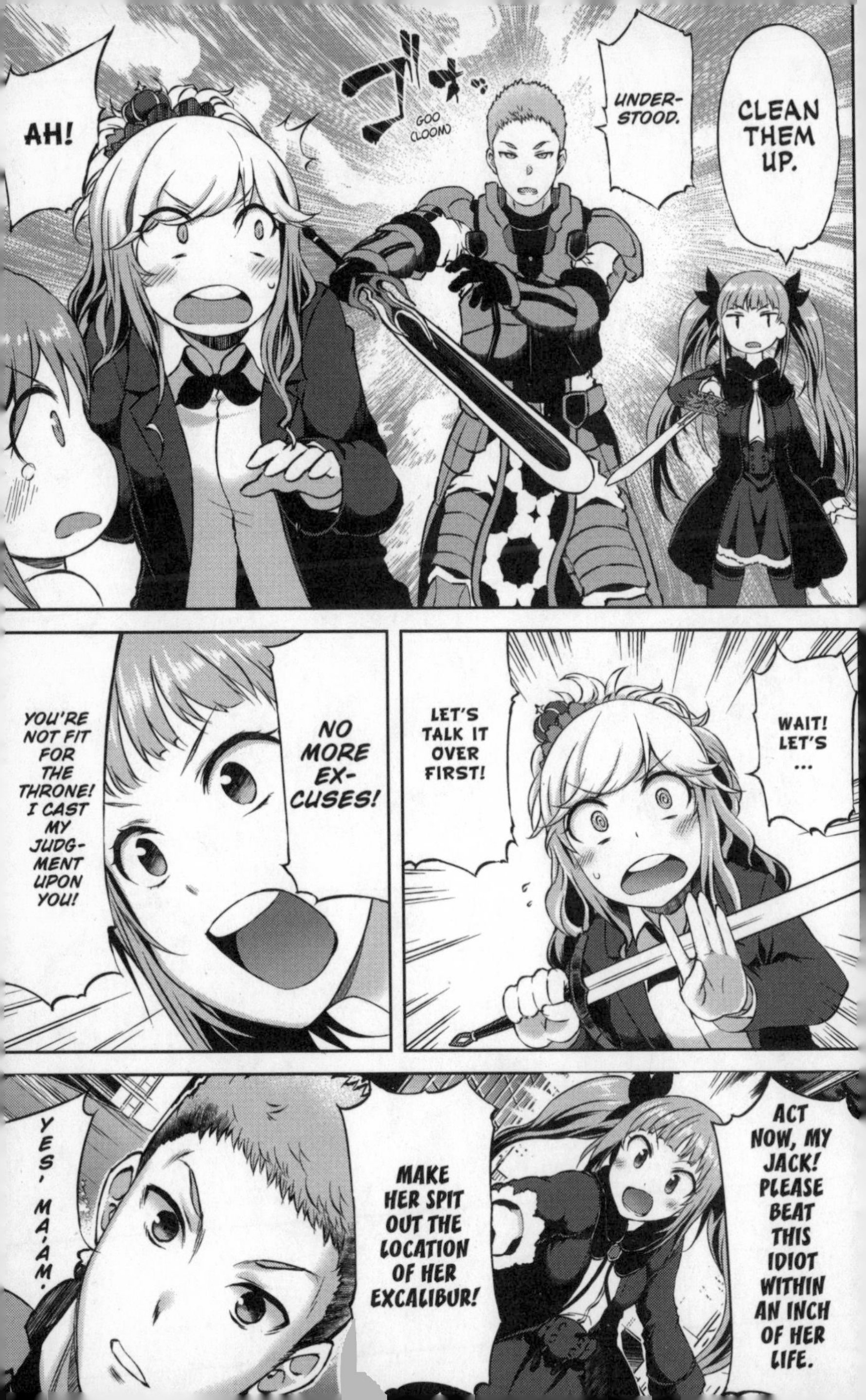
CLEAN THEM UP.
UNDER-STOOD.
GOO (LOOM)
AH!
WAIT! LET'S ...
LET'S TALK IT OVER FIRST!
NO MORE EX-CUSES!
YOU'RE NOT FIT FOR THE THRONE! I CAST MY JUDGMENT UPON YOU!
ACT NOW, MY JACK! PLEASE BEAT THIS IDIOT WITHIN AN INCH OF HER LIFE.
MAKE HER SPIT OUT THE LOCATION OF HER EXCALIBUR!
YES, MA'AM.

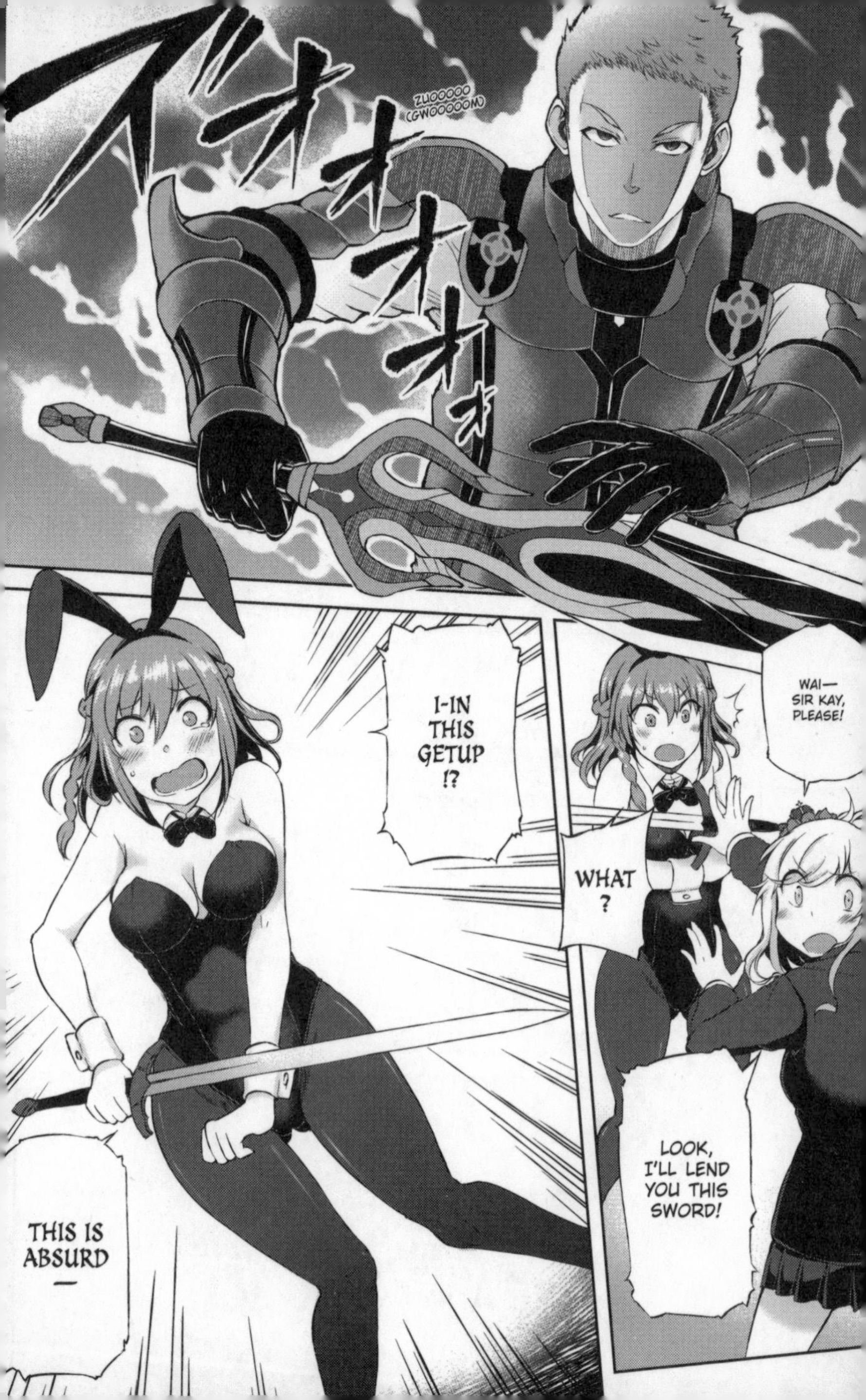
ズオオオオォ
ZUOOOOO (GWOOOOOM)
WAI— SIR KAY, PLEASE!
WHAT?
LOOK, I'LL LEND YOU THIS SWORD!
I-IN THIS GETUP!?
THIS IS ABSURD —

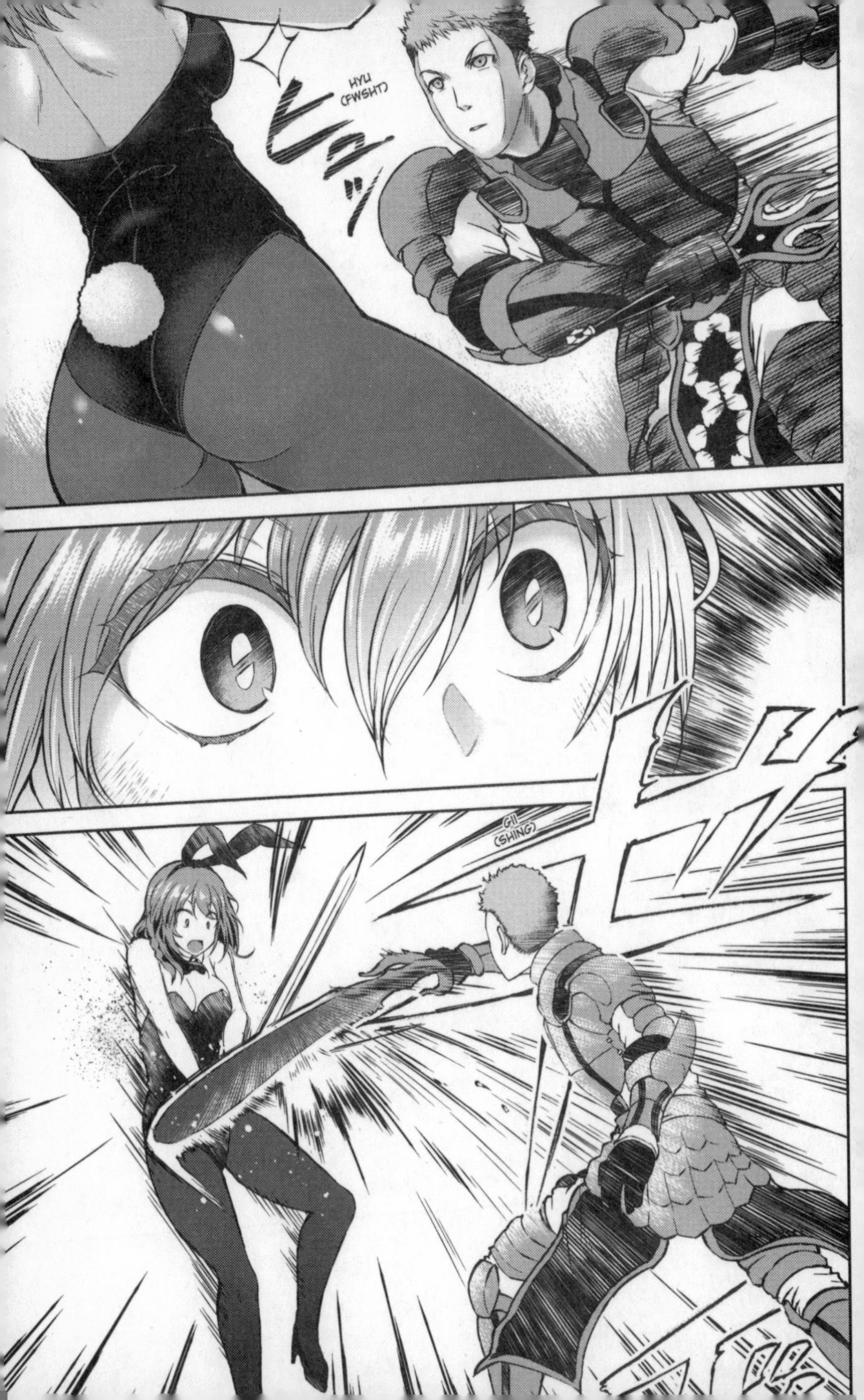
HYU
(FWSHT)
GII
(SHING)

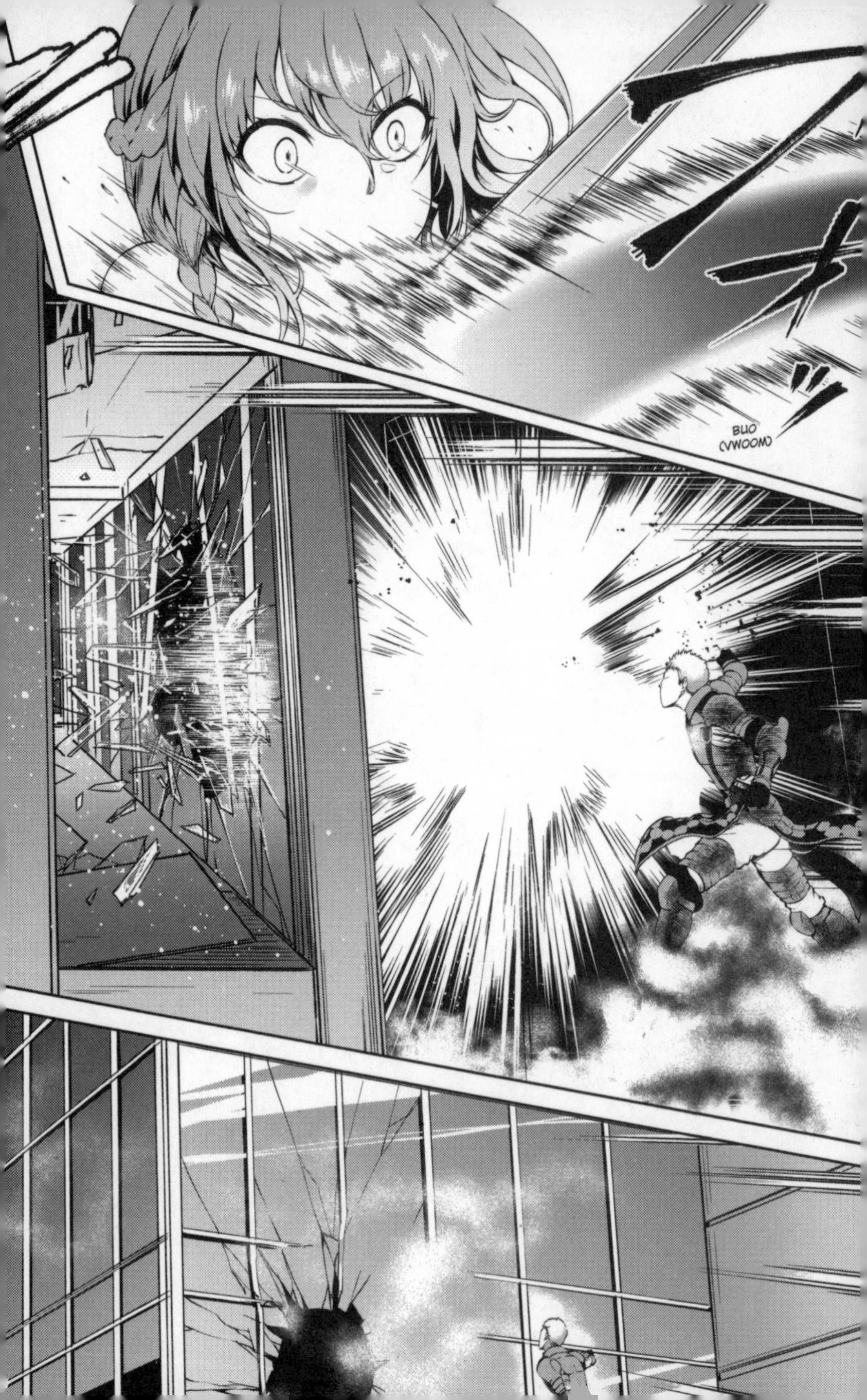
BUO
(VWOOM)

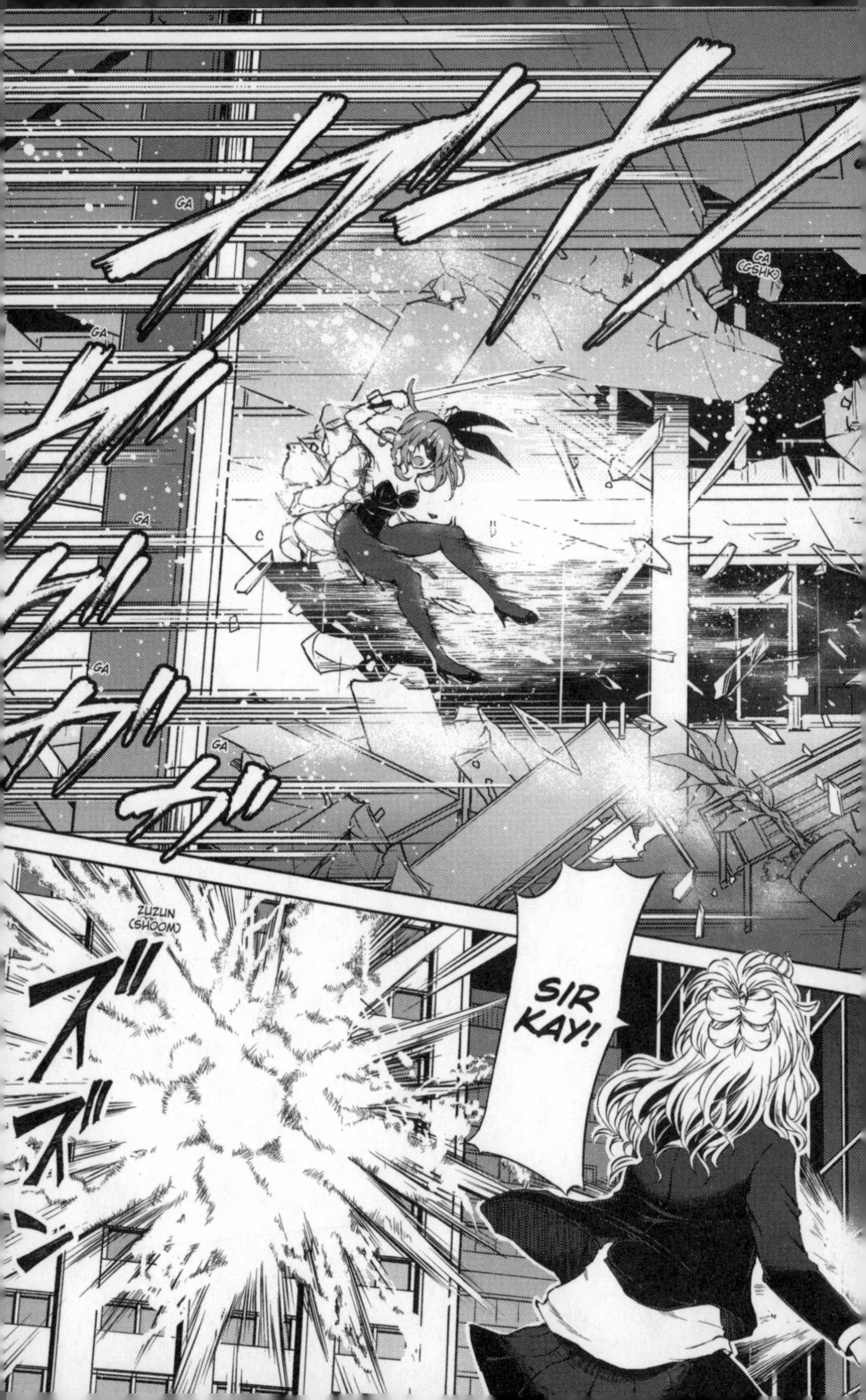
GA (GSHK)
GA
GA
GA
GA
GA
SIR KAY!
ZUZUN (SHOOM)

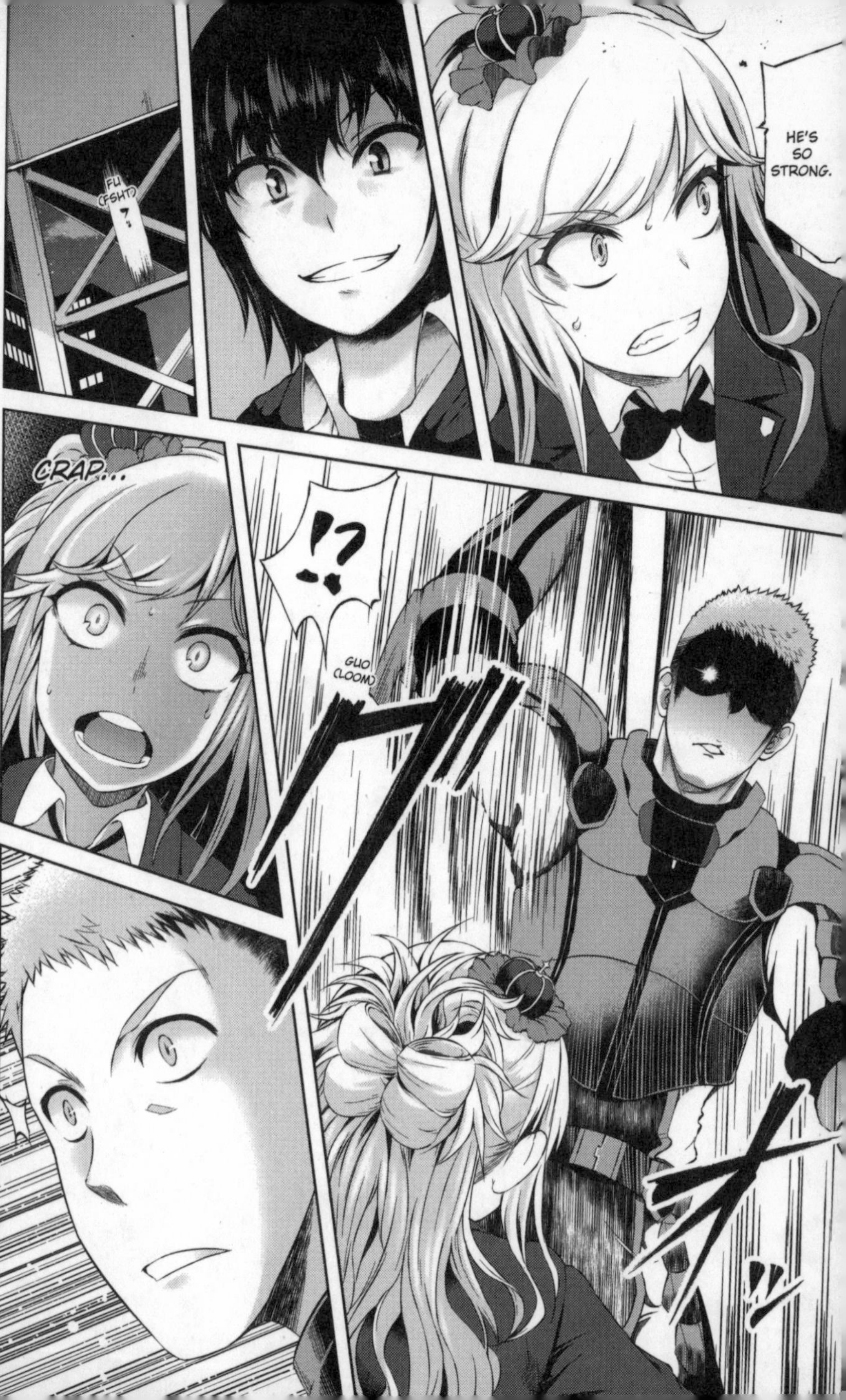
HE'S SO STRONG.
FU (FSHT)
!?
GUO (LOOM)
CRAP...

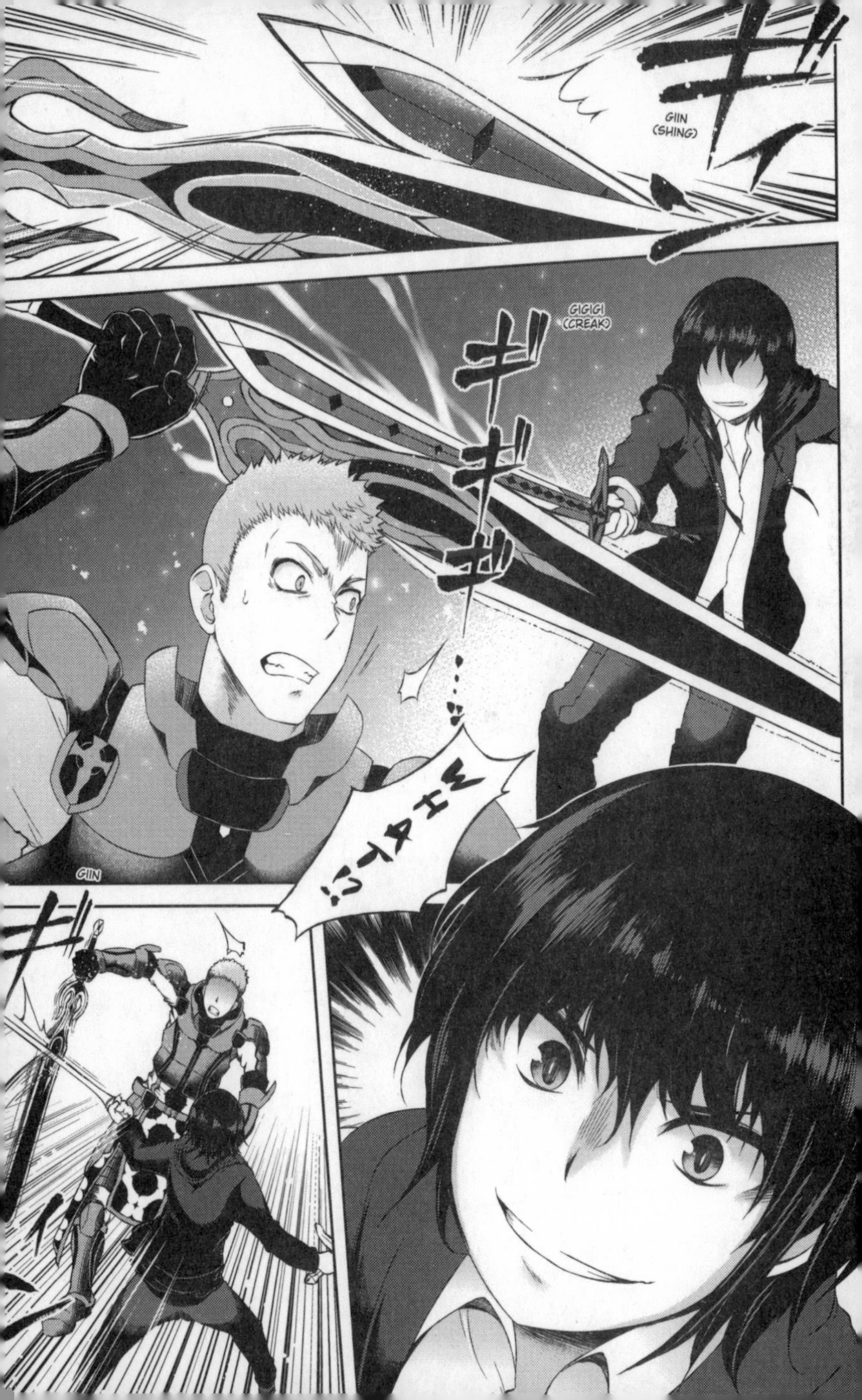
GIIN (SHING)
GIGIGI (CREAK)
GIIN
...!?
WHAT!?

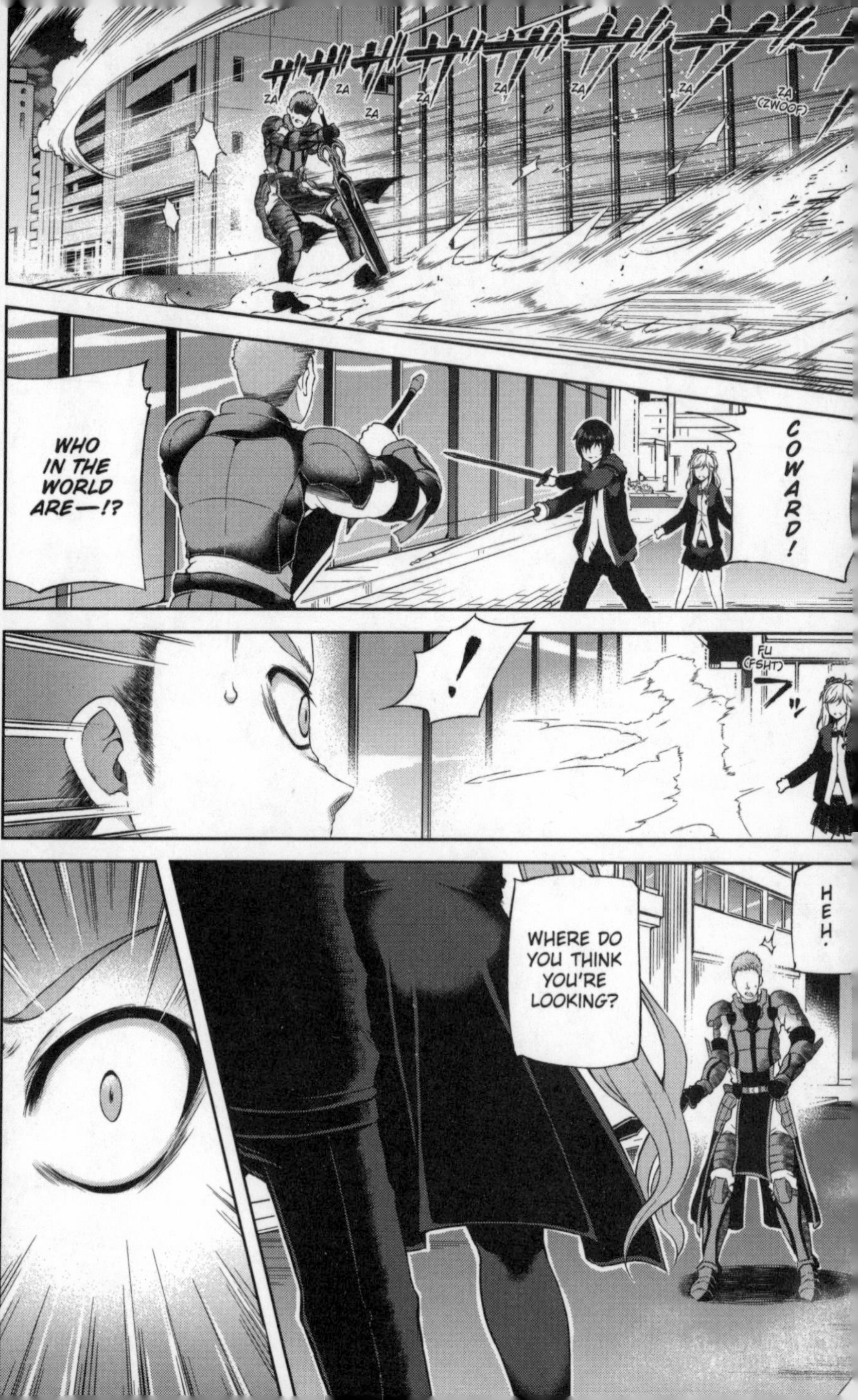
ZA (ZWOOF)
ZA ZA ZA ZA ZA ZA ZA
COWARD!
WHO IN THE WORLD ARE—!?
FU (FSHT)
!
HEH.
WHERE DO YOU THINK YOU'RE LOOKING?

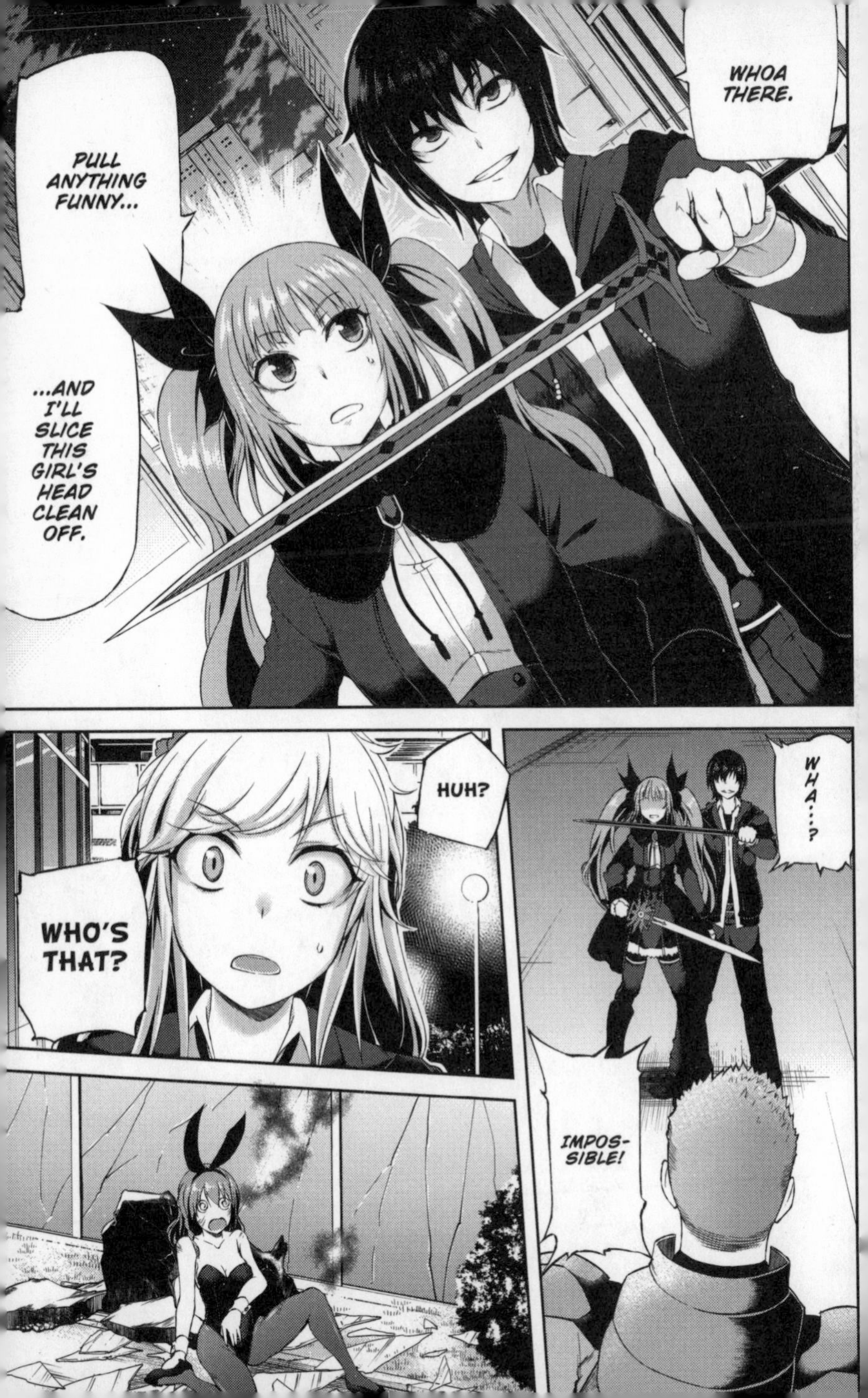
WHOA THERE.
PULL ANYTHING FUNNY...
...AND I'LL SLICE THIS GIRL'S HEAD CLEAN OFF.
WHA...?
IMPOS-SIBLE!
HUH?
WHO'S THAT?

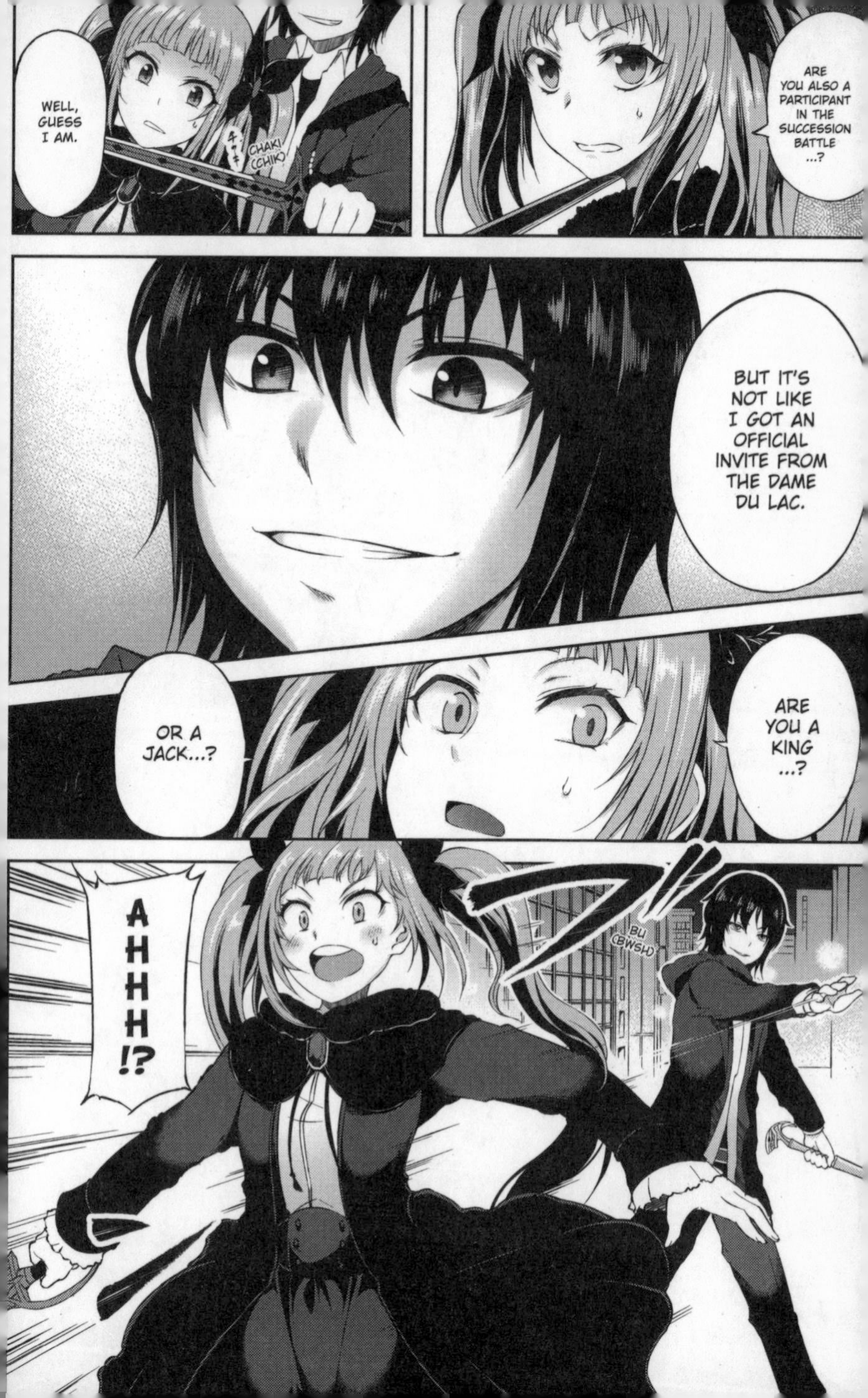
ARE YOU ALSO A PARTICIPANT IN THE SUCCESSION BATTLE ...?
WELL, GUESS I AM.
チャキ
CHAKI (CHIK)
BUT IT'S NOT LIKE I GOT AN OFFICIAL INVITE FROM THE DAME DU LAC.
ARE YOU A KING ...?
OR A JACK...?
BU (BWSH)
AHHHH!?

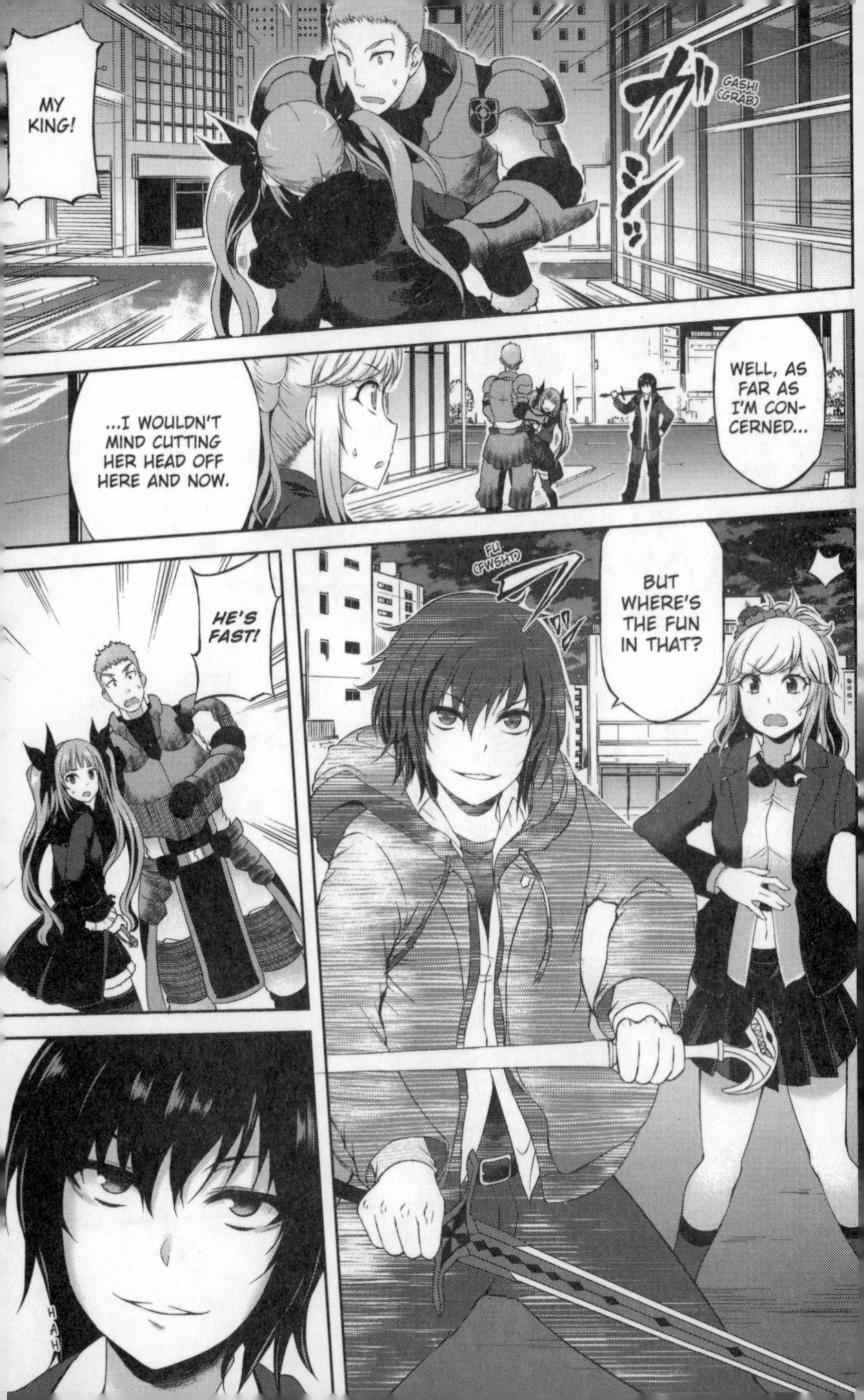
GASHI (GRAB)
MY KING!
WELL, AS FAR AS I'M CON- CERNED...
...I WOULDN'T MIND CUTTING HER HEAD OFF HERE AND NOW.
FU (FWSHT)
BUT WHERE'S THE FUN IN THAT?
HE'S FAST!
HAH

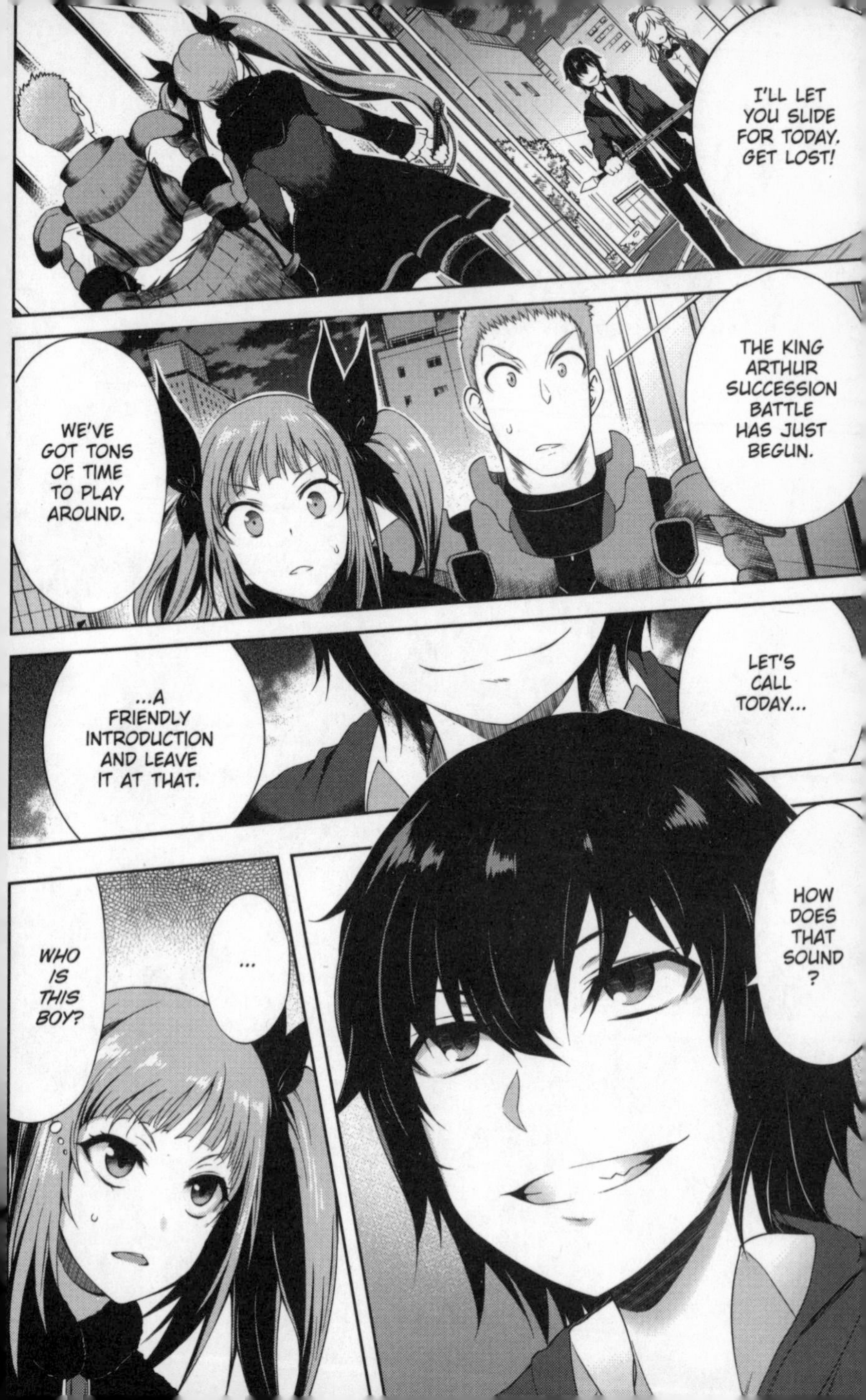
I'LL LET YOU SLIDE FOR TODAY. GET LOST!
THE KING ARTHUR SUCCESSION BATTLE HAS JUST BEGUN.
WE'VE GOT TONS OF TIME TO PLAY AROUND.
LET'S CALL TODAY...
...A FRIENDLY INTRODUCTION AND LEAVE IT AT THAT.
HOW DOES THAT SOUND?
...
WHO IS THIS BOY?

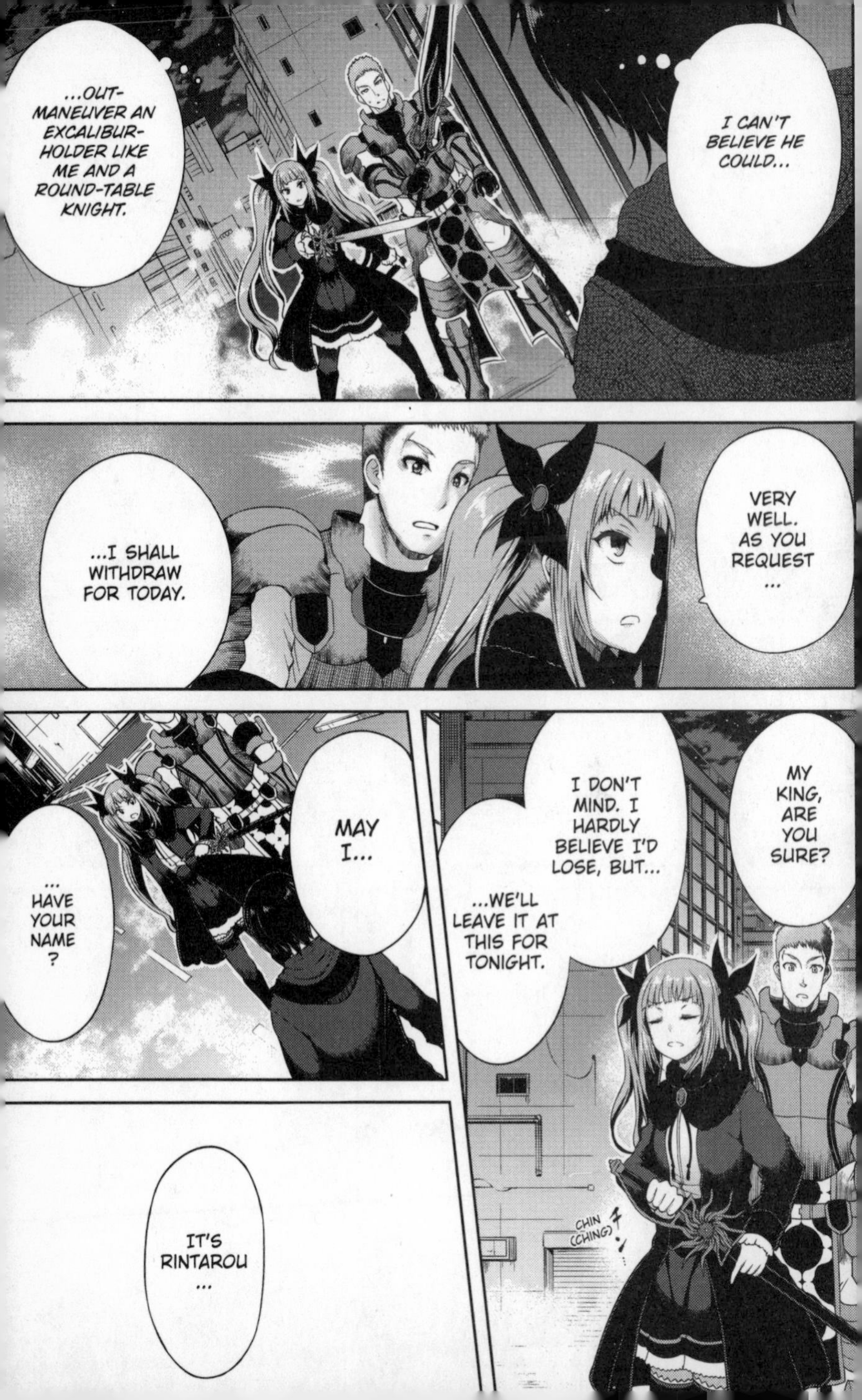
I CAN'T BELIEVE HE COULD...
...OUT-MANEUVER AN EXCALIBUR-HOLDER LIKE ME AND A ROUND-TABLE KNIGHT.
VERY WELL. AS YOU REQUEST ...
...I SHALL WITHDRAW FOR TODAY.
MY KING, ARE YOU SURE?
I DON'T MIND. I HARDLY BELIEVE I'D LOSE, BUT...
...WE'LL LEAVE IT AT THIS FOR TONIGHT.
CHIN (CHING)
MAY I...
...HAVE YOUR NAME?
IT'S RINTAROU ...

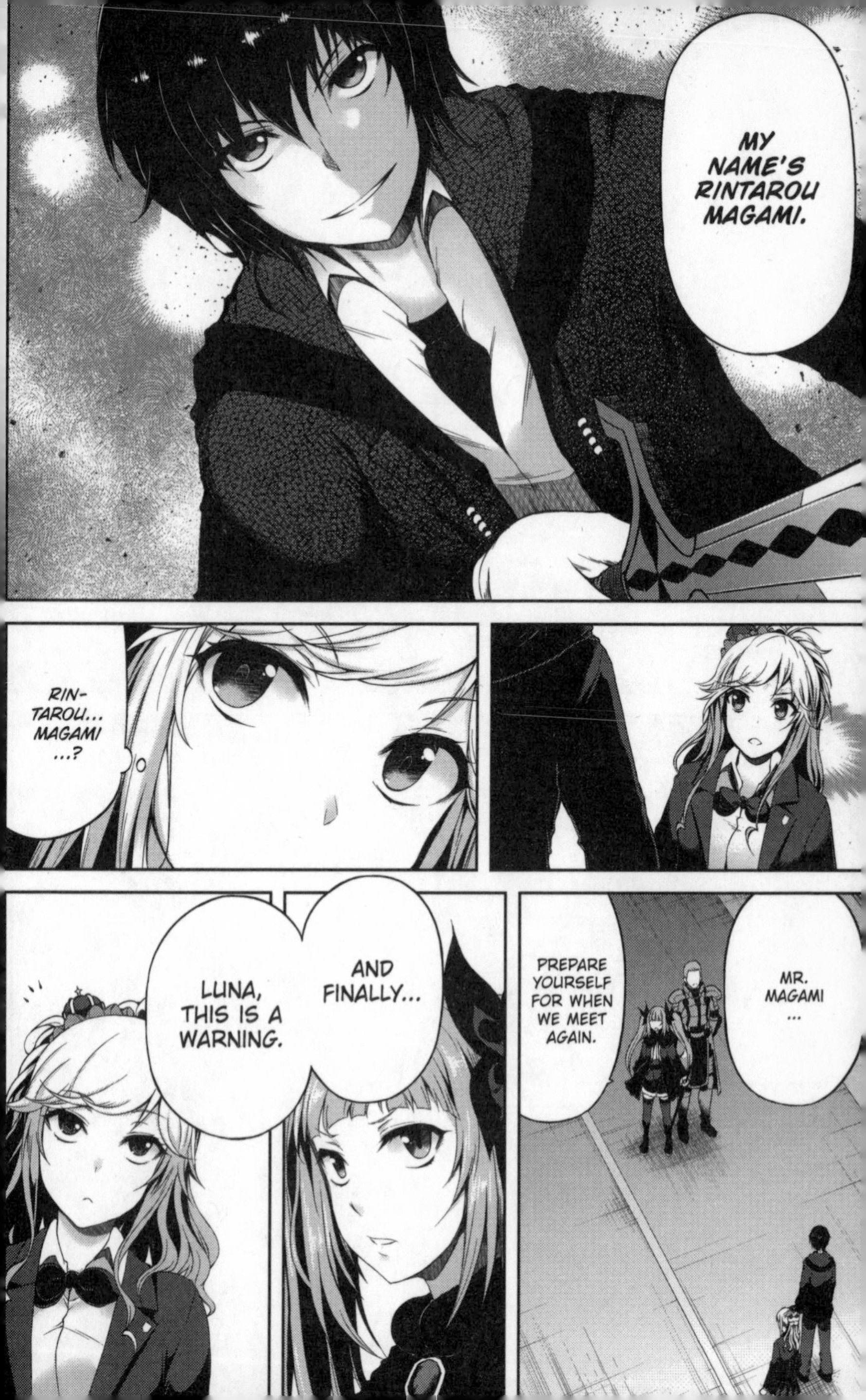
MY NAME'S RINTAROU MAGAMI.
RIN-TAROU... MAGAMI ...?
MR. MAGAMI ...
PREPARE YOURSELF FOR WHEN WE MEET AGAIN.
AND FINALLY...
LUNA, THIS IS A WARNING.

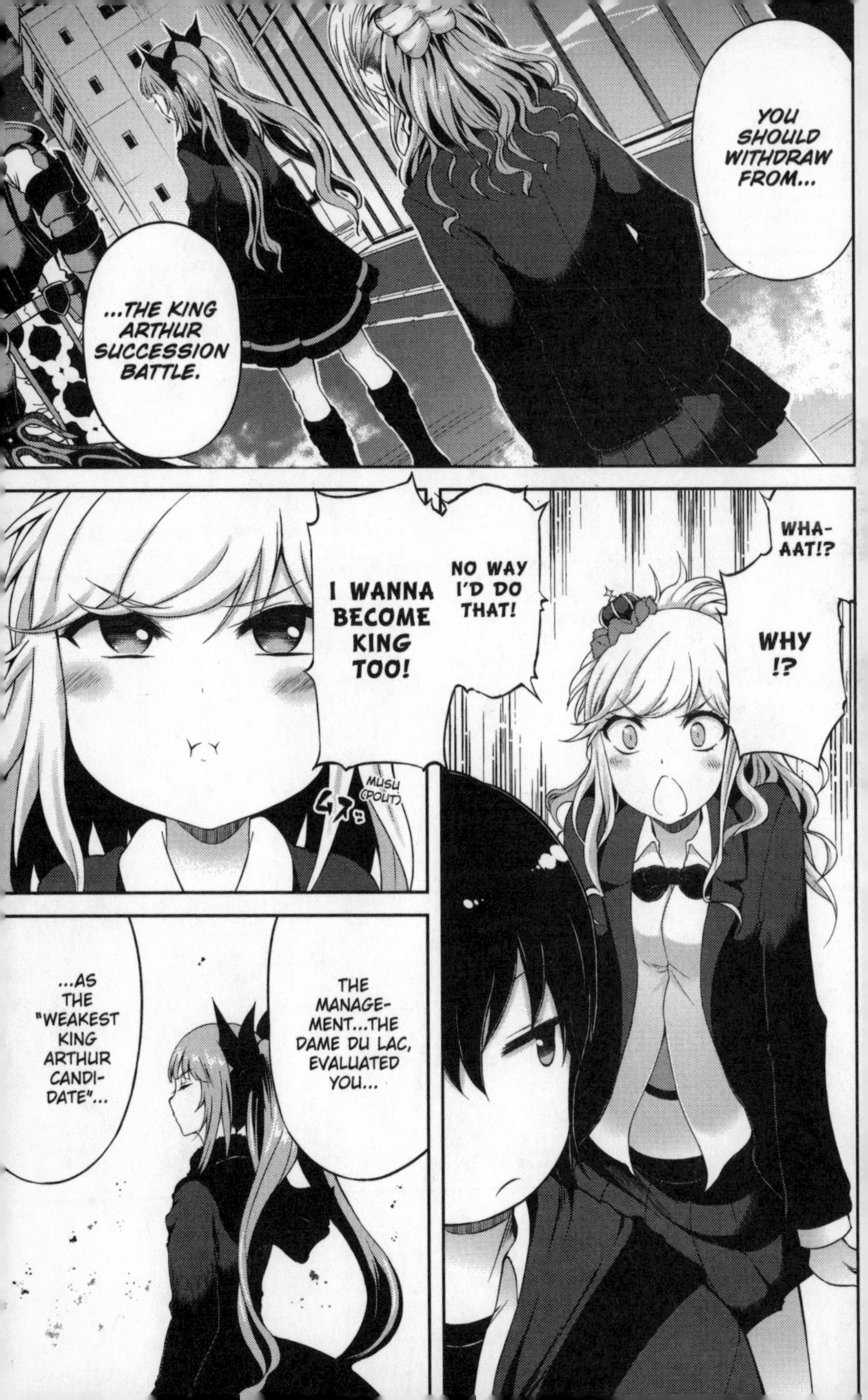
YOU SHOULD WITHDRAW FROM...
...THE KING ARTHUR SUCCESSION BATTLE.
WHA-AAT!?
WHY !?
NO WAY I'D DO THAT!
I WANNA BECOME KING TOO!
MUSU (POUT)
THE MANAGE-MENT...THE DAME DU LAC, EVALUATED YOU...
...AS THE "WEAKEST KING ARTHUR CANDI-DATE"...

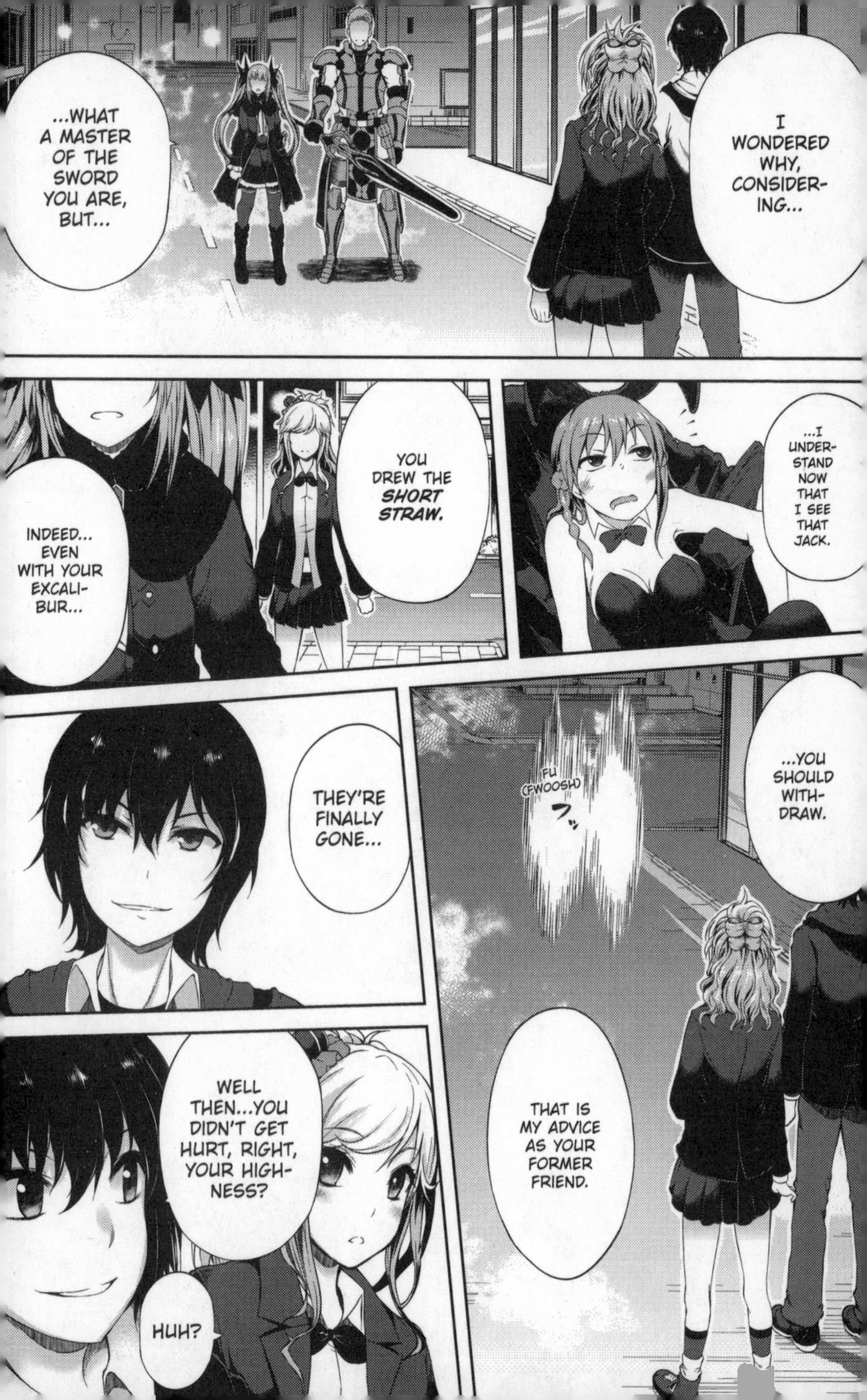
I WONDERED WHY, CONSIDERING...
...WHAT A MASTER OF THE SWORD YOU ARE, BUT...
...I UNDERSTAND NOW THAT I SEE THAT JACK.
YOU DREW THE SHORT STRAW.
INDEED... EVEN WITH YOUR EXCALIBUR...
...YOU SHOULD WITHDRAW.
FU (FWOOSH)
THAT IS MY ADVICE AS YOUR FORMER FRIEND.
THEY'RE FINALLY GONE...
WELL THEN...YOU DIDN'T GET HURT, RIGHT, YOUR HIGHNESS?
HUH?

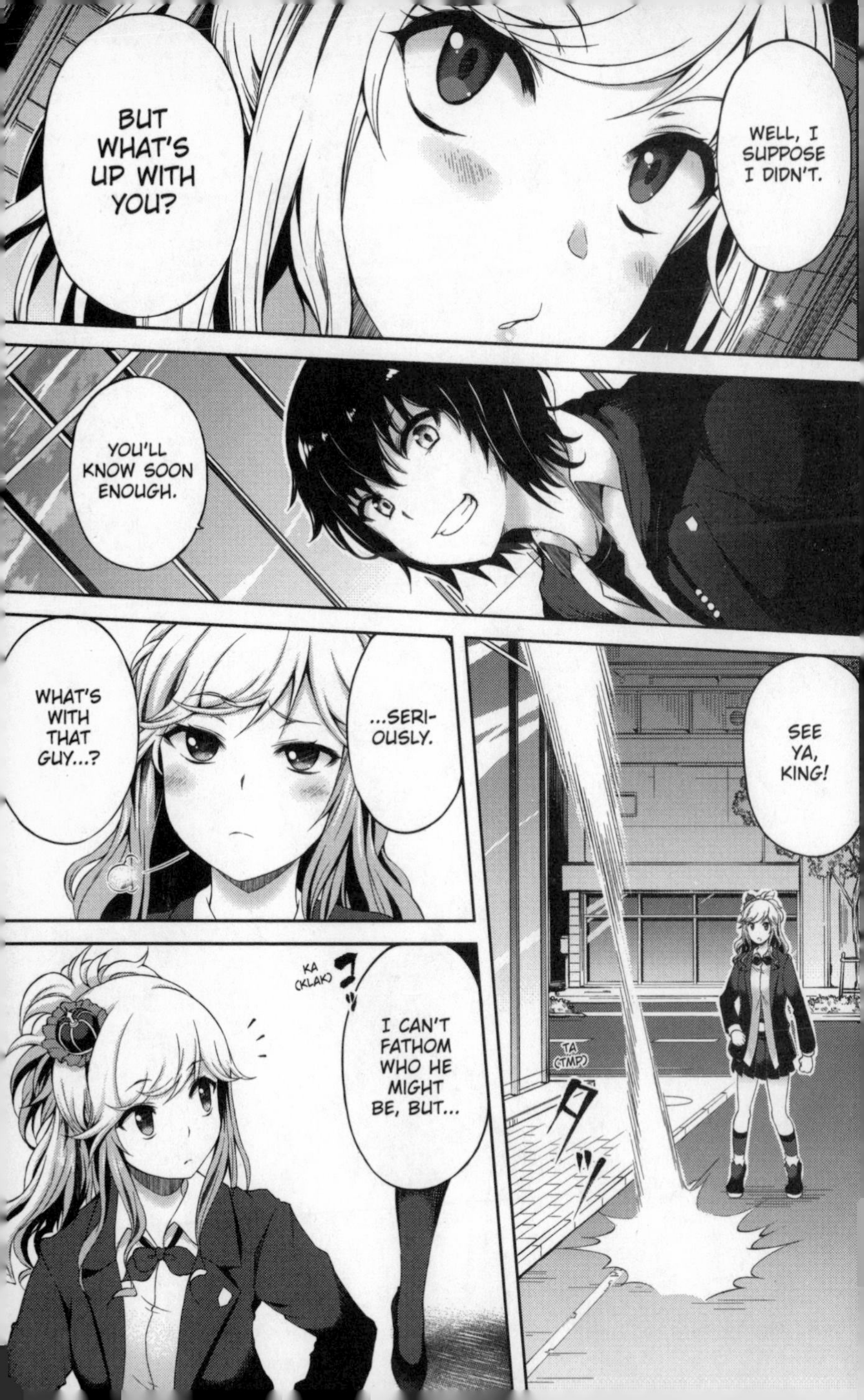
WELL, I SUPPOSE I DIDN'T.
BUT WHAT'S UP WITH YOU?
YOU'LL KNOW SOON ENOUGH.
SEE YA, KING!
TA (TMP)
...SERI-OUSLY.
WHAT'S WITH THAT GUY...?
KA (KLAK)
I CAN'T FATHOM WHO HE MIGHT BE, BUT...

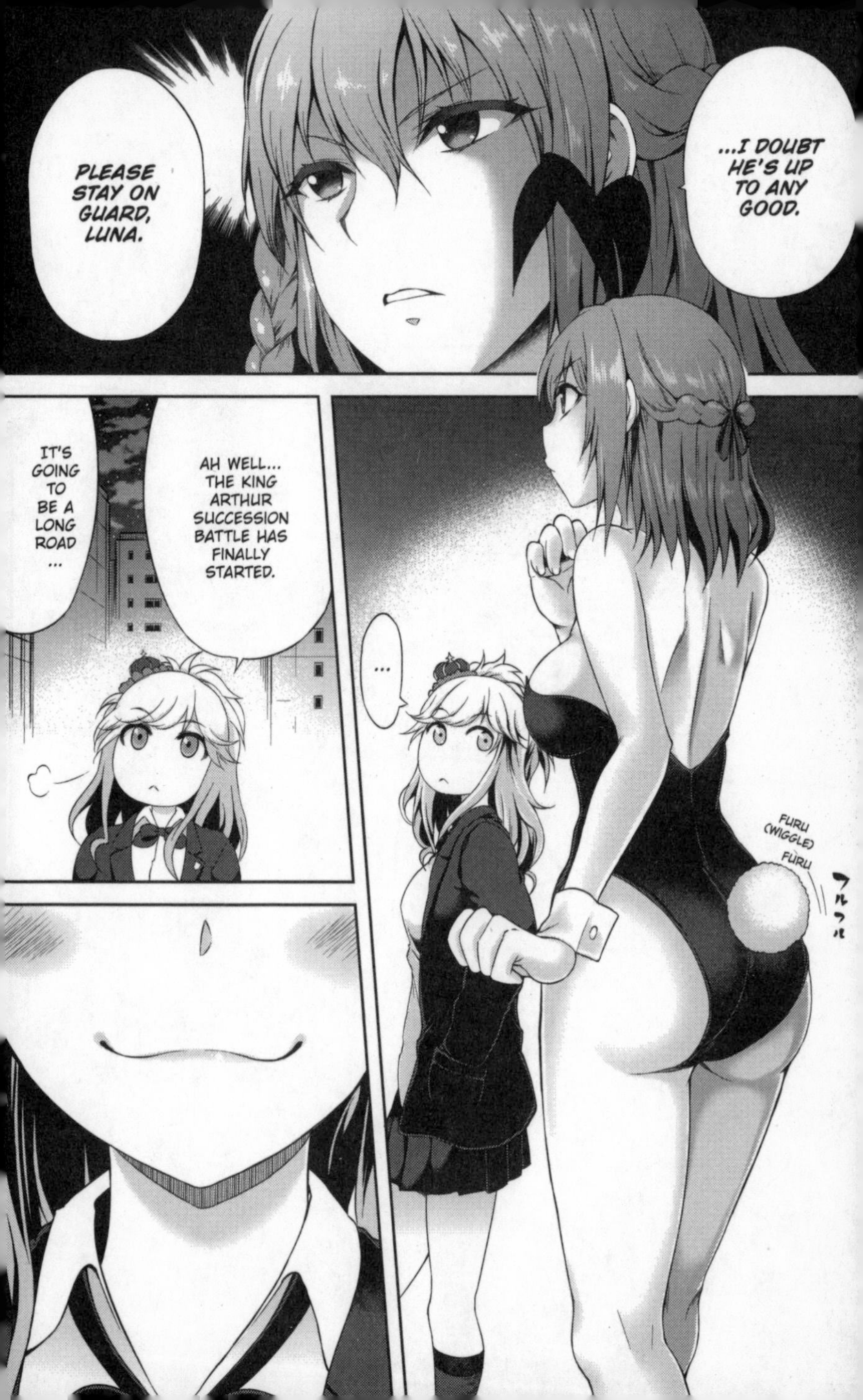
...I DOUBT HE'S UP TO ANY GOOD.
PLEASE STAY ON GUARD, LUNA.
...
FURU (WIGGLE) FURU
フルフル
AH WELL... THE KING ARTHUR SUCCESSION BATTLE HAS FINALLY STARTED.
IT'S GOING TO BE A LONG ROAD...

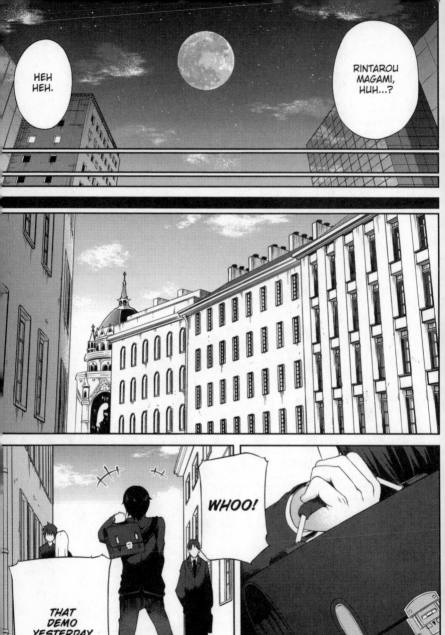

HEH HEH.

RINTAROU MAGAMI, HUH...?

WHOO!

THAT DEMO YESTERDAY WENT WITHOUT A HITCH!

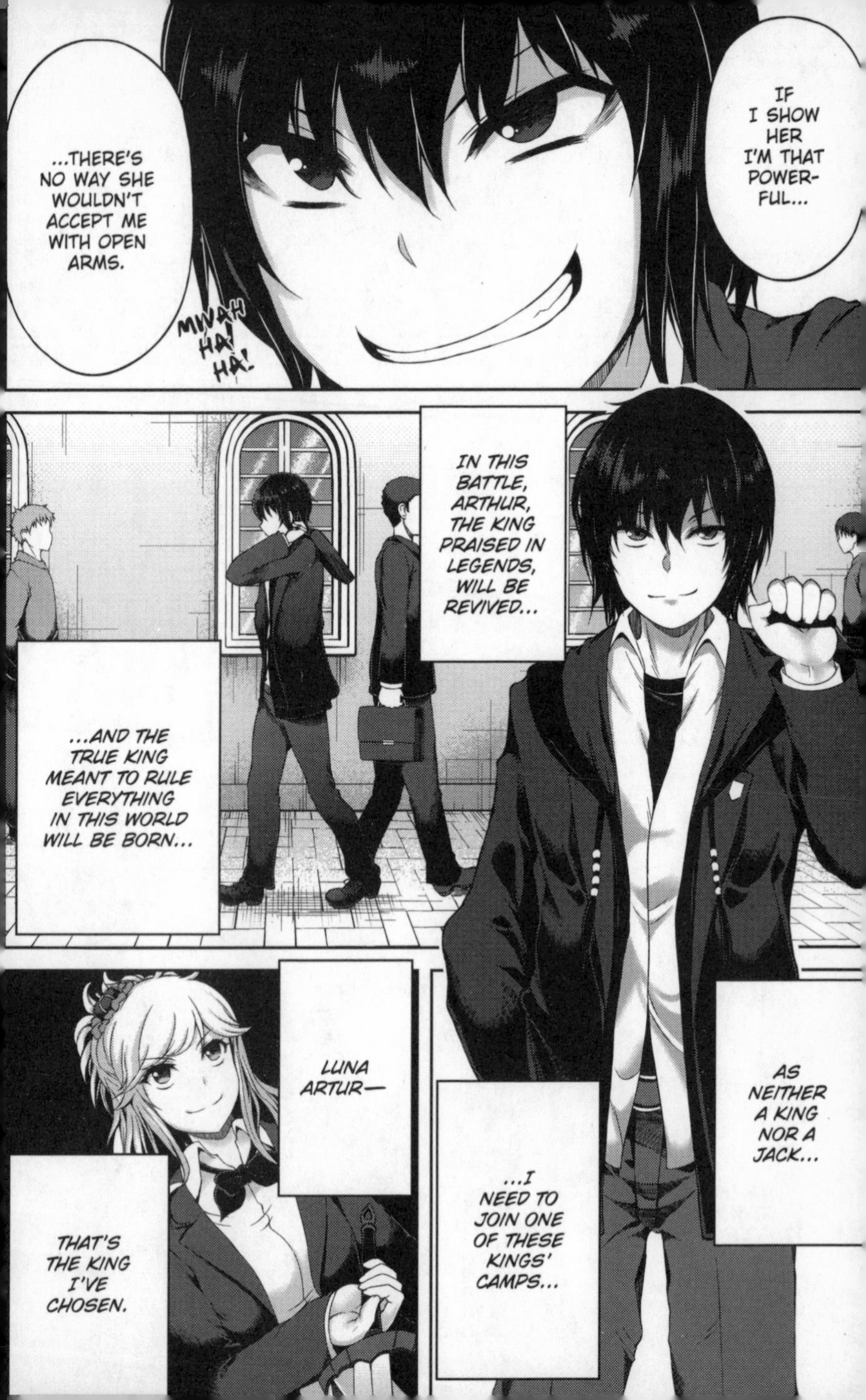
IF I SHOW HER I'M THAT POWER-FUL...
...THERE'S NO WAY SHE WOULDN'T ACCEPT ME WITH OPEN ARMS.
MWAH HA! HA!
IN THIS BATTLE, ARTHUR, THE KING PRAISED IN LEGENDS, WILL BE REVIVED...
...AND THE TRUE KING MEANT TO RULE EVERYTHING IN THIS WORLD WILL BE BORN...
AS NEITHER A KING NOR A JACK...
...I NEED TO JOIN ONE OF THESE KINGS' CAMPS...
LUNA ARTUR—
THAT'S THE KING I'VE CHOSEN.

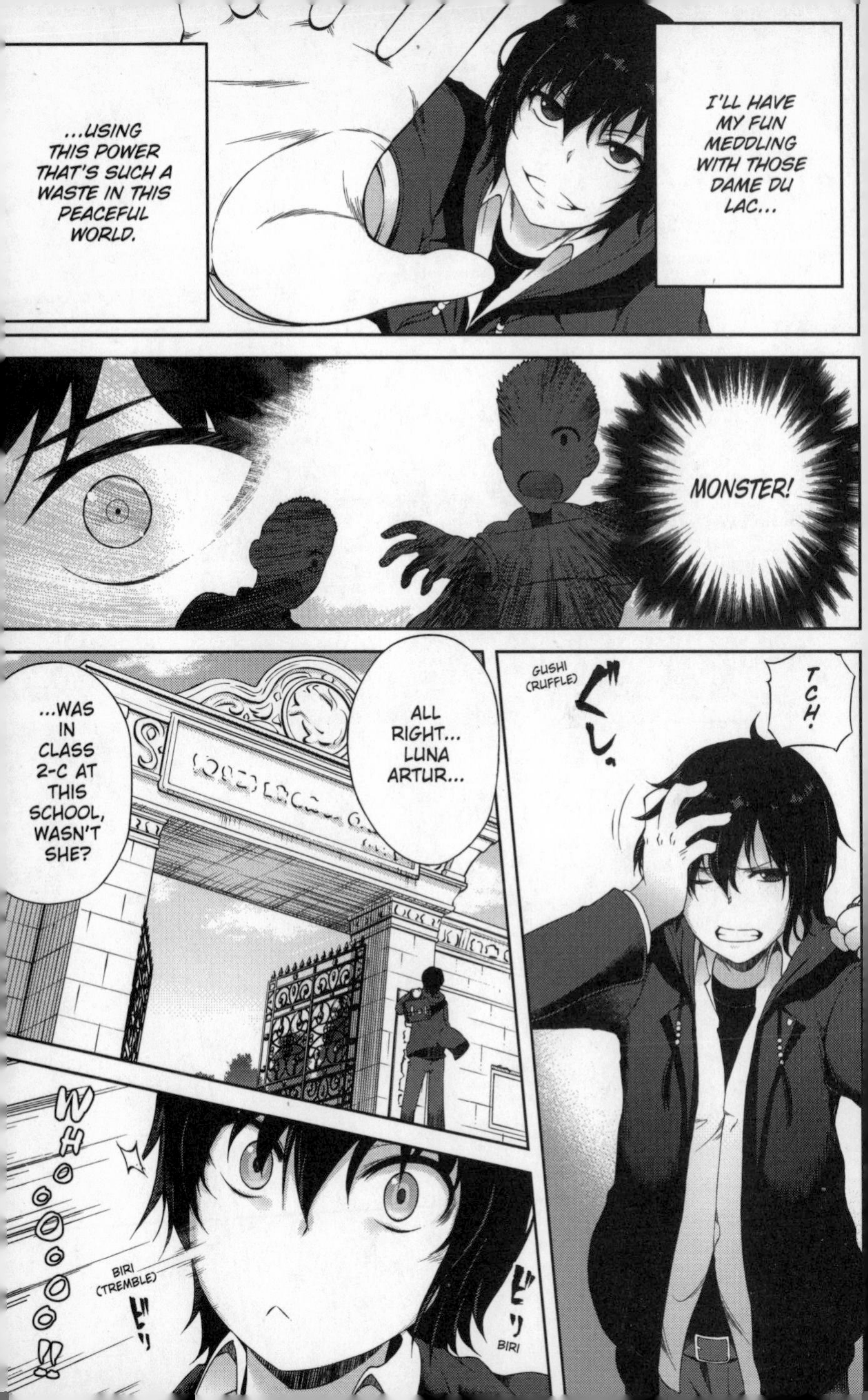
I'LL HAVE MY FUN MEDDLING WITH THOSE DAME DU LAC...
...USING THIS POWER THAT'S SUCH A WASTE IN THIS PEACEFUL WORLD.
MONSTER!
TCH!
GUSHI (RUFFLE)
ALL RIGHT... LUNA ARTUR...
...WAS IN CLASS 2-C AT THIS SCHOOL, WASN'T SHE?
BIRI
BIRI (TREMBLE)
WHOOOOOOO!!

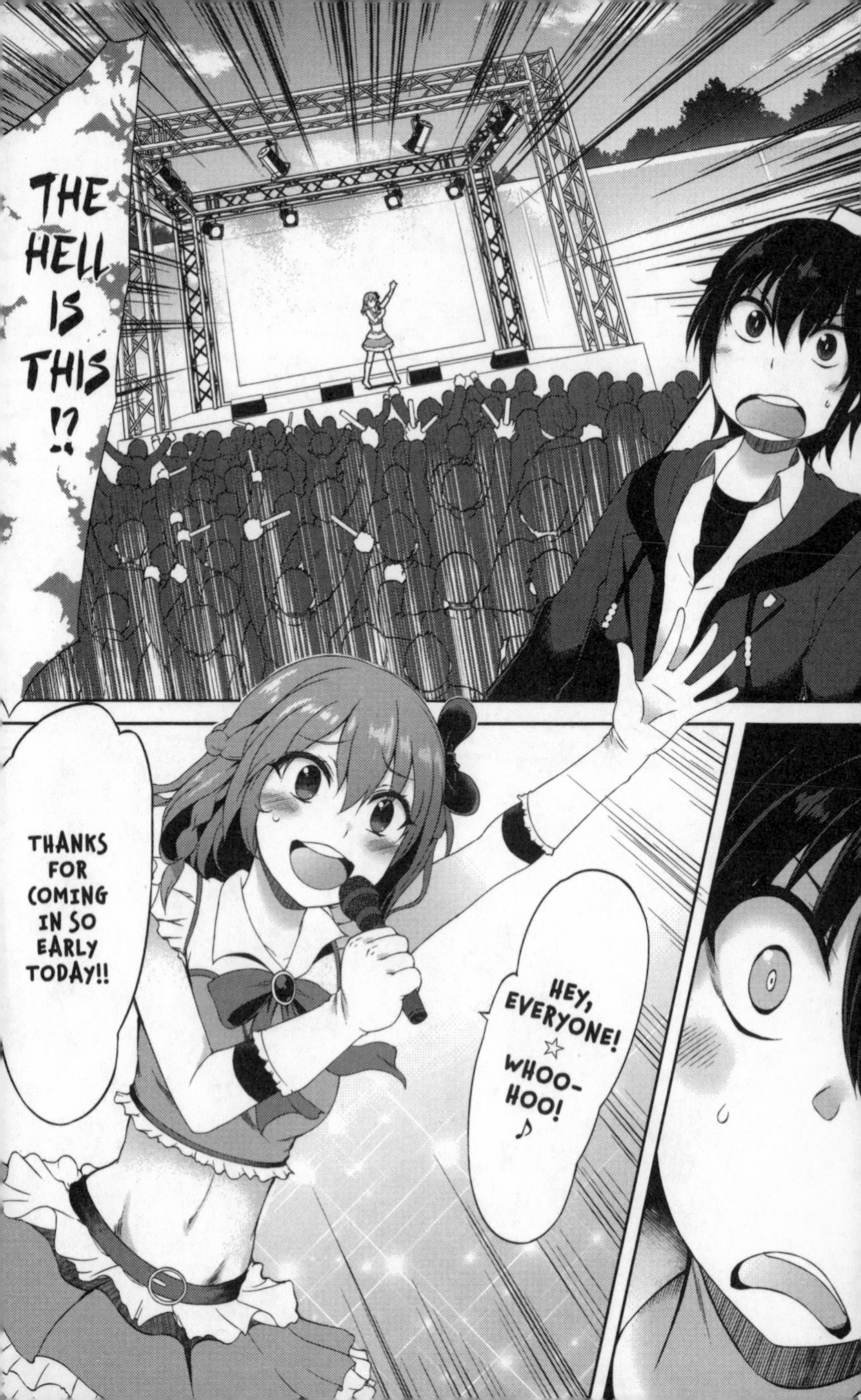
THE HELL IS THIS!?
HEY, EVERYONE! ☆ WHOO-HOO! ♪
THANKS FOR COMING IN SO EARLY TODAY!!

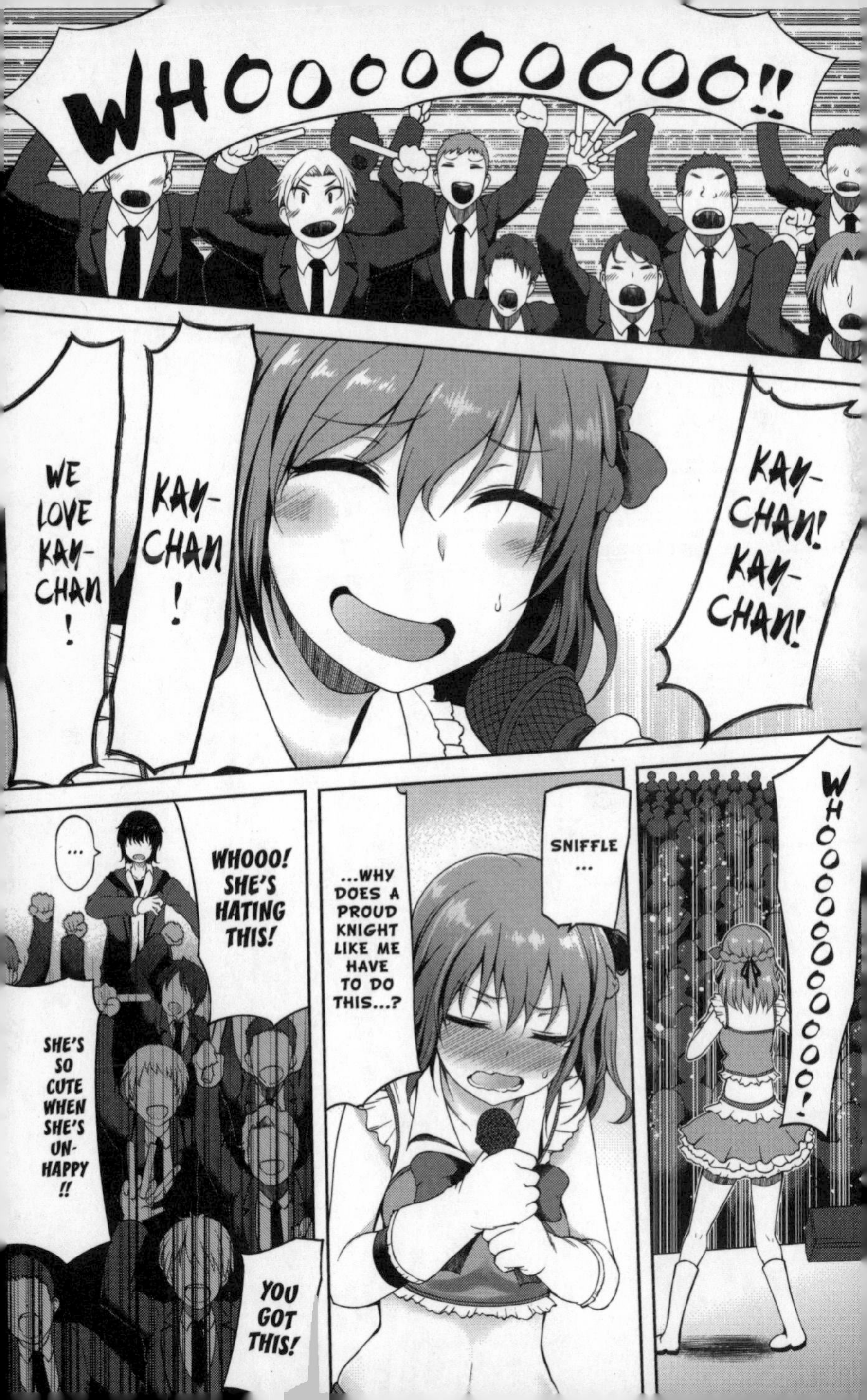
WHOOOOOOOOOO!!
KAY-CHAN! KAY-CHAN!
KAY-CHAN!
WE LOVE KAY-CHAN!
WHOOOOOOOOOOOO!
SNIFFLE...
...WHY DOES A PROUD KNIGHT LIKE ME HAVE TO DO THIS...?
WHOOO! SHE'S HATING THIS!
...
SHE'S SO CUTE WHEN SHE'S UNHAPPY!!
YOU GOT THIS!

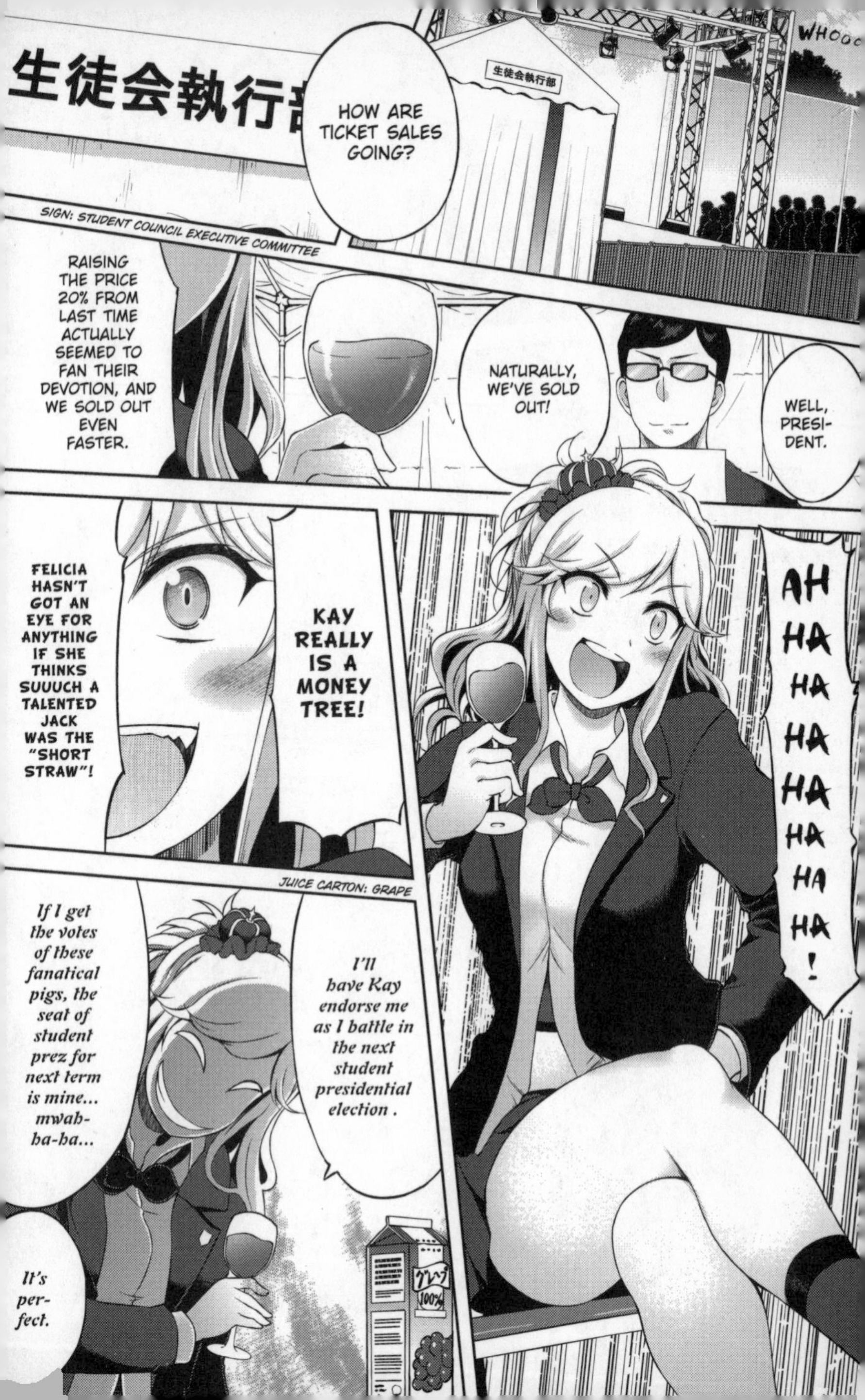

WHOOO
生徒会執行部
HOW ARE TICKET SALES GOING?
生徒会執行部
SIGN: STUDENT COUNCIL EXECUTIVE COMMITTEE
WELL, PRESIDENT.
NATURALLY, WE'VE SOLD OUT!
RAISING THE PRICE 20% FROM LAST TIME ACTUALLY SEEMED TO FAN THEIR DEVOTION, AND WE SOLD OUT EVEN FASTER.
AH HA HA HA HA HA HA HA HA!
KAY REALLY IS A MONEY TREE!
FELICIA HASN'T GOT AN EYE FOR ANYTHING IF SHE THINKS SUUUCH A TALENTED JACK WAS THE "SHORT STRAW"!
JUICE CARTON: GRAPE
グレープ
100%
I'll have Kay endorse me as I battle in the next student presidential election .
If I get the votes of these fanatical pigs, the seat of student prez for next term is mine... mwah-ha-ha...
It's per-fect.

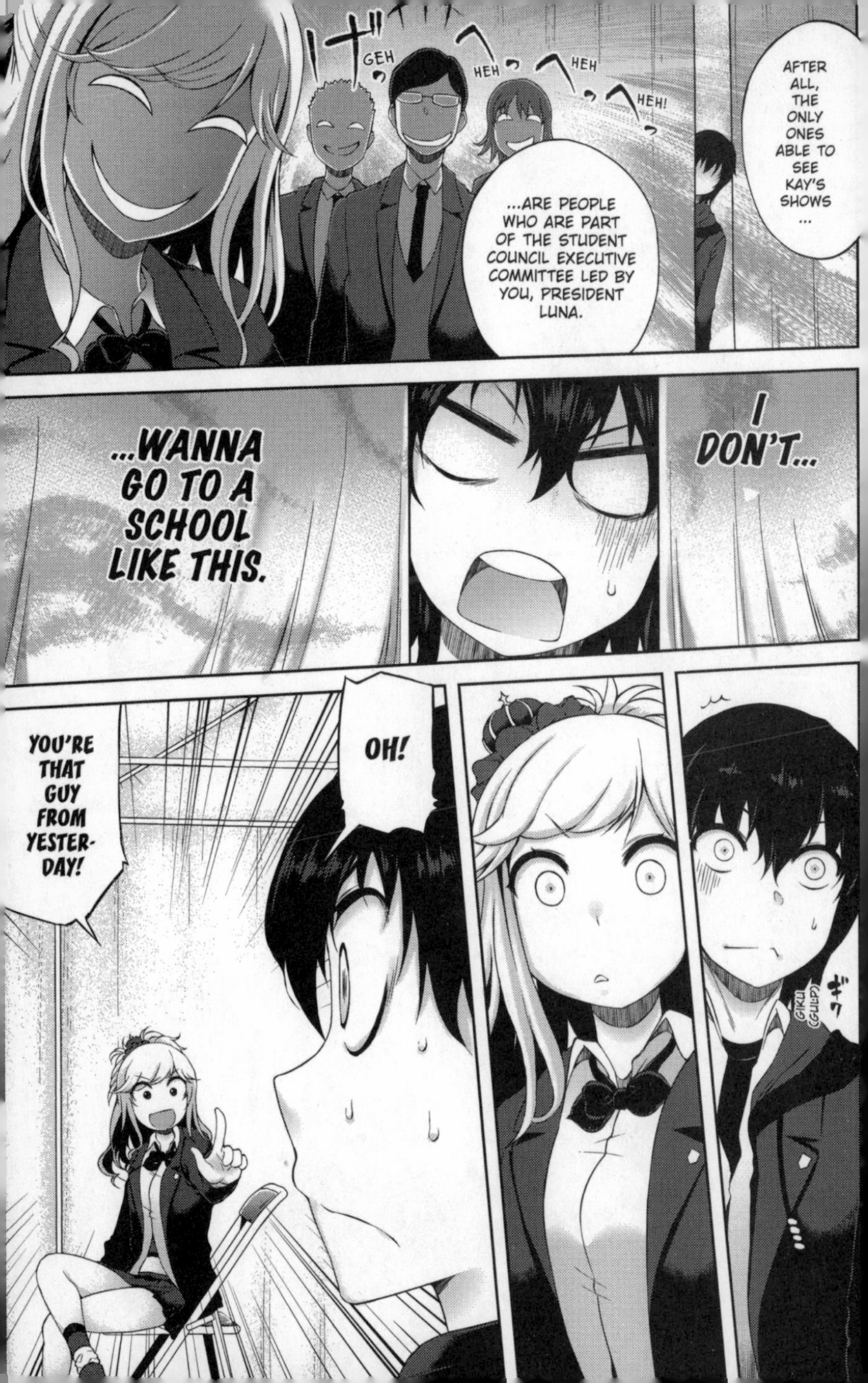
AFTER ALL, THE ONLY ONES ABLE TO SEE KAY'S SHOWS ...
HEH!
HEH
HEH
GEH
...ARE PEOPLE WHO ARE PART OF THE STUDENT COUNCIL EXECUTIVE COMMITTEE LED BY YOU, PRESIDENT LUNA.
I DON'T...
...WANNA GO TO A SCHOOL LIKE THIS.
GIKU (GULP)
OH!
YOU'RE THAT GUY FROM YESTER-DAY!

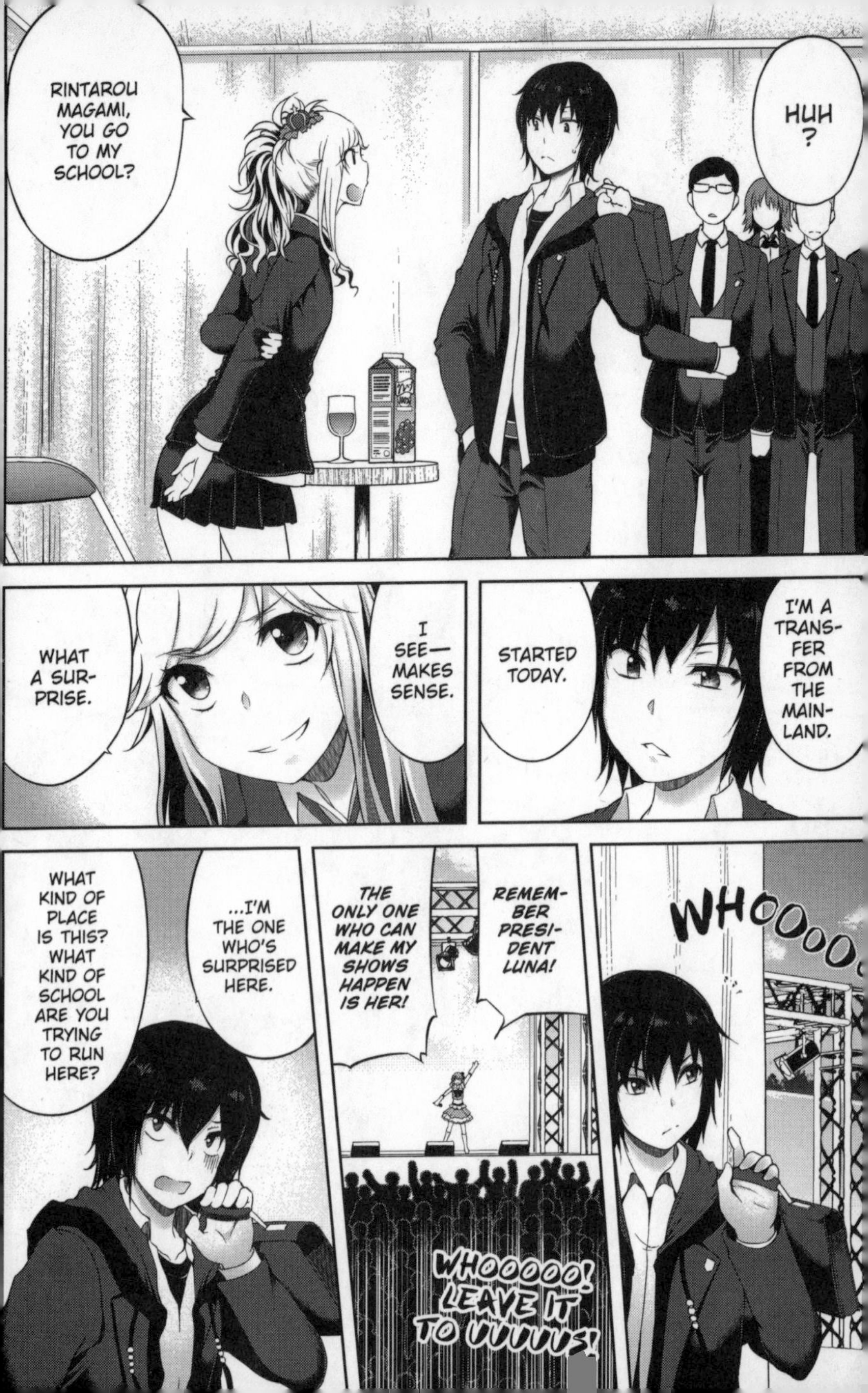
HUH?
RINTAROU MAGAMI, YOU GO TO MY SCHOOL?
I'M A TRANSFER FROM THE MAINLAND.
STARTED TODAY.
I SEE—MAKES SENSE.
WHAT A SURPRISE.
WHOOOOO
REMEMBER PRESIDENT LUNA!
THE ONLY ONE WHO CAN MAKE MY SHOWS HAPPEN IS HER!
WHOOOOOO! LEAVE IT TO UUUUUS!
...I'M THE ONE WHO'S SURPRISED HERE.
WHAT KIND OF PLACE IS THIS? WHAT KIND OF SCHOOL ARE YOU TRYING TO RUN HERE?

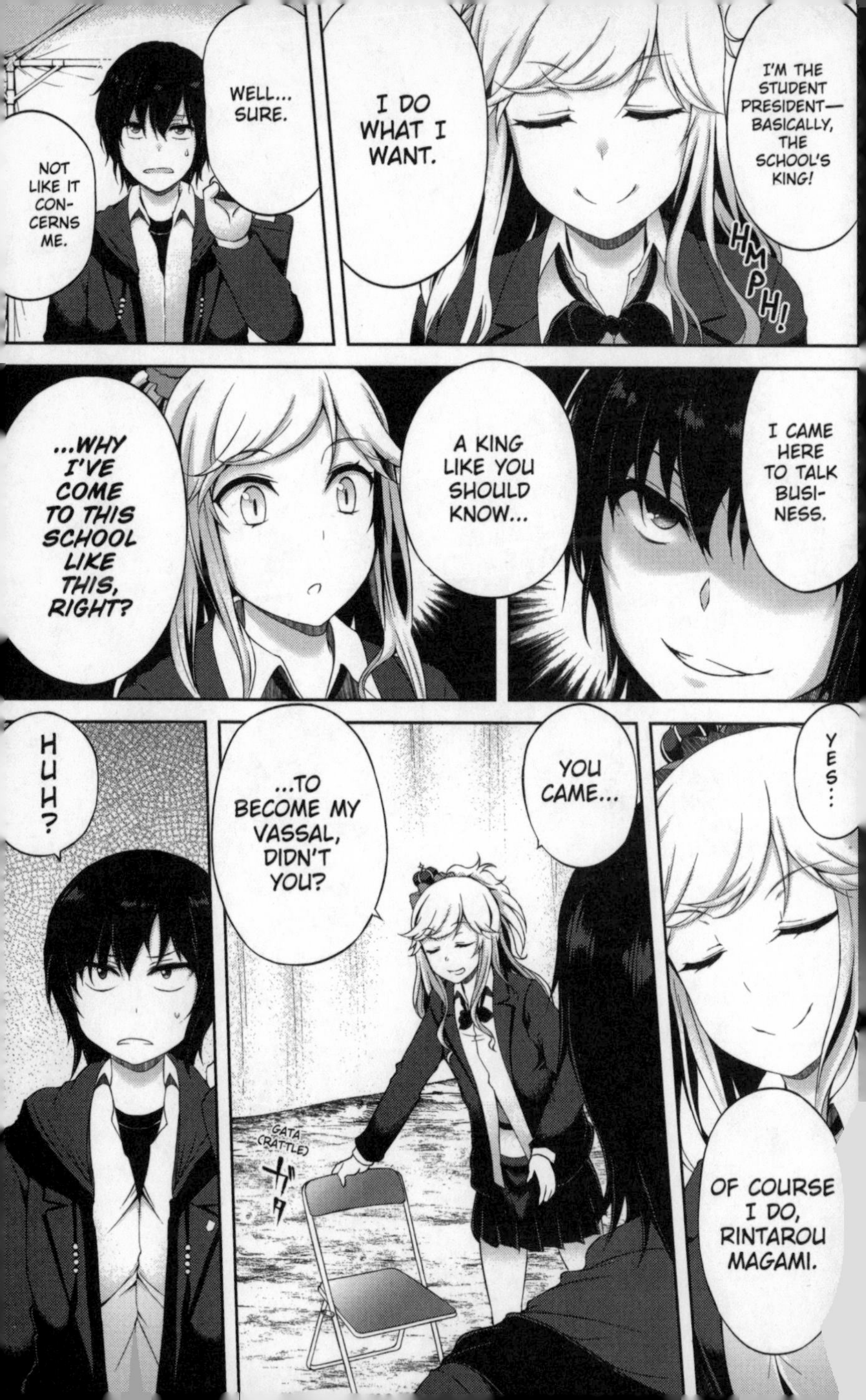
I'M THE STUDENT PRESIDENT—BASICALLY, THE SCHOOL'S KING!
HMPH!
I DO WHAT I WANT.
WELL... SURE.
NOT LIKE IT CONCERNS ME.
I CAME HERE TO TALK BUSINESS.
A KING LIKE YOU SHOULD KNOW...
...WHY I'VE COME TO THIS SCHOOL LIKE THIS, RIGHT?
YES...
OF COURSE I DO, RINTAROU MAGAMI.
YOU CAME...
...TO BECOME MY VASSAL, DIDN'T YOU?
GATA (RATTLE)
HUH?

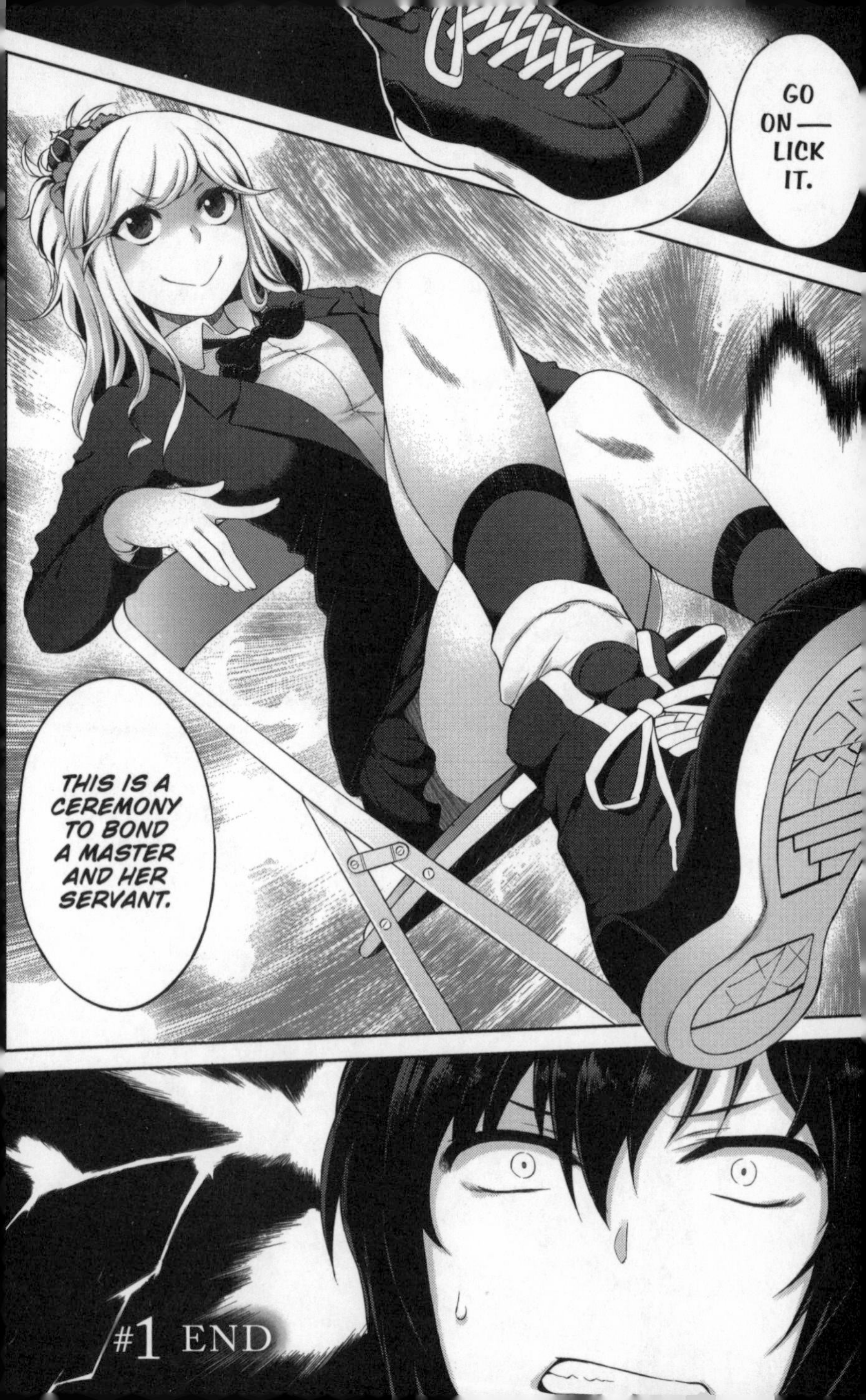
GO ON— LICK IT.
THIS IS A CEREMONY TO BOND A MASTER AND HER SERVANT.
#1 END

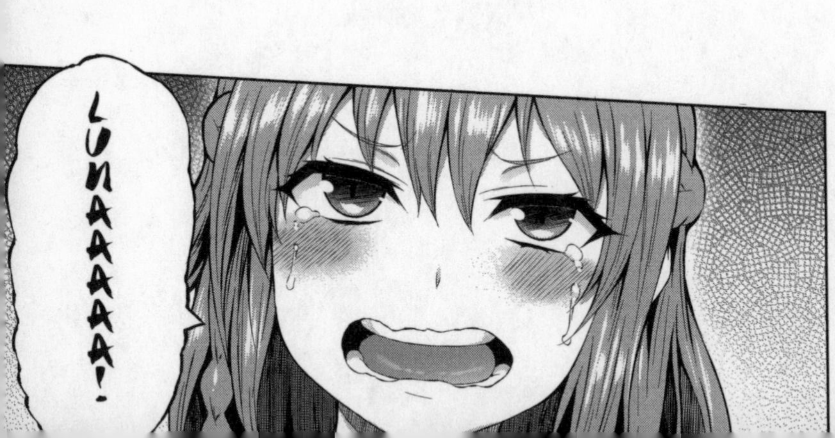
LUNAAAAA!

LAST ROUND
ARTHURS

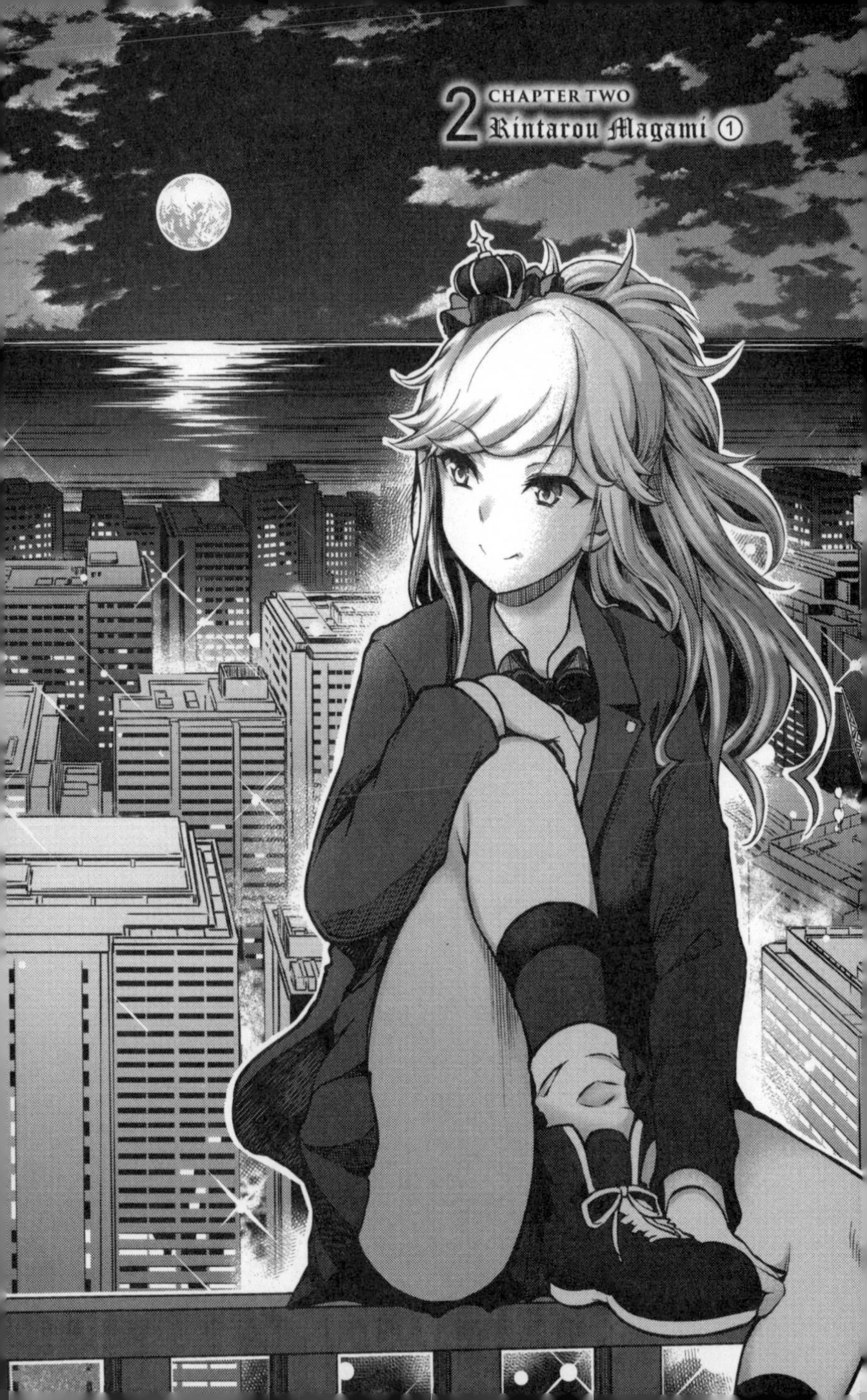
2 CHAPTER TWO
Rintarou Magami ①

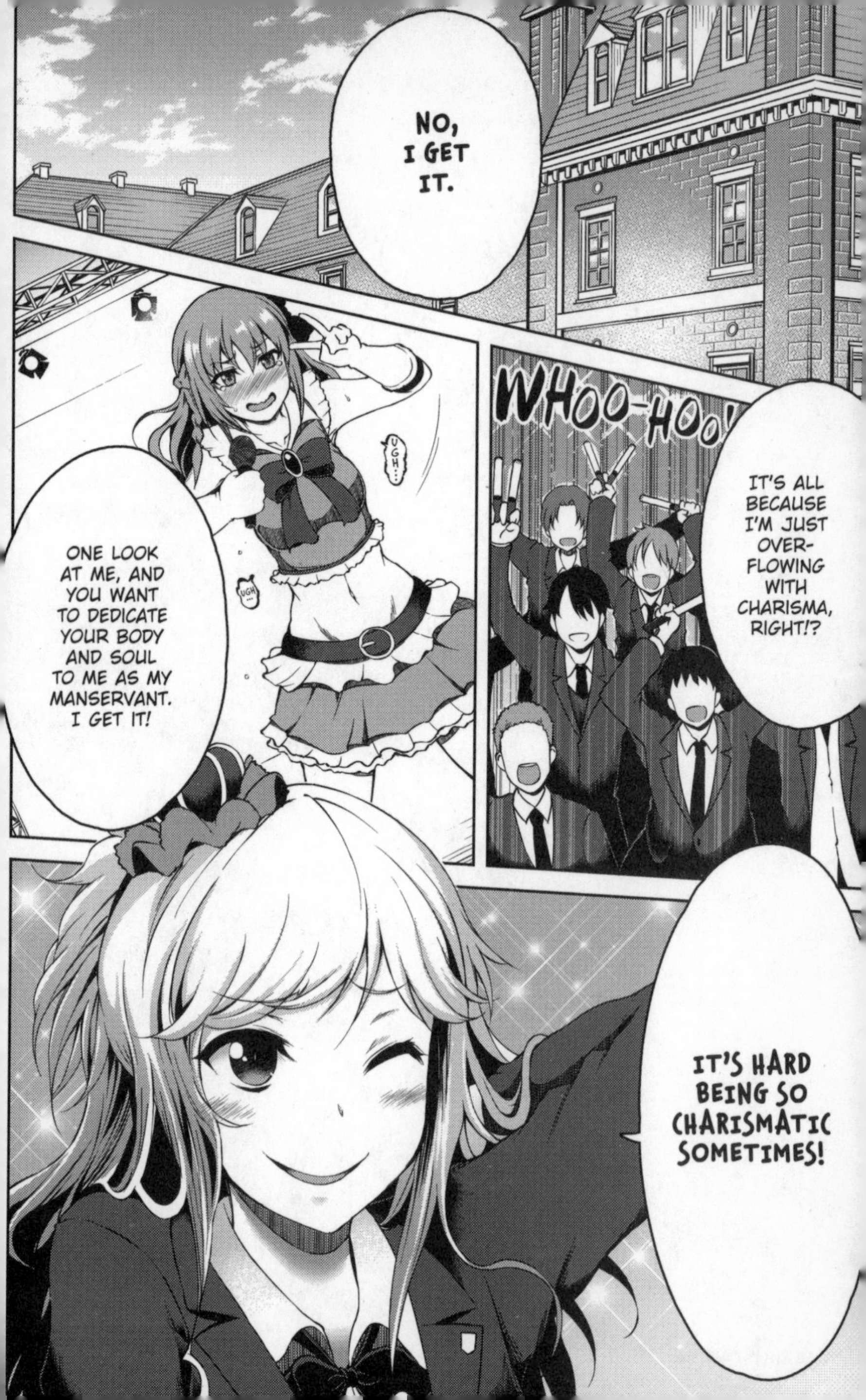
NO, I GET IT.
WHOO-HOO!
IT'S ALL BECAUSE I'M JUST OVER-FLOWING WITH CHARISMA, RIGHT!?
UGH...
UGH...
ONE LOOK AT ME, AND YOU WANT TO DEDICATE YOUR BODY AND SOUL TO ME AS MY MANSERVANT. I GET IT!
IT'S HARD BEING SO CHARISMATIC SOMETIMES!

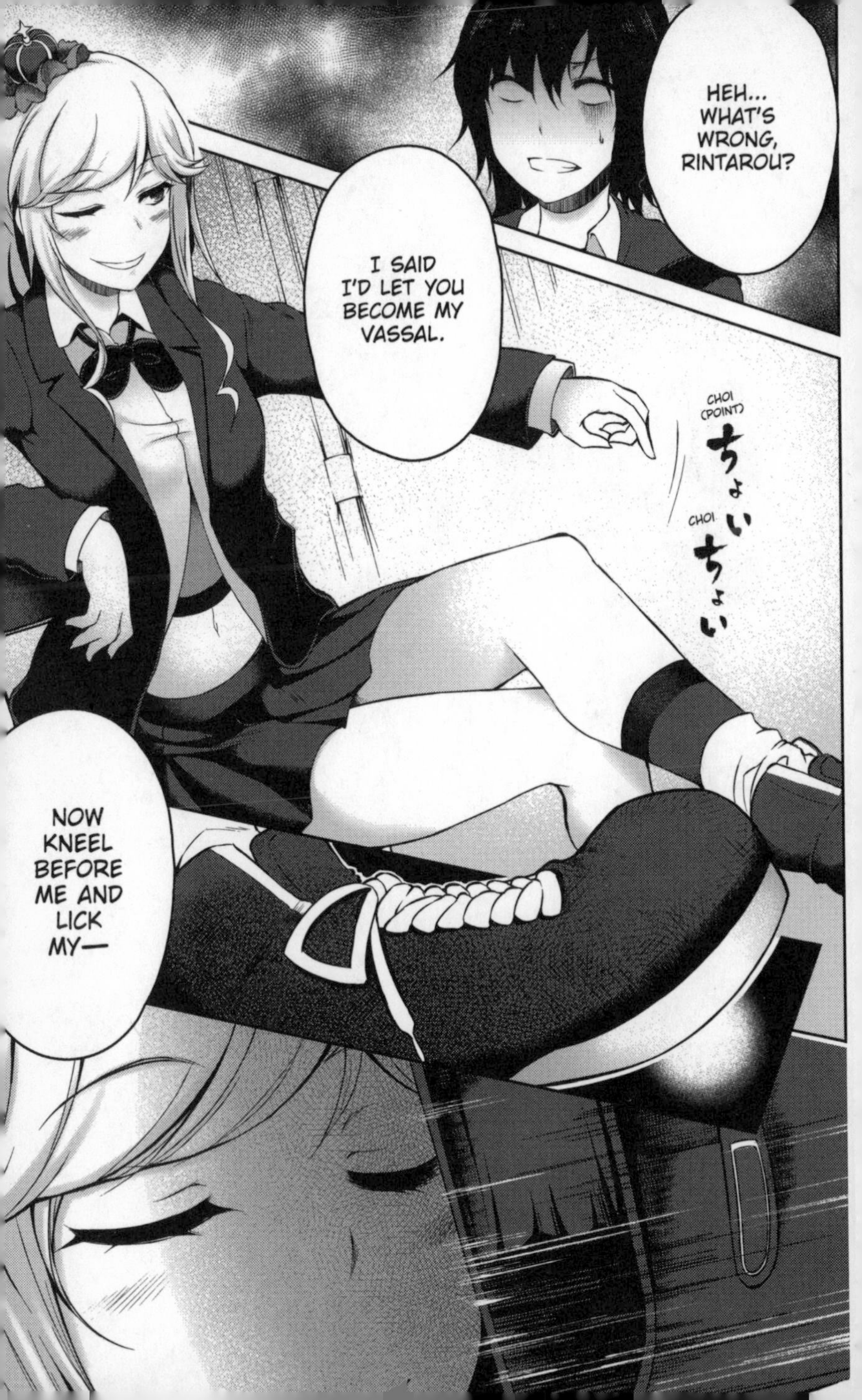
HEH... WHAT'S WRONG, RINTAROU?
I SAID I'D LET YOU BECOME MY VASSAL.
CHOI (POINT)
ちょい
CHOI
ちょい
NOW KNEEL BEFORE ME AND LICK MY—

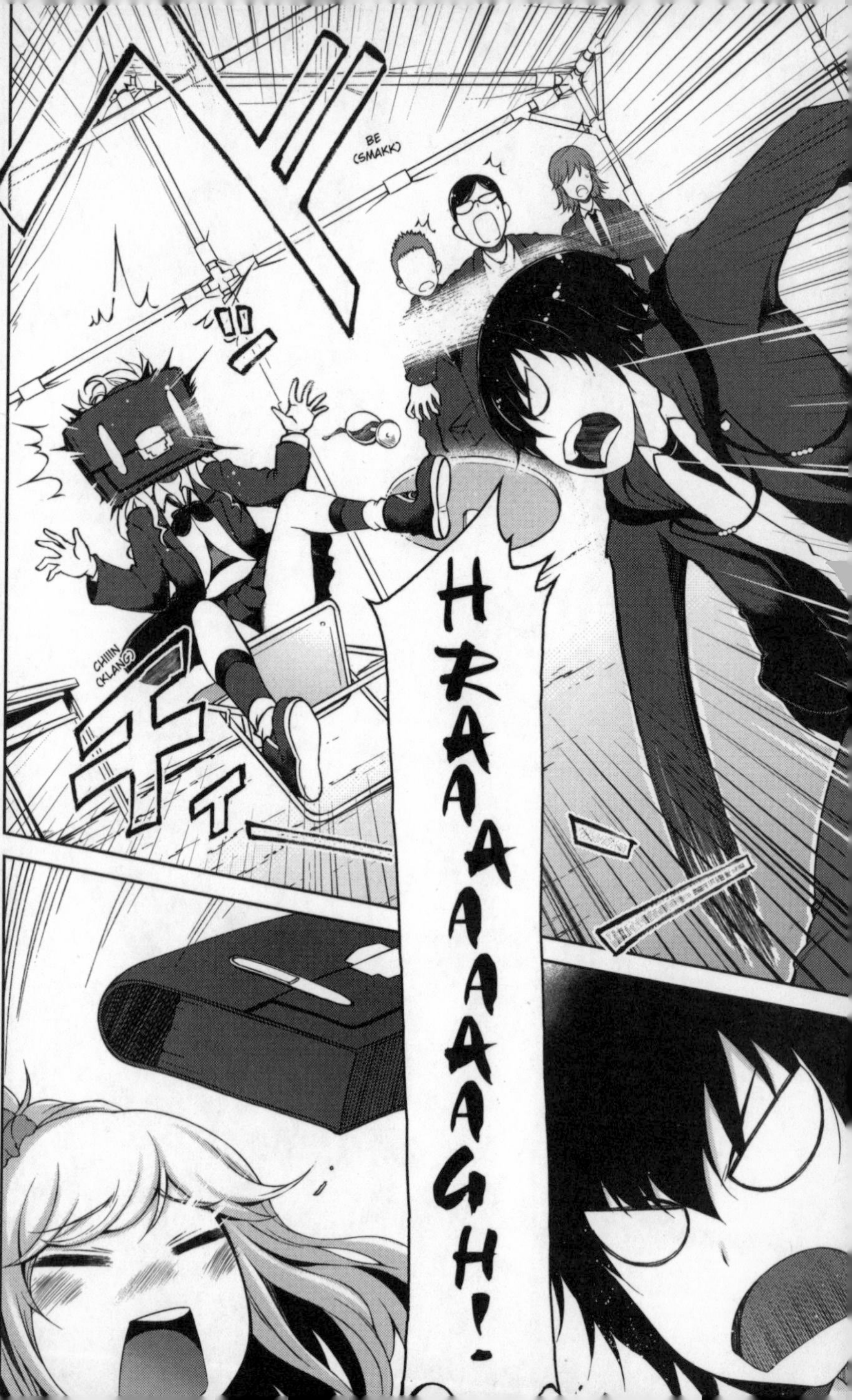
BE
(SMAKK)
CHIIIN
(KLANG)
HRAAAAAAAGH!

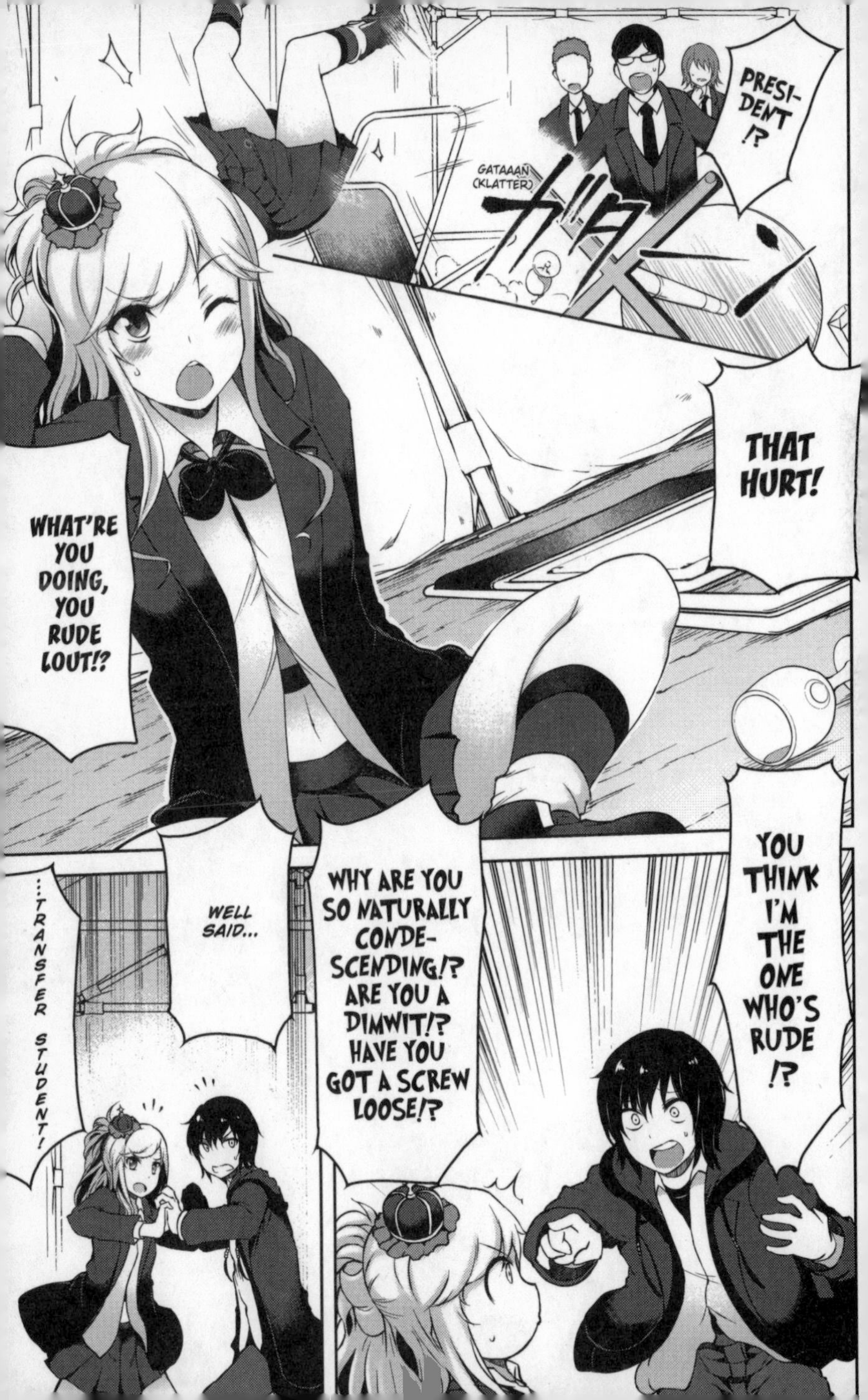
PRESIDENT!?
GATAAAN (KLATTER)
THAT HURT!
WHAT'RE YOU DOING, YOU RUDE LOUT!?
YOU THINK I'M THE ONE WHO'S RUDE!?
WHY ARE YOU SO NATURALLY CONDE-SCENDING!? ARE YOU A DIMWIT!? HAVE YOU GOT A SCREW LOOSE!?
WELL SAID...
...TRANSFER STUDENT!

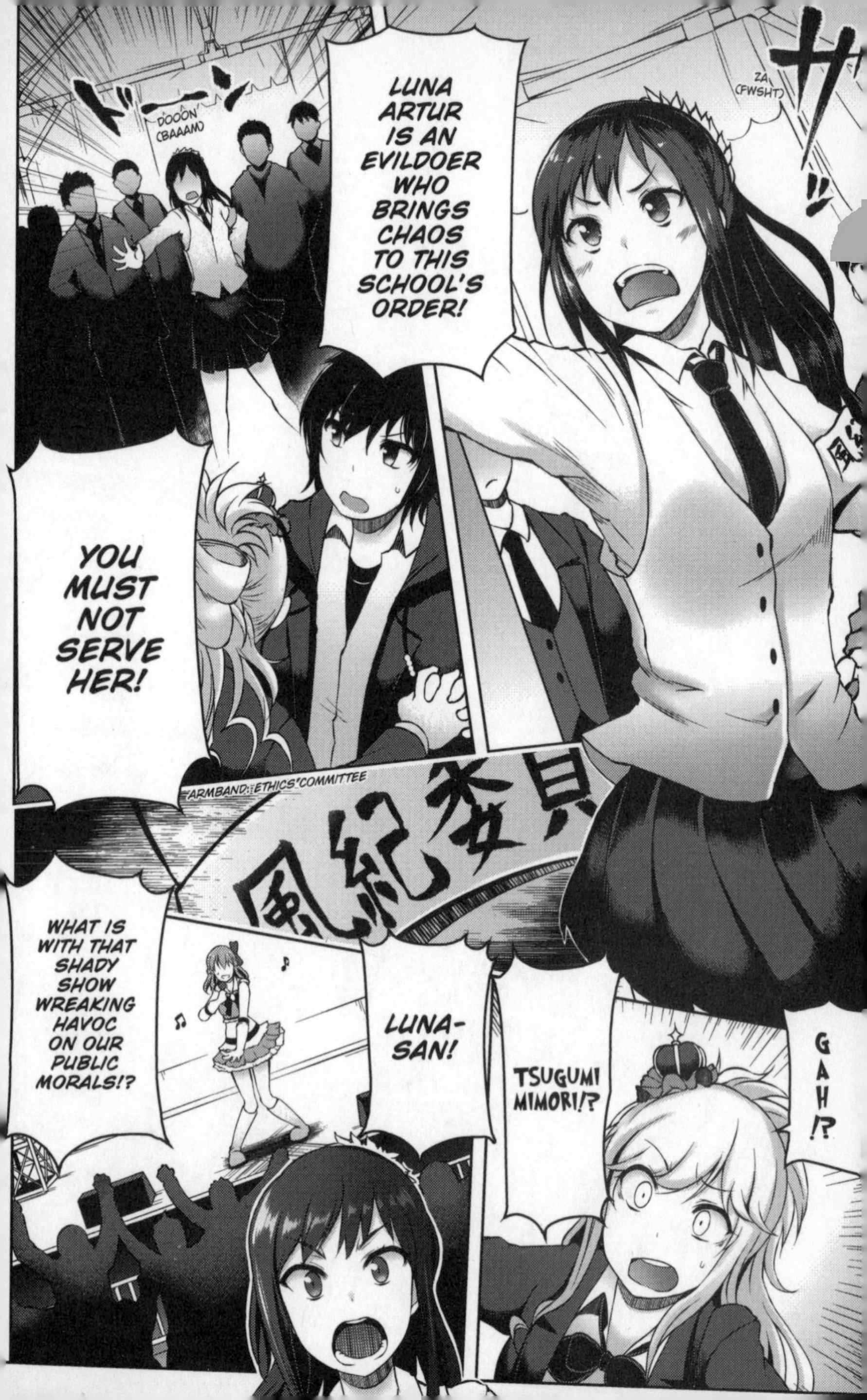
ZA (FWSHT)
LUNA ARTUR IS AN EVILDOER WHO BRINGS CHAOS TO THIS SCHOOL'S ORDER!
ARMBAND: ETHICS COMMITTEE
DOOON (BAAAM)
YOU MUST NOT SERVE HER!
GAH!?
TSUGUMI MIMORI!?
LUNA-SAN!
WHAT IS WITH THAT SHADY SHOW WREAKING HAVOC ON OUR PUBLIC MORALS!?

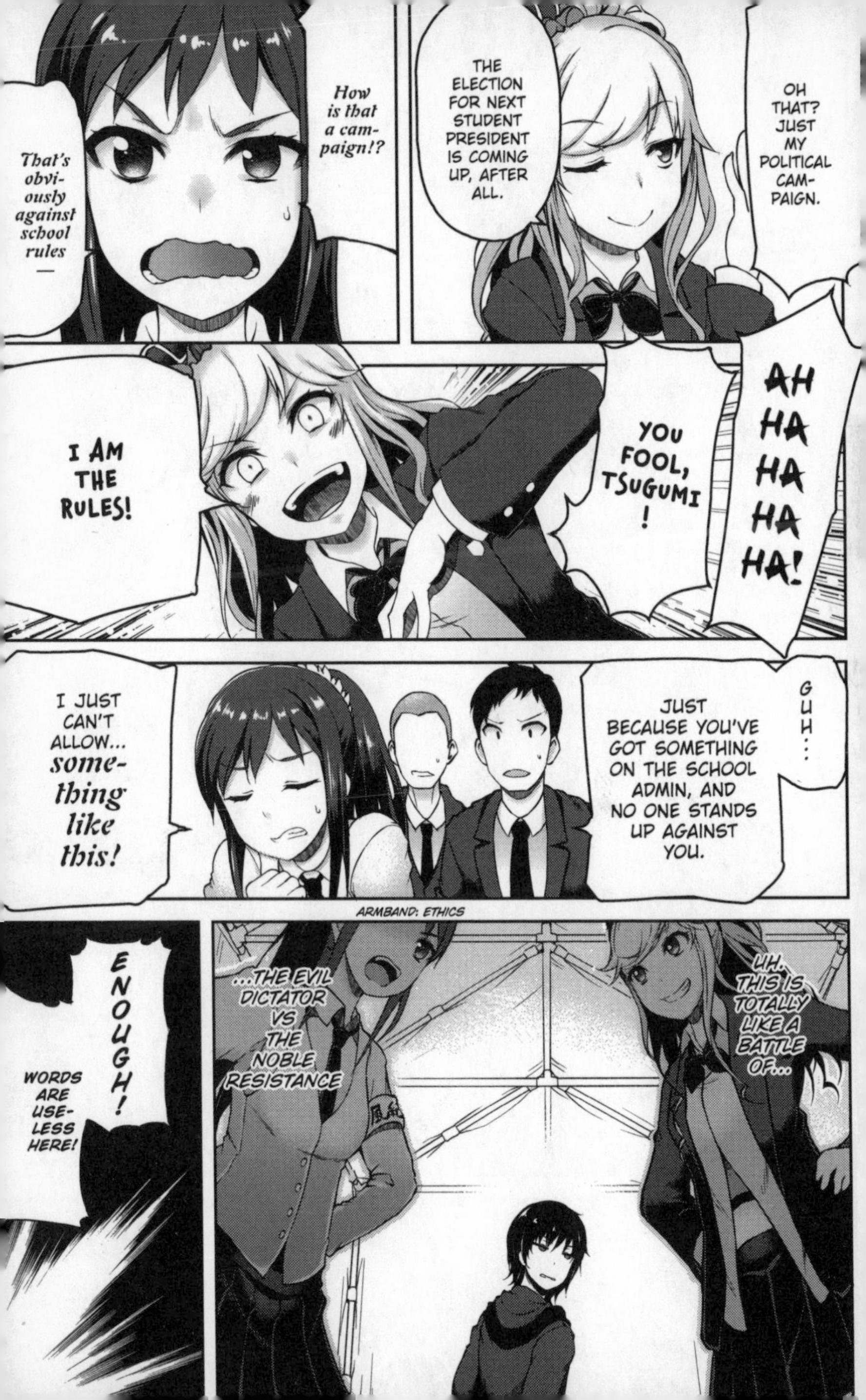
OH THAT? JUST MY POLITICAL CAMPAIGN.
THE ELECTION FOR NEXT STUDENT PRESIDENT IS COMING UP, AFTER ALL.
How is that a campaign!?
That's obviously against school rules —
AH HA HA HA HA!
YOU FOOL, TSUGUMI!
I AM THE RULES!
GUH...
JUST BECAUSE YOU'VE GOT SOMETHING ON THE SCHOOL ADMIN, AND NO ONE STANDS UP AGAINST YOU.
I JUST CAN'T ALLOW... something like this!
ARMBAND: ETHICS
UH. THIS IS TOTALLY LIKE A BATTLE OF...
...THE EVIL DICTATOR VS THE NOBLE RESISTANCE
ENOUGH!
WORDS ARE USELESS HERE!

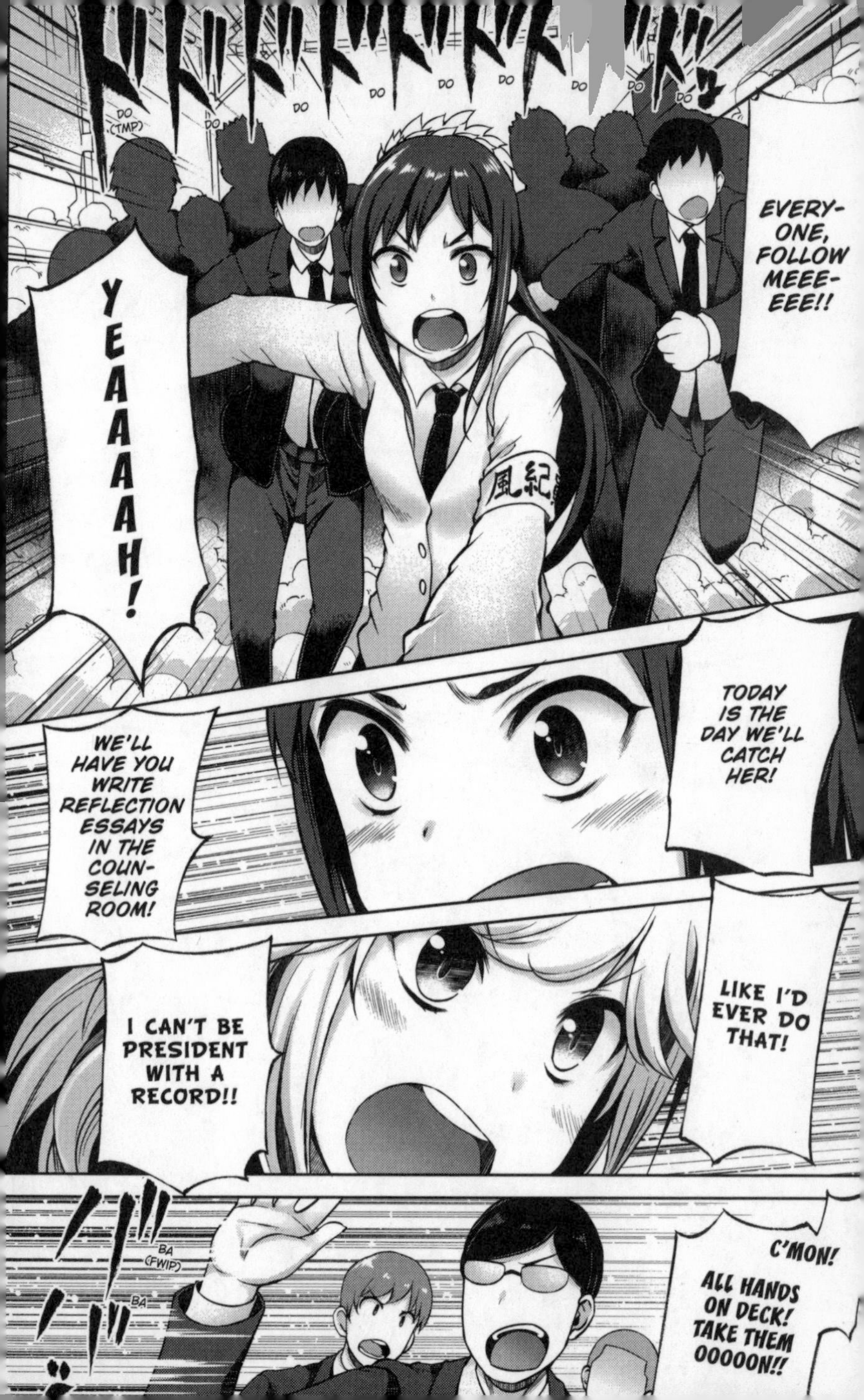
DO DO DO DO DO DO DO
DO (TMP)
EVERYONE, FOLLOW MEEEEEE!!
YEAAAAAAH!
TODAY IS THE DAY WE'LL CATCH HER!
WE'LL HAVE YOU WRITE REFLECTION ESSAYS IN THE COUNSELING ROOM!
LIKE I'D EVER DO THAT!
I CAN'T BE PRESIDENT WITH A RECORD!!
C'MON!
ALL HANDS ON DECK! TAKE THEM OOOOON!!
BA (FWIP)
BA

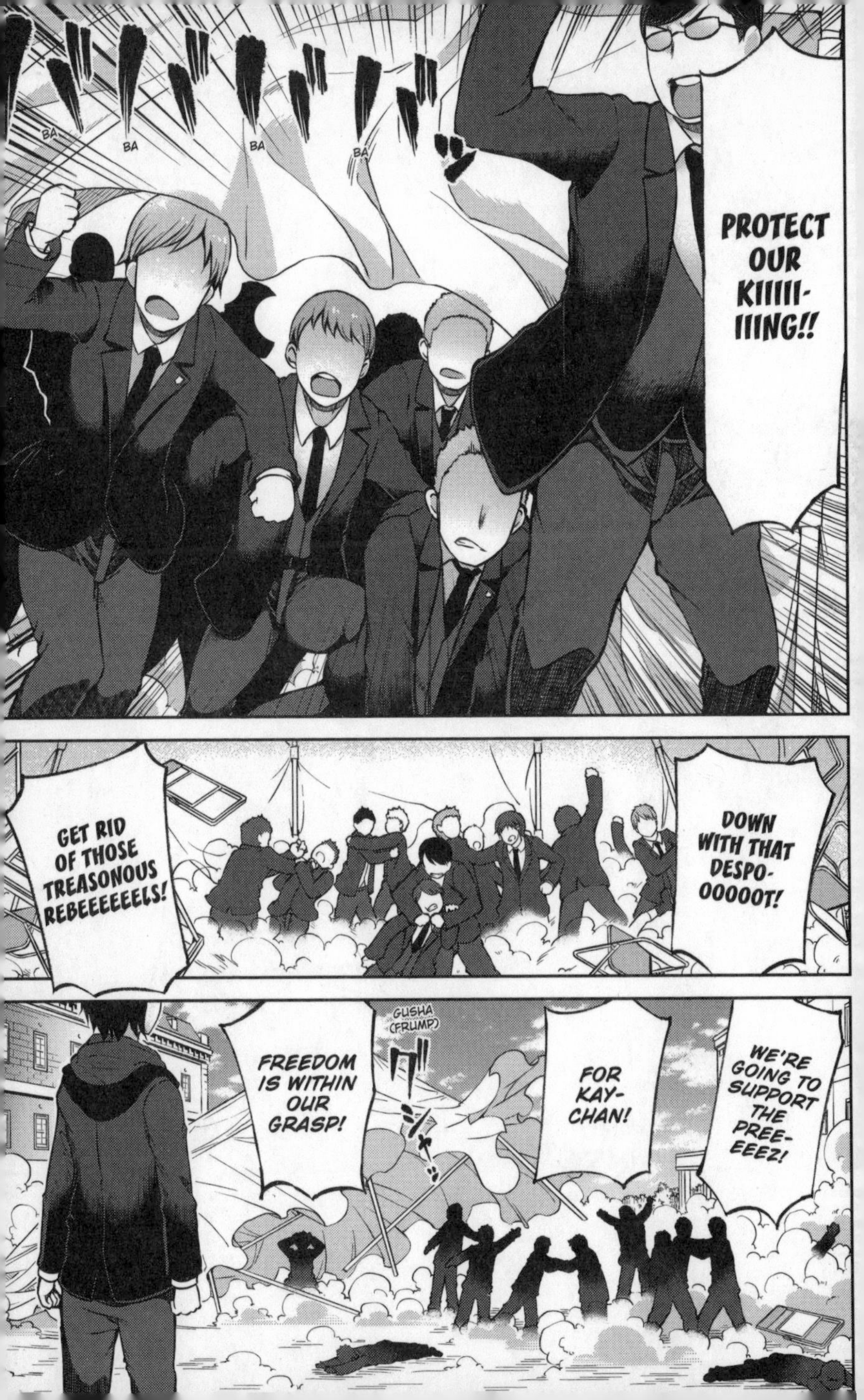

BA
BA
BA
BA
PROTECT OUR KIIIII-IIING!!
DOWN WITH THAT DESPO-OOOOOT!
GET RID OF THOSE TREASONOUS REBEEEEEELS!
WE'RE GOING TO SUPPORT THE PREE-EEEZ!
FOR KAY-CHAN!
GUSHA (FRUMP)
FREEDOM IS WITHIN OUR GRASP!

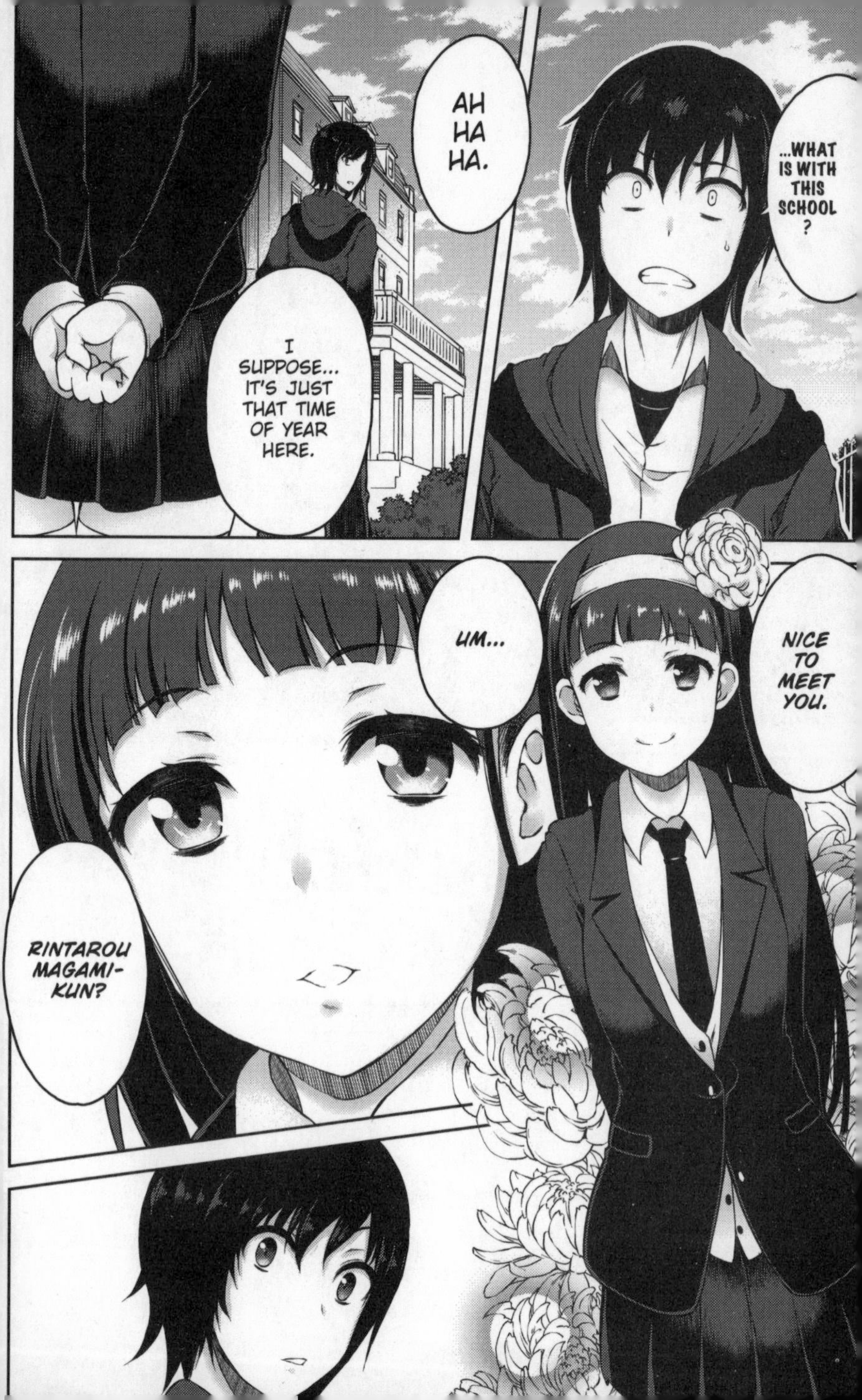
...WHAT IS WITH THIS SCHOOL?
AH HA HA.
I SUPPOSE... IT'S JUST THAT TIME OF YEAR HERE.
NICE TO MEET YOU.
UM...
RINTAROU MAGAMI-KUN?

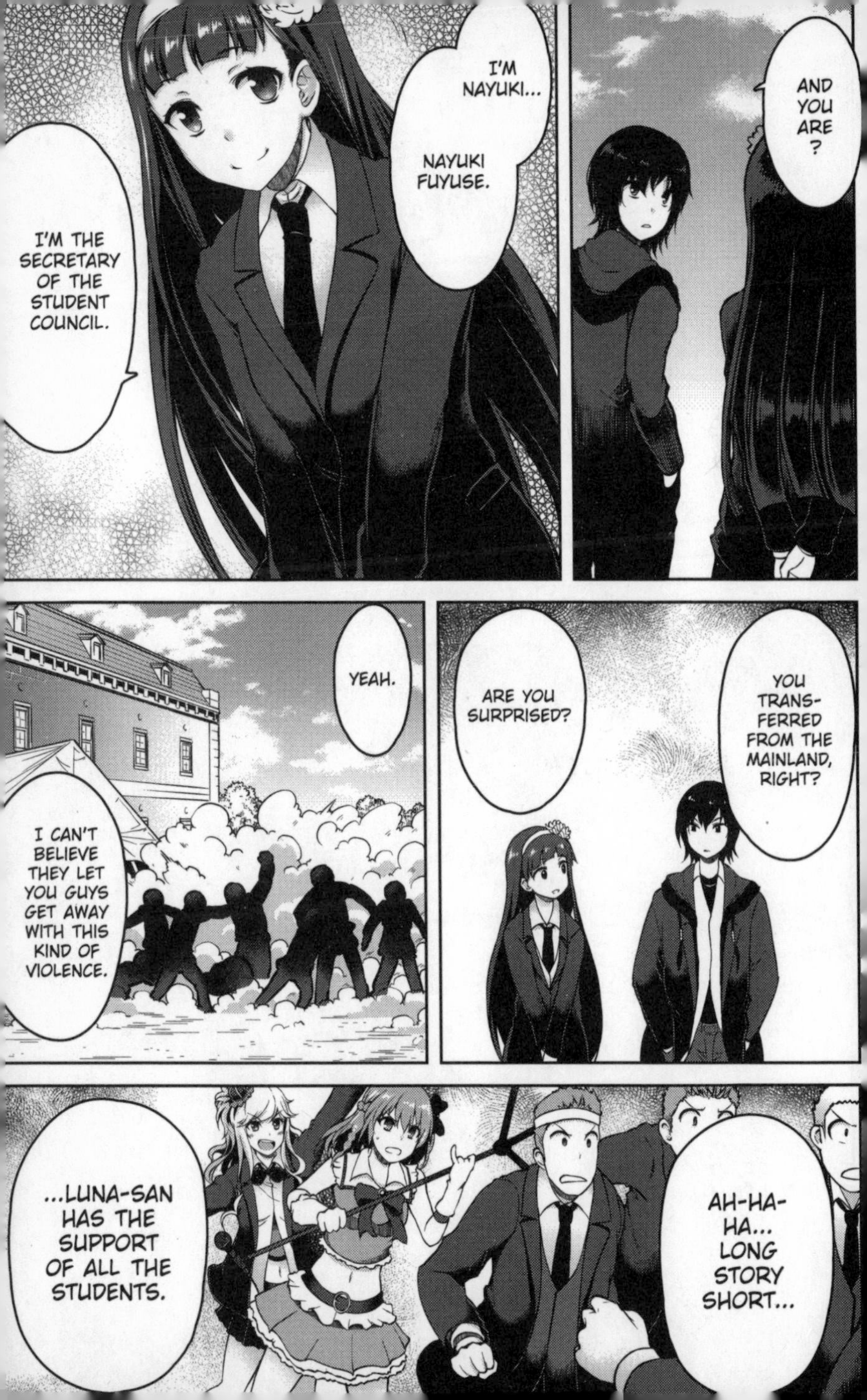
AND YOU ARE?
I'M NAYUKI...
NAYUKI FUYUSE.
I'M THE SECRETARY OF THE STUDENT COUNCIL.
YOU TRANSFERRED FROM THE MAINLAND, RIGHT?
ARE YOU SURPRISED?
YEAH.
I CAN'T BELIEVE THEY LET YOU GUYS GET AWAY WITH THIS KIND OF VIOLENCE.
AH-HA-HA... LONG STORY SHORT...
...LUNA-SAN HAS THE SUPPORT OF ALL THE STUDENTS.

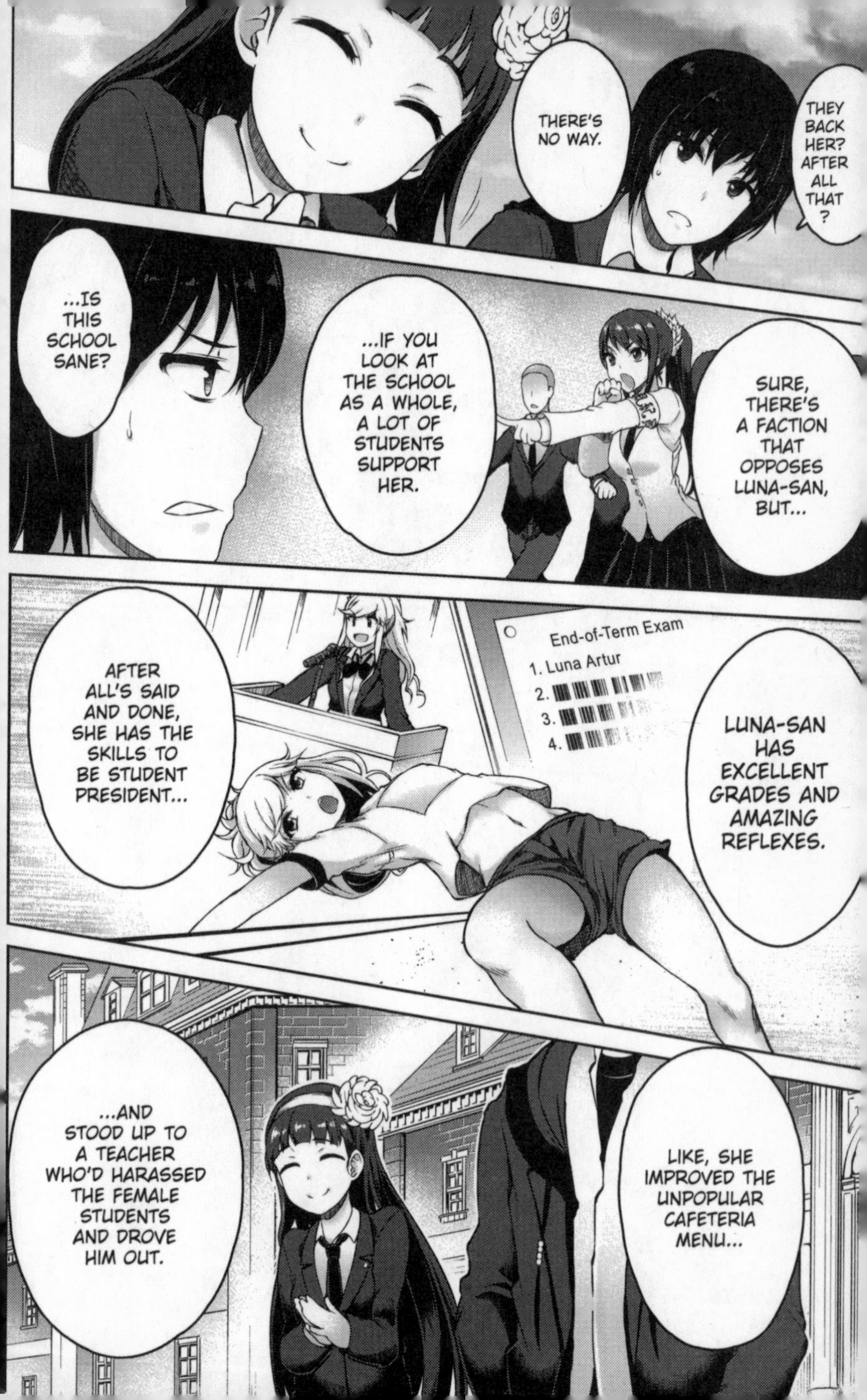
THEY BACK HER? AFTER ALL THAT?
THERE'S NO WAY.
SURE, THERE'S A FACTION THAT OPPOSES LUNA-SAN, BUT...
...IF YOU LOOK AT THE SCHOOL AS A WHOLE, A LOT OF STUDENTS SUPPORT HER.
...IS THIS SCHOOL SANE?
End-of-Term Exam
1. Luna Artur
LUNA-SAN HAS EXCELLENT GRADES AND AMAZING REFLEXES.
AFTER ALL'S SAID AND DONE, SHE HAS THE SKILLS TO BE STUDENT PRESIDENT...
LIKE, SHE IMPROVED THE UNPOPULAR CAFETERIA MENU...
...AND STOOD UP TO A TEACHER WHO'D HARASSED THE FEMALE STUDENTS AND DROVE HIM OUT.

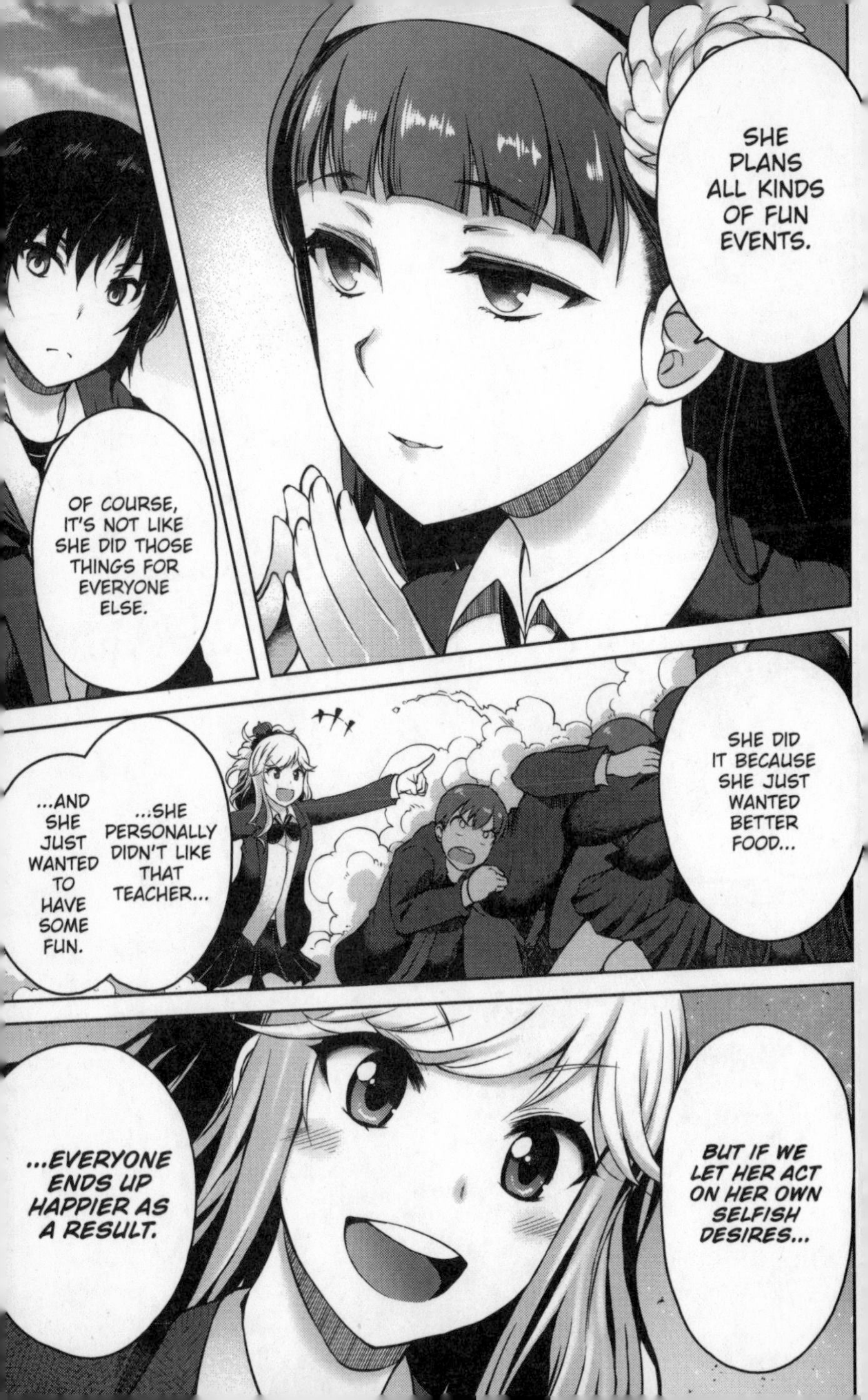
SHE PLANS ALL KINDS OF FUN EVENTS.
OF COURSE, IT'S NOT LIKE SHE DID THOSE THINGS FOR EVERYONE ELSE.
SHE DID IT BECAUSE SHE JUST WANTED BETTER FOOD...
...SHE PERSONALLY DIDN'T LIKE THAT TEACHER...
...AND SHE JUST WANTED TO HAVE SOME FUN.
BUT IF WE LET HER ACT ON HER OWN SELFISH DESIRES...
...EVERYONE ENDS UP HAPPIER AS A RESULT.

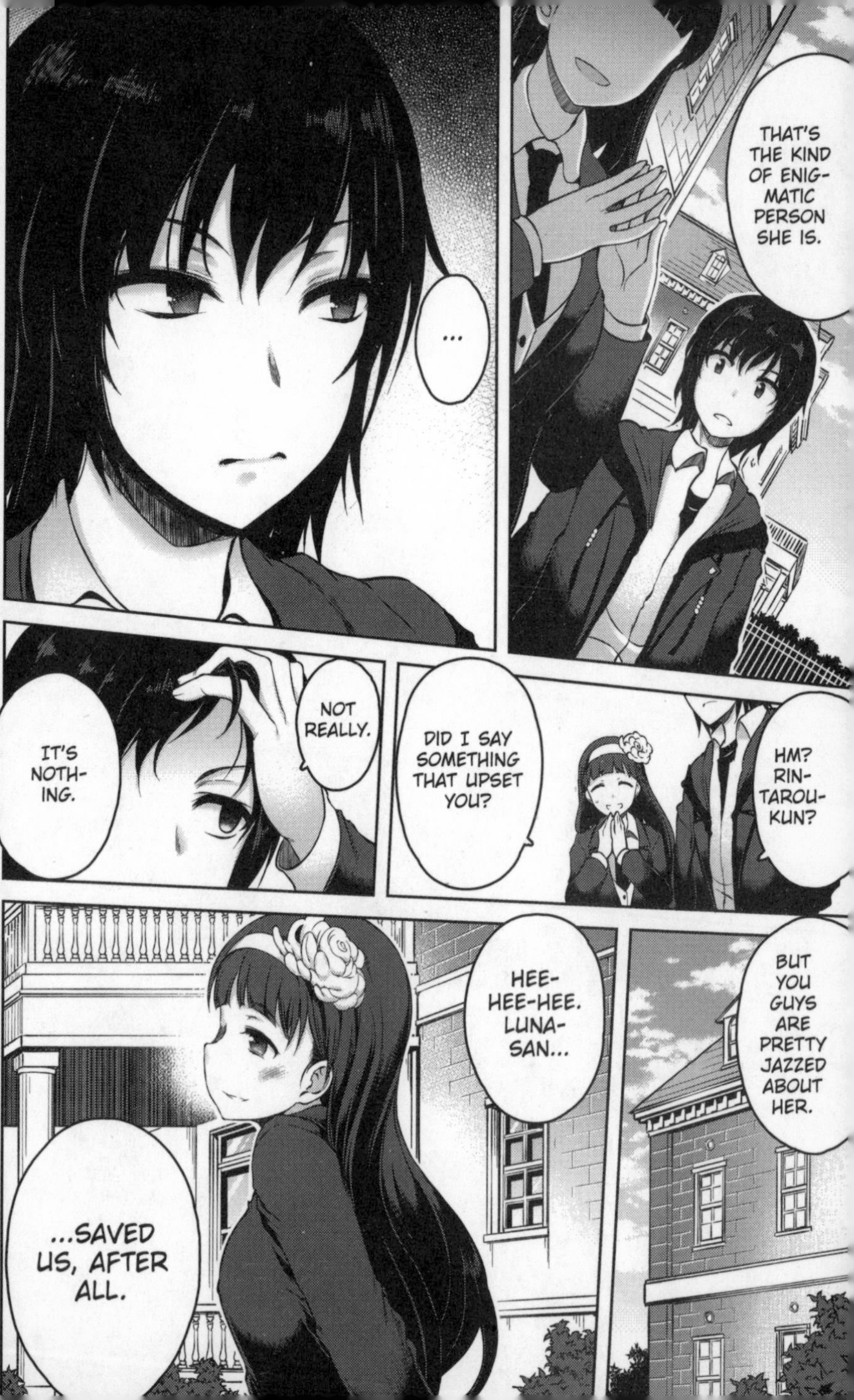

THAT'S THE KIND OF ENIGMATIC PERSON SHE IS.
...
HM? RINTAROU-KUN?
DID I SAY SOMETHING THAT UPSET YOU?
NOT REALLY.
IT'S NOTHING.
BUT YOU GUYS ARE PRETTY JAZZED ABOUT HER.
HEE-HEE-HEE. LUNA-SAN...
...SAVED US, AFTER ALL.

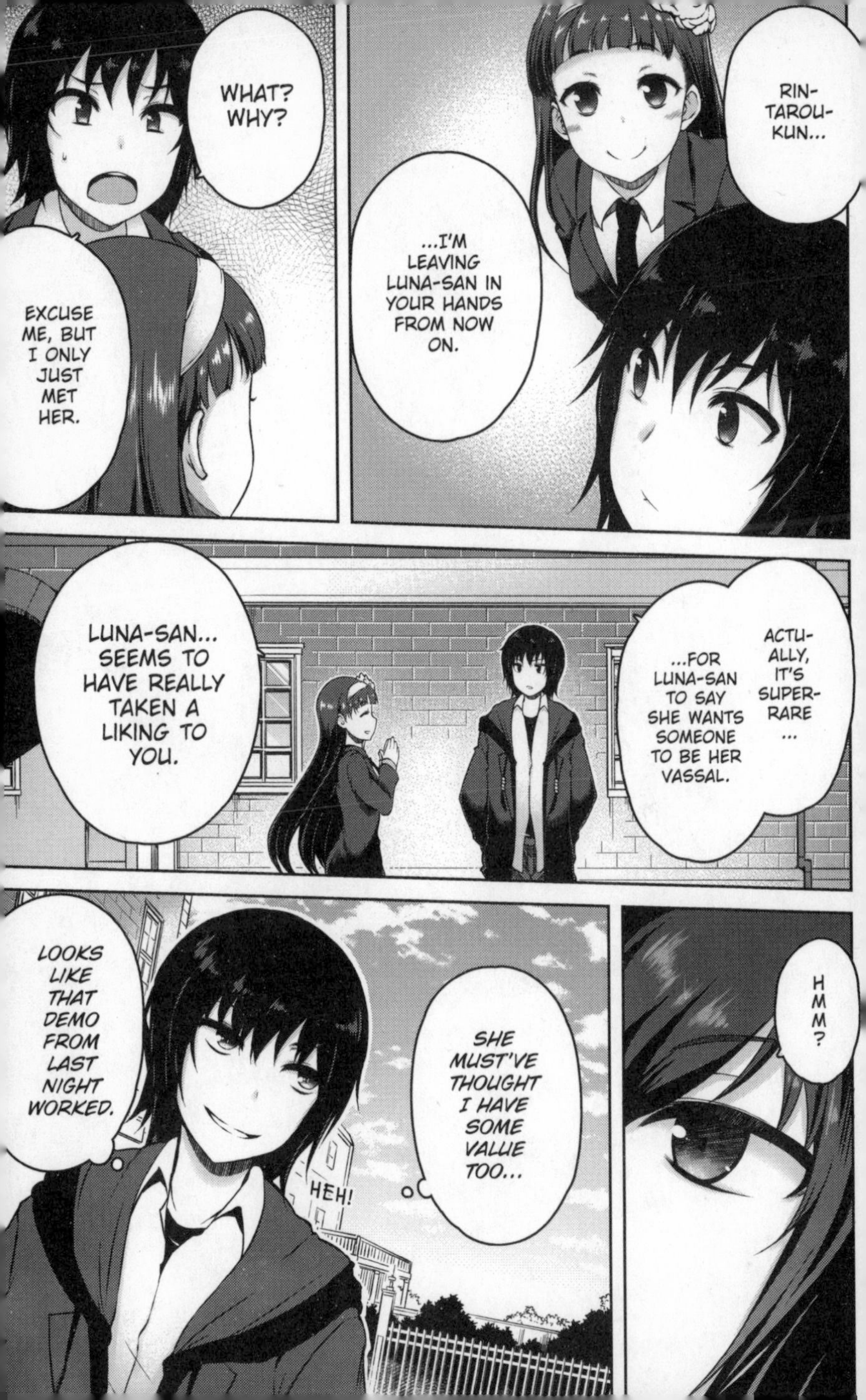
RIN-TAROU-KUN...
...I'M LEAVING LUNA-SAN IN YOUR HANDS FROM NOW ON.
WHAT? WHY?
EXCUSE ME, BUT I ONLY JUST MET HER.
ACTU-ALLY, IT'S SUPER-RARE...
...FOR LUNA-SAN TO SAY SHE WANTS SOMEONE TO BE HER VASSAL.
LUNA-SAN... SEEMS TO HAVE REALLY TAKEN A LIKING TO YOU.
HMM?
SHE MUST'VE THOUGHT I HAVE SOME VALUE TOO...
LOOKS LIKE THAT DEMO FROM LAST NIGHT WORKED.
HEH!

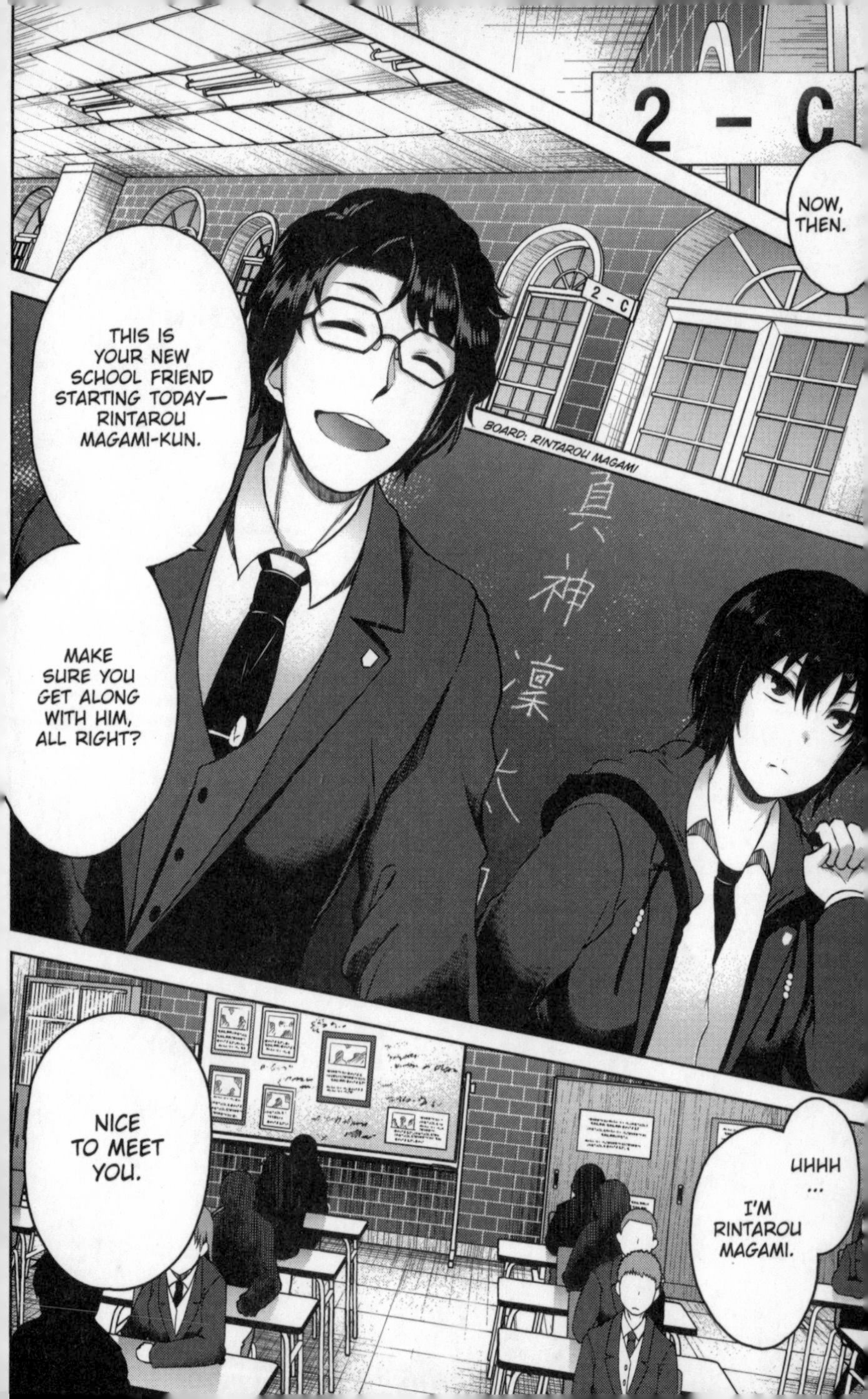
2-C
NOW, THEN.
THIS IS YOUR NEW SCHOOL FRIEND STARTING TODAY—RINTAROU MAGAMI-KUN.
BOARD: RINTAROU MAGAMI
MAKE SURE YOU GET ALONG WITH HIM, ALL RIGHT?
UHHH ... I'M RINTAROU MAGAMI.
NICE TO MEET YOU.

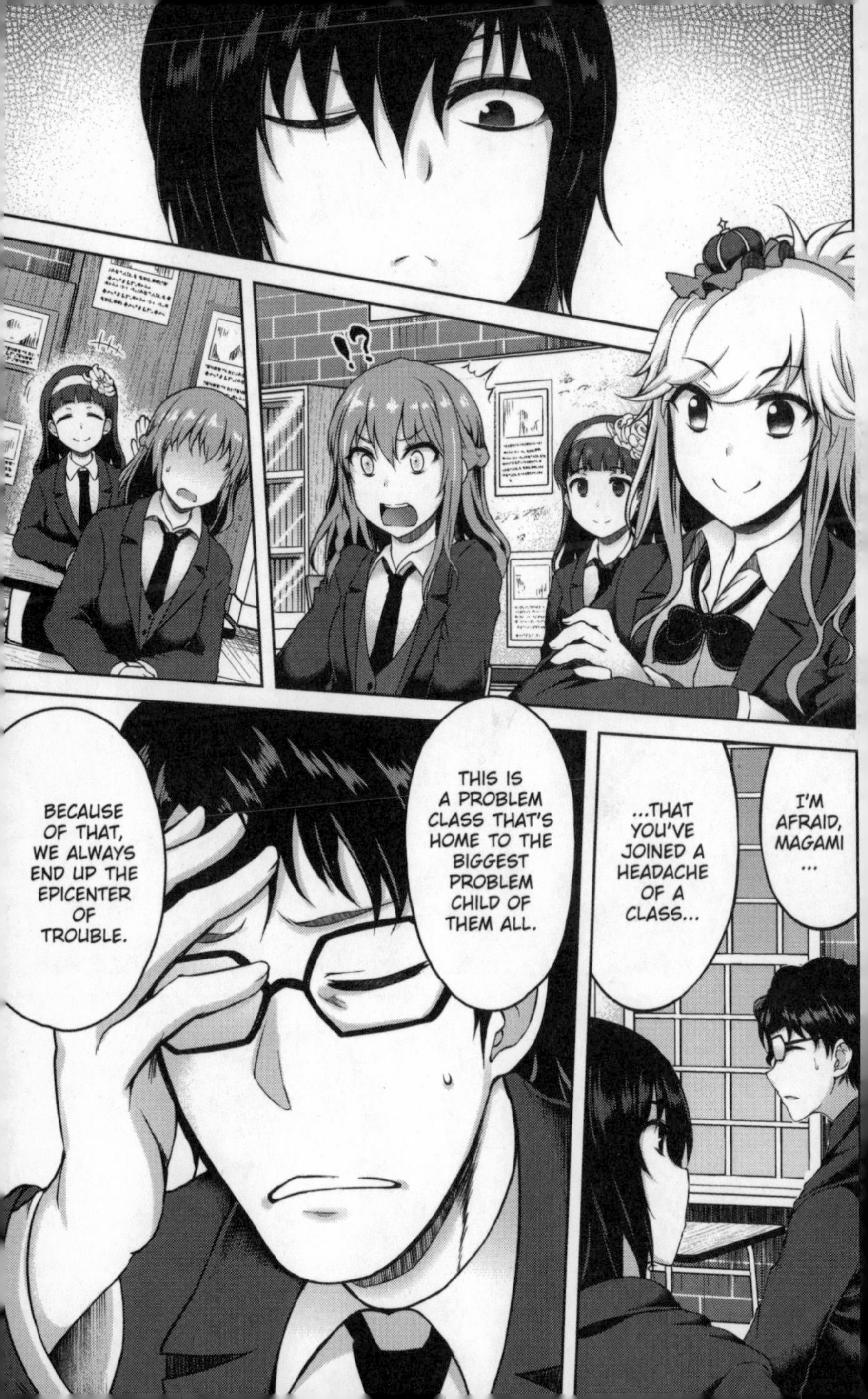
!?
I'M AFRAID, MAGAMI...
...THAT YOU'VE JOINED A HEADACHE OF A CLASS...
THIS IS A PROBLEM CLASS THAT'S HOME TO THE BIGGEST PROBLEM CHILD OF THEM ALL.
BECAUSE OF THAT, WE ALWAYS END UP THE EPICENTER OF TROUBLE.

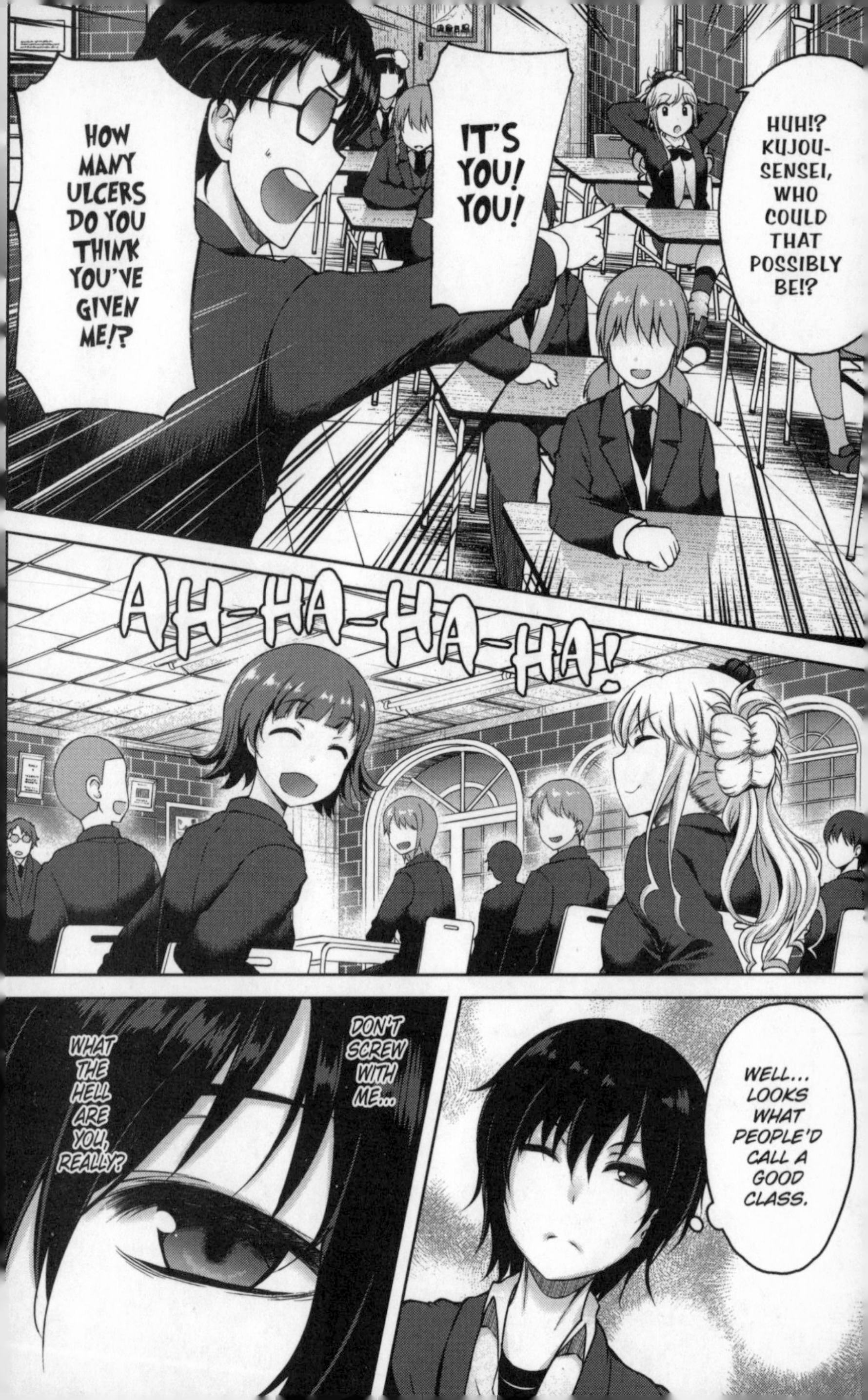
HUH!? KUJOU-SENSEI, WHO COULD THAT POSSIBLY BE!?
IT'S YOU! YOU!
HOW MANY ULCERS DO YOU THINK YOU'VE GIVEN ME!?
AH-HA-HA-HA-HA!
WELL... LOOKS WHAT PEOPLE'D CALL A GOOD CLASS.
DON'T SCREW WITH ME...
WHAT THE HELL ARE YOU, REALLY?

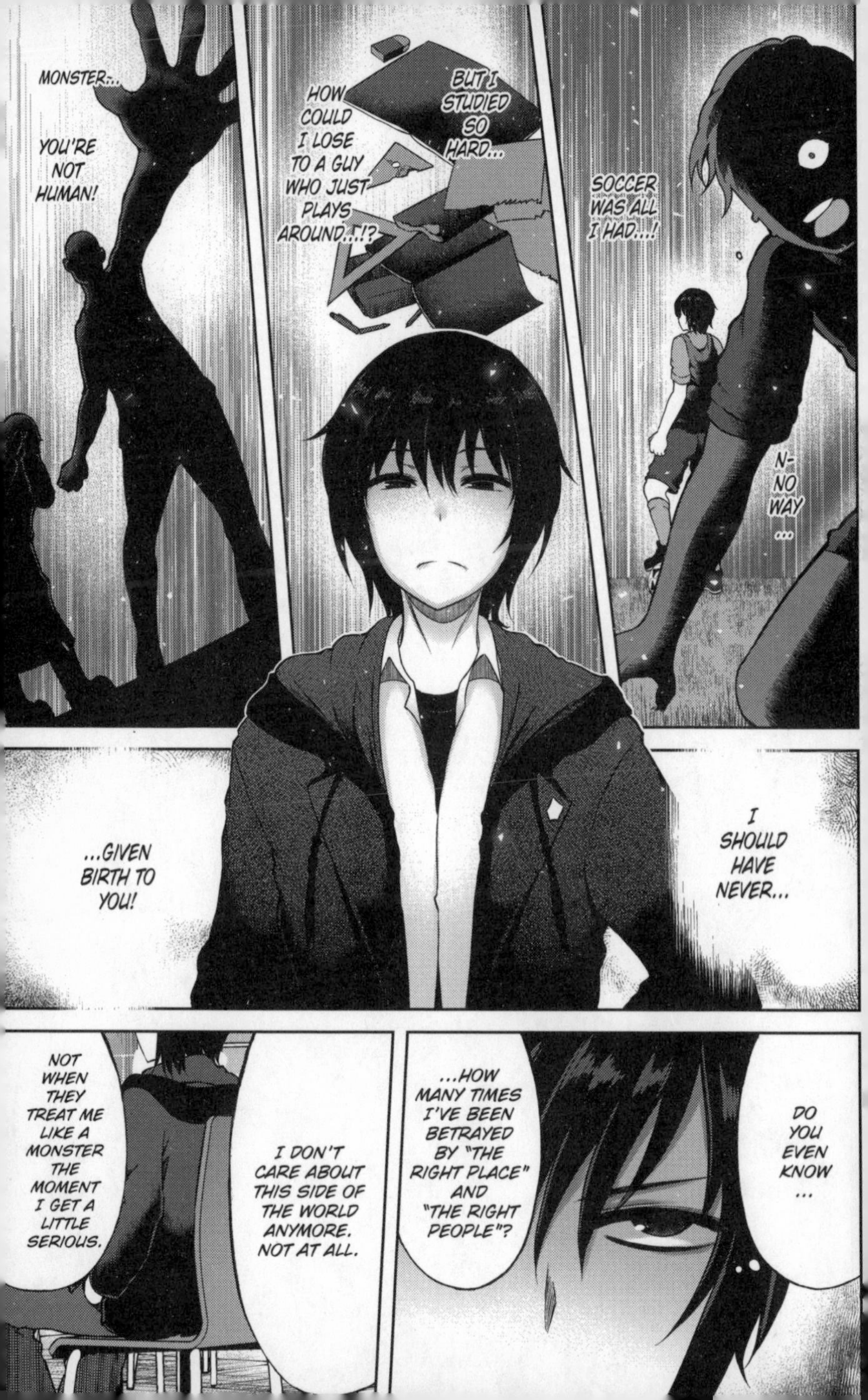
SOCCER WAS ALL I HAD...!
N-NO WAY...
BUT I STUDIED SO HARD...
HOW COULD I LOSE TO A GUY WHO JUST PLAYS AROUND...!?
MONSTER...
YOU'RE NOT HUMAN!
I SHOULD HAVE NEVER...
...GIVEN BIRTH TO YOU!
DO YOU EVEN KNOW...
...HOW MANY TIMES I'VE BEEN BETRAYED BY "THE RIGHT PLACE" AND "THE RIGHT PEOPLE"?
I DON'T CARE ABOUT THIS SIDE OF THE WORLD ANYMORE. NOT AT ALL.
NOT WHEN THEY TREAT ME LIKE A MONSTER THE MOMENT I GET A LITTLE SERIOUS.

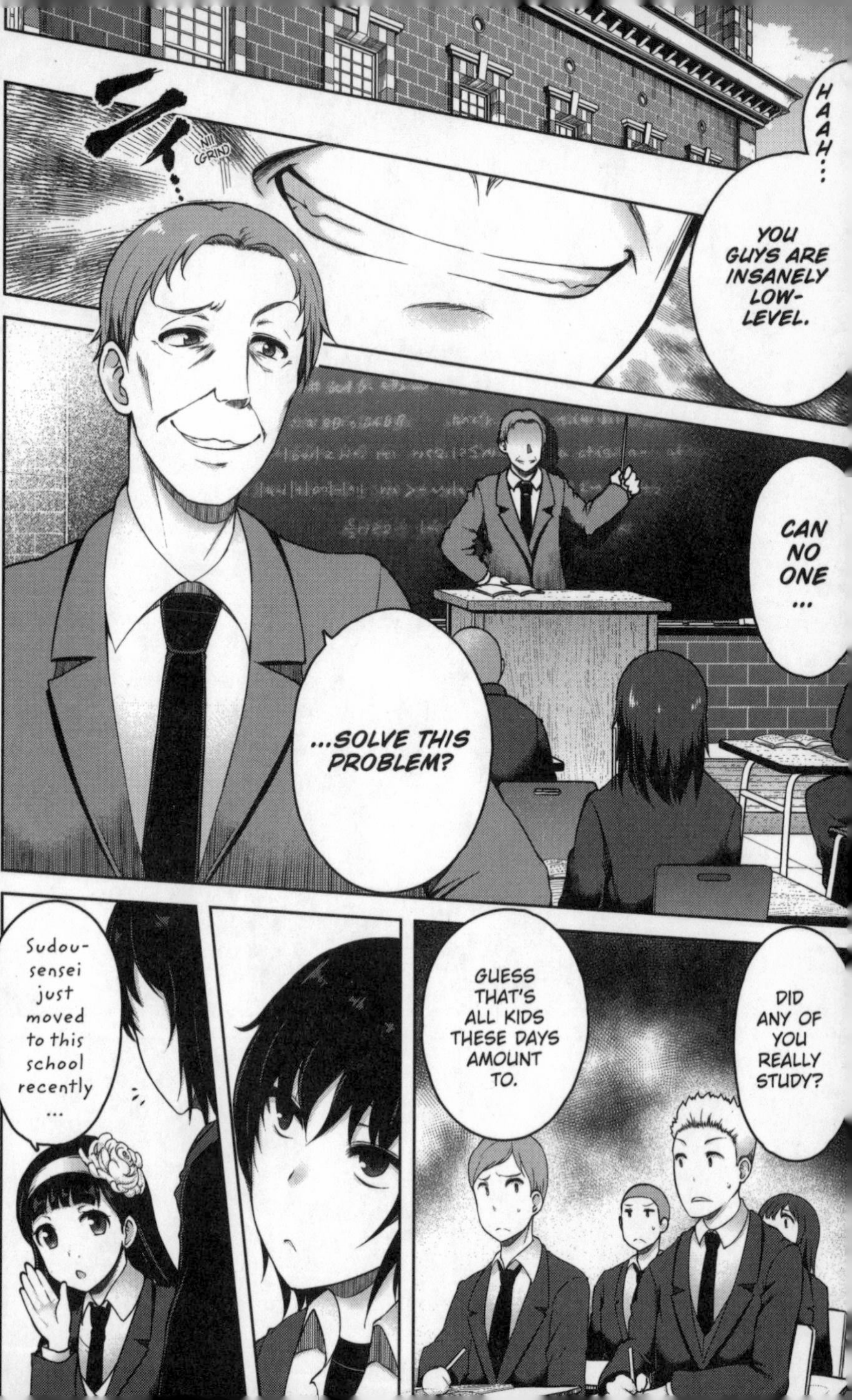
HAAAH...
YOU GUYS ARE INSANELY LOW-LEVEL.
NII (GRIN)
CAN NO ONE...
...SOLVE THIS PROBLEM?
DID ANY OF YOU REALLY STUDY?
GUESS THAT'S ALL KIDS THESE DAYS AMOUNT TO.
Sudou-sensei just moved to this school recently...

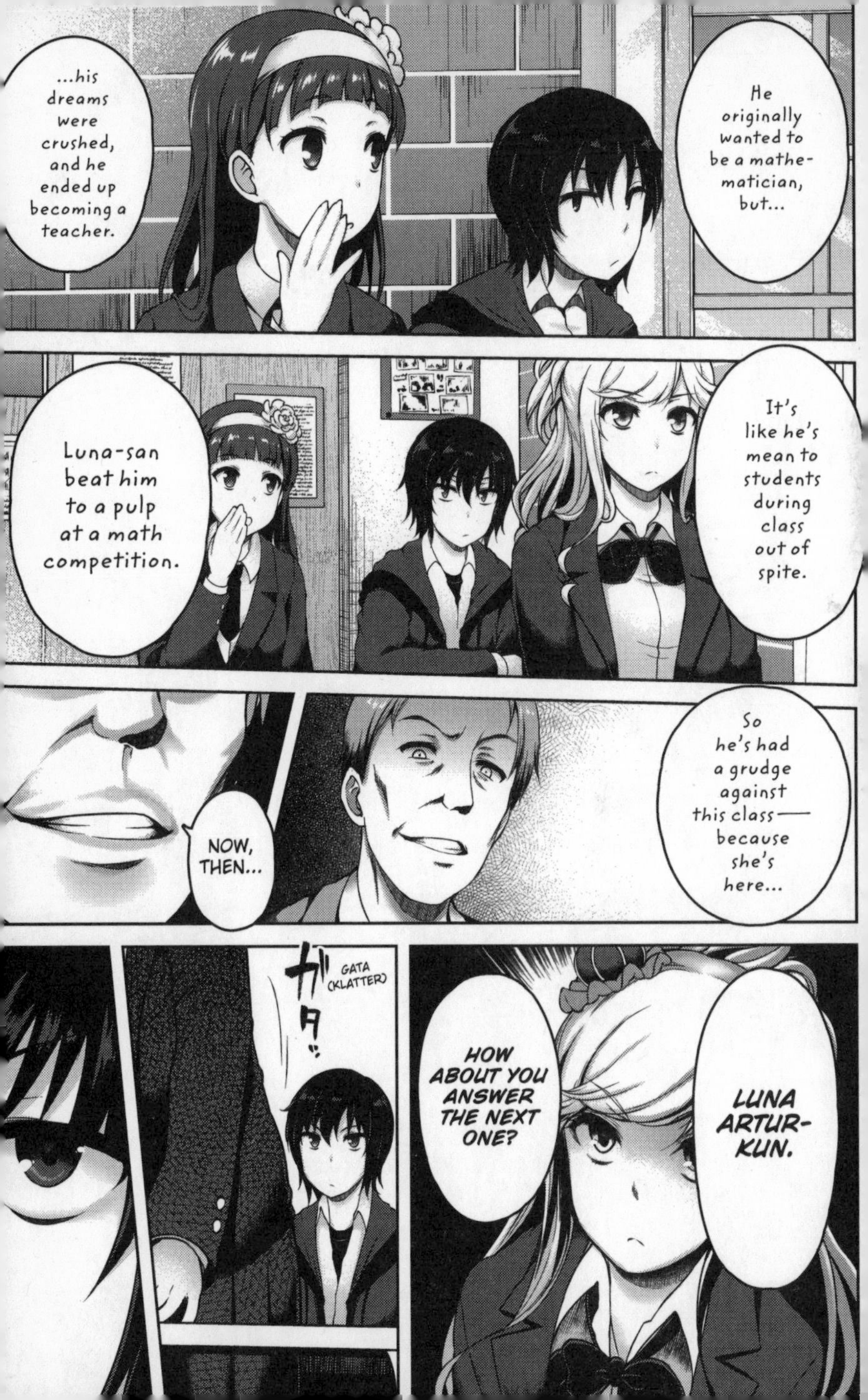
He originally wanted to be a mathematician, but...
...his dreams were crushed, and he ended up becoming a teacher.
It's like he's mean to students during class out of spite.
Luna-san beat him to a pulp at a math competition.
So he's had a grudge against this class—because she's here...
NOW, THEN...
LUNA ARTUR-KUN.
HOW ABOUT YOU ANSWER THE NEXT ONE?
GATA (KLATTER)

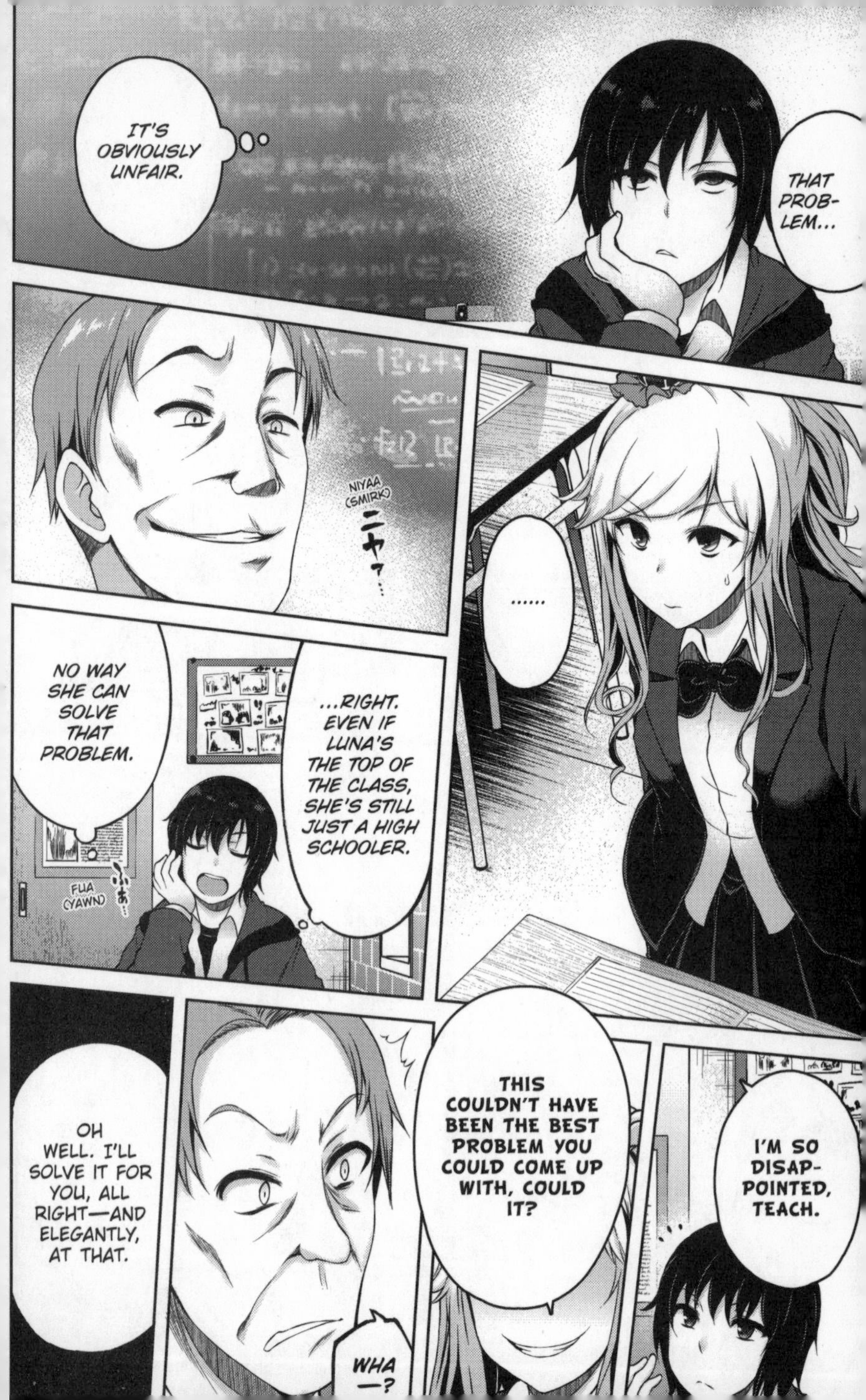
THAT PROB-LEM...
IT'S OBVIOUSLY UNFAIR.
......
NIYAA (SMIRK)
ニヤァ…
...RIGHT. EVEN IF LUNA'S THE TOP OF THE CLASS, SHE'S STILL JUST A HIGH SCHOOLER.
NO WAY SHE CAN SOLVE THAT PROBLEM.
FUA (YAWN)
ふあ…
I'M SO DISAP-POINTED, TEACH.
THIS COULDN'T HAVE BEEN THE BEST PROBLEM YOU COULD COME UP WITH, COULD IT?
WHA—?
OH WELL. I'LL SOLVE IT FOR YOU, ALL RIGHT—AND ELEGANTLY, AT THAT.

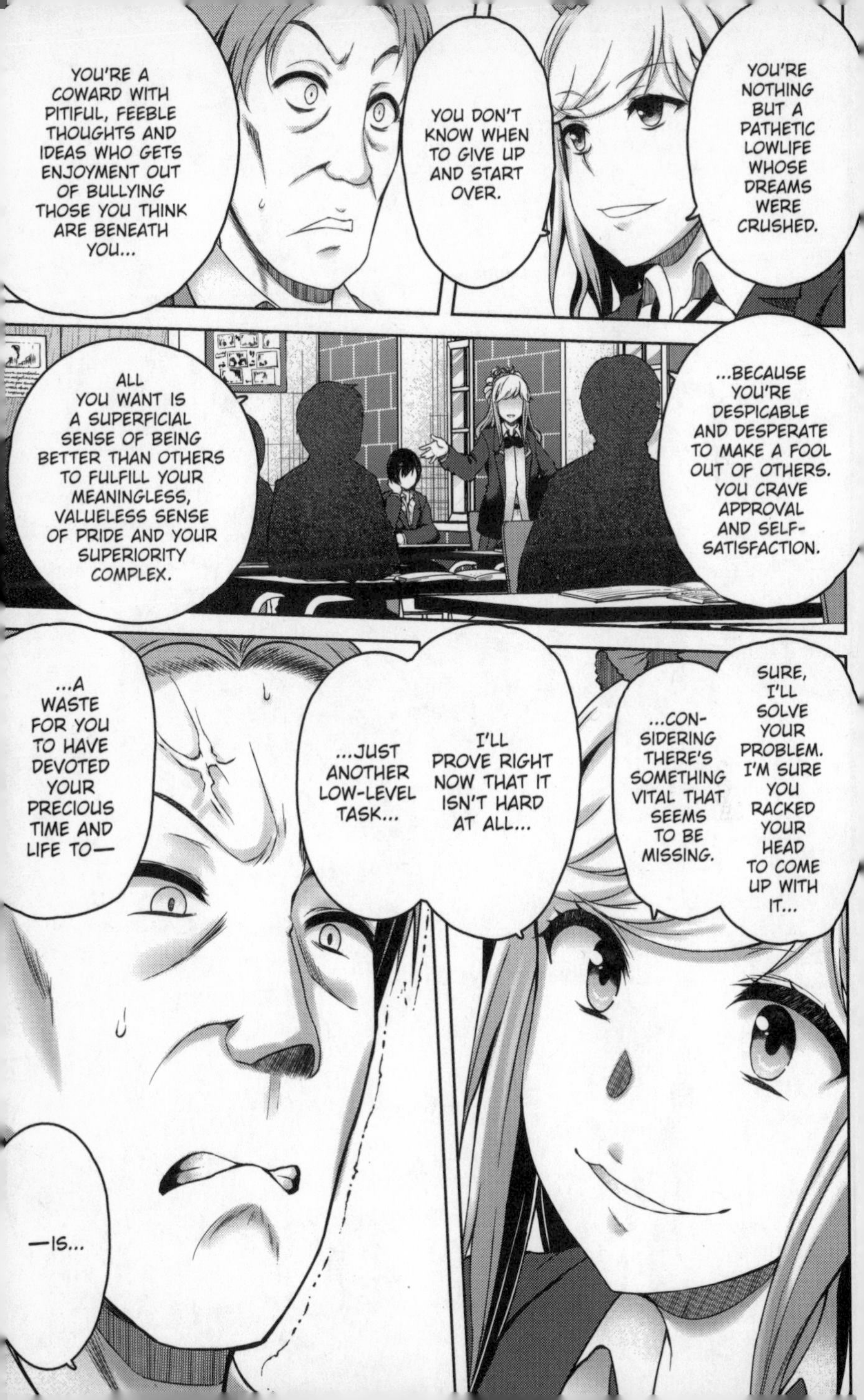
YOU'RE NOTHING BUT A PATHETIC LOWLIFE WHOSE DREAMS WERE CRUSHED.
YOU DON'T KNOW WHEN TO GIVE UP AND START OVER.
YOU'RE A COWARD WITH PITIFUL, FEEBLE THOUGHTS AND IDEAS WHO GETS ENJOYMENT OUT OF BULLYING THOSE YOU THINK ARE BENEATH YOU...
...BECAUSE YOU'RE DESPICABLE AND DESPERATE TO MAKE A FOOL OUT OF OTHERS. YOU CRAVE APPROVAL AND SELF-SATISFACTION.
ALL YOU WANT IS A SUPERFICIAL SENSE OF BEING BETTER THAN OTHERS TO FULFILL YOUR MEANINGLESS, VALUELESS SENSE OF PRIDE AND YOUR SUPERIORITY COMPLEX.
SURE, I'LL SOLVE YOUR PROBLEM. I'M SURE YOU RACKED YOUR HEAD TO COME UP WITH IT...
...CONSIDERING THERE'S SOMETHING VITAL THAT SEEMS TO BE MISSING.
I'LL PROVE RIGHT NOW THAT IT ISN'T HARD AT ALL...
...JUST ANOTHER LOW-LEVEL TASK...
...A WASTE FOR YOU TO HAVE DEVOTED YOUR PRECIOUS TIME AND LIFE TO—
—IS...

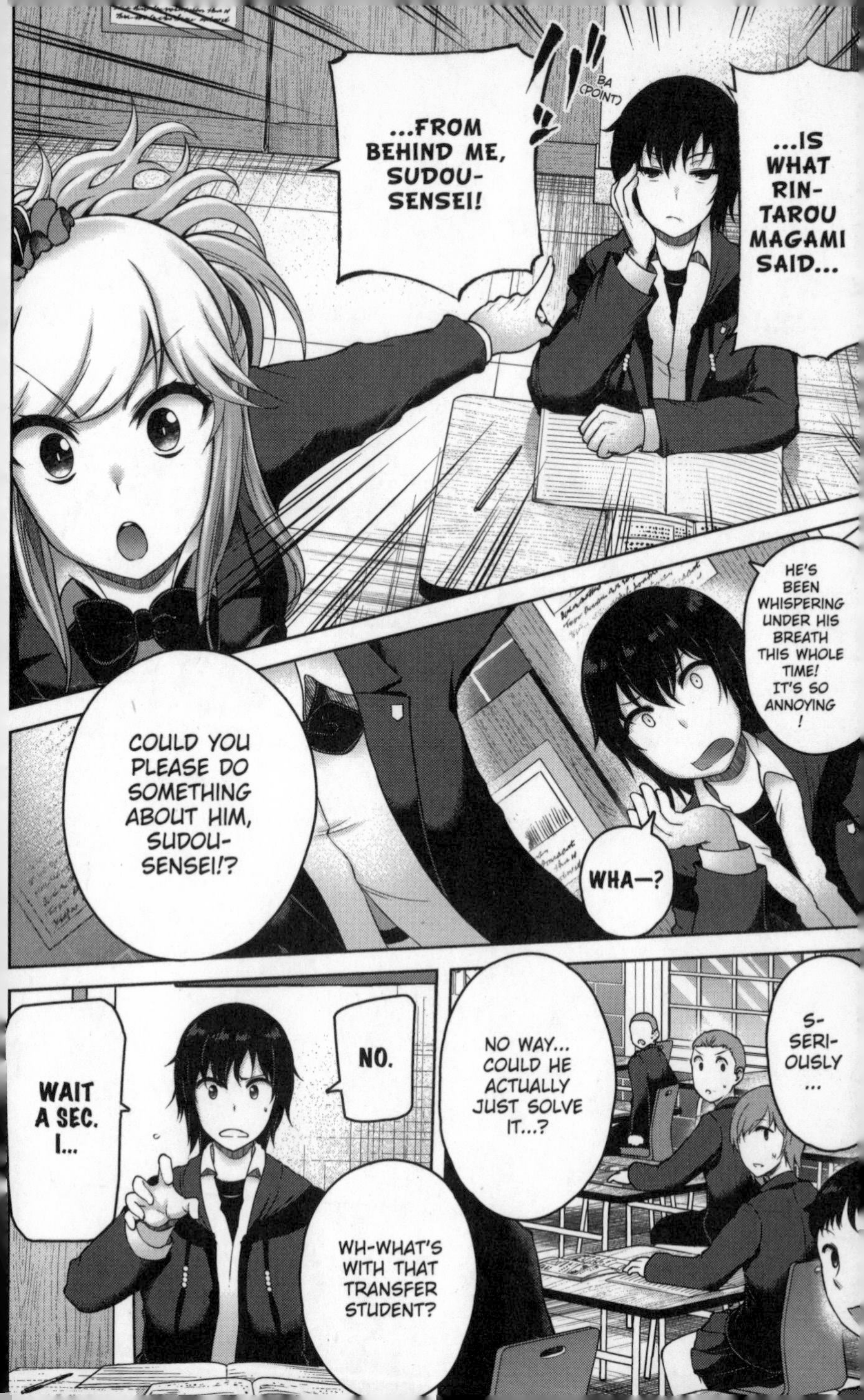
...IS WHAT RIN-TAROU MAGAMI SAID...
BA (POINT)
...FROM BEHIND ME, SUDOU-SENSEI!
HE'S BEEN WHISPERING UNDER HIS BREATH THIS WHOLE TIME! IT'S SO ANNOYING!
WHA—?
COULD YOU PLEASE DO SOMETHING ABOUT HIM, SUDOU-SENSEI!?
S-SERI-OUSLY...
NO WAY... COULD HE ACTUALLY JUST SOLVE IT...?
NO.
WAIT A SEC. I...
WH-WHAT'S WITH THAT TRANSFER STUDENT?

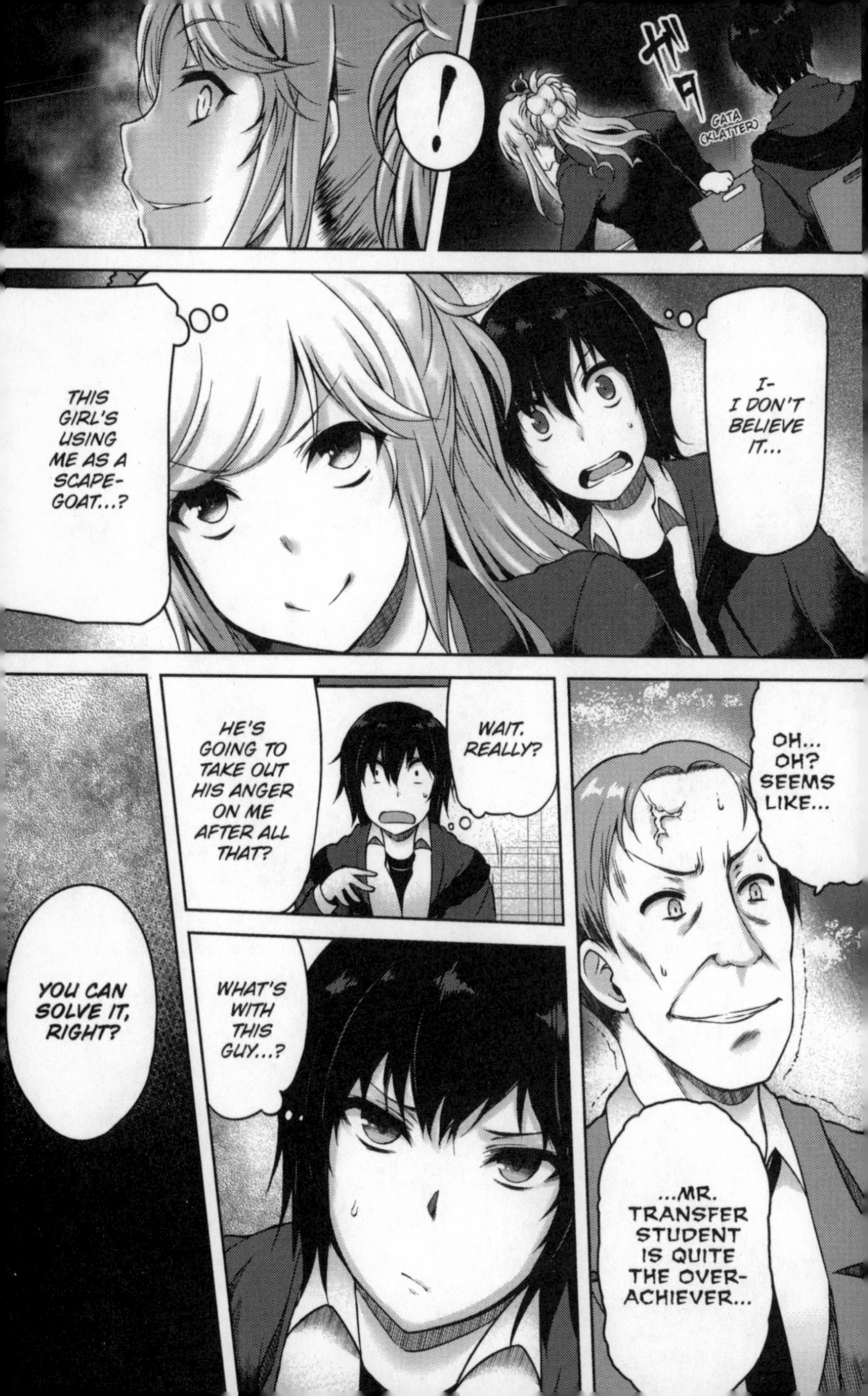

ガタ
GATA (KLATTER)
!
I- I DON'T BELIEVE IT...
THIS GIRL'S USING ME AS A SCAPE-GOAT...?
OH... OH? SEEMS LIKE...
...MR. TRANSFER STUDENT IS QUITE THE OVER-ACHIEVER...
WAIT. REALLY?
HE'S GOING TO TAKE OUT HIS ANGER ON ME AFTER ALL THAT?
WHAT'S WITH THIS GUY...?
YOU CAN SOLVE IT, RIGHT?

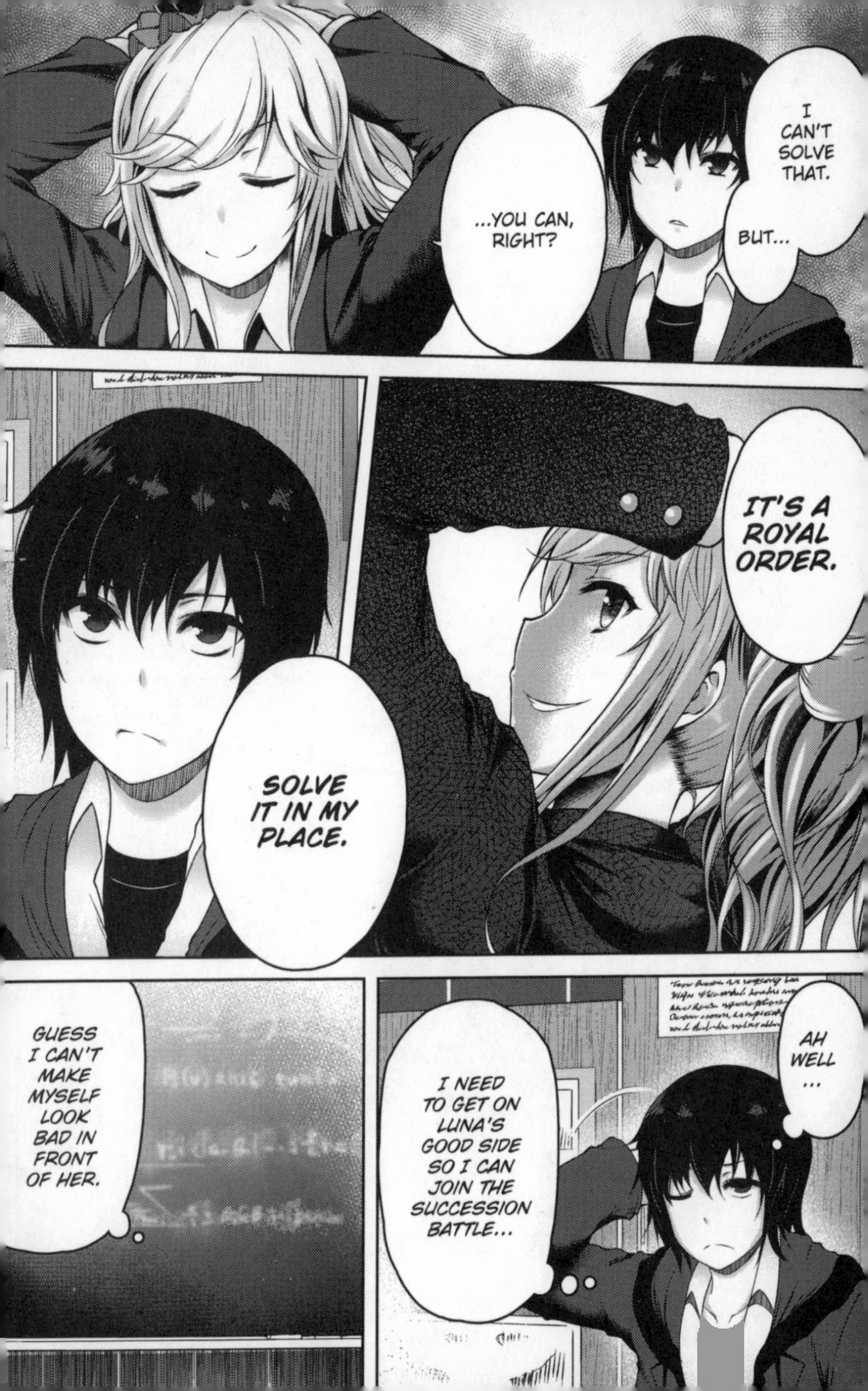
I CAN'T SOLVE THAT.
BUT...
...YOU CAN, RIGHT?
IT'S A ROYAL ORDER.
SOLVE IT IN MY PLACE.
AH WELL...
I NEED TO GET ON LUNA'S GOOD SIDE SO I CAN JOIN THE SUCCESSION BATTLE...
GUESS I CAN'T MAKE MYSELF LOOK BAD IN FRONT OF HER.

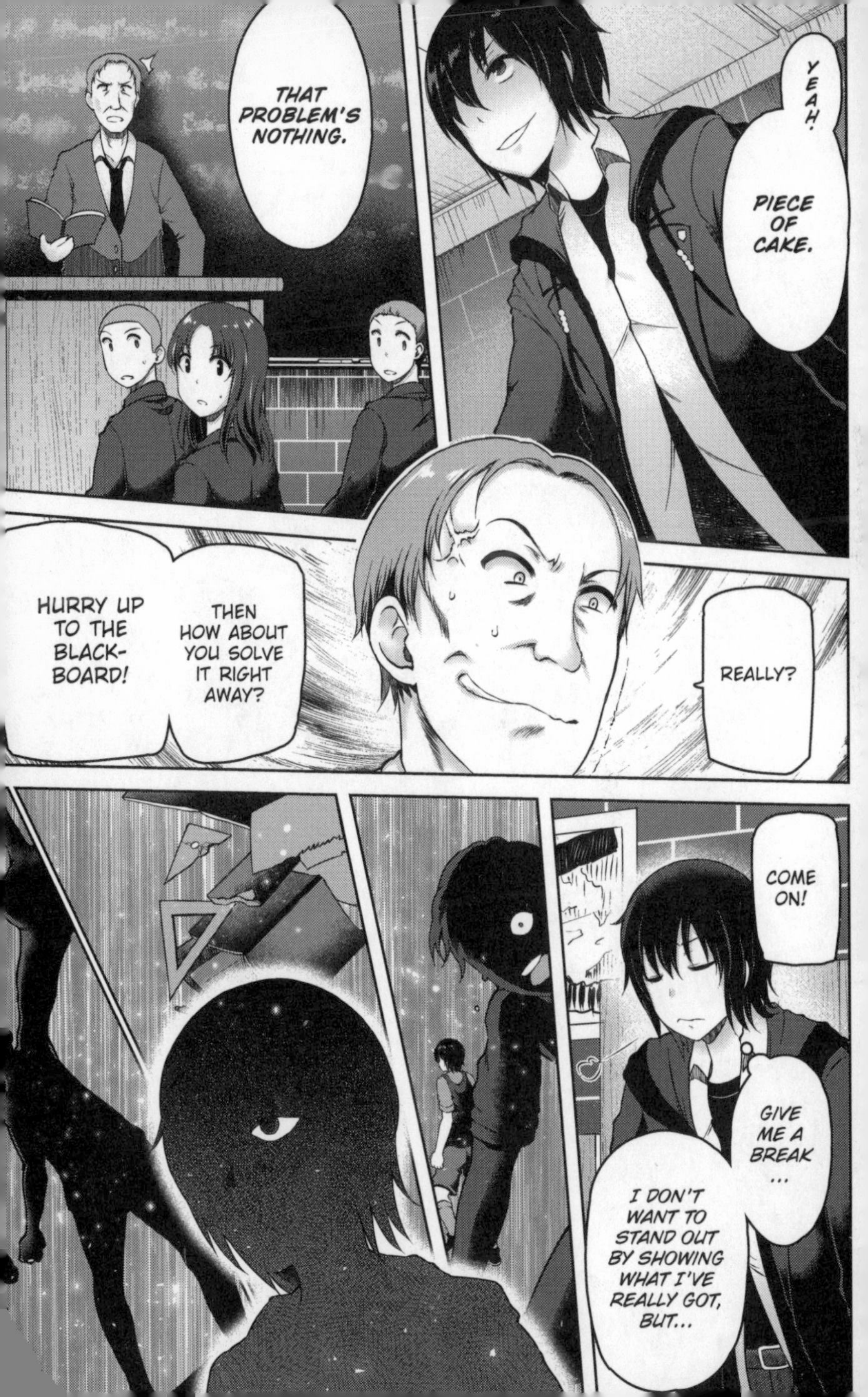
YEAH! PIECE OF CAKE.
THAT PROBLEM'S NOTHING.
REALLY?
THEN HOW ABOUT YOU SOLVE IT RIGHT AWAY?
HURRY UP TO THE BLACK-BOARD!
COME ON!
GIVE ME A BREAK...
I DON'T WANT TO STAND OUT BY SHOWING WHAT I'VE REALLY GOT, BUT...

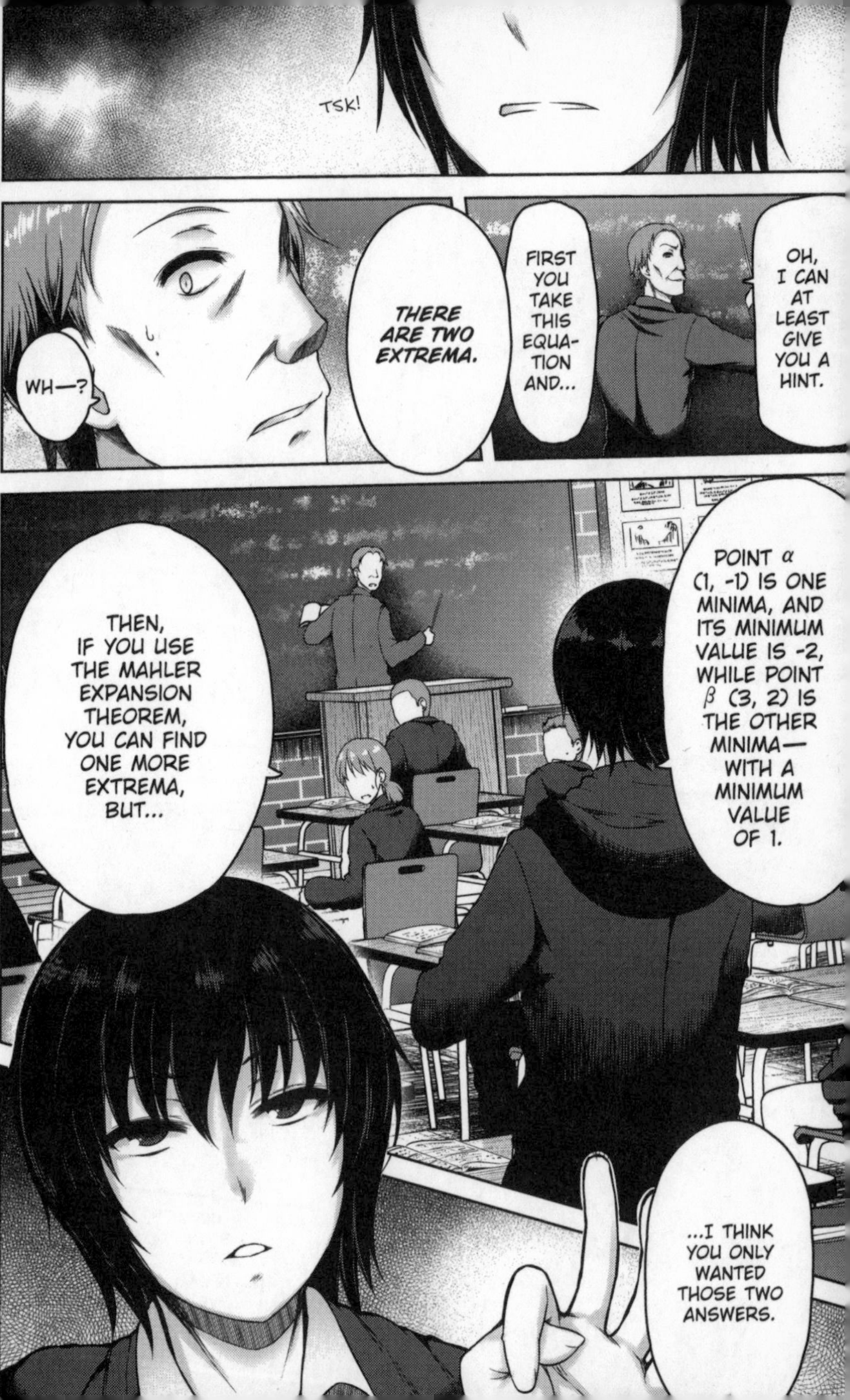
TSK!
OH, I CAN AT LEAST GIVE YOU A HINT.
FIRST YOU TAKE THIS EQUA-TION AND...
THERE ARE TWO EXTREMA.
WH—?
POINT α (1, -1) IS ONE MINIMA, AND ITS MINIMUM VALUE IS -2, WHILE POINT β (3, 2) IS THE OTHER MINIMA—WITH A MINIMUM VALUE OF 1.
THEN, IF YOU USE THE MAHLER EXPANSION THEOREM, YOU CAN FIND ONE MORE EXTREMA, BUT...
...I THINK YOU ONLY WANTED THOSE TWO ANSWERS.

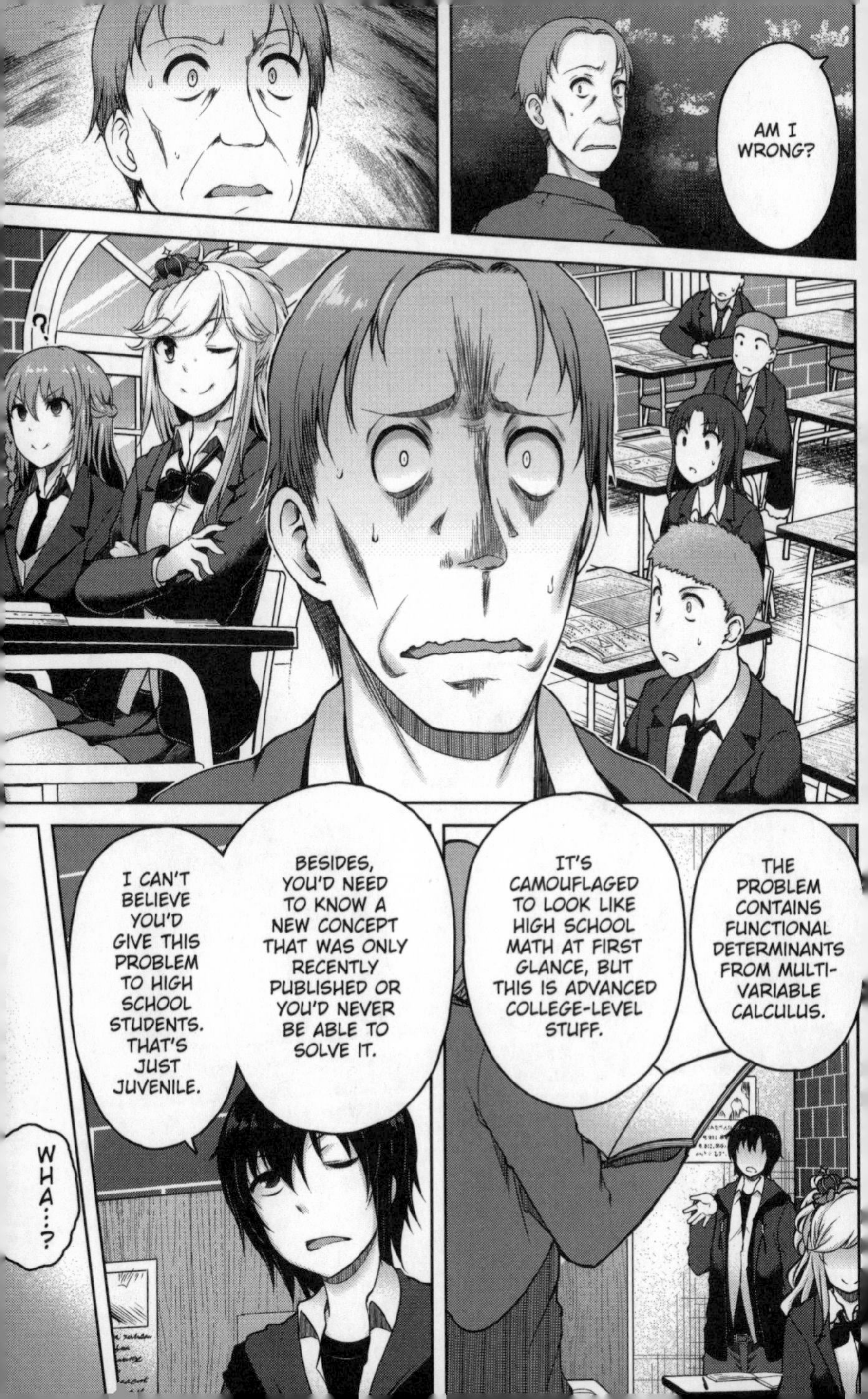
AM I WRONG?
?
THE PROBLEM CONTAINS FUNCTIONAL DETERMINANTS FROM MULTI-VARIABLE CALCULUS.
IT'S CAMOUFLAGED TO LOOK LIKE HIGH SCHOOL MATH AT FIRST GLANCE, BUT THIS IS ADVANCED COLLEGE-LEVEL STUFF.
BESIDES, YOU'D NEED TO KNOW A NEW CONCEPT THAT WAS ONLY RECENTLY PUBLISHED OR YOU'D NEVER BE ABLE TO SOLVE IT.
I CAN'T BELIEVE YOU'D GIVE THIS PROBLEM TO HIGH SCHOOL STUDENTS. THAT'S JUST JUVENILE.
WHA...?

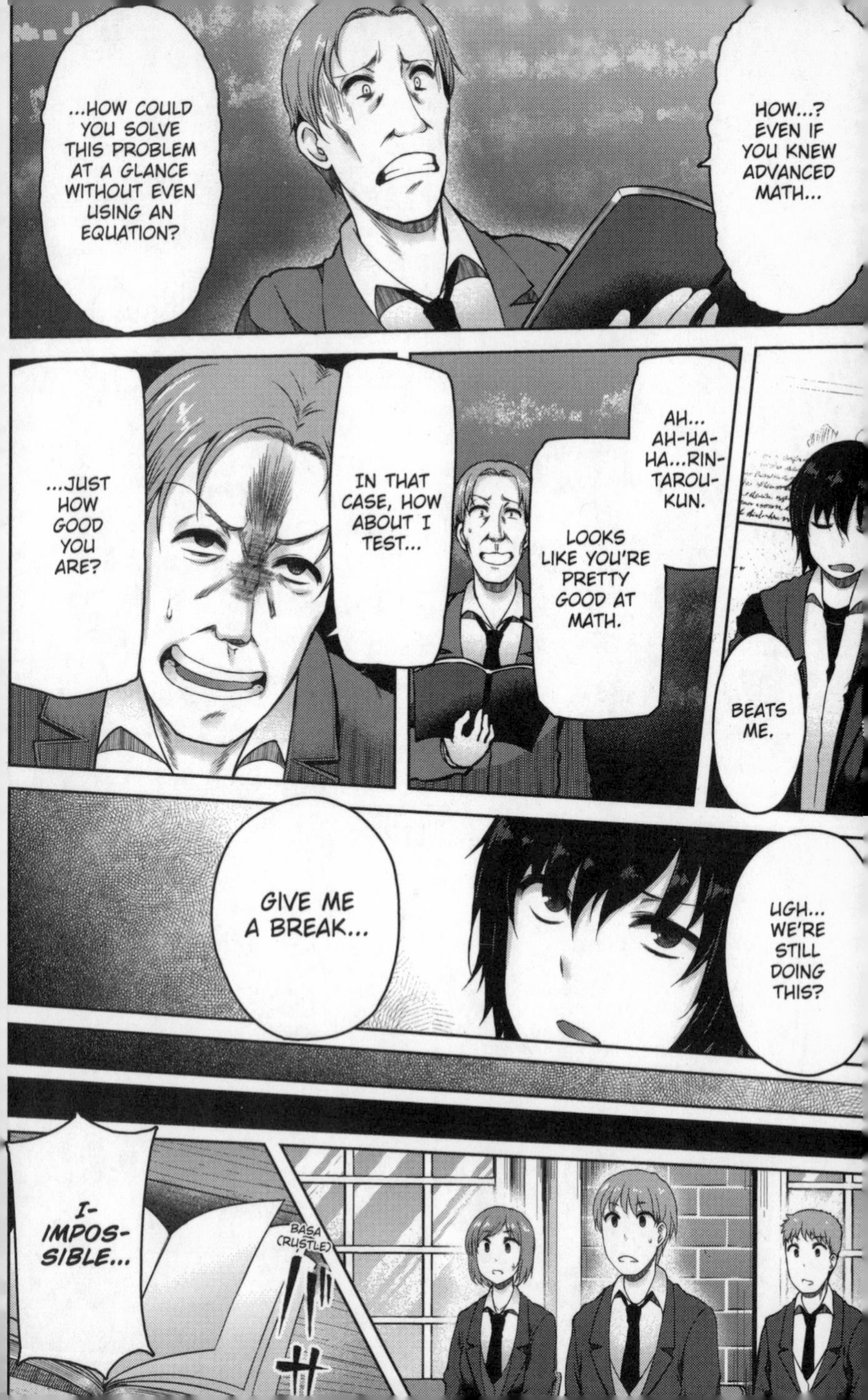
HOW...? EVEN IF YOU KNEW ADVANCED MATH...
...HOW COULD YOU SOLVE THIS PROBLEM AT A GLANCE WITHOUT EVEN USING AN EQUATION?
BEATS ME.
AH... AH-HA-HA...RIN-TAROU-KUN.
LOOKS LIKE YOU'RE PRETTY GOOD AT MATH.
IN THAT CASE, HOW ABOUT I TEST...
...JUST HOW GOOD YOU ARE?
UGH... WE'RE STILL DOING THIS?
GIVE ME A BREAK...
BASA (RUSTLE)
I-IMPOSSIBLE...

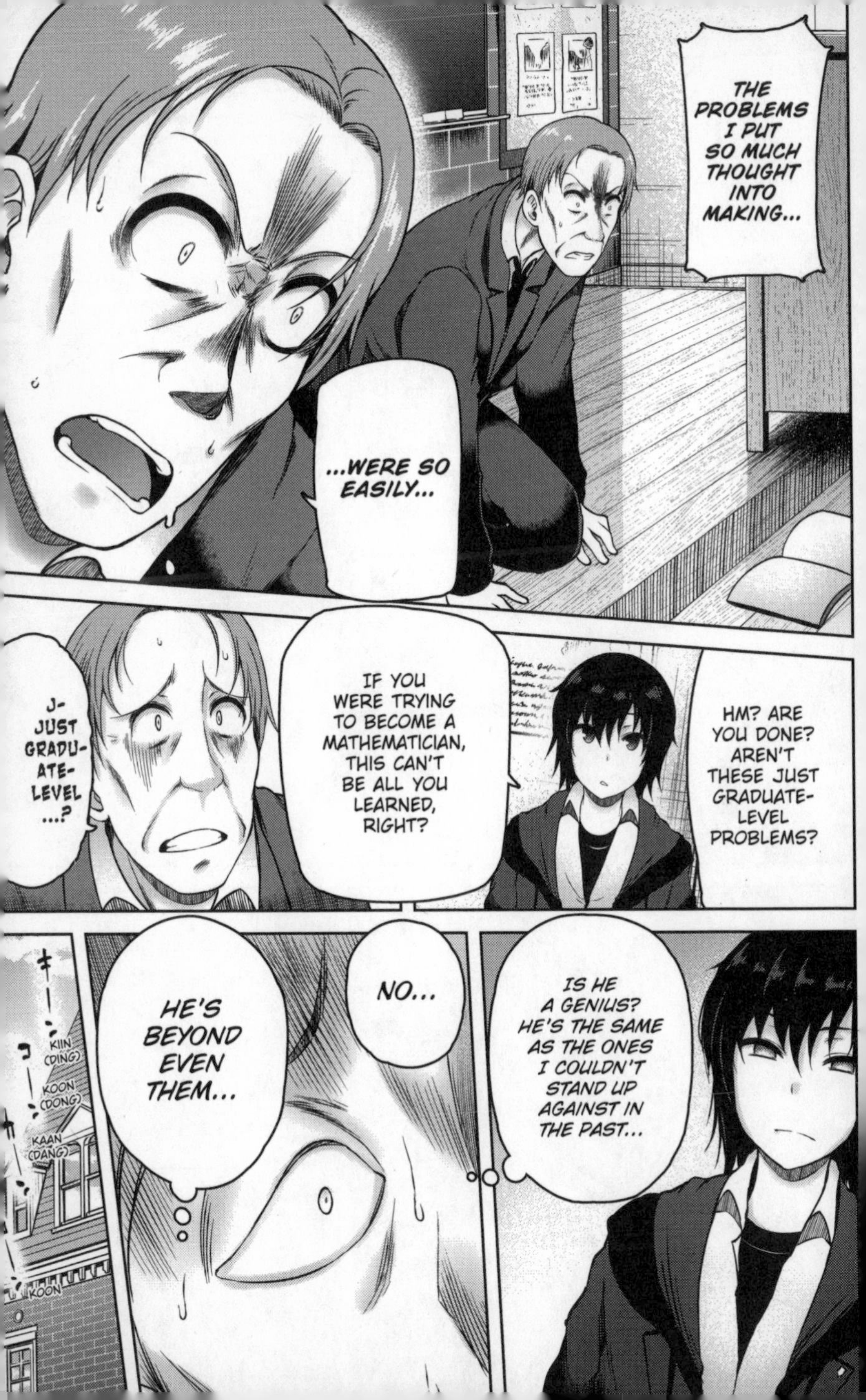
THE PROBLEMS I PUT SO MUCH THOUGHT INTO MAKING...
...WERE SO EASILY...
HM? ARE YOU DONE? AREN'T THESE JUST GRADUATE-LEVEL PROBLEMS?
IF YOU WERE TRYING TO BECOME A MATHEMATICIAN, THIS CAN'T BE ALL YOU LEARNED, RIGHT?
J-JUST GRADUATE-LEVEL ...?
IS HE A GENIUS? HE'S THE SAME AS THE ONES I COULDN'T STAND UP AGAINST IN THE PAST...
NO...
HE'S BEYOND EVEN THEM...
KIIN (DING)
KOON (DONG)
KAAN (DANG)
KOON

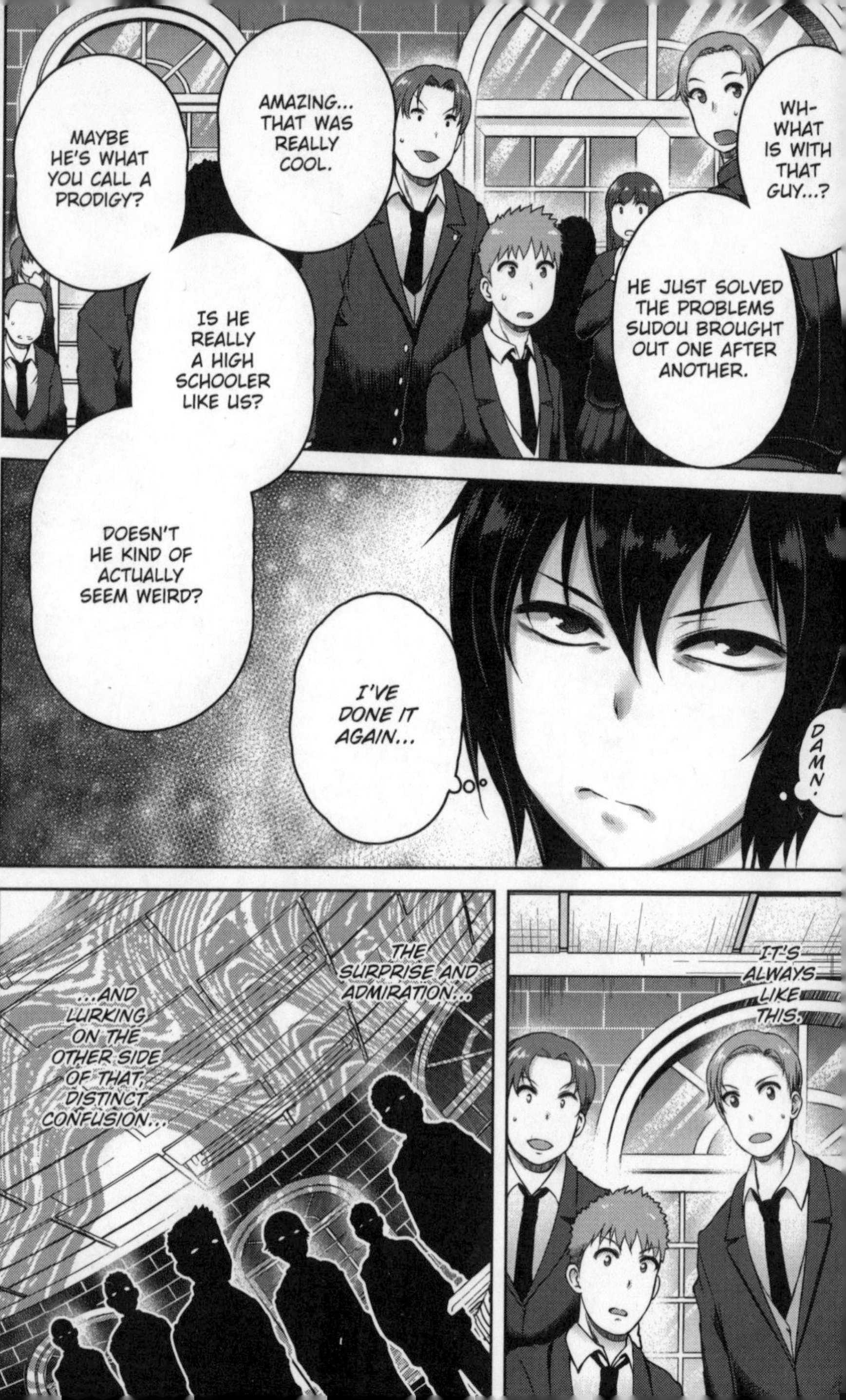
WH-WHAT IS WITH THAT GUY...?
HE JUST SOLVED THE PROBLEMS SUDOU BROUGHT OUT ONE AFTER ANOTHER.
AMAZING... THAT WAS REALLY COOL.
MAYBE HE'S WHAT YOU CALL A PRODIGY?
IS HE REALLY A HIGH SCHOOLER LIKE US?
DOESN'T HE KIND OF ACTUALLY SEEM WEIRD?
DAMN.
I'VE DONE IT AGAIN...
IT'S ALWAYS LIKE THIS.
THE SURPRISE AND ADMIRATION...
...AND LURKING ON THE OTHER SIDE OF THAT, DISTINCT CONFUSION...

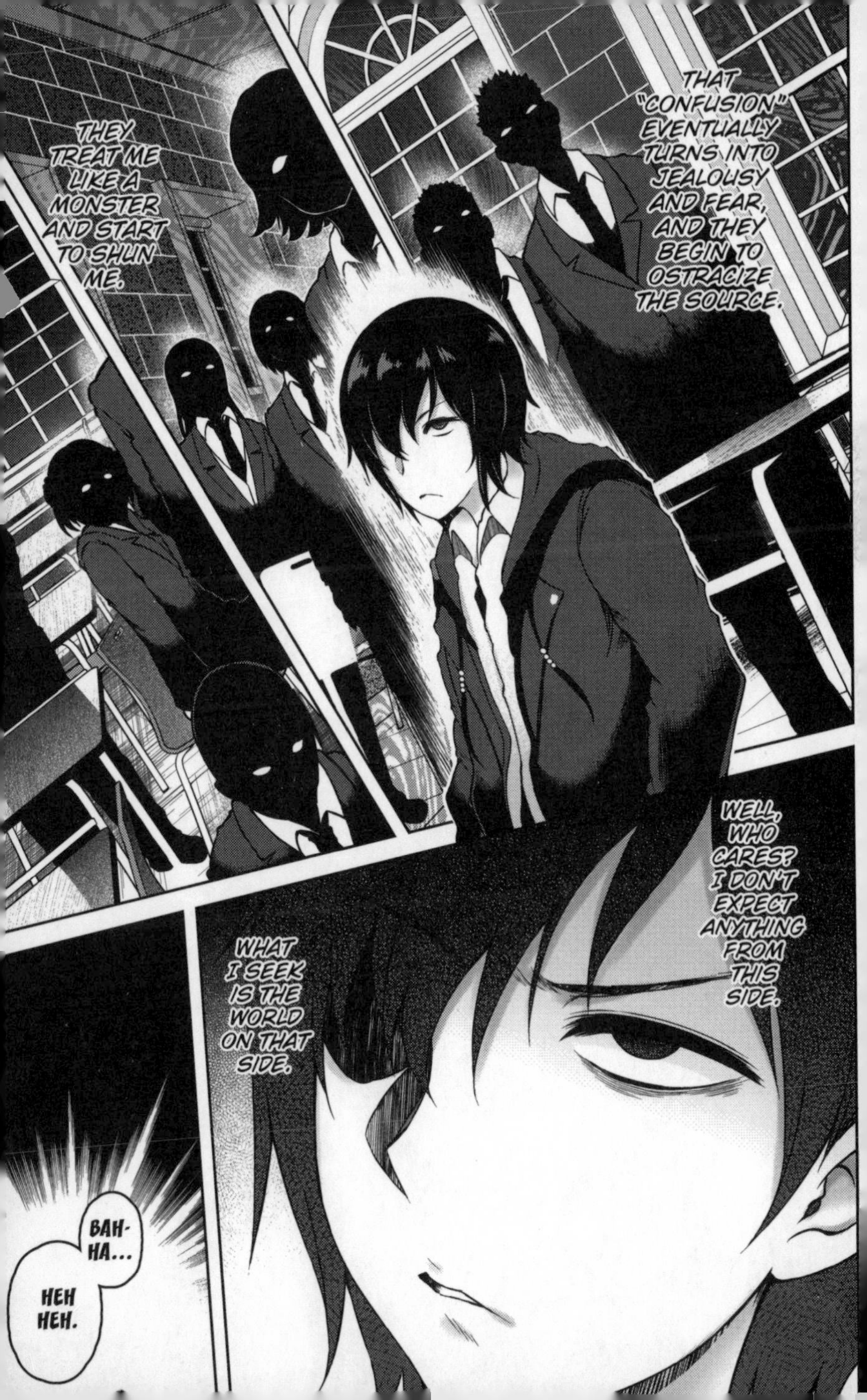
THAT "CONFUSION" EVENTUALLY TURNS INTO JEALOUSY AND FEAR, AND THEY BEGIN TO OSTRACIZE THE SOURCE.
THEY TREAT ME LIKE A MONSTER AND START TO SHUN ME.
WELL, WHO CARES? I DON'T EXPECT ANYTHING FROM THIS SIDE.
WHAT I SEEK IS THE WORLD ON THAT SIDE.
BAH-HA... HEH HEH.

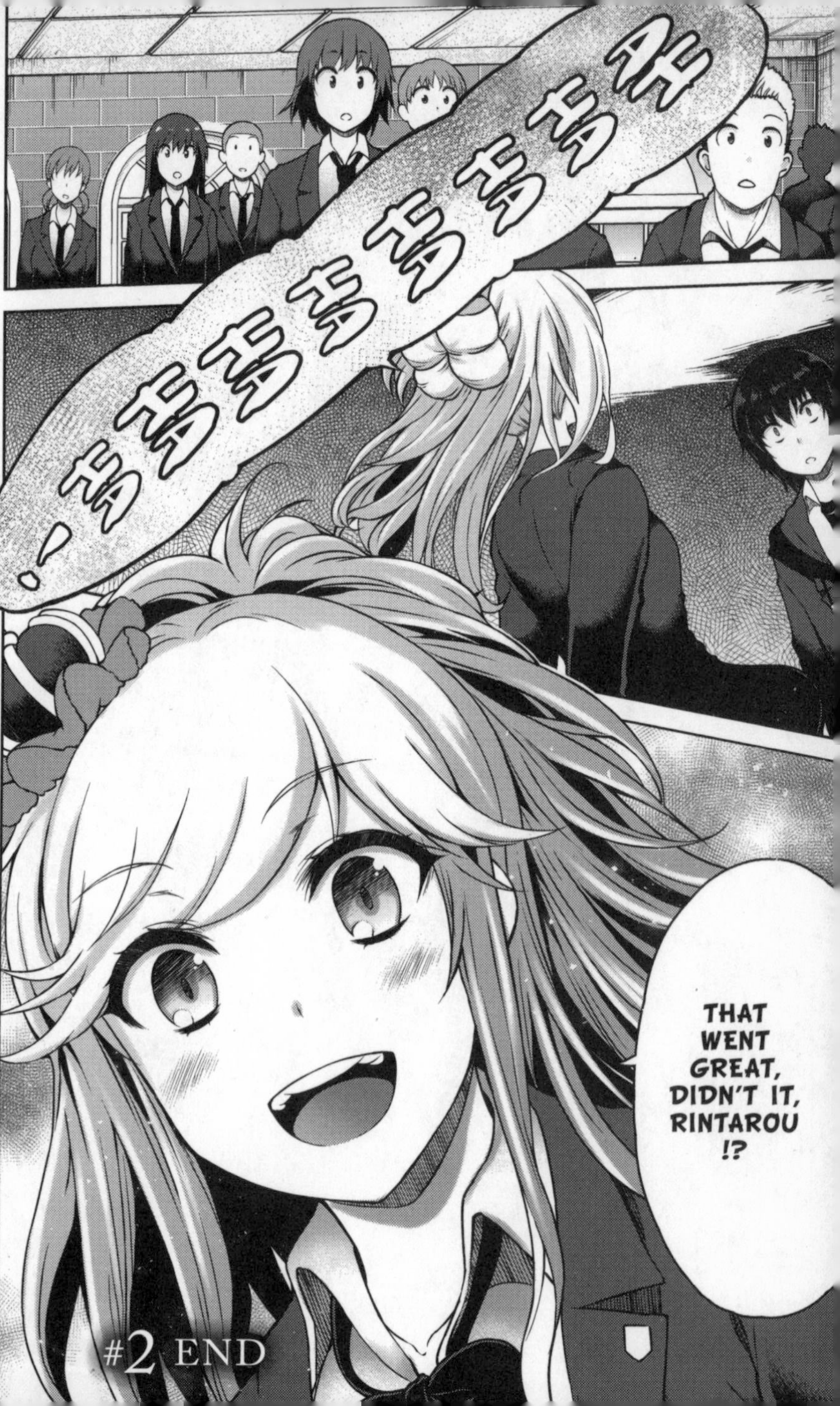
THAT WENT GREAT, DIDN'T IT, RINTAROU!?
#2 END

LAST ROUND

ARTHURS

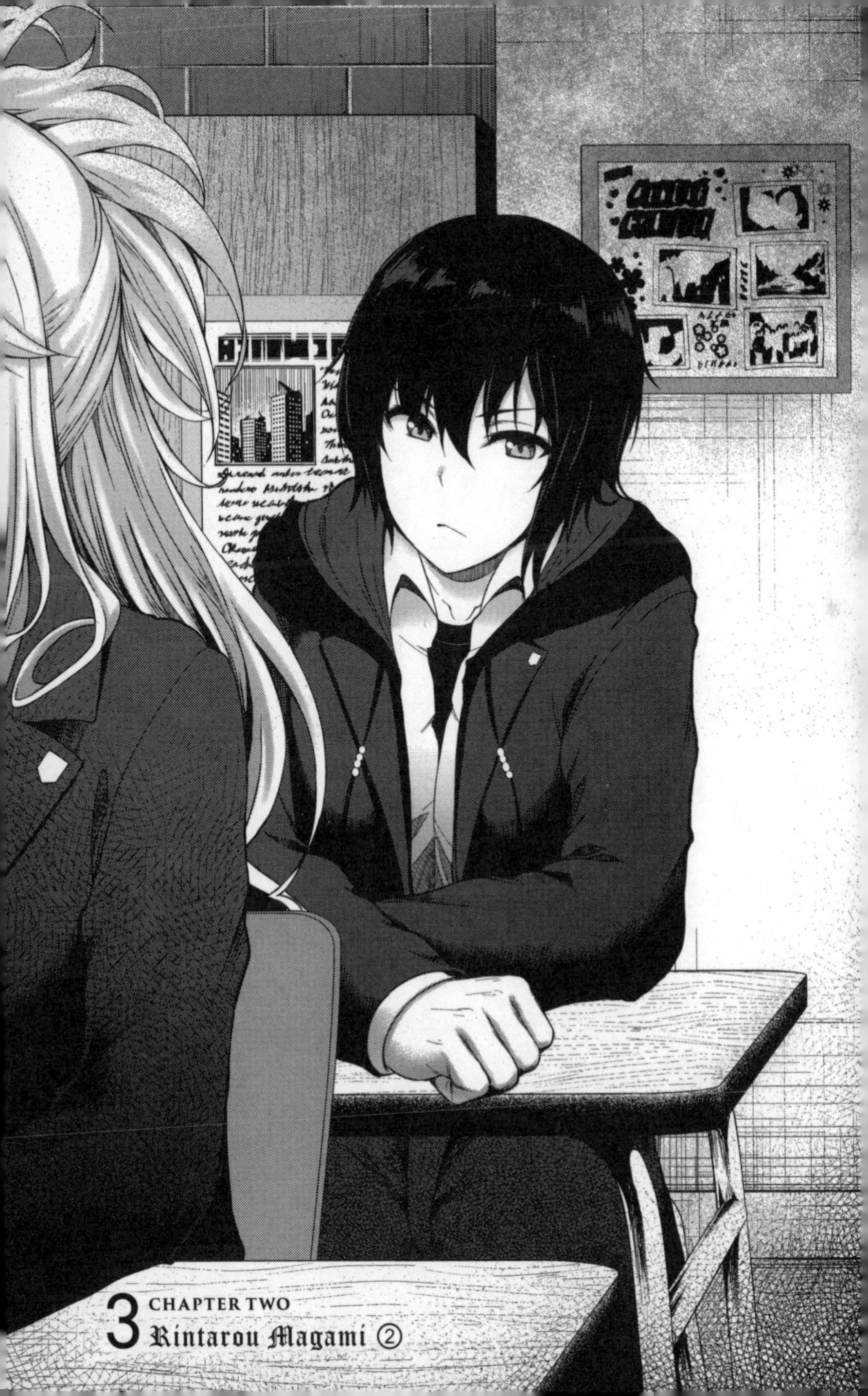

3 CHAPTER TWO

Rintarou Magami ②

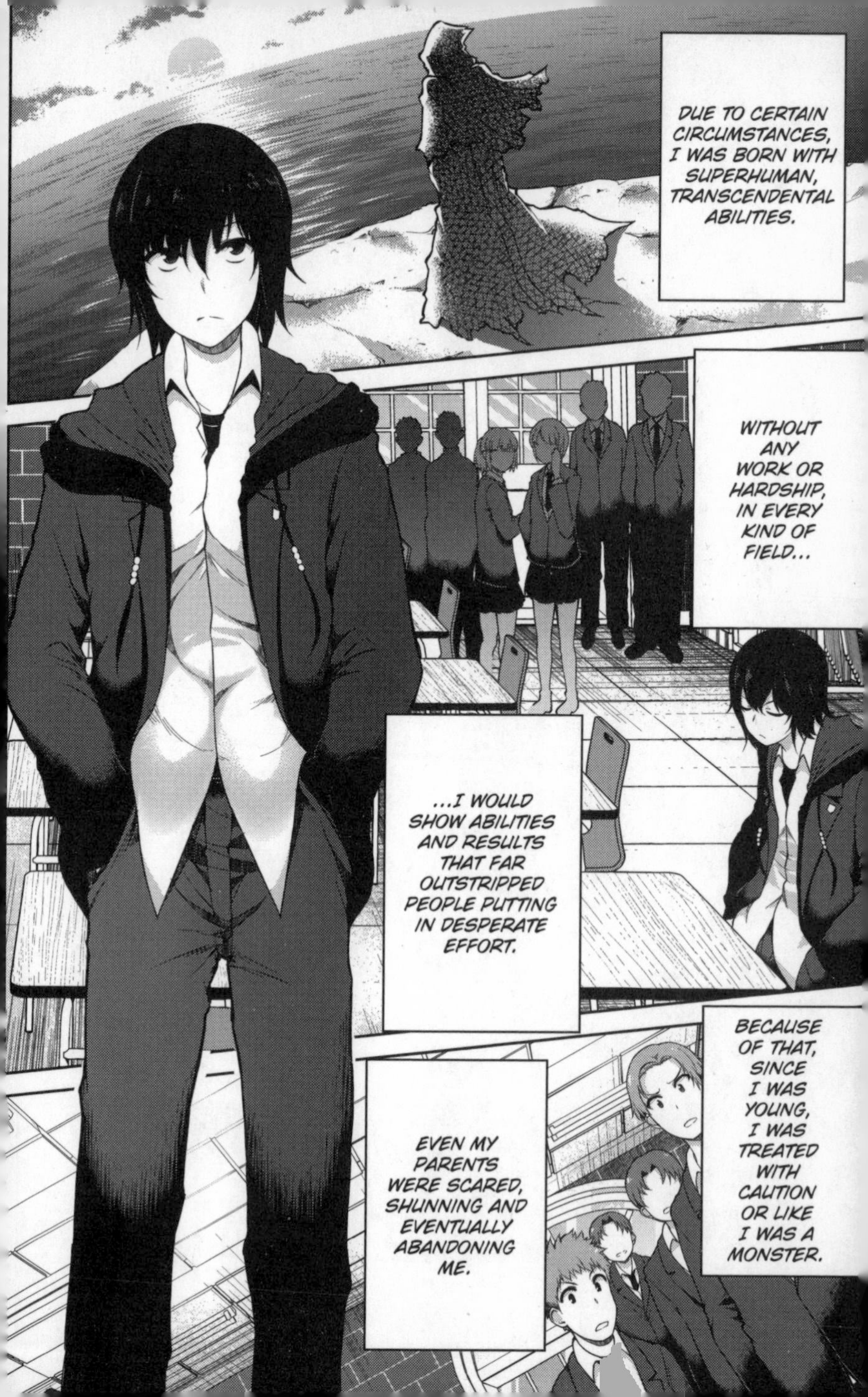
DUE TO CERTAIN CIRCUMSTANCES, I WAS BORN WITH SUPERHUMAN, TRANSCENDENTAL ABILITIES.
WITHOUT ANY WORK OR HARDSHIP, IN EVERY KIND OF FIELD...
...I WOULD SHOW ABILITIES AND RESULTS THAT FAR OUTSTRIPPED PEOPLE PUTTING IN DESPERATE EFFORT.
BECAUSE OF THAT, SINCE I WAS YOUNG, I WAS TREATED WITH CAUTION OR LIKE I WAS A MONSTER.
EVEN MY PARENTS WERE SCARED, SHUNNING AND EVENTUALLY ABANDONING ME.

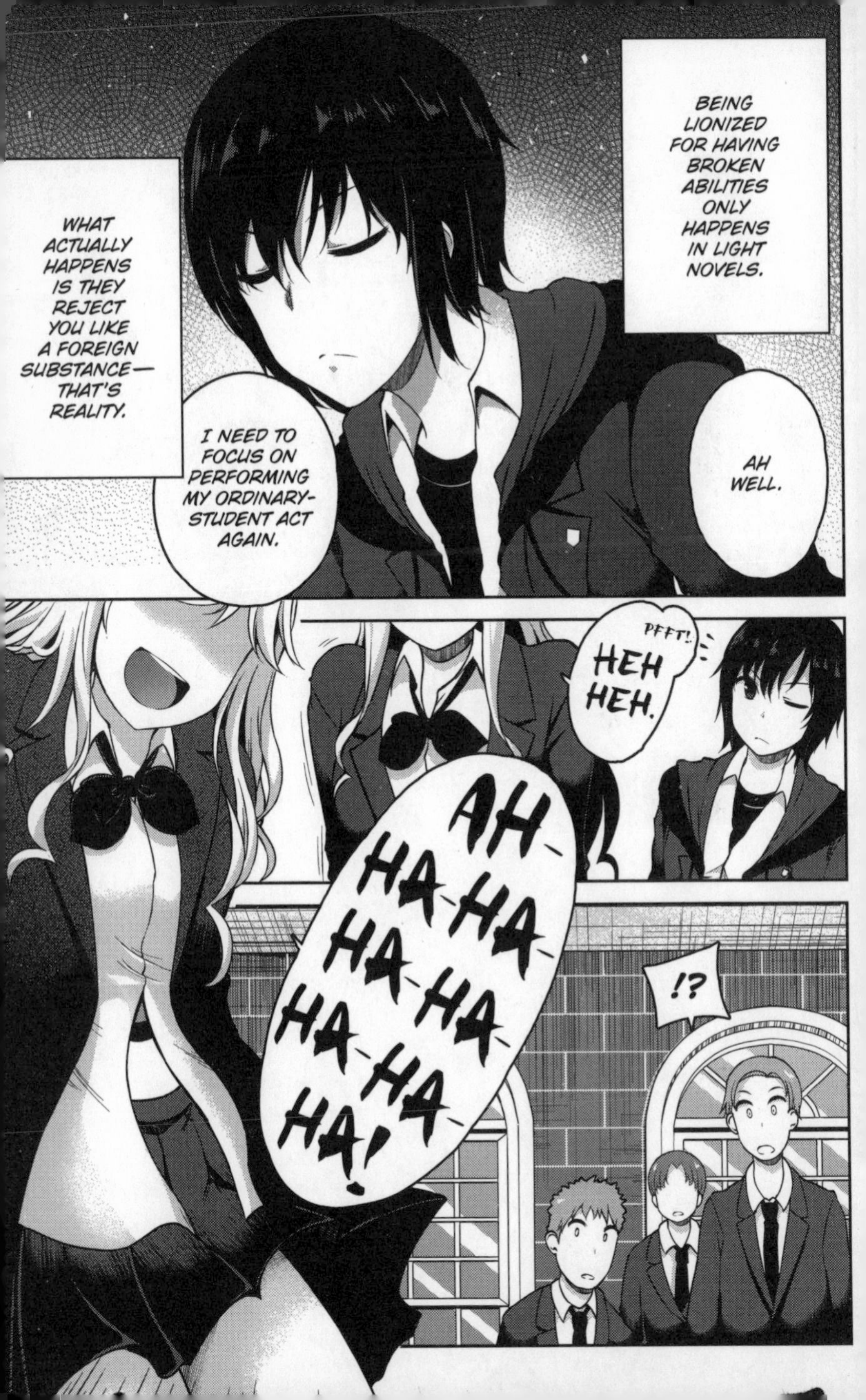
BEING LIONIZED FOR HAVING BROKEN ABILITIES ONLY HAPPENS IN LIGHT NOVELS.
AH WELL.
WHAT ACTUALLY HAPPENS IS THEY REJECT YOU LIKE A FOREIGN SUBSTANCE—THAT'S REALITY.
I NEED TO FOCUS ON PERFORMING MY ORDINARY-STUDENT ACT AGAIN.
PFFT!
HEH HEH.
AH-HA-HA-HA-HA-HA-HA-HA-HA-HA-HA!
!?

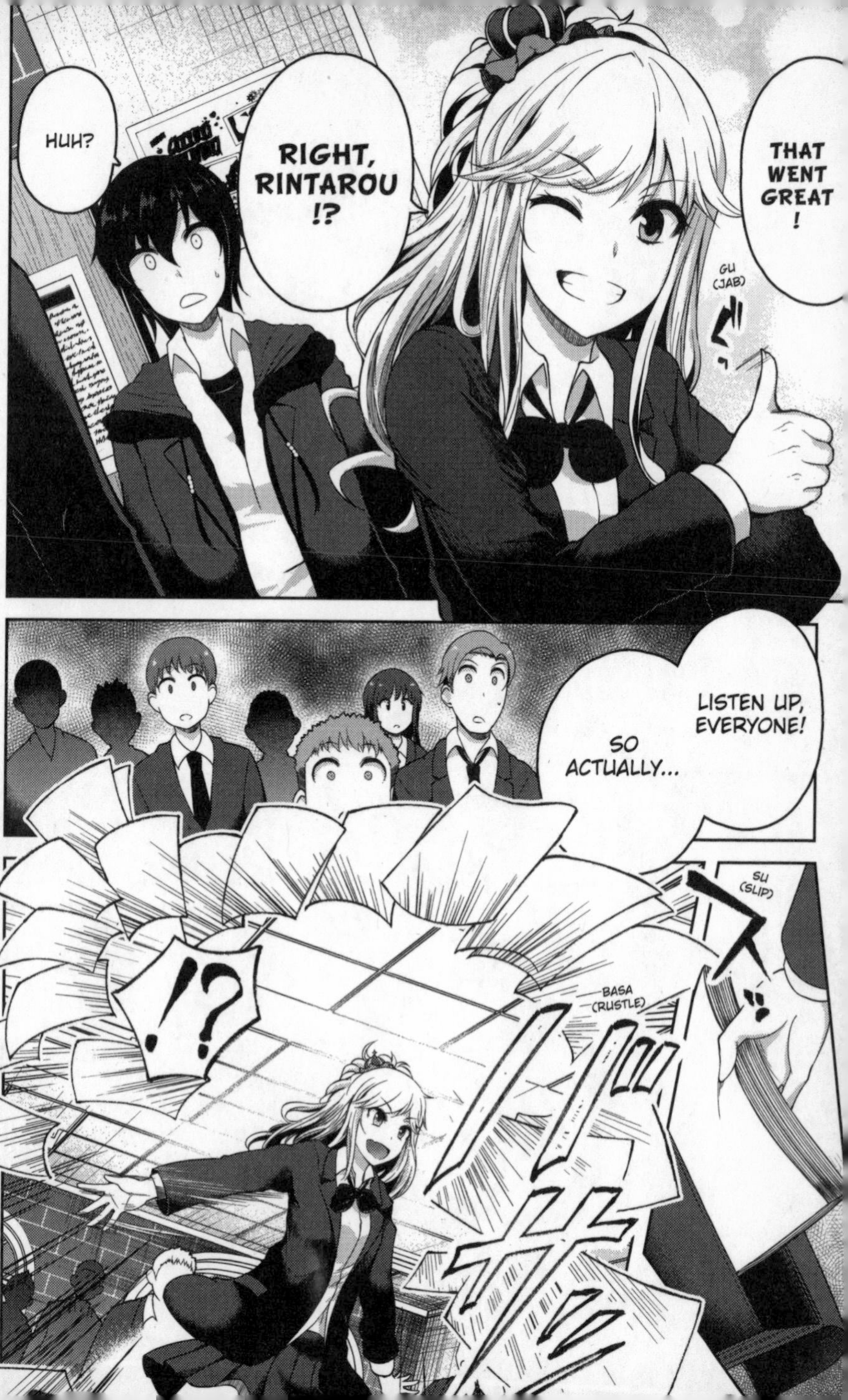
THAT WENT GREAT!
GU (JAB)
RIGHT, RINTAROU!?
HUH?
LISTEN UP, EVERYONE!
SO ACTUALLY...
SU (SLIP)
BASA (RUSTLE)
!?

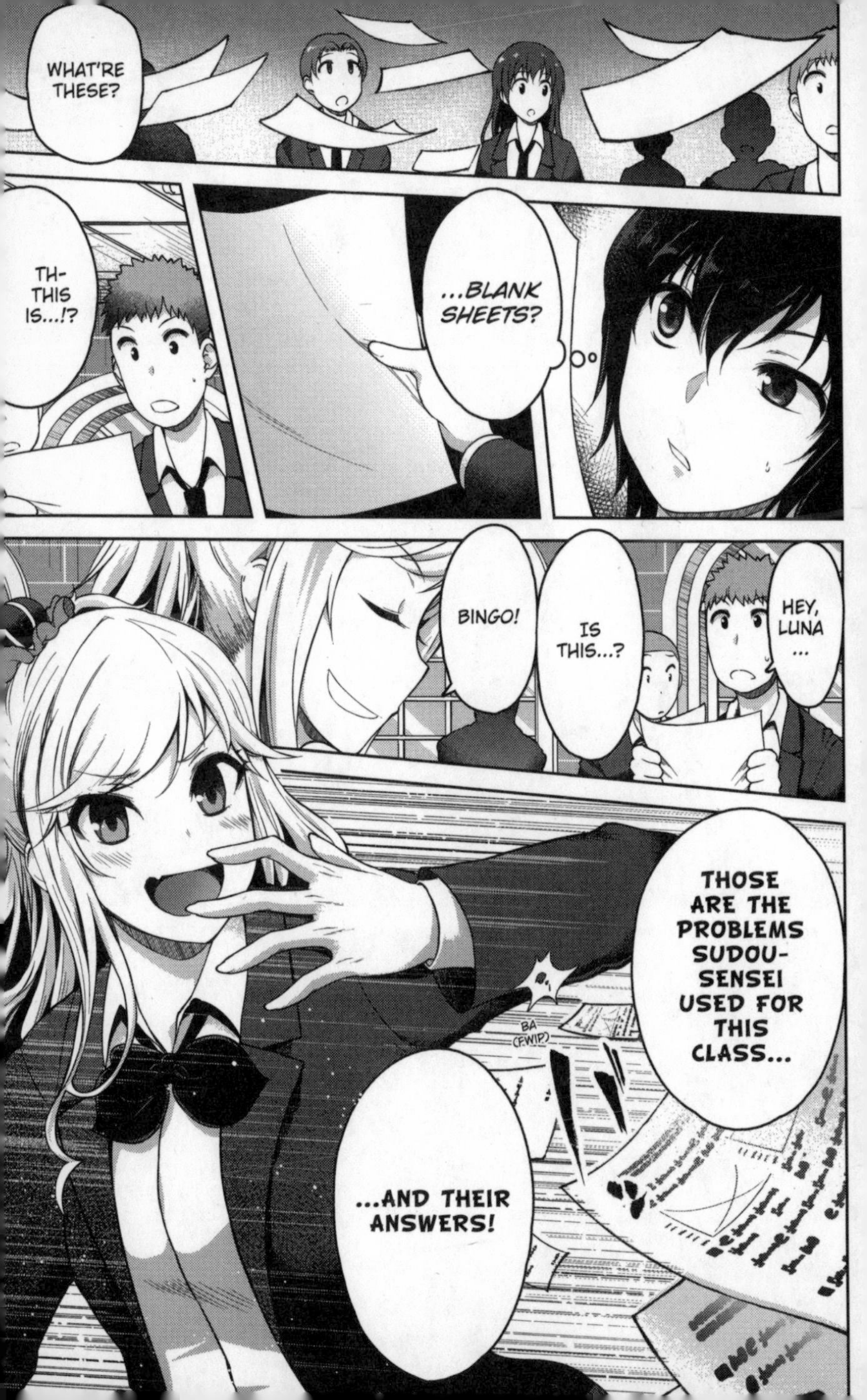
WHAT'RE THESE?
...BLANK SHEETS?
TH- THIS IS...!?
HEY, LUNA ...
IS THIS...?
BINGO!
THOSE ARE THE PROBLEMS SUDOU-SENSEI USED FOR THIS CLASS...
BA (F.WIP)
...AND THEIR ANSWERS!

THEY'RE THE QUESTIONS WE JUST SAW!

IT'S TRUE!

THIS GIRL...

SHE REALLY WENT AND DID THAT!?

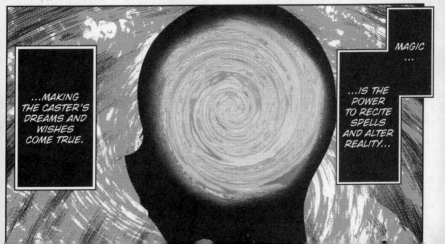

MAGIC...

...IS THE POWER TO RECITE SPELLS AND ALTER REALITY...

...MAKING THE CASTER'S DREAMS AND WISHES COME TRUE.

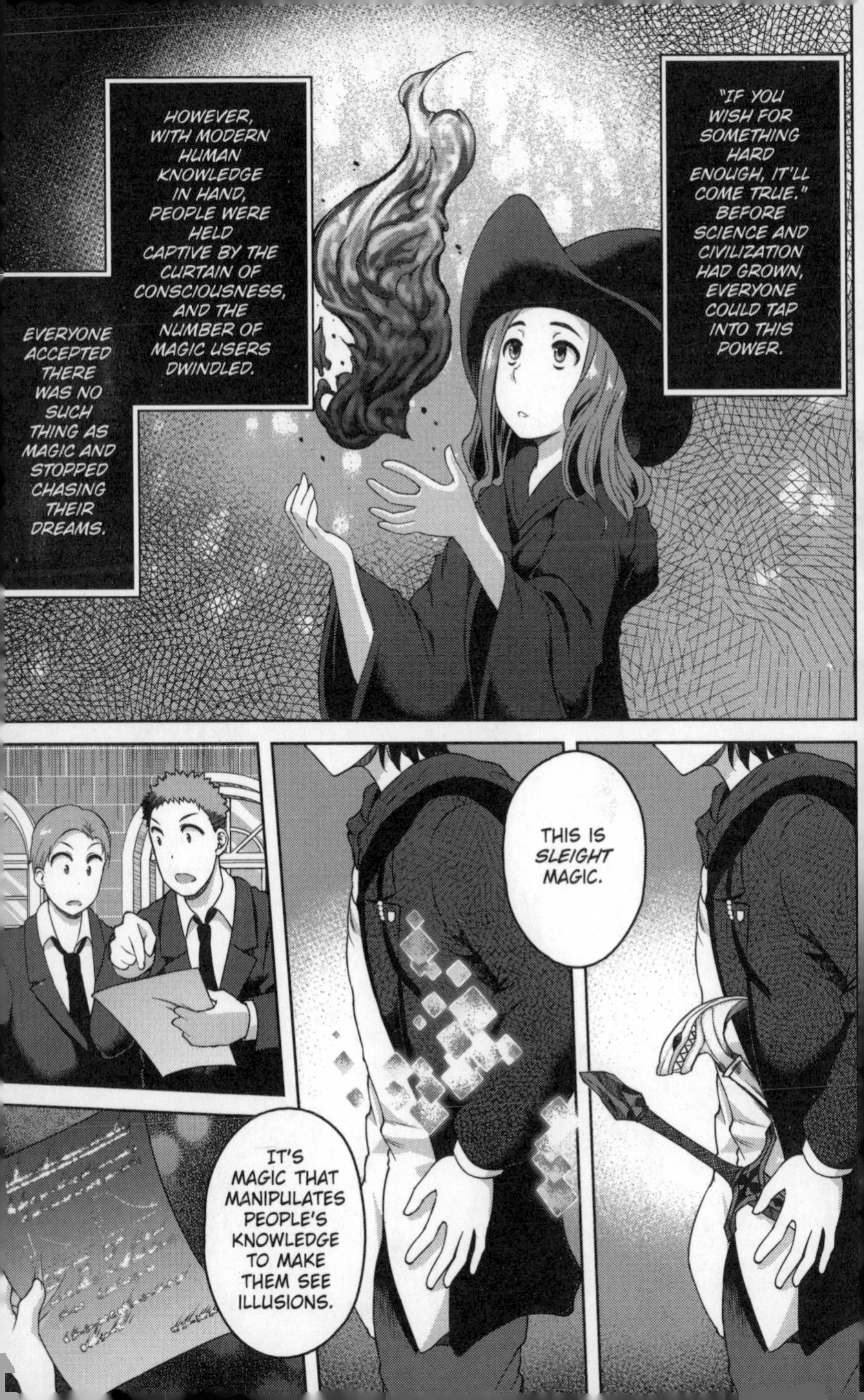
"IF YOU WISH FOR SOMETHING HARD ENOUGH, IT'LL COME TRUE." BEFORE SCIENCE AND CIVILIZATION HAD GROWN, EVERYONE COULD TAP INTO THIS POWER.
HOWEVER, WITH MODERN HUMAN KNOWLEDGE IN HAND, PEOPLE WERE HELD CAPTIVE BY THE CURTAIN OF CONSCIOUSNESS, AND THE NUMBER OF MAGIC USERS DWINDLED.
EVERYONE ACCEPTED THERE WAS NO SUCH THING AS MAGIC AND STOPPED CHASING THEIR DREAMS.
THIS IS *SLEIGHT* MAGIC.
IT'S MAGIC THAT MANIPULATES PEOPLE'S KNOWLEDGE TO MAKE THEM SEE ILLUSIONS.

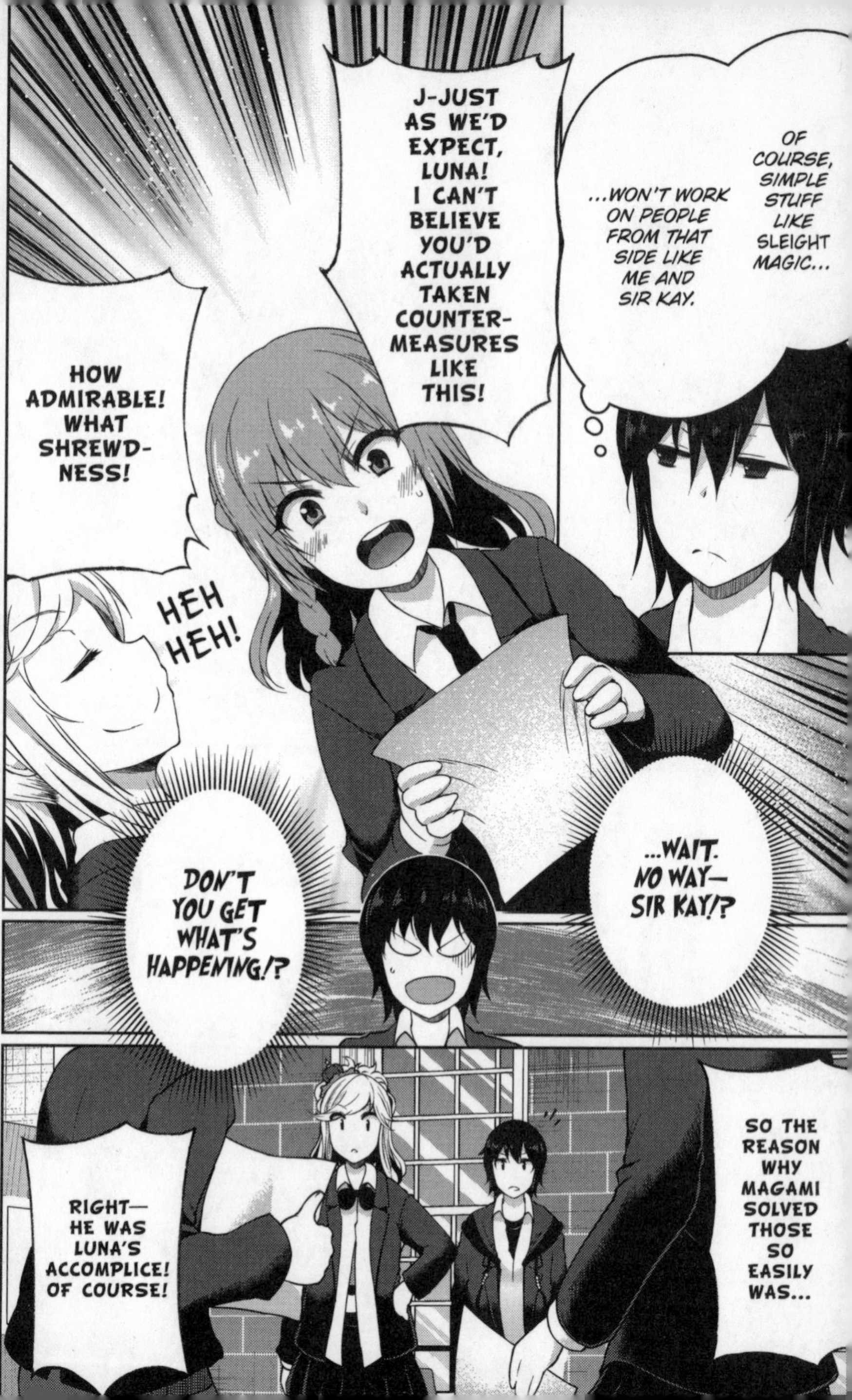
OF COURSE, SIMPLE STUFF LIKE SLEIGHT MAGIC...
...WON'T WORK ON PEOPLE FROM THAT SIDE LIKE ME AND SIR KAY.
J-JUST AS WE'D EXPECT, LUNA! I CAN'T BELIEVE YOU'D ACTUALLY TAKEN COUNTER-MEASURES LIKE THIS!
HOW ADMIRABLE! WHAT SHREWD-NESS!
HEH HEH!
...WAIT. NO WAY— SIR KAY!?
DON'T YOU GET WHAT'S HAPPENING!?
SO THE REASON WHY MAGAMI SOLVED THOSE SO EASILY WAS...
RIGHT— HE WAS LUNA'S ACCOMPLICE! OF COURSE!

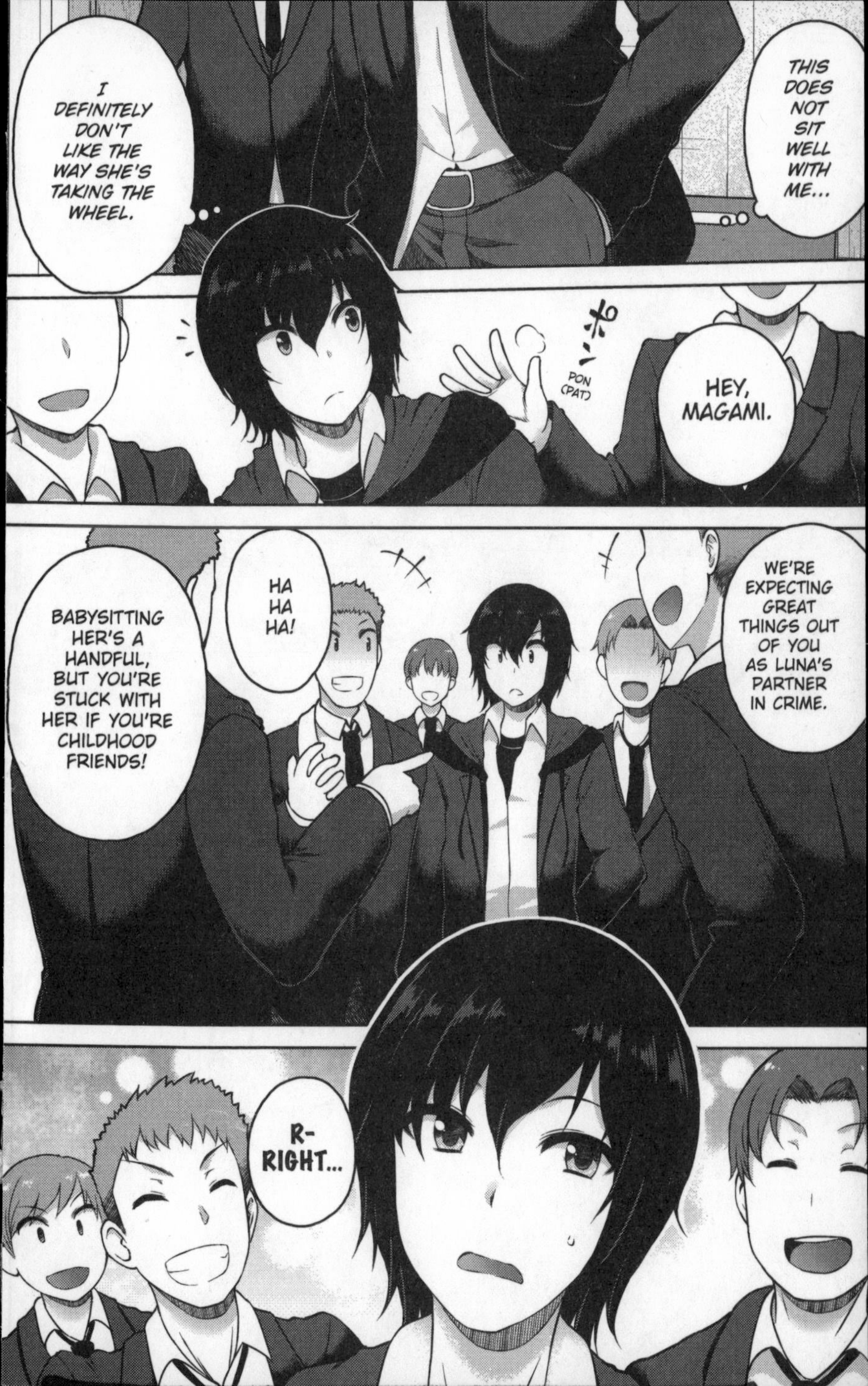
THIS DOES NOT SIT WELL WITH ME...
I DEFINITELY DON'T LIKE THE WAY SHE'S TAKING THE WHEEL.
HEY, MAGAMI.
PON (PAT)
WE'RE EXPECTING GREAT THINGS OUT OF YOU AS LUNA'S PARTNER IN CRIME.
HA HA HA!
BABYSITTING HER'S A HANDFUL, BUT YOU'RE STUCK WITH HER IF YOU'RE CHILDHOOD FRIENDS!
R-RIGHT...

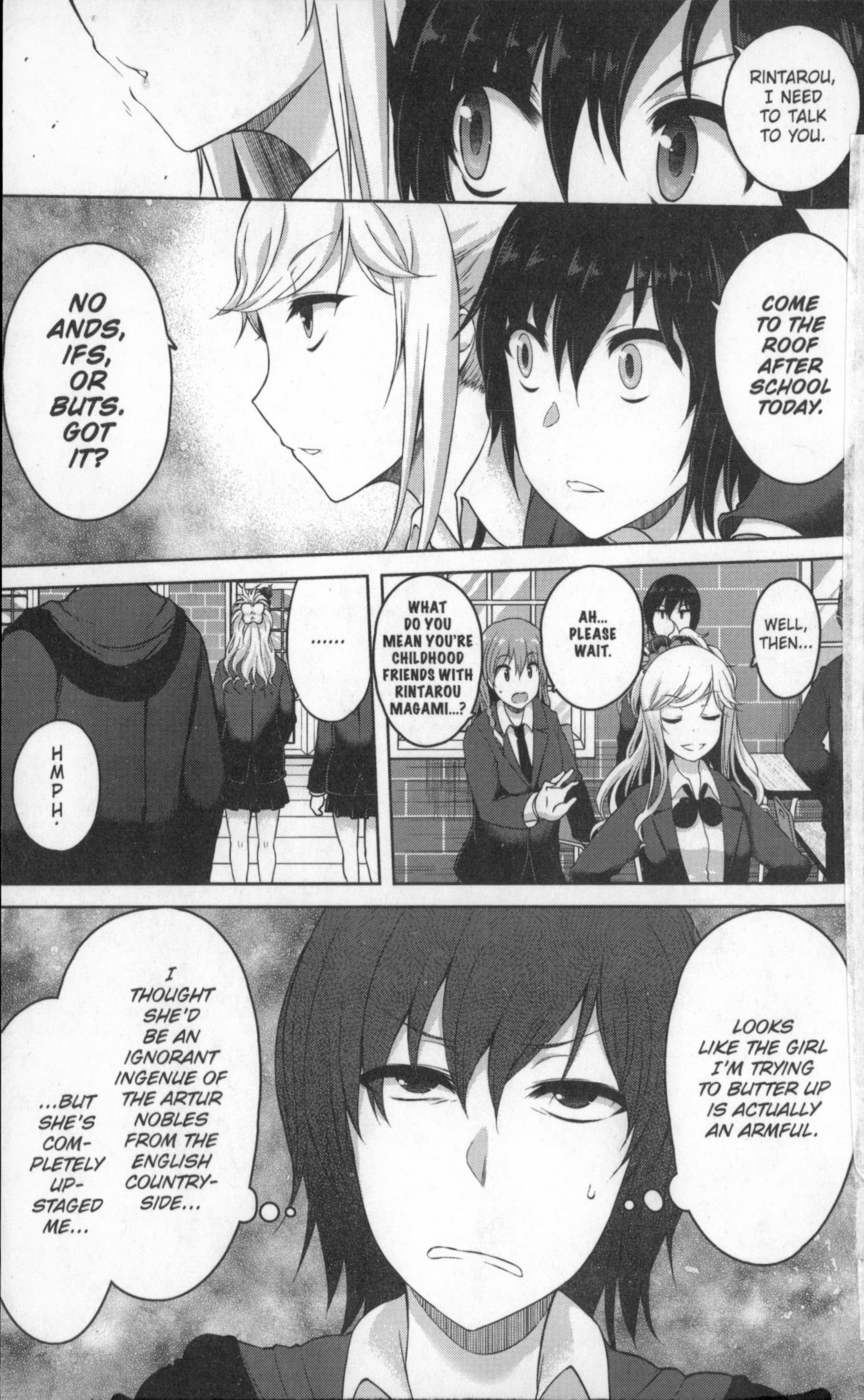
RINTAROU, I NEED TO TALK TO YOU.
COME TO THE ROOF AFTER SCHOOL TODAY.
NO ANDS, IFS, OR BUTS. GOT IT?
WELL, THEN...
AH... PLEASE WAIT.
WHAT DO YOU MEAN YOU'RE CHILDHOOD FRIENDS WITH RINTAROU MAGAMI...?
......
HMPH.
LOOKS LIKE THE GIRL I'M TRYING TO BUTTER UP IS ACTUALLY AN ARMFUL.
I THOUGHT SHE'D BE AN IGNORANT INGENUE OF THE ARTUR NOBLES FROM THE ENGLISH COUNTRY-SIDE...
...BUT SHE'S COM-PLETELY UP-STAGED ME...

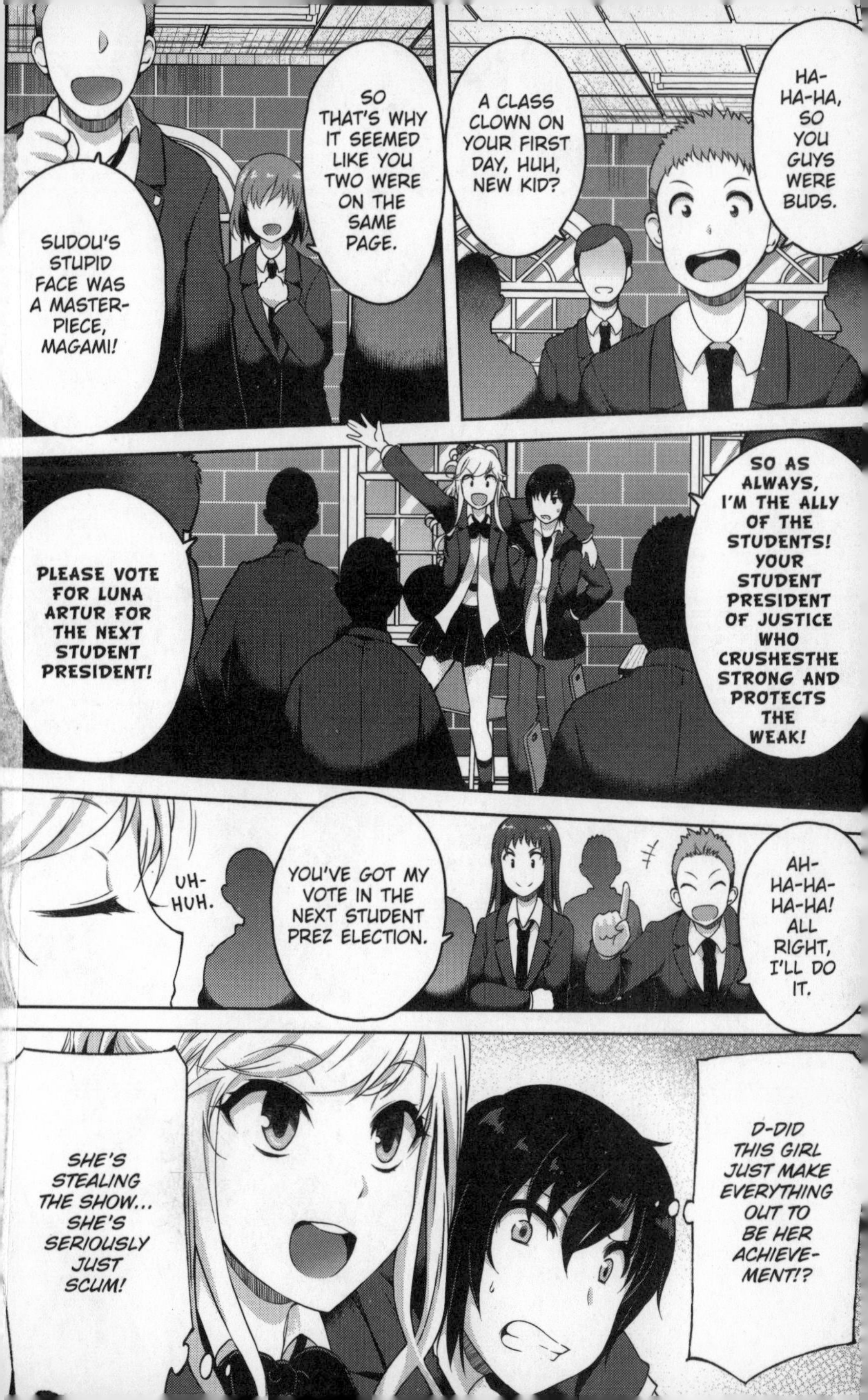
HA-HA-HA, SO YOU GUYS WERE BUDS.
A CLASS CLOWN ON YOUR FIRST DAY, HUH, NEW KID?
SO THAT'S WHY IT SEEMED LIKE YOU TWO WERE ON THE SAME PAGE.
SUDOU'S STUPID FACE WAS A MASTER-PIECE, MAGAMI!
SO AS ALWAYS, I'M THE ALLY OF THE STUDENTS! YOUR STUDENT PRESIDENT OF JUSTICE WHO CRUSHESTHE STRONG AND PROTECTS THE WEAK!
PLEASE VOTE FOR LUNA ARTUR FOR THE NEXT STUDENT PRESIDENT!
AH-HA-HA-HA-HA! ALL RIGHT, I'LL DO IT.
YOU'VE GOT MY VOTE IN THE NEXT STUDENT PREZ ELECTION.
UH-HUH.
D-DID THIS GIRL JUST MAKE EVERYTHING OUT TO BE HER ACHIEVE-MENT!?
SHE'S STEALING THE SHOW... SHE'S SERIOUSLY JUST SCUM!

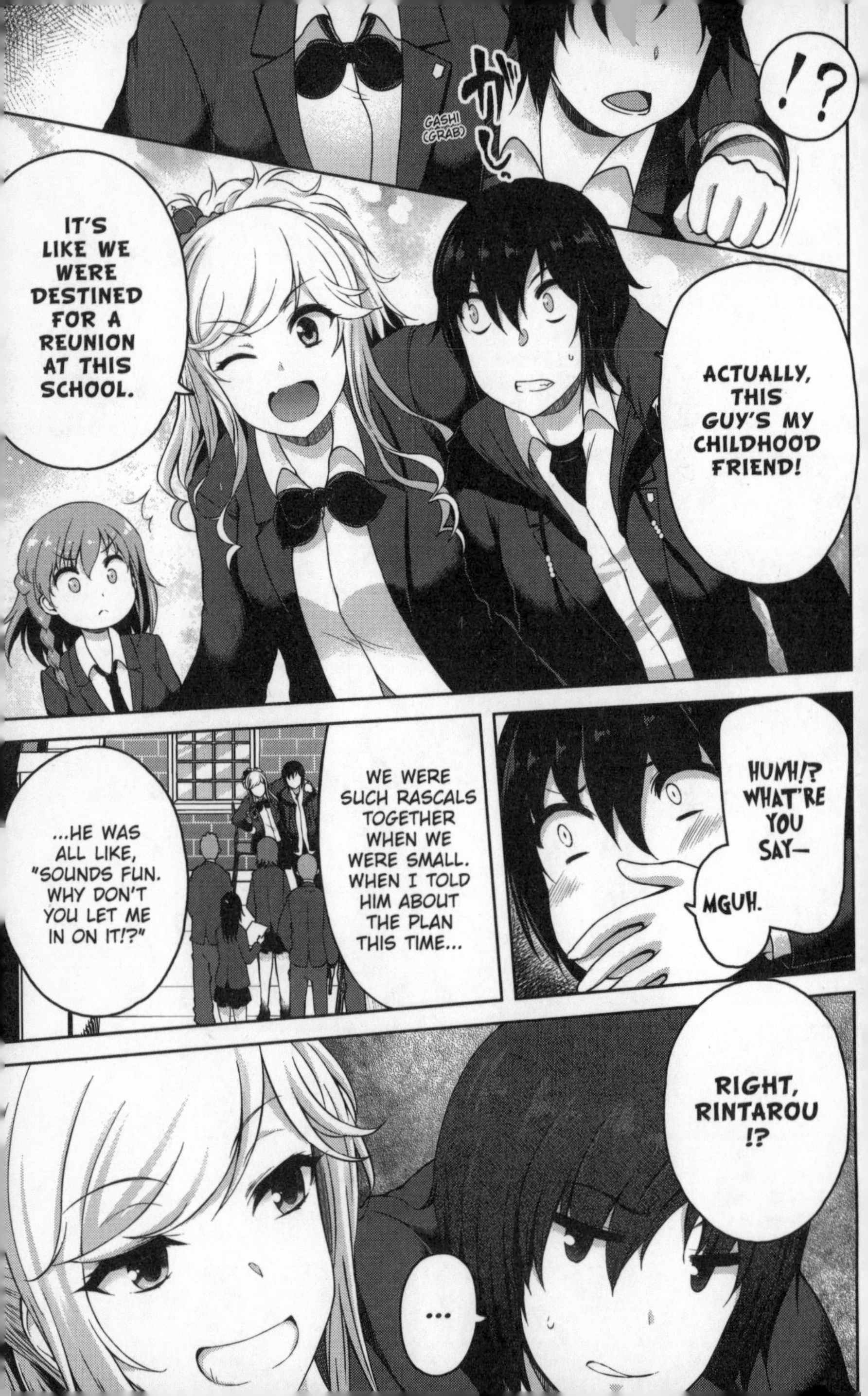
!?
GASHI (GRAB)
ACTUALLY, THIS GUY'S MY CHILDHOOD FRIEND!
IT'S LIKE WE WERE DESTINED FOR A REUNION AT THIS SCHOOL.
HUNH!? WHAT'RE YOU SAY—
MGUH.
WE WERE SUCH RASCALS TOGETHER WHEN WE WERE SMALL. WHEN I TOLD HIM ABOUT THE PLAN THIS TIME...
...HE WAS ALL LIKE, "SOUNDS FUN. WHY DON'T YOU LET ME IN ON IT!?"
RIGHT, RINTAROU!?
...

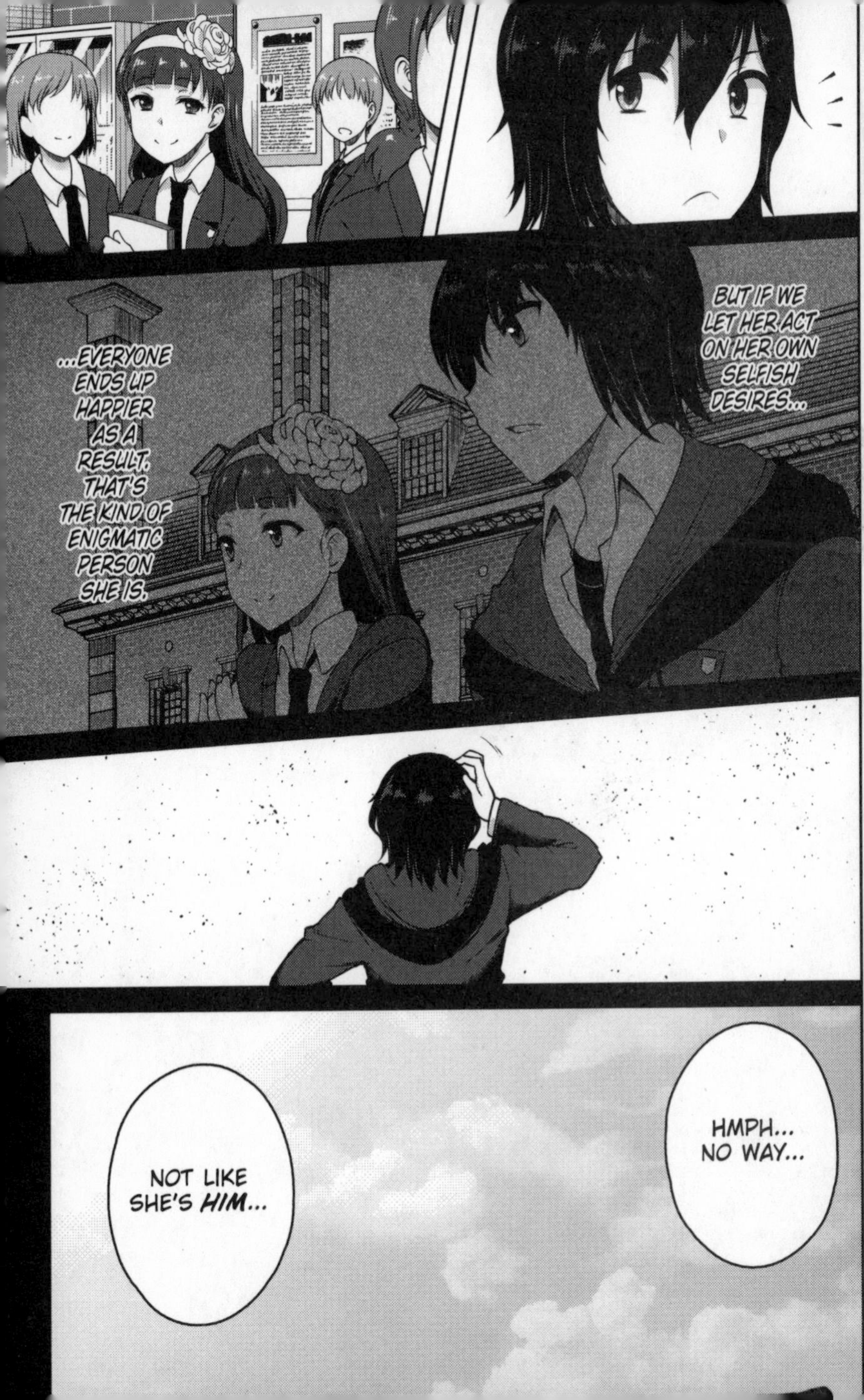
BUT IF WE LET HER ACT ON HER OWN SELFISH DESIRES...
...EVERYONE ENDS UP HAPPIER AS A RESULT. THAT'S THE KIND OF ENIGMATIC PERSON SHE IS.
HMPH... NO WAY...
NOT LIKE SHE'S *HIM*...

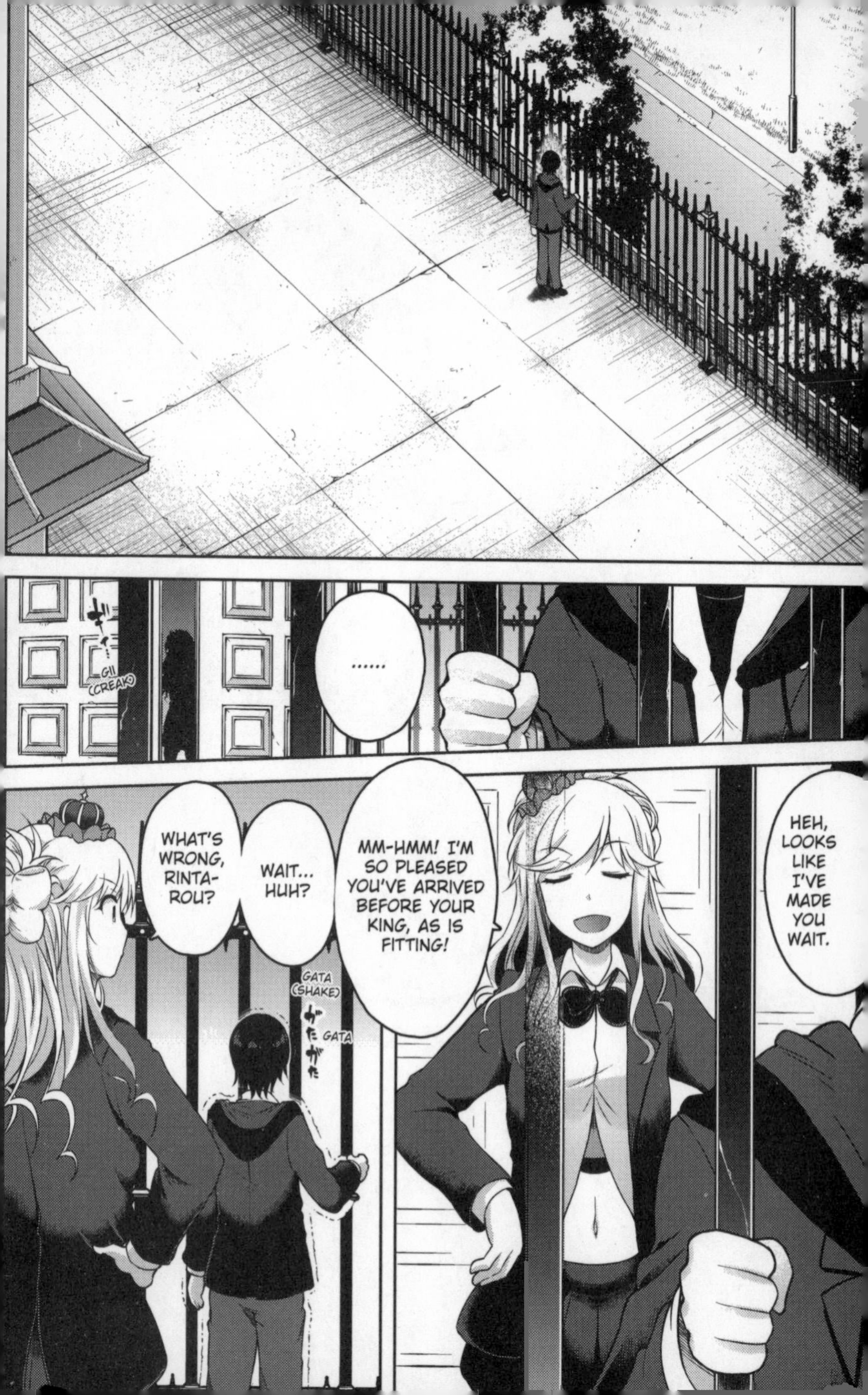
......
GII (CREAK)
HEH, LOOKS LIKE I'VE MADE YOU WAIT.
MM-HMM! I'M SO PLEASED YOU'VE ARRIVED BEFORE YOUR KING, AS IS FITTING!
WAIT... HUH?
GATA (SHAKE) GATA
WHAT'S WRONG, RINTAROU?

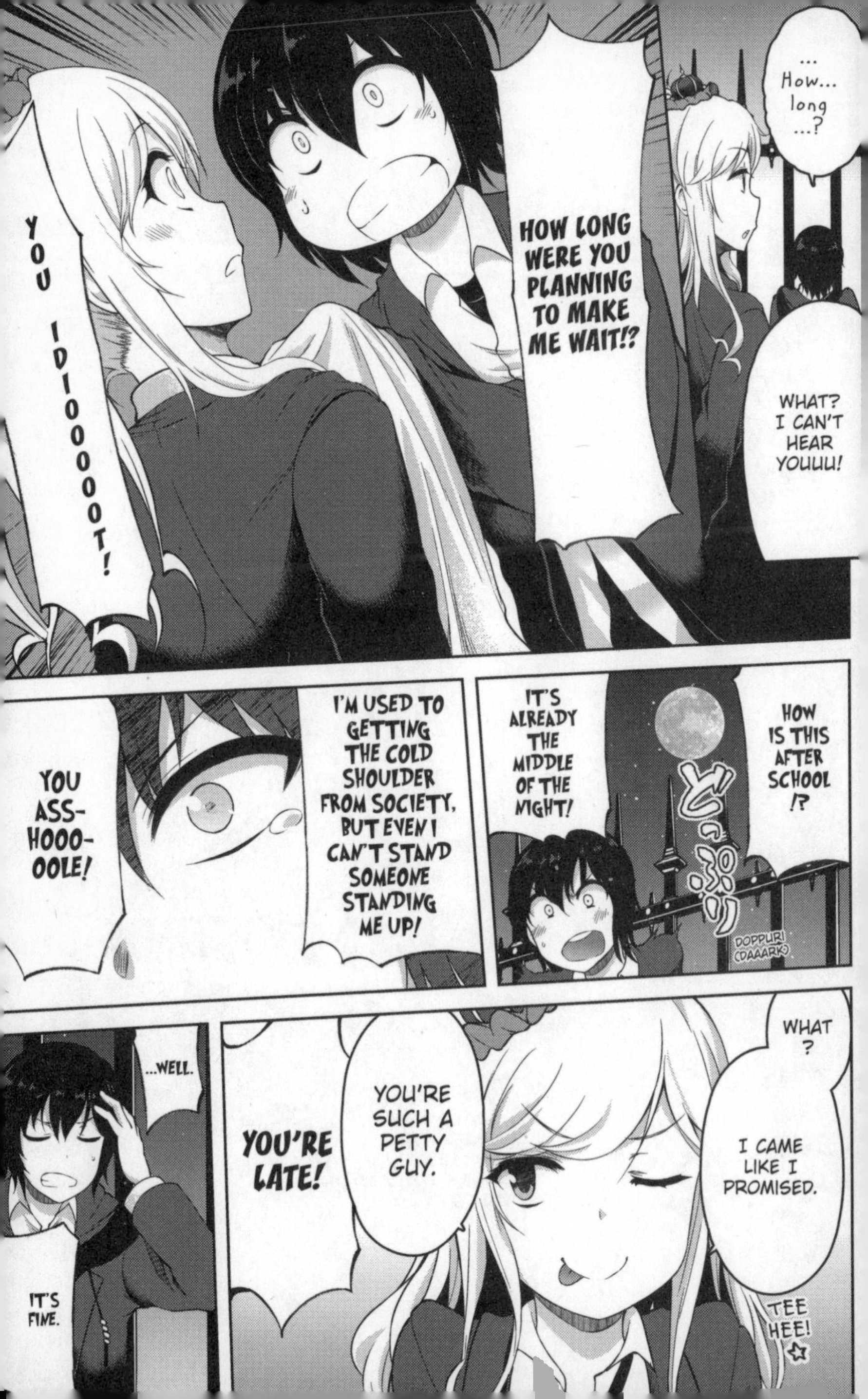

...How...long...?
WHAT? I CAN'T HEAR YOUUU!
HOW LONG WERE YOU PLANNING TO MAKE ME WAIT!?
YOU IDIOOOOOOT!
HOW IS THIS AFTER SCHOOL!?
IT'S ALREADY THE MIDDLE OF THE NIGHT!
DOPPURI (DAAARK)
I'M USED TO GETTING THE COLD SHOULDER FROM SOCIETY, BUT EVEN I CAN'T STAND SOMEONE STANDING ME UP!
YOU ASS-HOOOOOLE!
WHAT?
I CAME LIKE I PROMISED.
TEE HEE! ☆
YOU'RE SUCH A PETTY GUY.
YOU'RE LATE!
...WELL.
IT'S FINE.

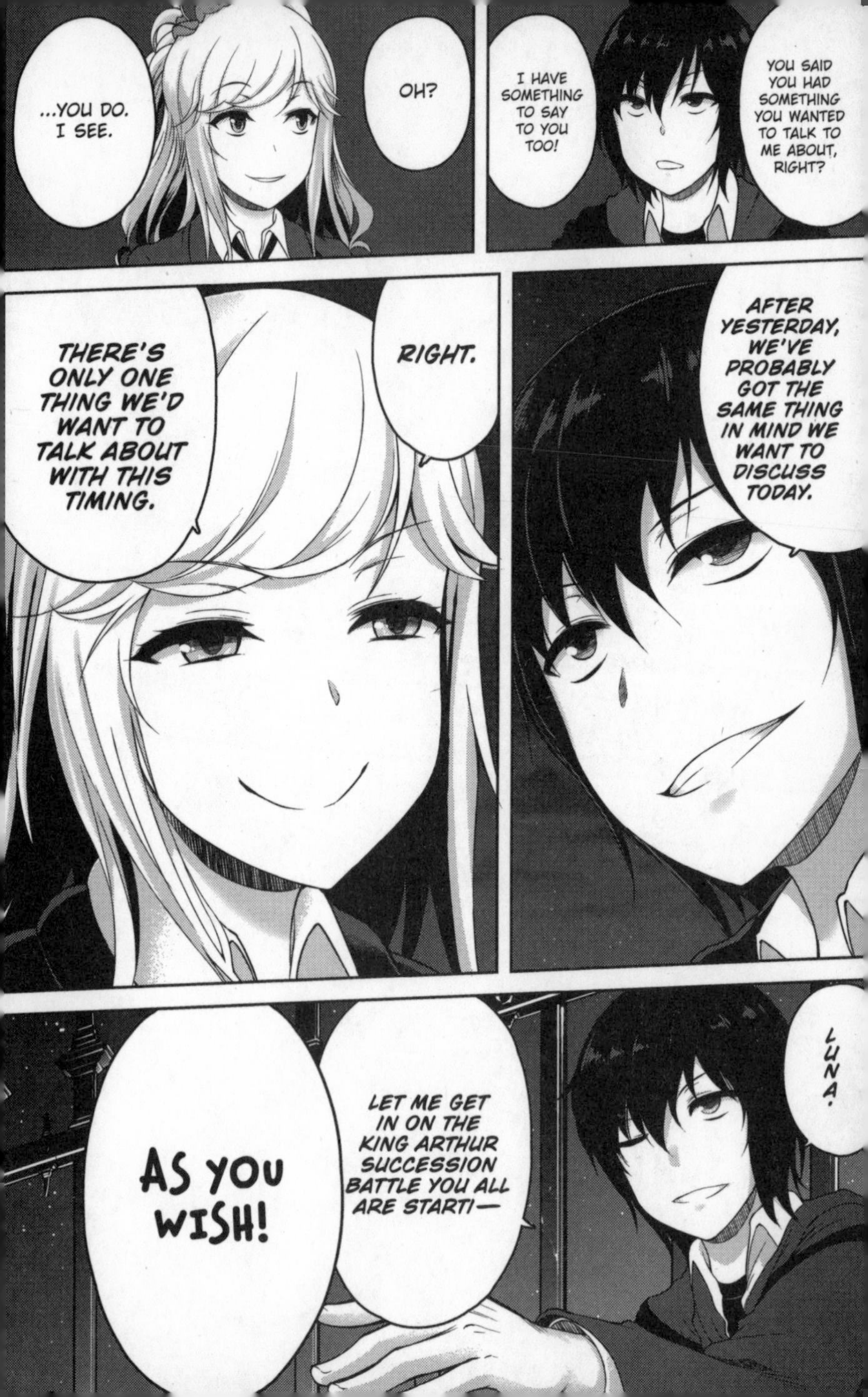
YOU SAID YOU HAD SOMETHING YOU WANTED TO TALK TO ME ABOUT, RIGHT?
I HAVE SOMETHING TO SAY TO YOU TOO!
OH?
...YOU DO. I SEE.
AFTER YESTERDAY, WE'VE PROBABLY GOT THE SAME THING IN MIND WE WANT TO DISCUSS TODAY.
RIGHT.
THERE'S ONLY ONE THING WE'D WANT TO TALK ABOUT WITH THIS TIMING.
LUNA.
LET ME GET IN ON THE KING ARTHUR SUCCESSION BATTLE YOU ALL ARE STARTI—
AS YOU WISH!

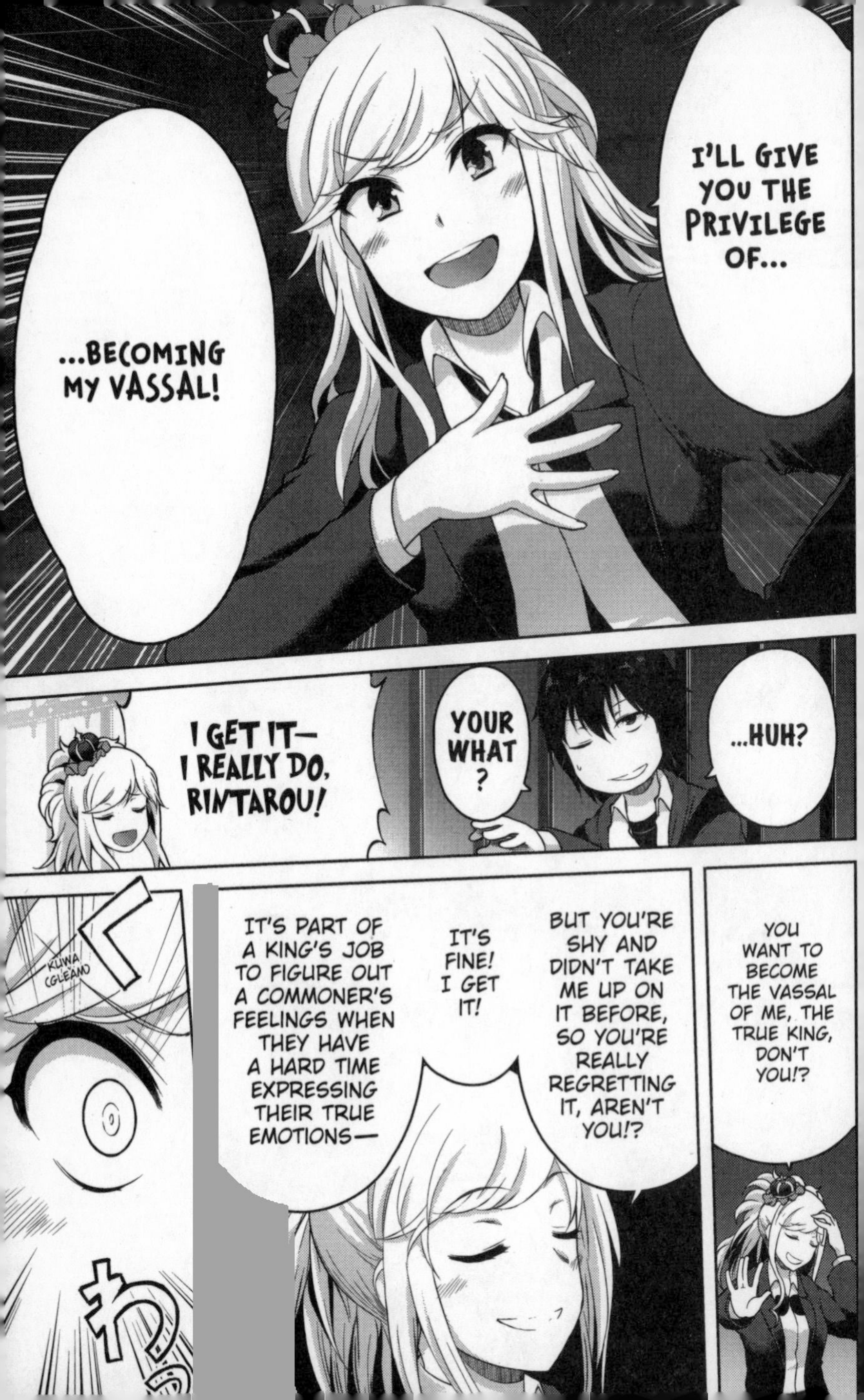
I'LL GIVE YOU THE PRIVILEGE OF...
...BECOMING MY VASSAL!
...HUH?
YOUR WHAT?
I GET IT— I REALLY DO, RINTAROU!
YOU WANT TO BECOME THE VASSAL OF ME, THE TRUE KING, DON'T YOU!?
BUT YOU'RE SHY AND DIDN'T TAKE ME UP ON IT BEFORE, SO YOU'RE REALLY REGRETTING IT, AREN'T YOU!?
IT'S FINE! I GET IT!
IT'S PART OF A KING'S JOB TO FIGURE OUT A COMMONER'S FEELINGS WHEN THEY HAVE A HARD TIME EXPRESSING THEIR TRUE EMOTIONS—
KUWA (GLEAM)

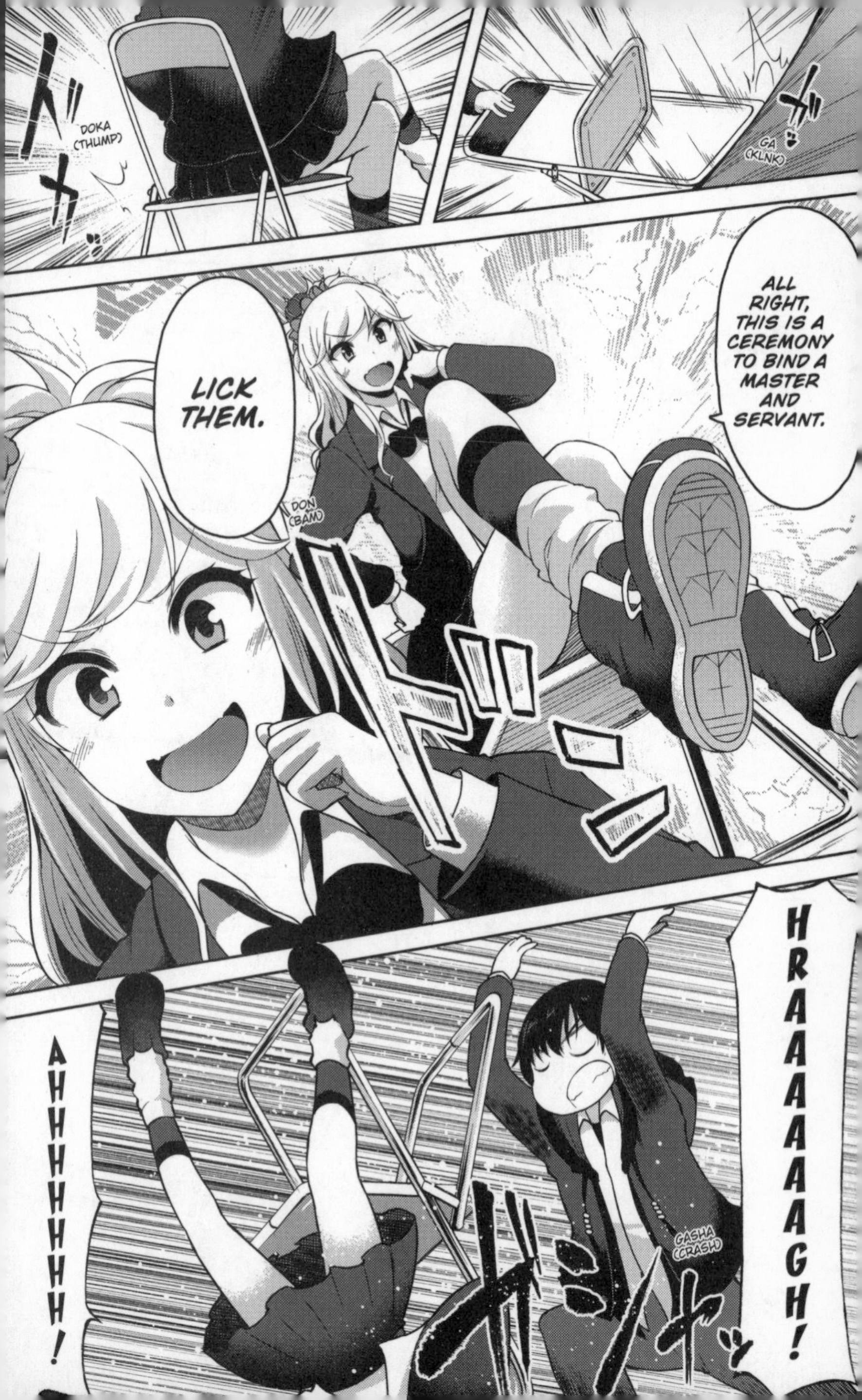
GA (KLNK)
DOKA (THUMP)
ALL RIGHT, THIS IS A CEREMONY TO BIND A MASTER AND SERVANT.
LICK THEM.
DON (BAM)
HRAAAAAAGH!
GASHA (CRASH)
AHHHHHHH!

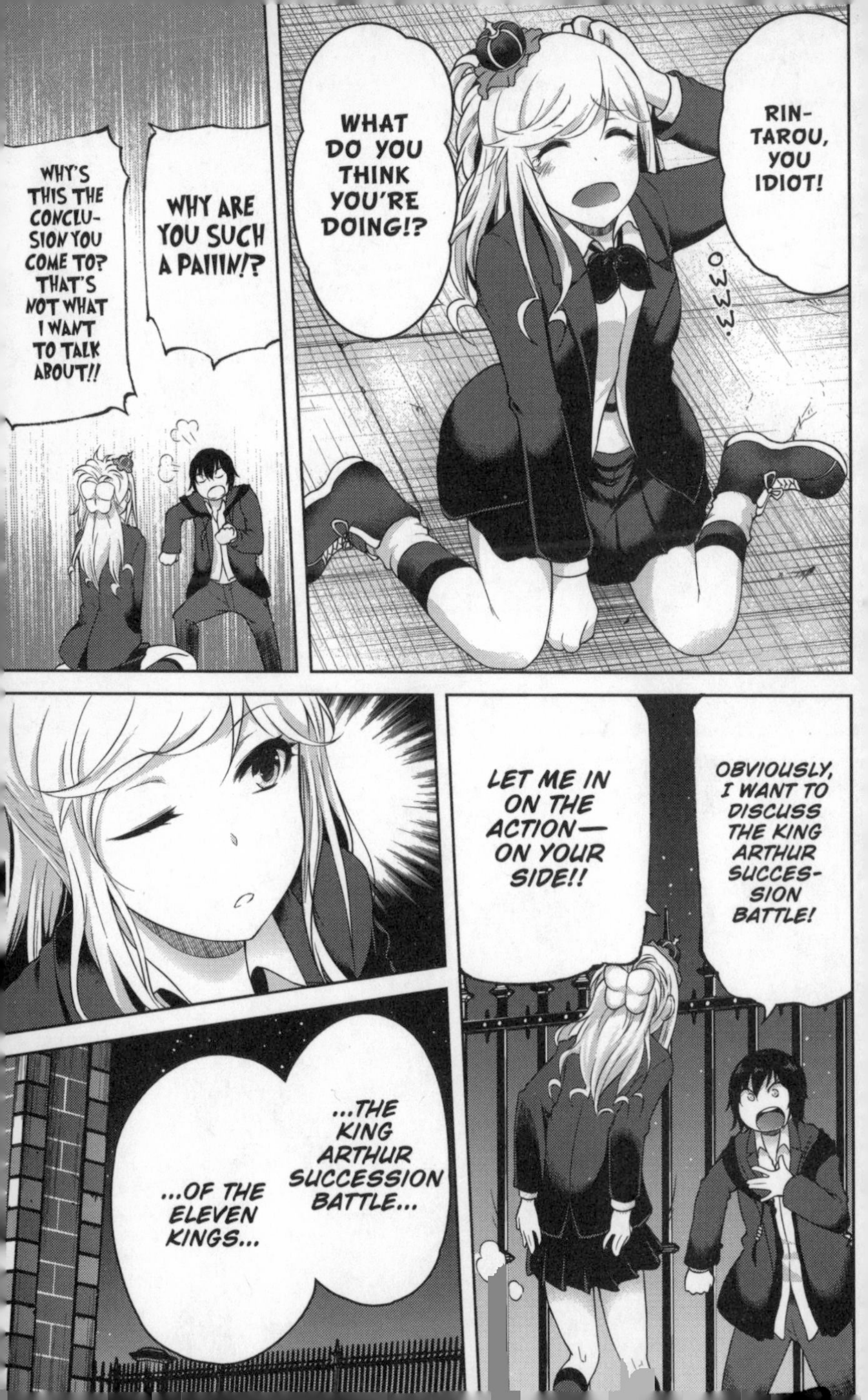
RIN-TAROU, YOU IDIOT!
OWWW..
WHAT DO YOU THINK YOU'RE DOING!?
WHY ARE YOU SUCH A PAIIIN!?
WHY'S THIS THE CONCLUSION YOU COME TO? THAT'S NOT WHAT I WANT TO TALK ABOUT!!
OBVIOUSLY, I WANT TO DISCUSS THE KING ARTHUR SUCCESSION BATTLE!
LET ME IN ON THE ACTION—ON YOUR SIDE!!
...THE KING ARTHUR SUCCESSION BATTLE...
...OF THE ELEVEN KINGS...

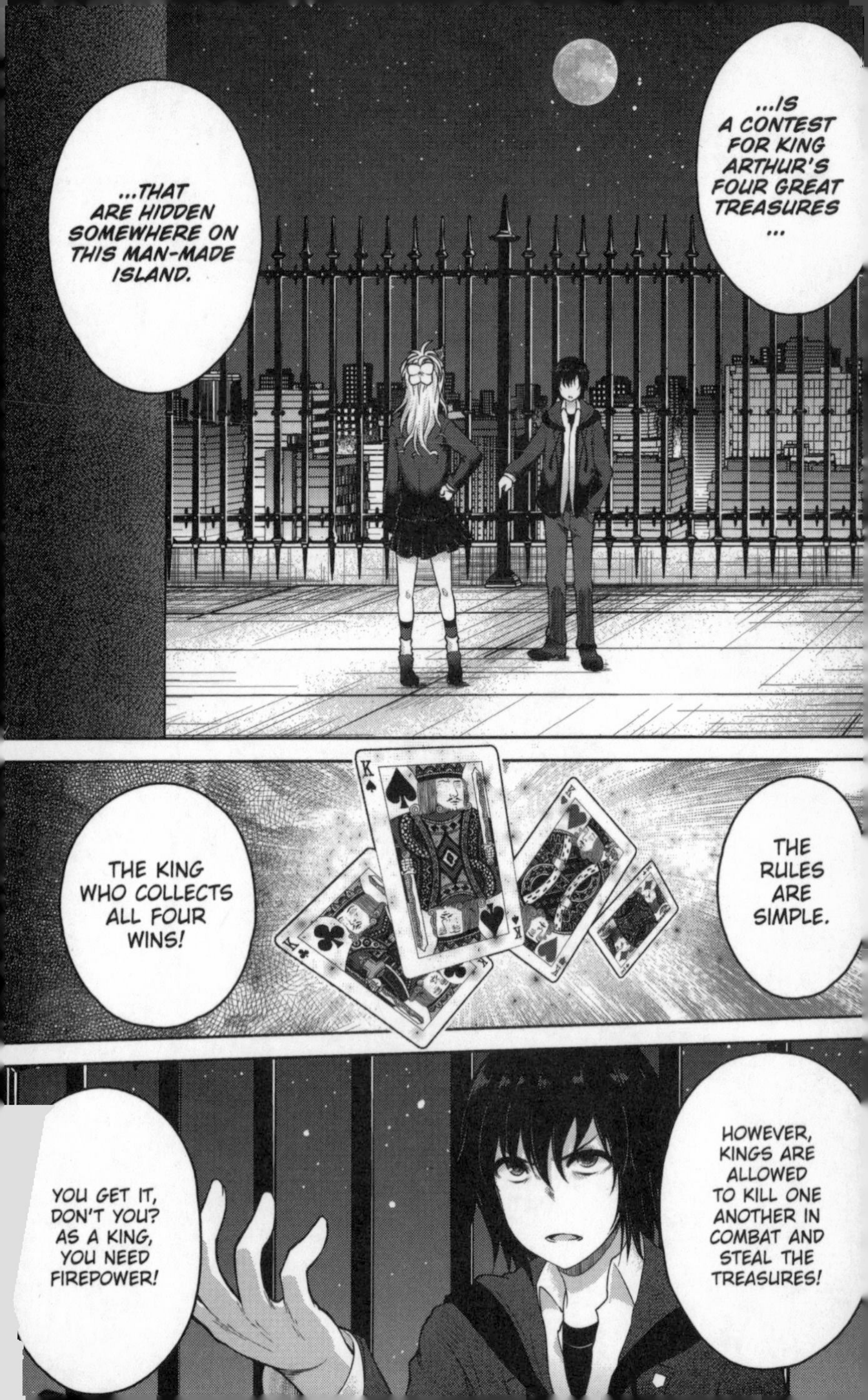
...IS A CONTEST FOR KING ARTHUR'S FOUR GREAT TREASURES ...
...THAT ARE HIDDEN SOMEWHERE ON THIS MAN-MADE ISLAND.
THE RULES ARE SIMPLE.
THE KING WHO COLLECTS ALL FOUR WINS!
HOWEVER, KINGS ARE ALLOWED TO KILL ONE ANOTHER IN COMBAT AND STEAL THE TREASURES!
YOU GET IT, DON'T YOU? AS A KING, YOU NEED FIREPOWER!

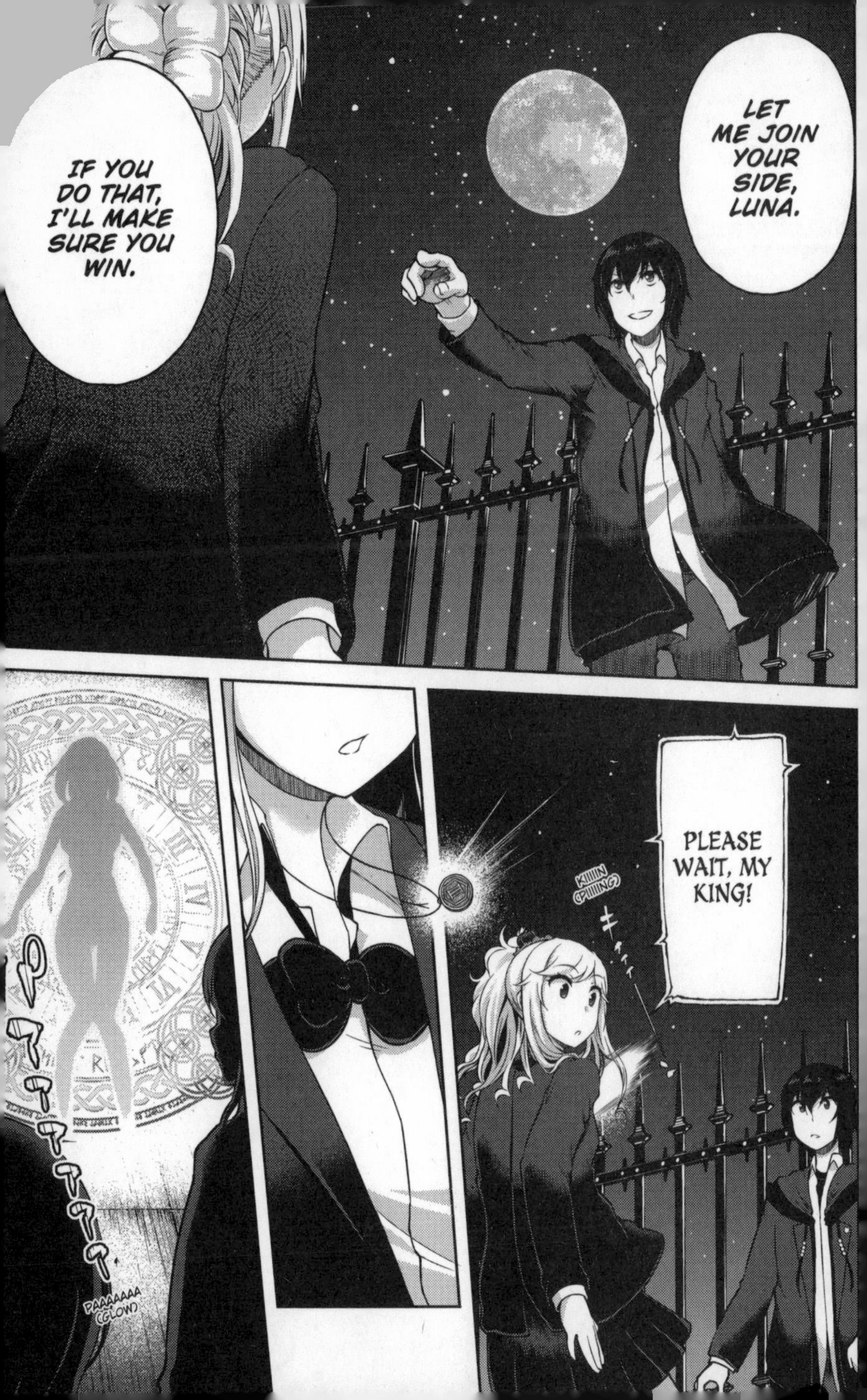
LET ME JOIN YOUR SIDE, LUNA.
IF YOU DO THAT, I'LL MAKE SURE YOU WIN.
PLEASE WAIT, MY KING!
KIIIIN (PIIIING)
PAAAAAAA (GLOW)

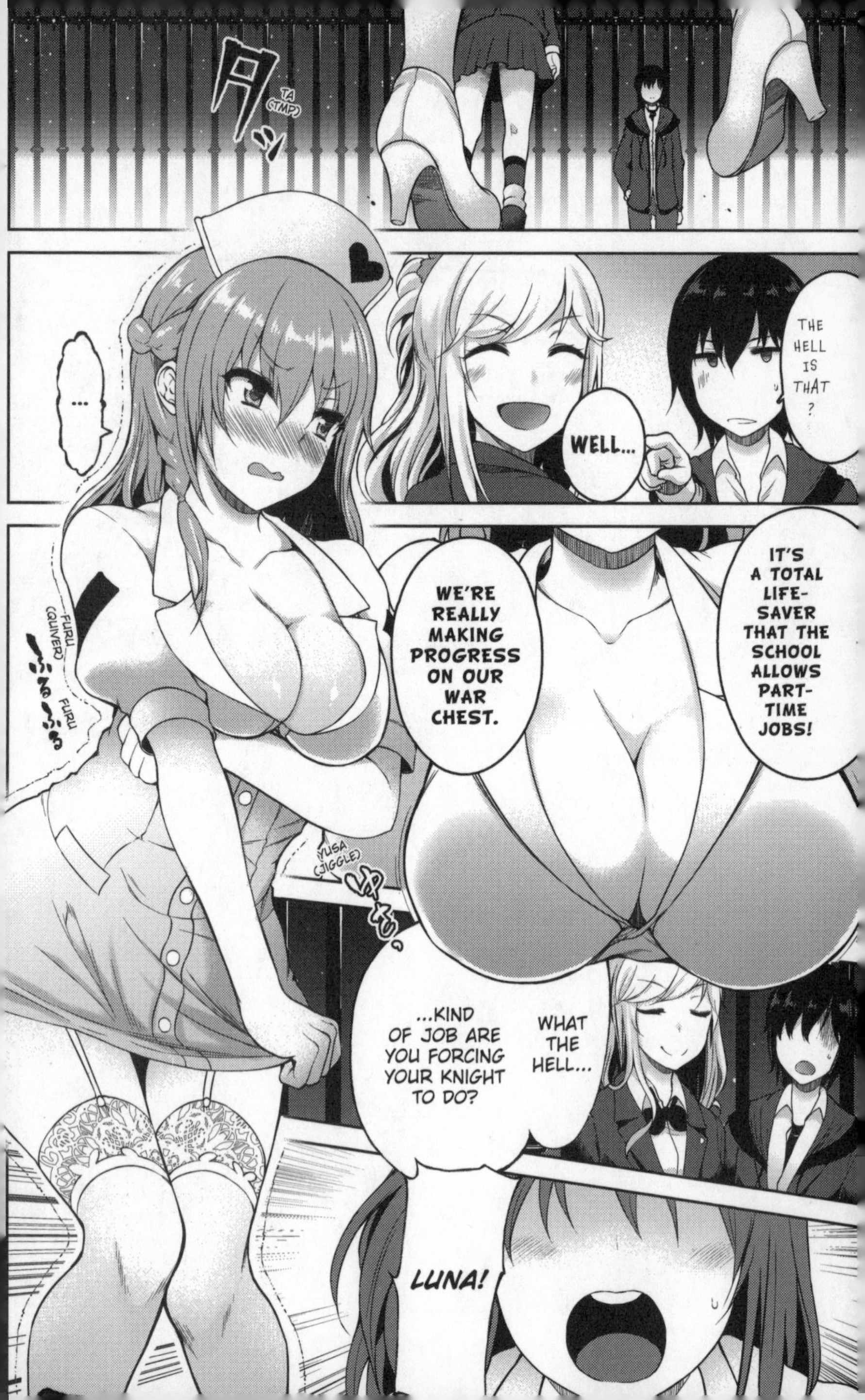
TA (TMP)
THE HELL IS THAT?
WELL...
...
IT'S A TOTAL LIFE-SAVER THAT THE SCHOOL ALLOWS PART-TIME JOBS!
WE'RE REALLY MAKING PROGRESS ON OUR WAR CHEST.
FURU (QUIVER) FURU
ふるふる
YUSA (JIGGLE)
WHAT THE HELL...
...KIND OF JOB ARE YOU FORCING YOUR KNIGHT TO DO?
LUNA!

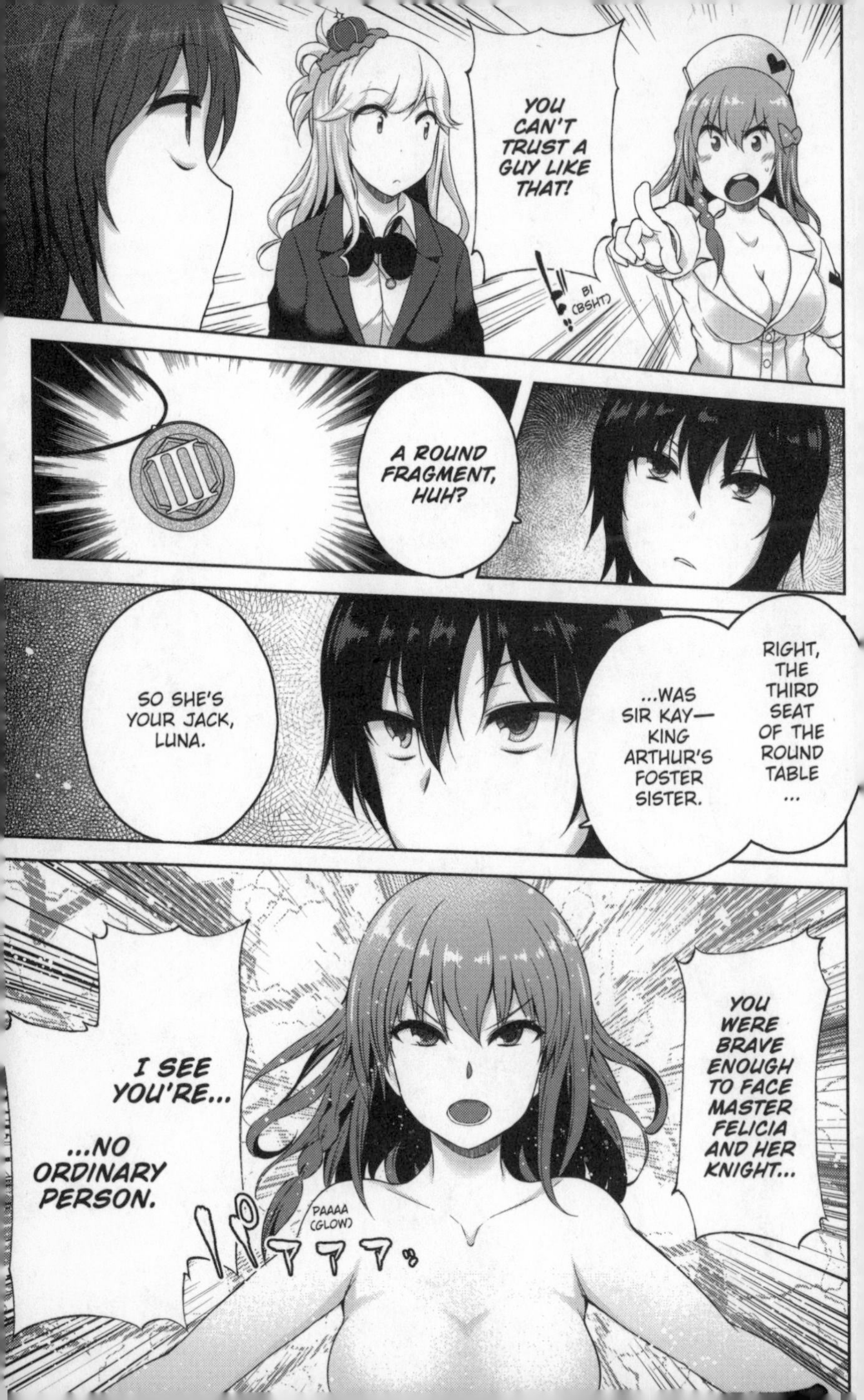
YOU CAN'T TRUST A GUY LIKE THAT!
BI (BSHT)
A ROUND FRAGMENT, HUH?
RIGHT, THE THIRD SEAT OF THE ROUND TABLE ...
...WAS SIR KAY—KING ARTHUR'S FOSTER SISTER.
SO SHE'S YOUR JACK, LUNA.
YOU WERE BRAVE ENOUGH TO FACE MASTER FELICIA AND HER KNIGHT...
I SEE YOU'RE...
...NO ORDINARY PERSON.
PAAAA (GLOW)

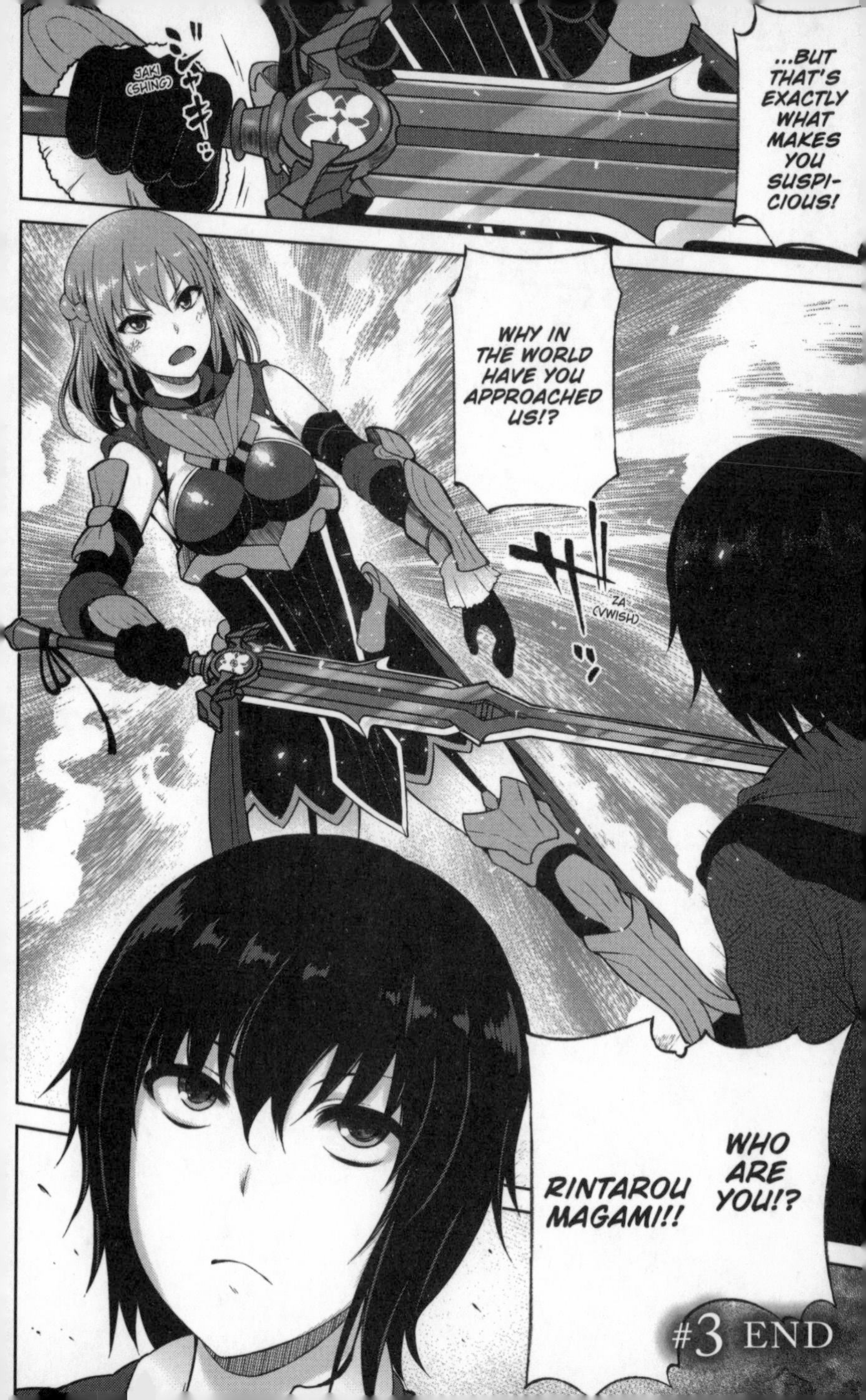
...BUT THAT'S EXACTLY WHAT MAKES YOU SUSPICIOUS!
JAKI (SHING)
WHY IN THE WORLD HAVE YOU APPROACHED US!?
ZA (VWISH)
WHO ARE YOU!?
RINTAROU MAGAMI!!
#3 END

LAST ROUND ARTHURS

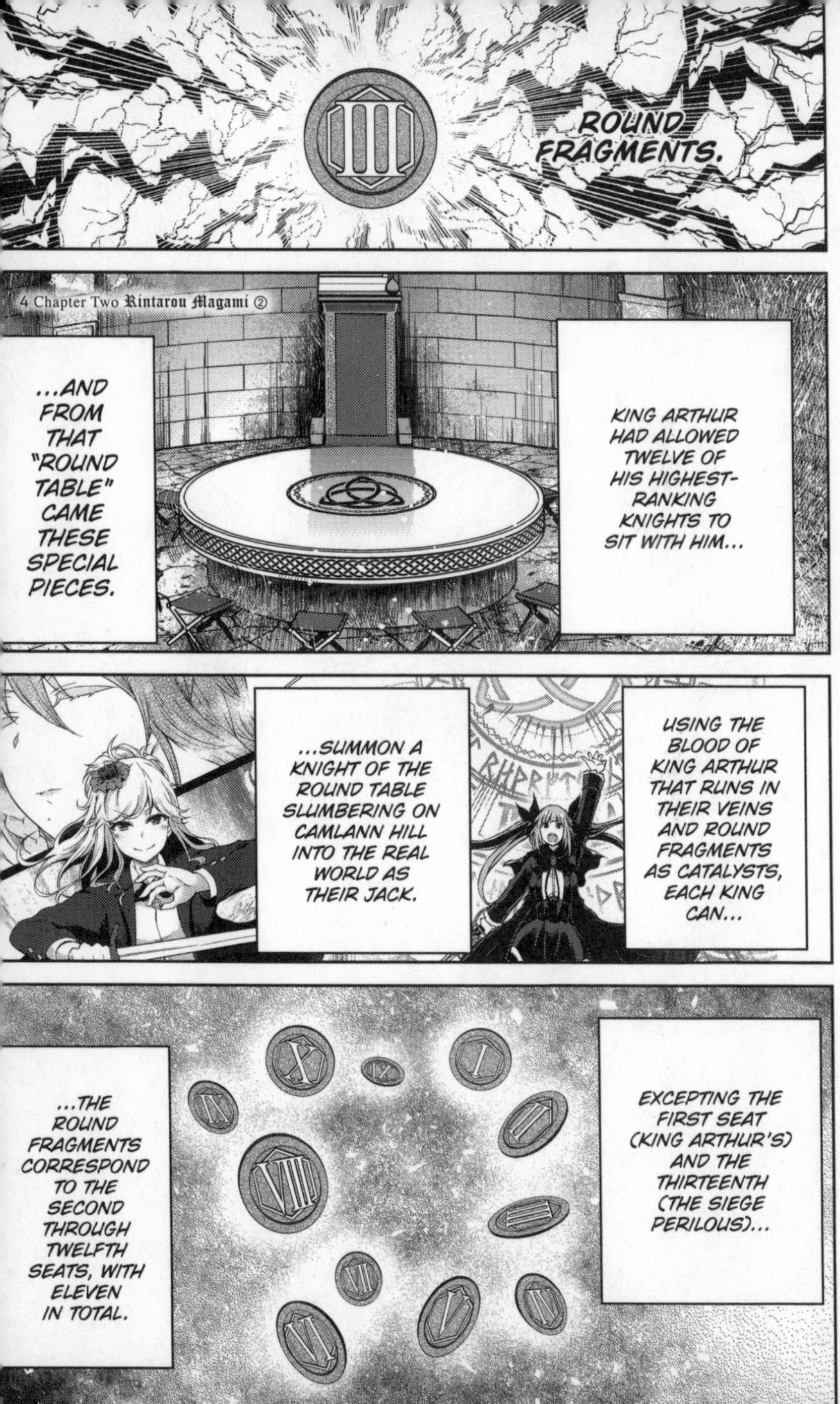
ROUND FRAGMENTS.
KING ARTHUR HAD ALLOWED TWELVE OF HIS HIGHEST-RANKING KNIGHTS TO SIT WITH HIM...
...AND FROM THAT "ROUND TABLE" CAME THESE SPECIAL PIECES.
USING THE BLOOD OF KING ARTHUR THAT RUNS IN THEIR VEINS AND ROUND FRAGMENTS AS CATALYSTS, EACH KING CAN...
...SUMMON A KNIGHT OF THE ROUND TABLE SLUMBERING ON CAMLANN HILL INTO THE REAL WORLD AS THEIR JACK.
EXCEPTING THE FIRST SEAT (KING ARTHUR'S) AND THE THIRTEENTH (THE SIEGE PERILOUS)...
...THE ROUND FRAGMENTS CORRESPOND TO THE SECOND THROUGH TWELFTH SEATS, WITH ELEVEN IN TOTAL.

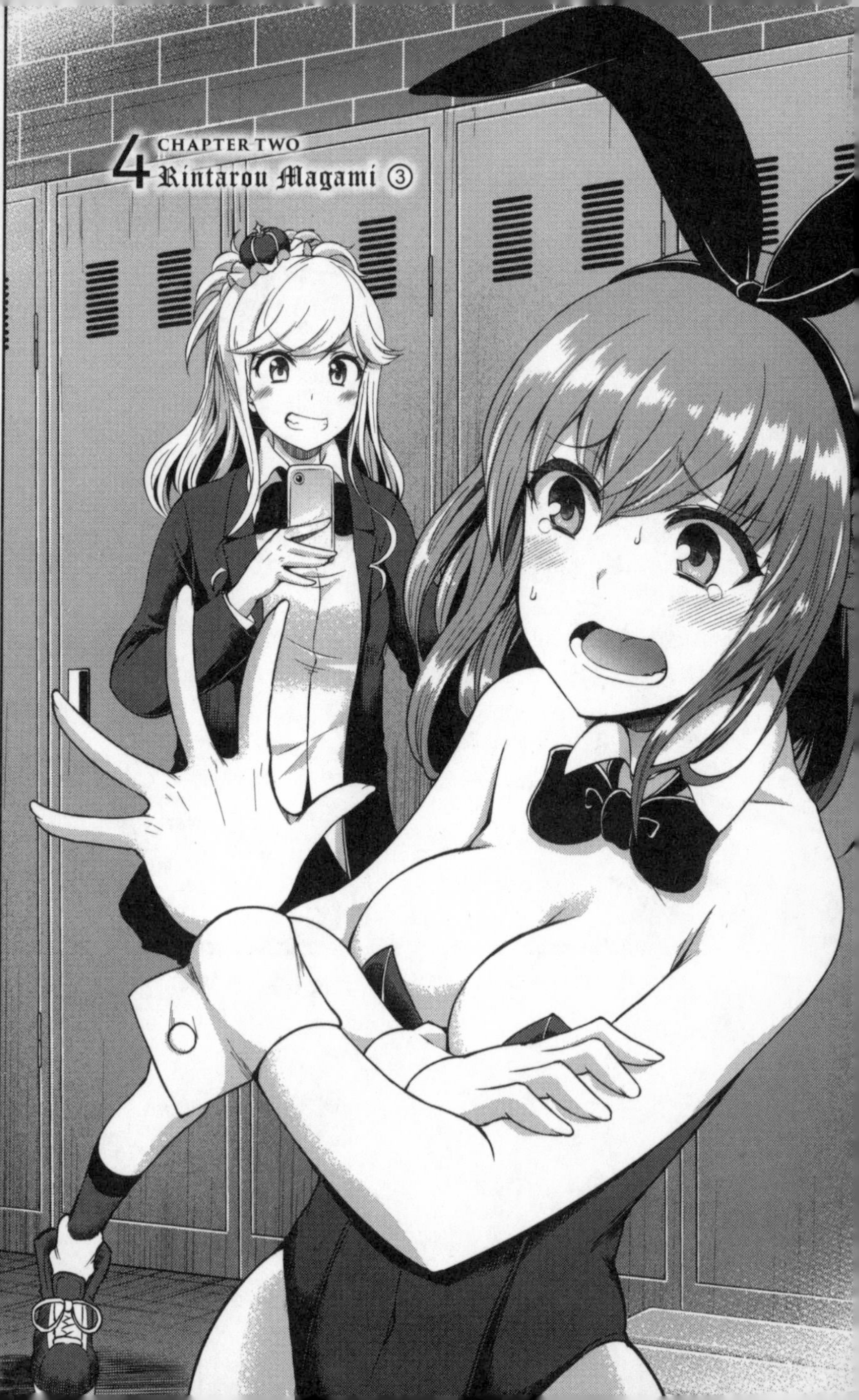
4 CHAPTER TWO
Rintarou Magami ③

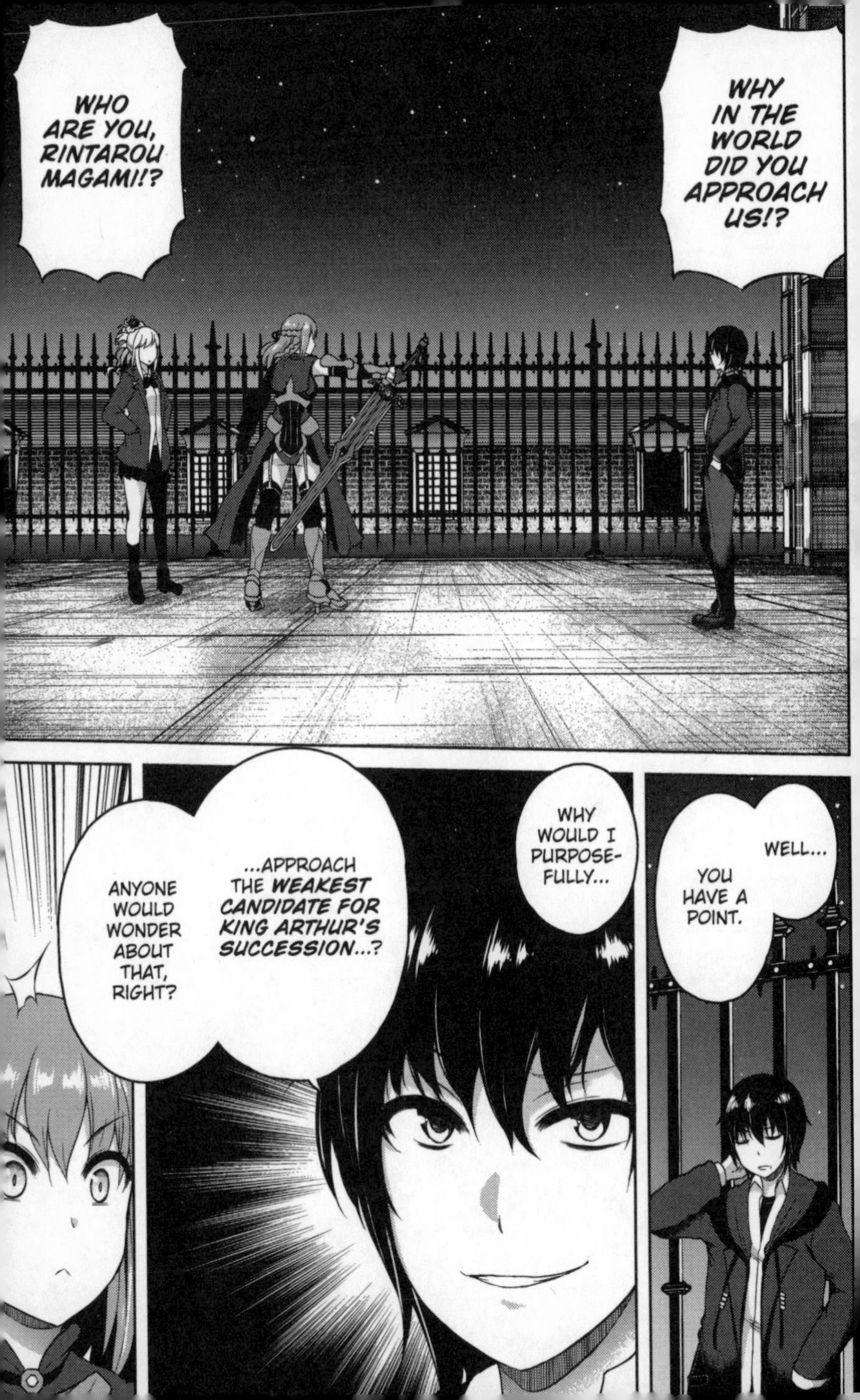
WHY IN THE WORLD DID YOU APPROACH US!?
WHO ARE YOU, RINTAROU MAGAMI!?
WELL...
YOU HAVE A POINT.
WHY WOULD I PURPOSE-FULLY...
...APPROACH THE WEAKEST CANDIDATE FOR KING ARTHUR'S SUCCESSION...?
ANYONE WOULD WONDER ABOUT THAT, RIGHT?

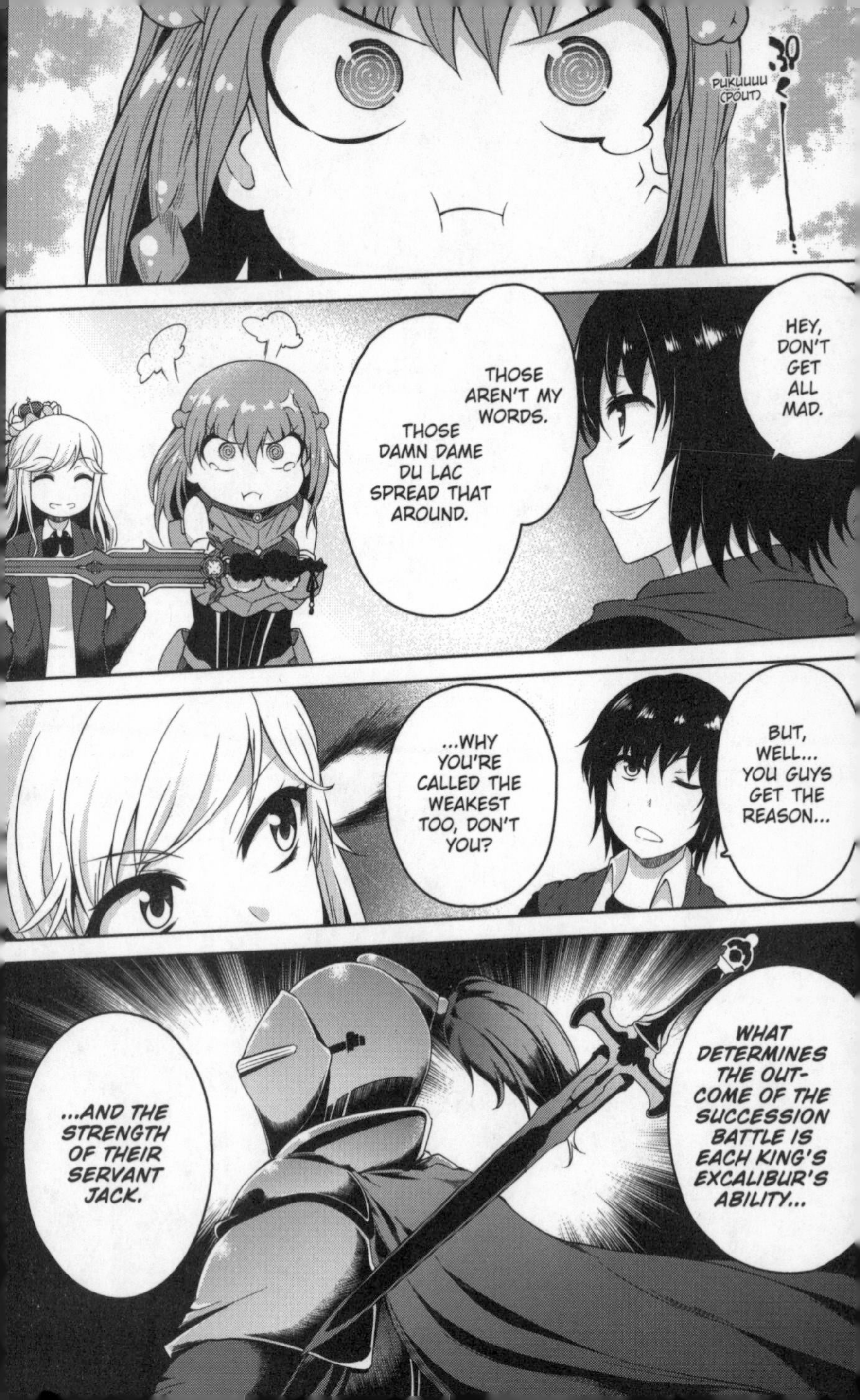
PUKUUUU (POUT)
HEY, DON'T GET ALL MAD.
THOSE AREN'T MY WORDS.
THOSE DAMN DAME DU LAC SPREAD THAT AROUND.
BUT, WELL... YOU GUYS GET THE REASON...
...WHY YOU'RE CALLED THE WEAKEST TOO, DON'T YOU?
WHAT DETERMINES THE OUT-COME OF THE SUCCESSION BATTLE IS EACH KING'S EXCALIBUR'S ABILITY...
...AND THE STRENGTH OF THEIR SERVANT JACK.

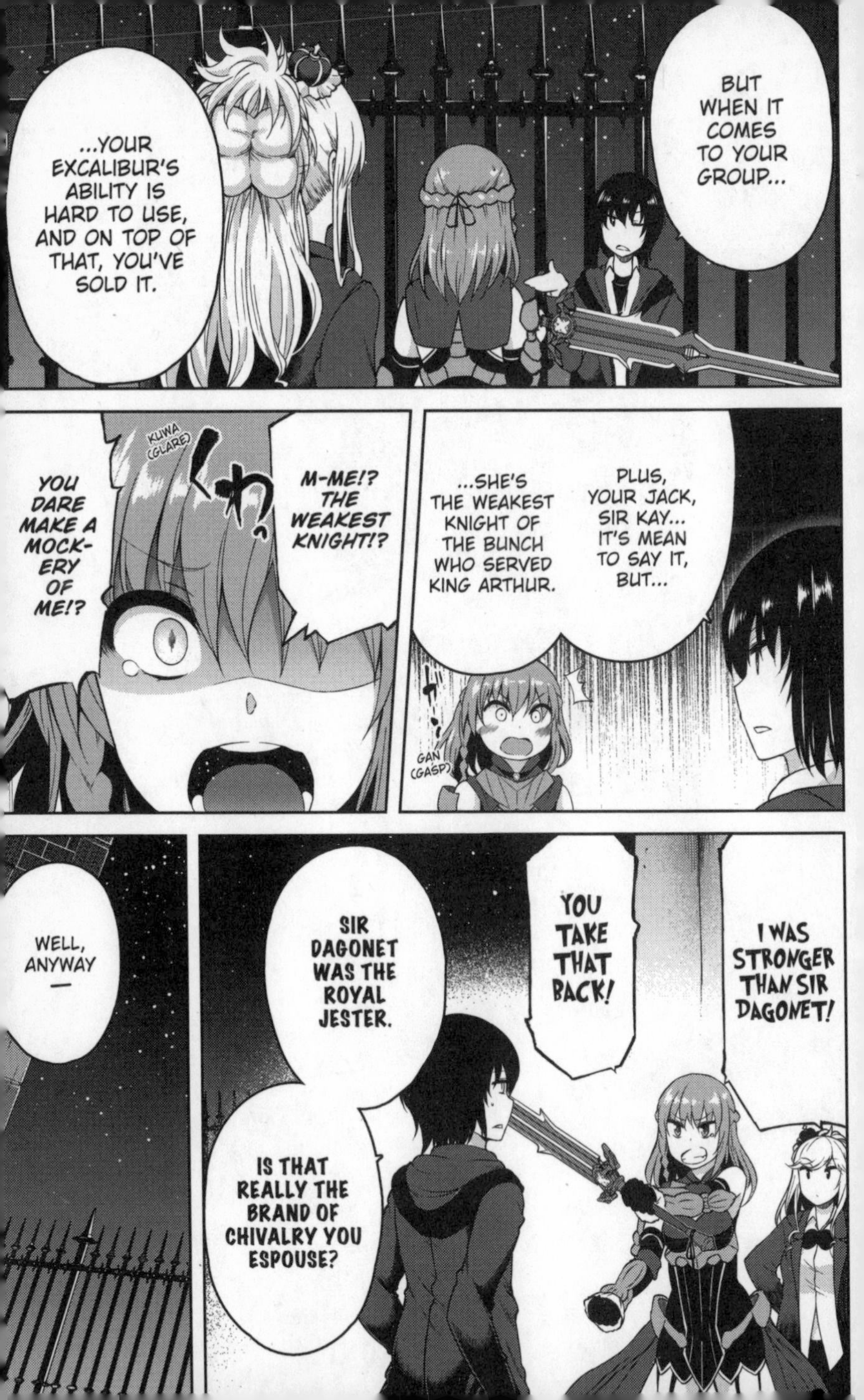

BUT WHEN IT COMES TO YOUR GROUP...
...YOUR EXCALIBUR'S ABILITY IS HARD TO USE, AND ON TOP OF THAT, YOU'VE SOLD IT.
PLUS, YOUR JACK, SIR KAY... IT'S MEAN TO SAY IT, BUT...
...SHE'S THE WEAKEST KNIGHT OF THE BUNCH WHO SERVED KING ARTHUR.
GAN (GASP)
M-ME!? THE WEAKEST KNIGHT!?
KUWA (GLARE)
YOU DARE MAKE A MOCK-ERY OF ME!?
I WAS STRONGER THAN SIR DAGONET!
YOU TAKE THAT BACK!
SIR DAGONET WAS THE ROYAL JESTER.
IS THAT REALLY THE BRAND OF CHIVALRY YOU ESPOUSE?
WELL, ANYWAY—

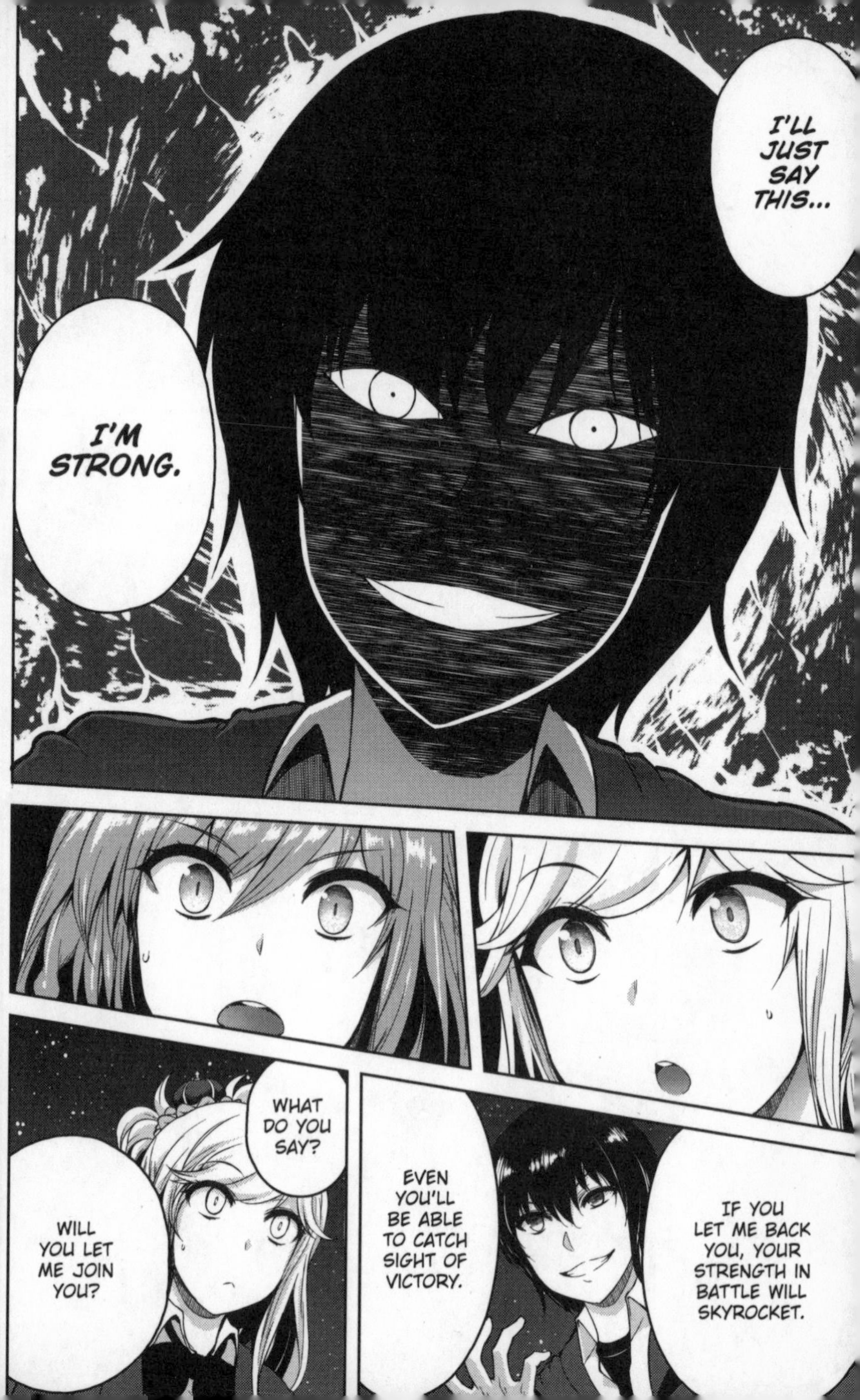
I'LL JUST SAY THIS...
I'M STRONG.
IF YOU LET ME BACK YOU, YOUR STRENGTH IN BATTLE WILL SKYROCKET.
EVEN YOU'LL BE ABLE TO CATCH SIGHT OF VICTORY.
WHAT DO YOU SAY?
WILL YOU LET ME JOIN YOU?

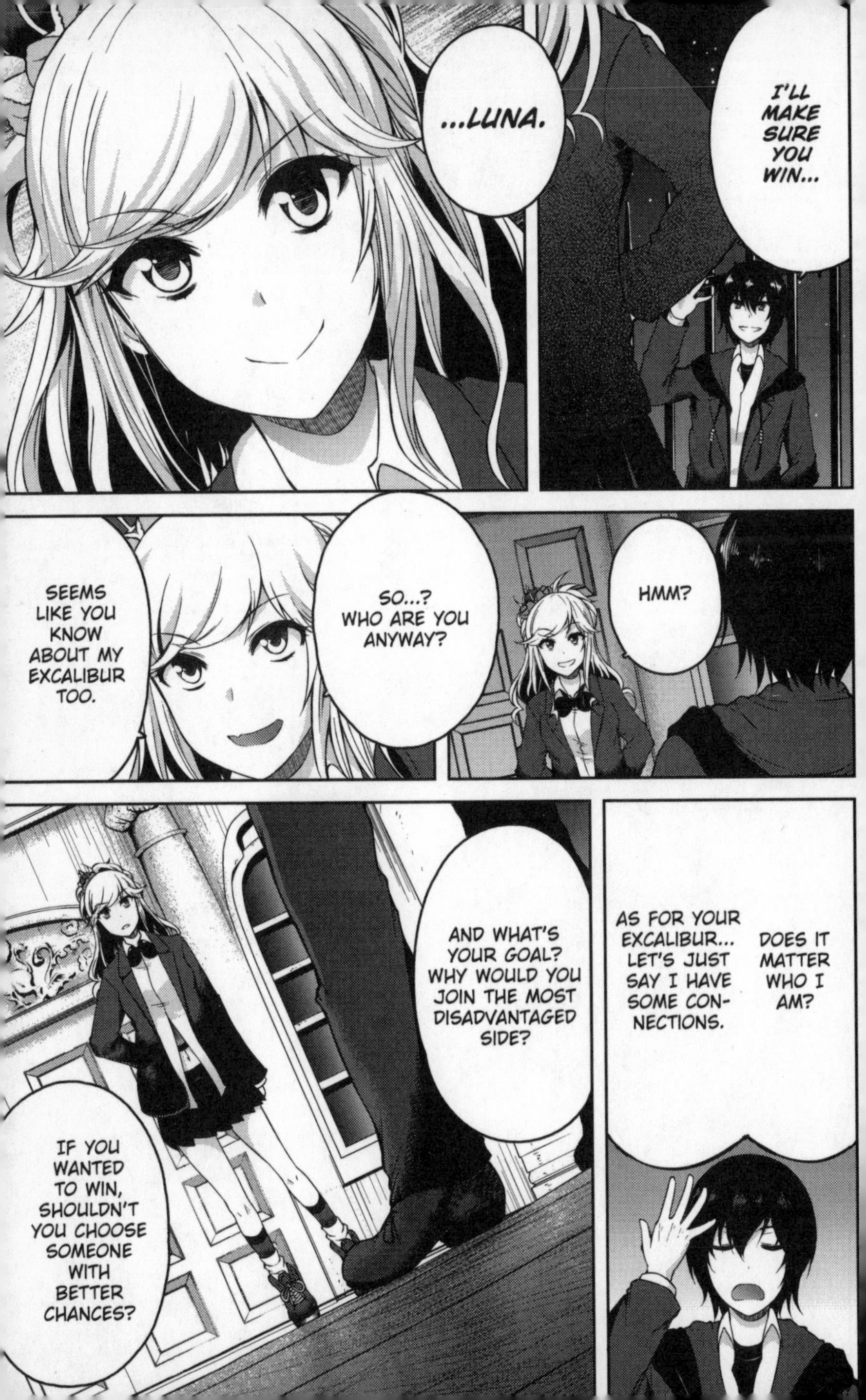
I'LL MAKE SURE YOU WIN...
...LUNA.
HMM?
SO...? WHO ARE YOU ANYWAY?
SEEMS LIKE YOU KNOW ABOUT MY EXCALIBUR TOO.
DOES IT MATTER WHO I AM?
AS FOR YOUR EXCALIBUR... LET'S JUST SAY I HAVE SOME CON-NECTIONS.
AND WHAT'S YOUR GOAL? WHY WOULD YOU JOIN THE MOST DISADVANTAGED SIDE?
IF YOU WANTED TO WIN, SHOULDN'T YOU CHOOSE SOMEONE WITH BETTER CHANCES?

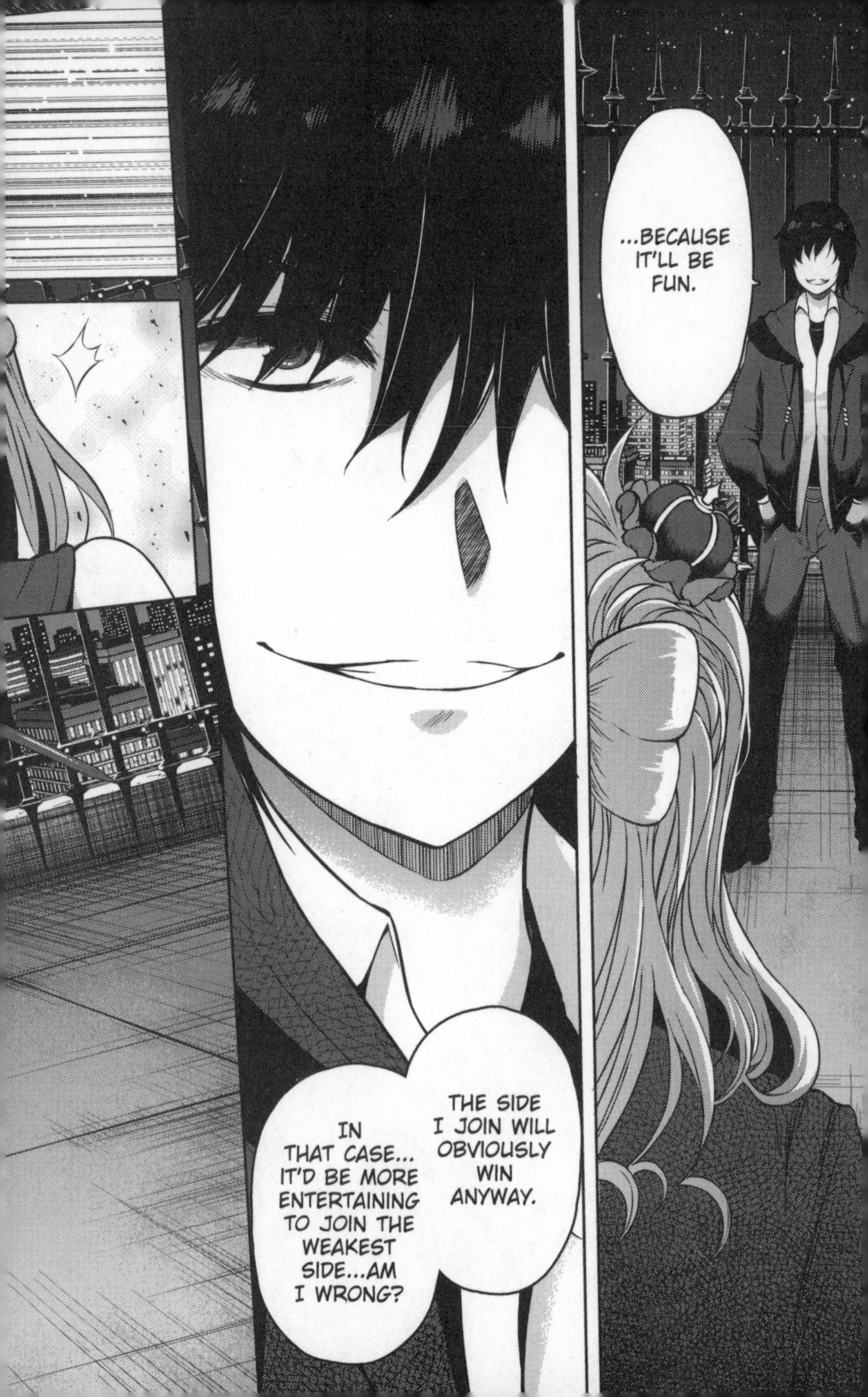
...BECAUSE IT'LL BE FUN.
THE SIDE I JOIN WILL OBVIOUSLY WIN ANYWAY.
IN THAT CASE... IT'D BE MORE ENTERTAINING TO JOIN THE WEAKEST SIDE...AM I WRONG?

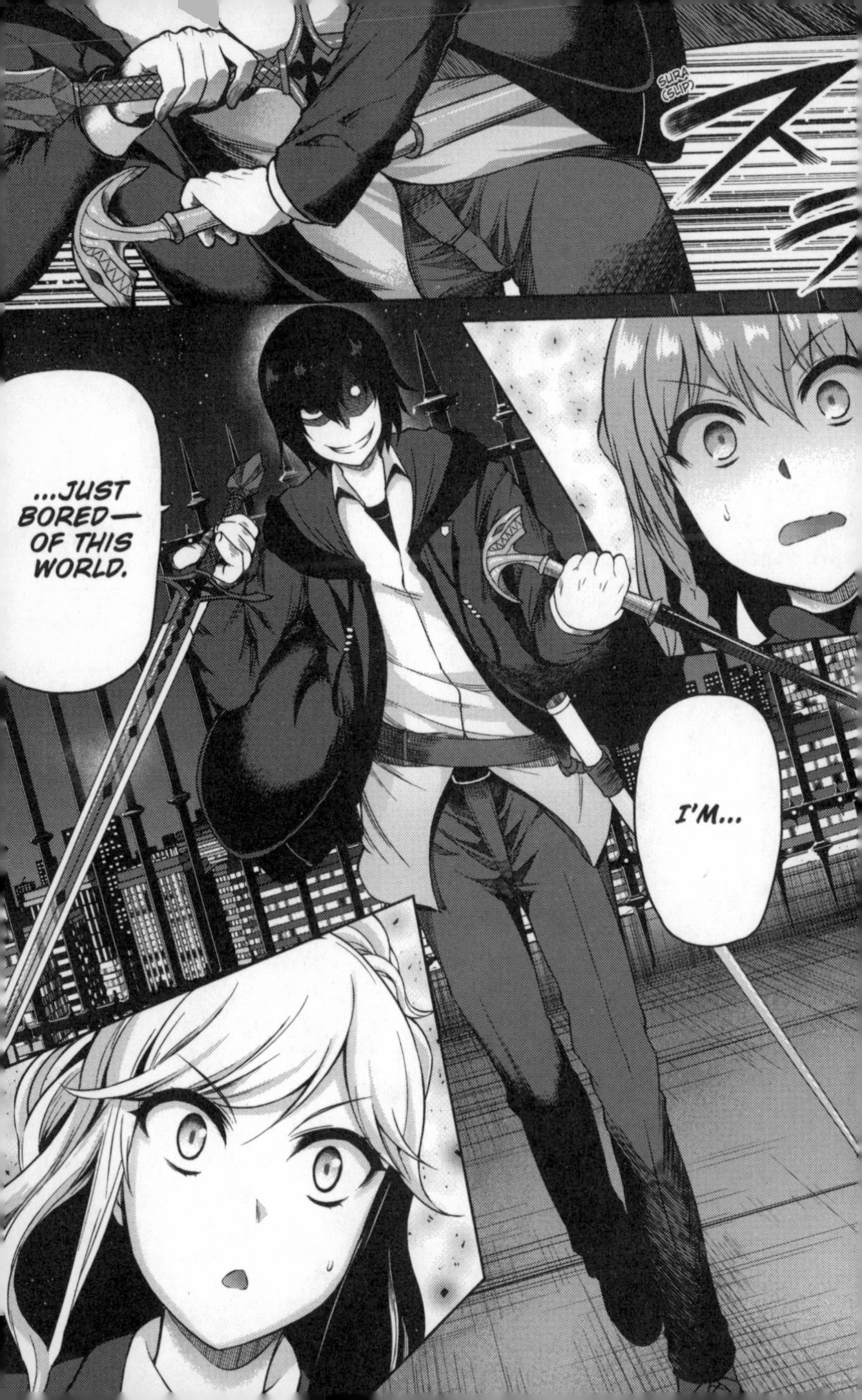
SURA (SLIP)
...JUST BORED— OF THIS WORLD.
I'M...

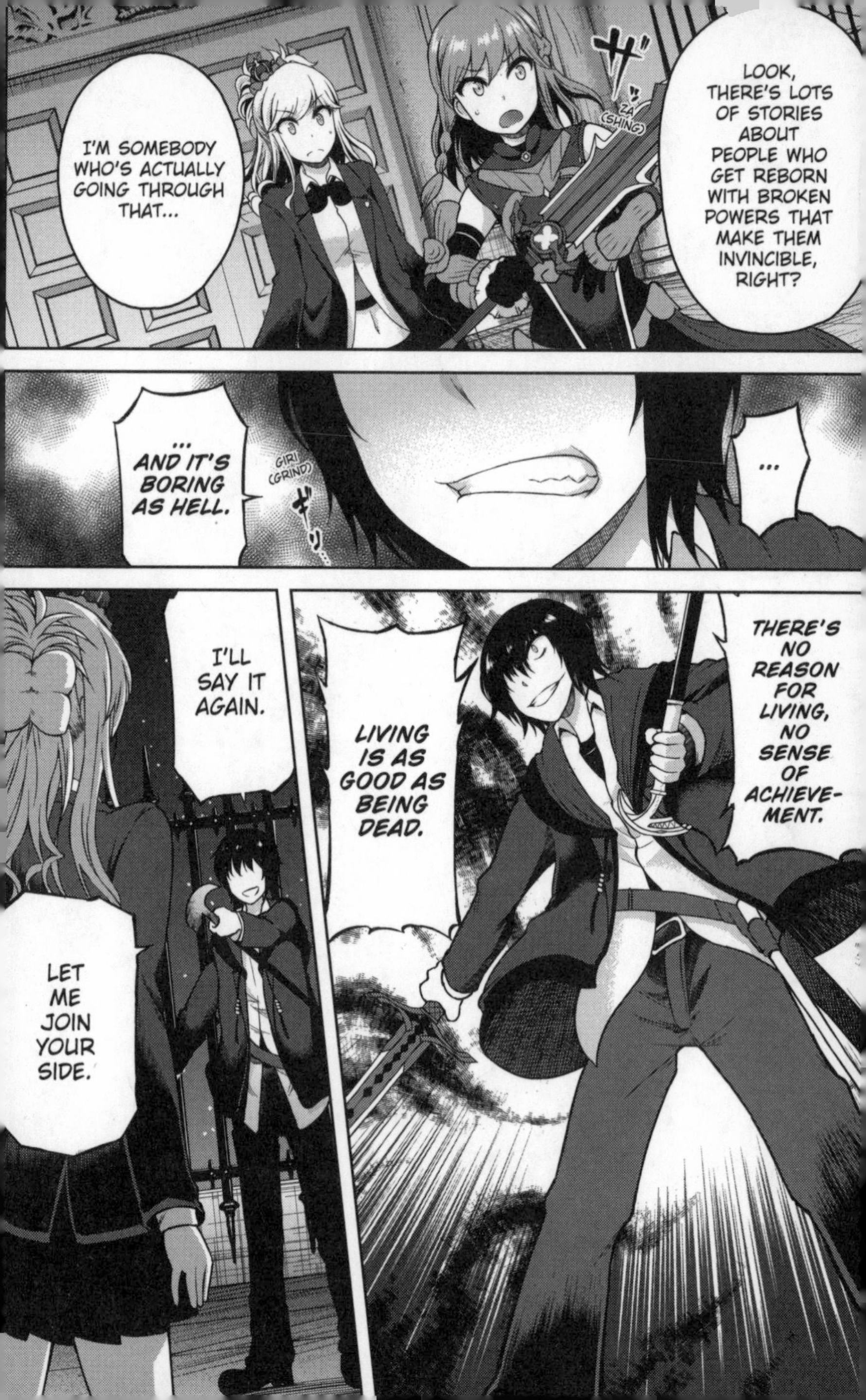
LOOK, THERE'S LOTS OF STORIES ABOUT PEOPLE WHO GET REBORN WITH BROKEN POWERS THAT MAKE THEM INVINCIBLE, RIGHT?
ZA (SHING)
I'M SOMEBODY WHO'S ACTUALLY GOING THROUGH THAT...
...
GIRI (GRIND)
... AND IT'S BORING AS HELL.
THERE'S NO REASON FOR LIVING, NO SENSE OF ACHIEVEMENT.
LIVING IS AS GOOD AS BEING DEAD.
I'LL SAY IT AGAIN.
LET ME JOIN YOUR SIDE.

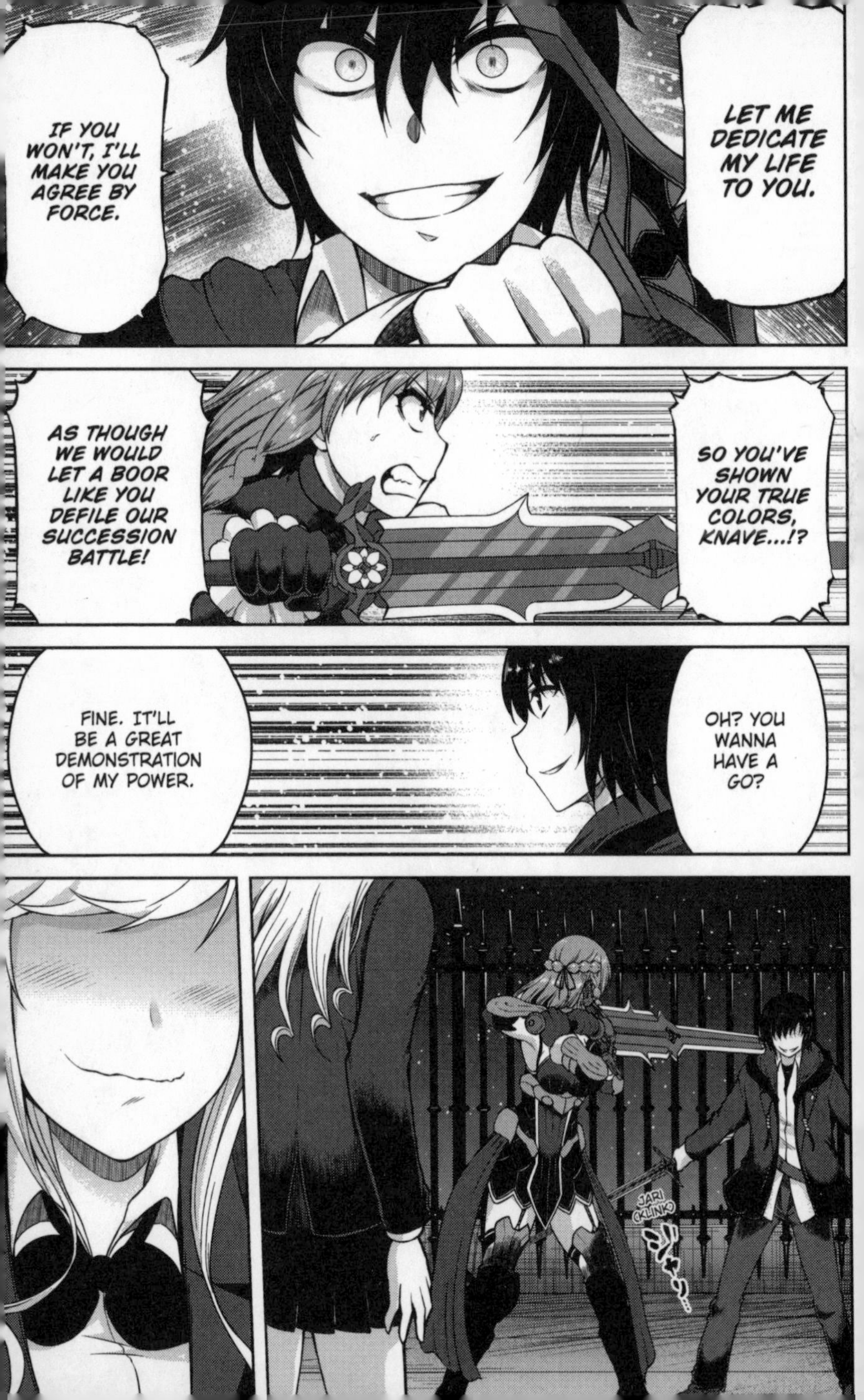
LET ME DEDICATE MY LIFE TO YOU.
IF YOU WON'T, I'LL MAKE YOU AGREE BY FORCE.
SO YOU'VE SHOWN YOUR TRUE COLORS, KNAVE...!?
AS THOUGH WE WOULD LET A BOOR LIKE YOU DEFILE OUR SUCCESSION BATTLE!
OH? YOU WANNA HAVE A GO?
FINE. IT'LL BE A GREAT DEMONSTRATION OF MY POWER.
JARI (KLINK)

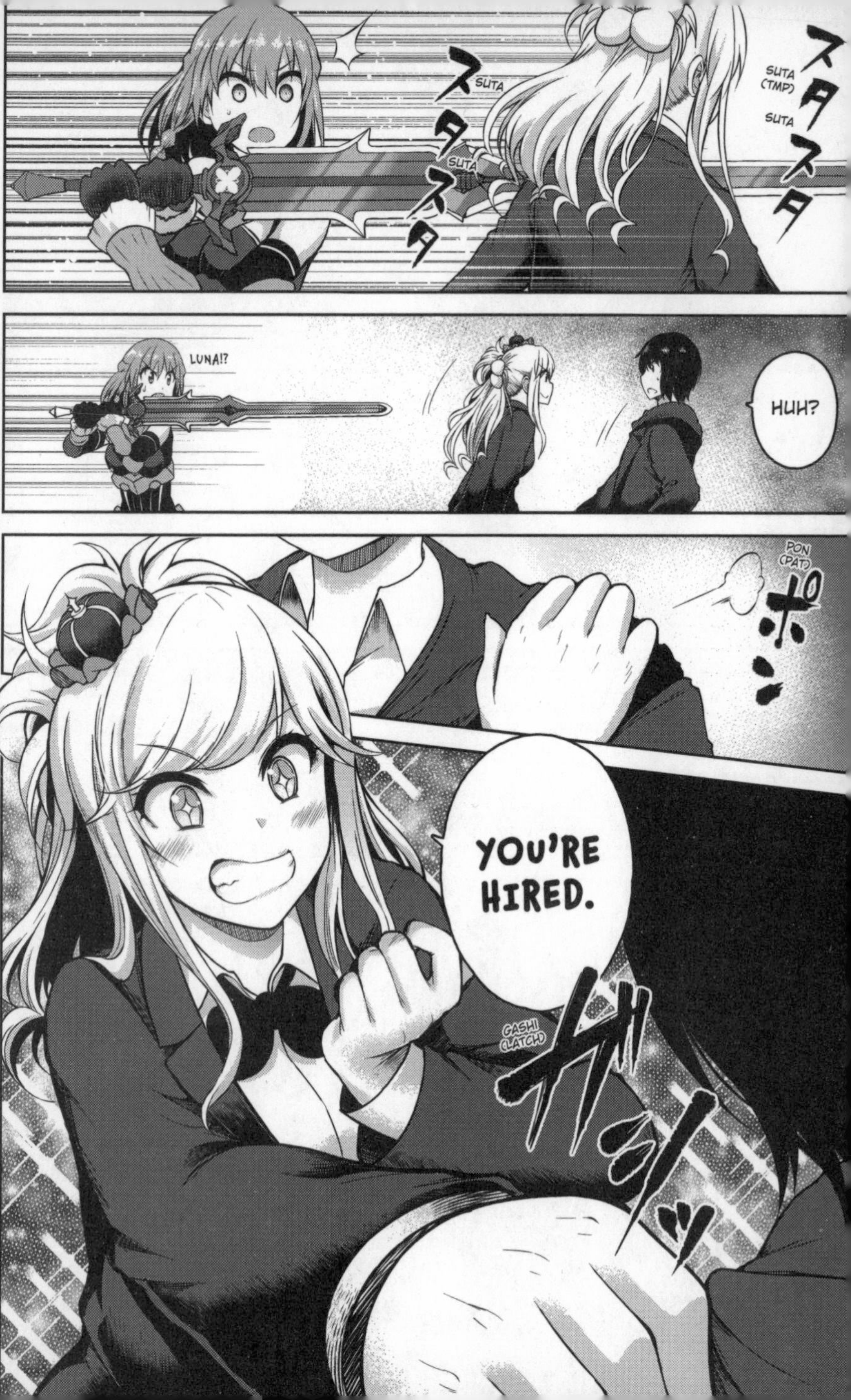
SUTA (TMP) SUTA
SUTA
SUTA
HUH?
LUNA!?
PON (PAT)
YOU'RE HIRED.
GASHI (LATCH)

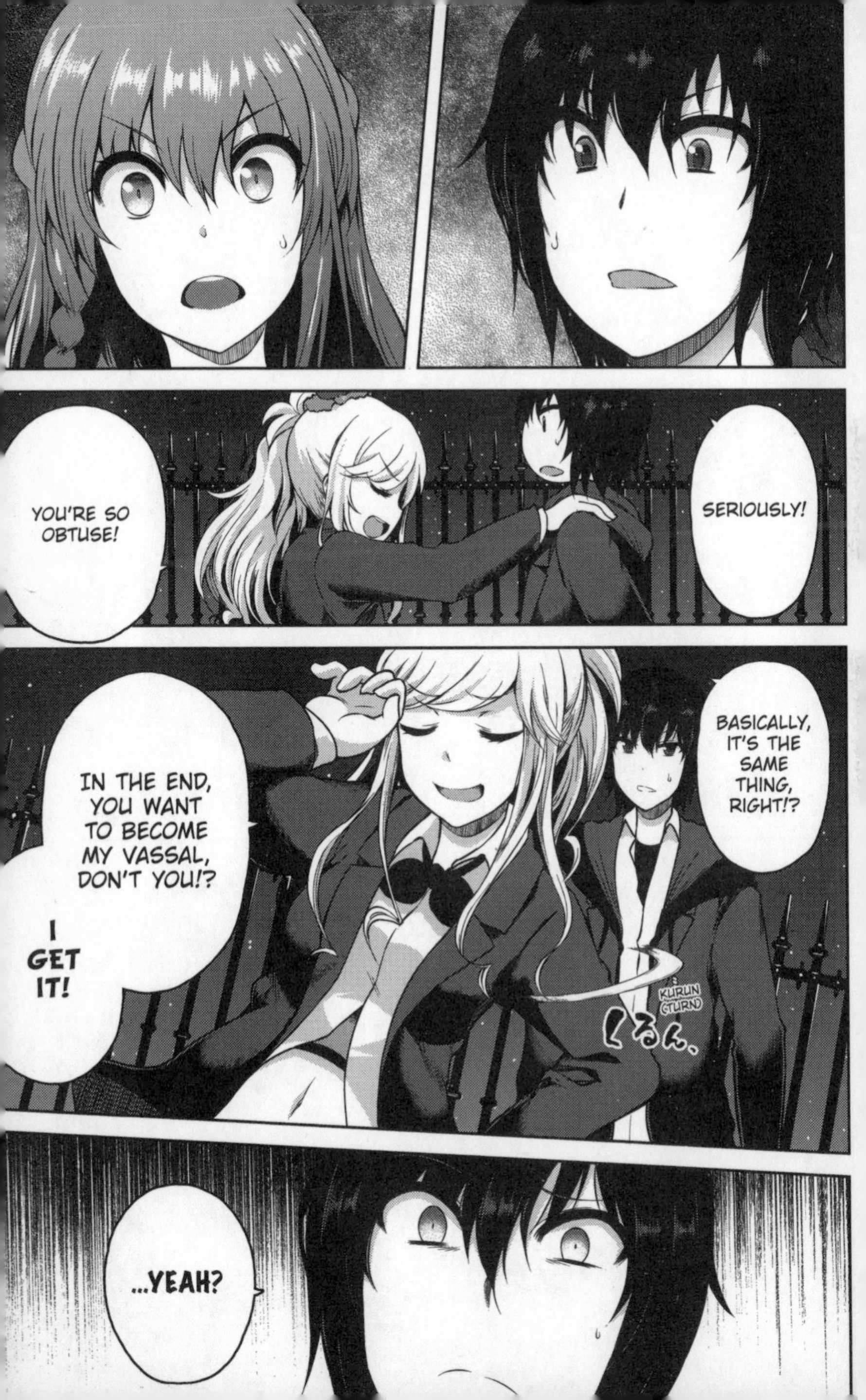
SERIOUSLY!
YOU'RE SO OBTUSE!
BASICALLY, IT'S THE SAME THING, RIGHT!?
KURUN (TURN)
くるん。
IN THE END, YOU WANT TO BECOME MY VASSAL, DON'T YOU!?
I GET IT!
...YEAH?

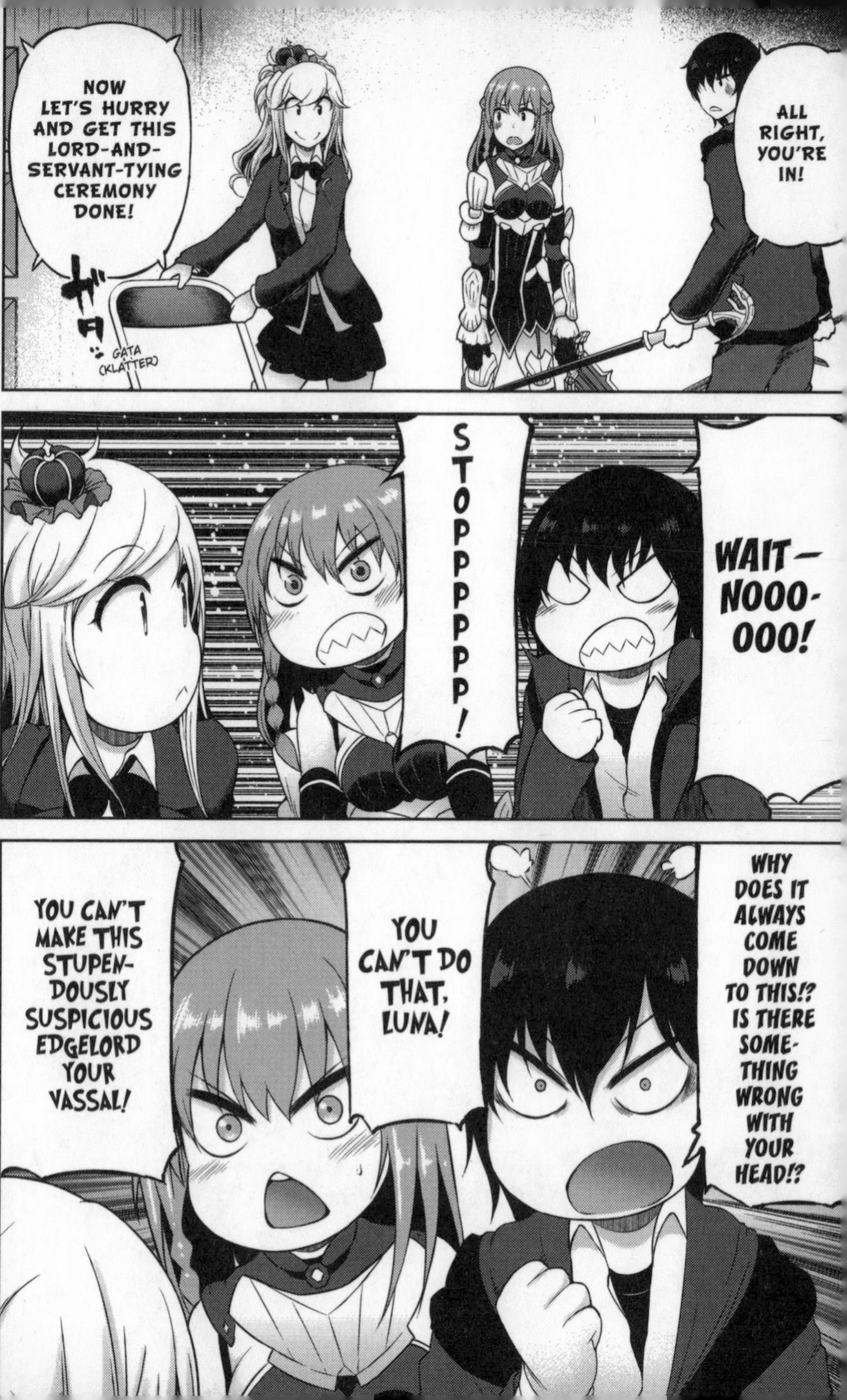
ALL RIGHT, YOU'RE IN!
NOW LET'S HURRY AND GET THIS LORD-AND-SERVANT-TYING CEREMONY DONE!
GATA (KLATTER)
WAIT—NOOOOOO!
STOPPPPPPP!
WHY DOES IT ALWAYS COME DOWN TO THIS!? IS THERE SOMETHING WRONG WITH YOUR HEAD!?
YOU CAN'T DO THAT, LUNA!
YOU CAN'T MAKE THIS STUPENDOUSLY SUSPICIOUS EDGELORD YOUR VASSAL!

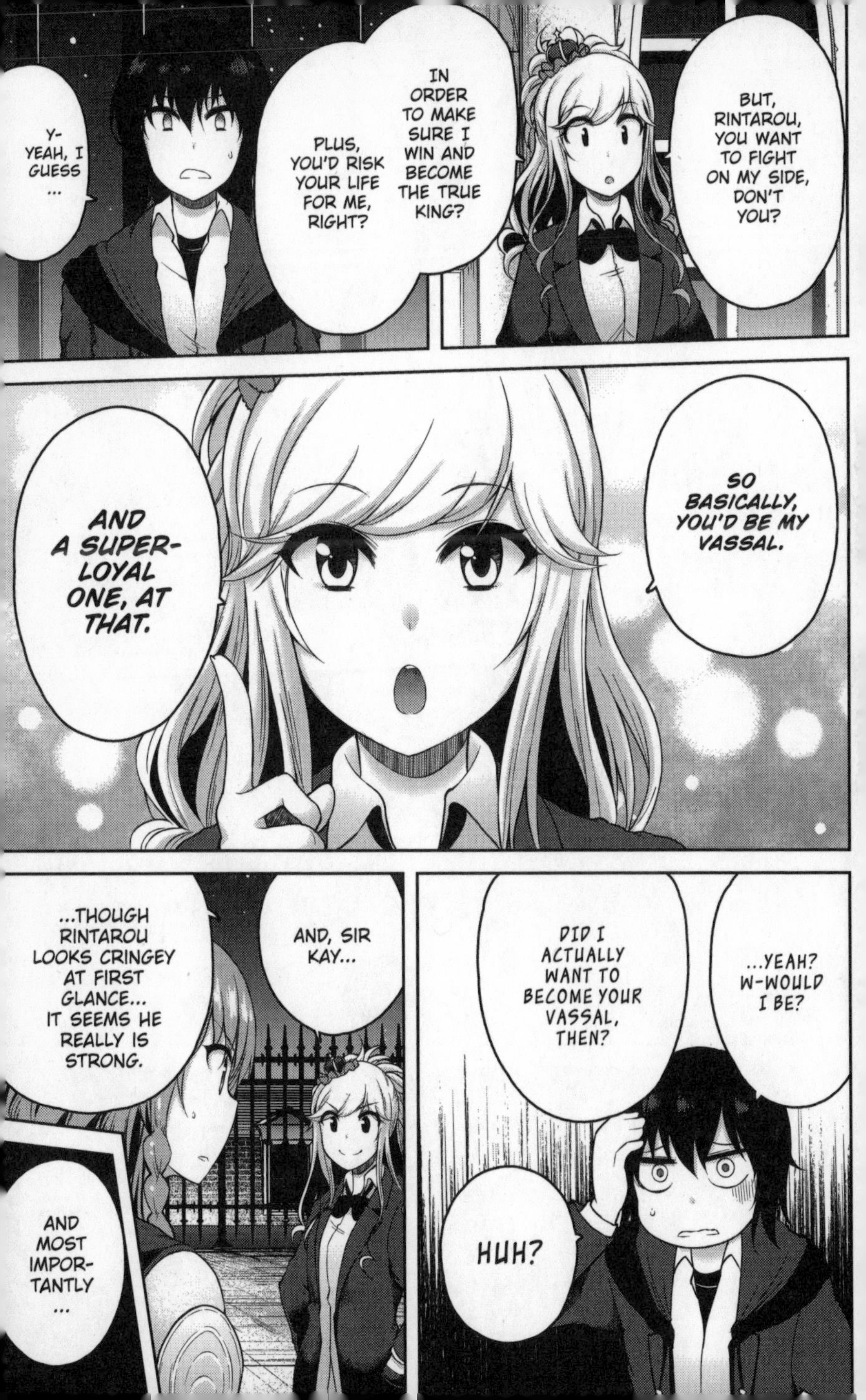
BUT, RINTAROU, YOU WANT TO FIGHT ON MY SIDE, DON'T YOU?
IN ORDER TO MAKE SURE I WIN AND BECOME THE TRUE KING?
PLUS, YOU'D RISK YOUR LIFE FOR ME, RIGHT?
Y-YEAH, I GUESS...
SO BASICALLY, YOU'D BE MY VASSAL.
AND A SUPER-LOYAL ONE, AT THAT.
...YEAH? W-WOULD I BE?
DID I ACTUALLY WANT TO BECOME YOUR VASSAL, THEN?
HUH?
AND, SIR KAY...
...THOUGH RINTAROU LOOKS CRINGEY AT FIRST GLANCE... IT SEEMS HE REALLY IS STRONG.
AND MOST IMPORTANTLY...

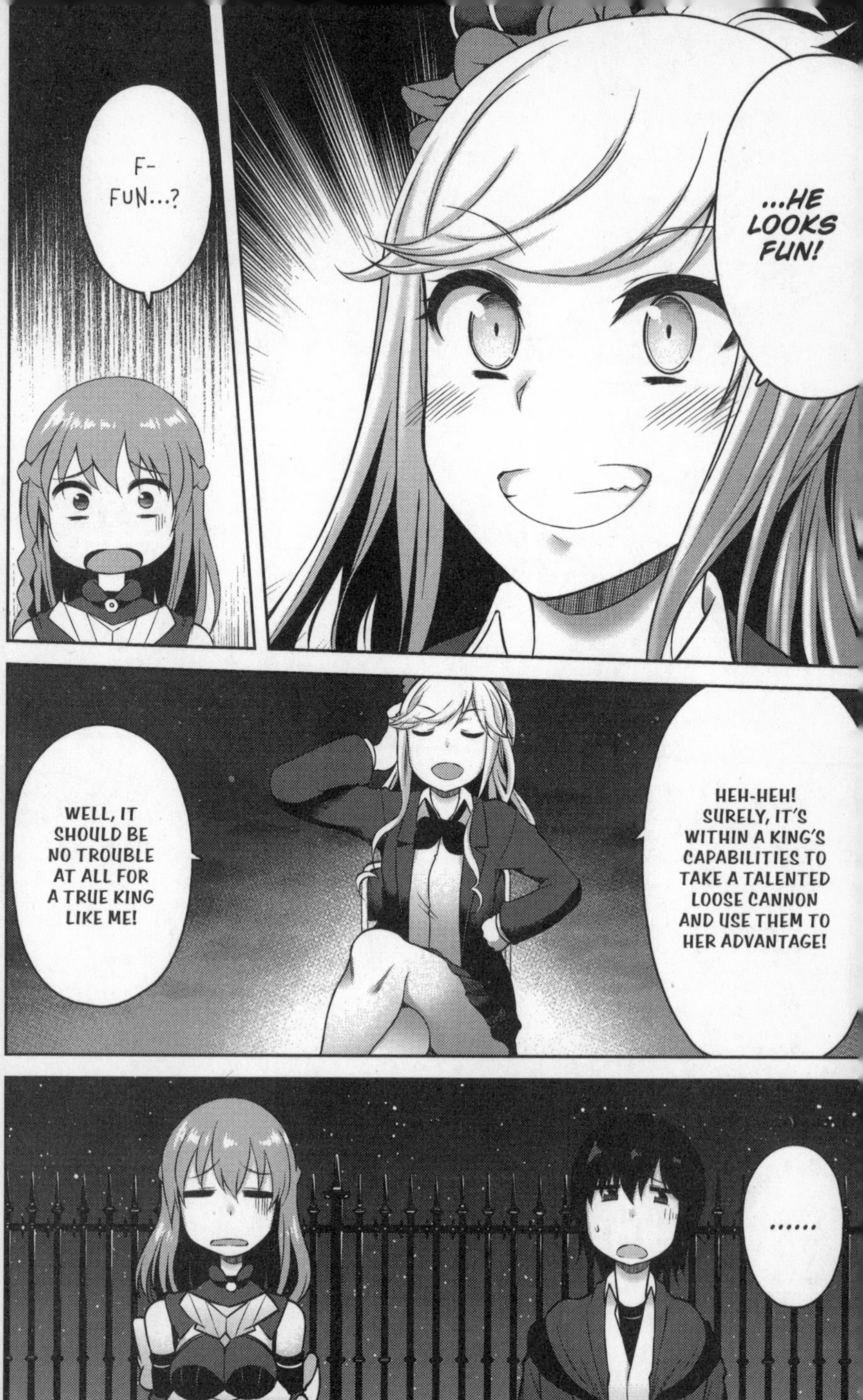
...HE LOOKS FUN!
F-FUN...?
HEH-HEH! SURELY, IT'S WITHIN A KING'S CAPABILITIES TO TAKE A TALENTED LOOSE CANNON AND USE THEM TO HER ADVANTAGE!
WELL, IT SHOULD BE NO TROUBLE AT ALL FOR A TRUE KING LIKE ME!
......

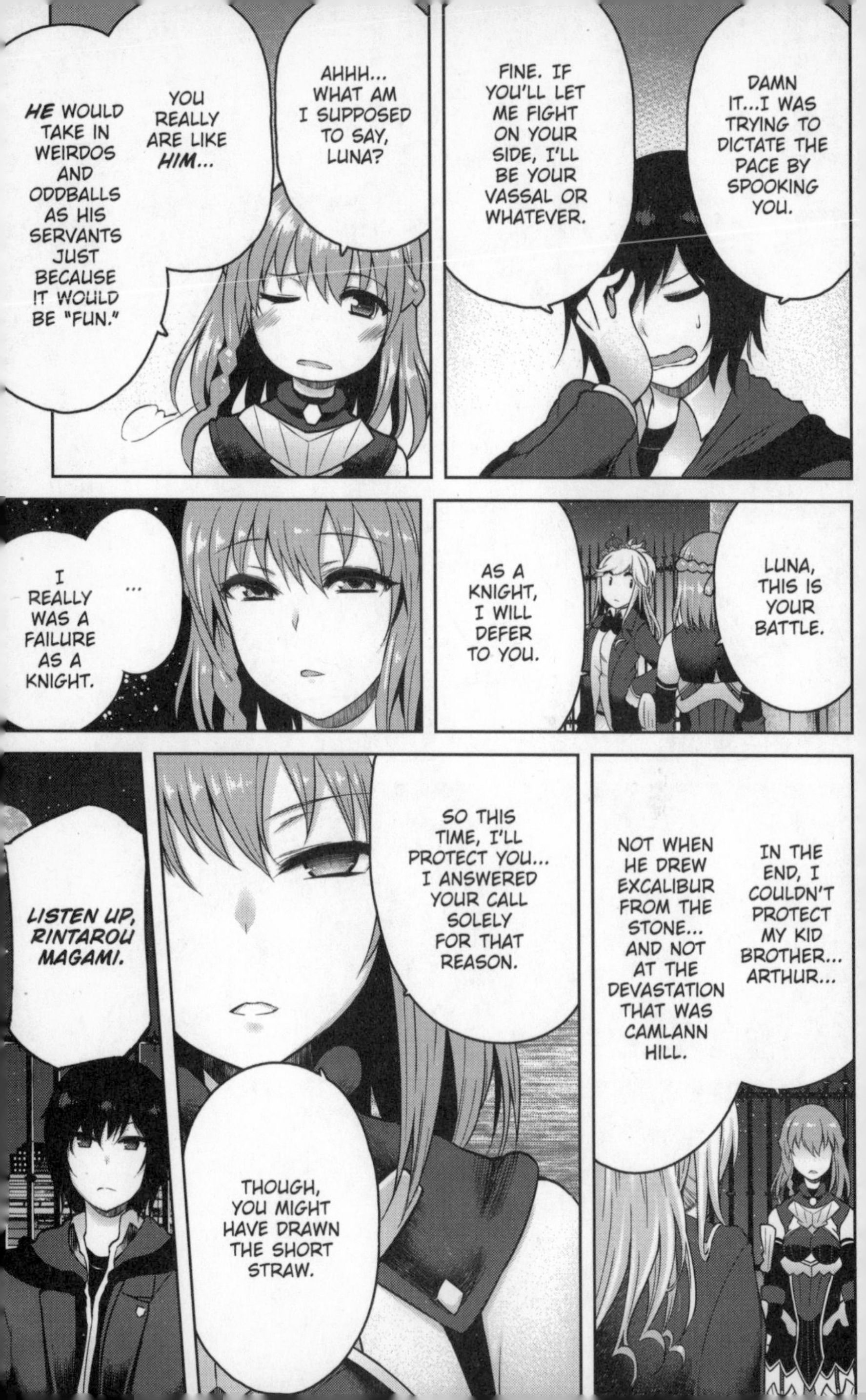
DAMN IT...I WAS TRYING TO DICTATE THE PACE BY SPOOKING YOU.
FINE. IF YOU'LL LET ME FIGHT ON YOUR SIDE, I'LL BE YOUR VASSAL OR WHATEVER.
AHHH... WHAT AM I SUPPOSED TO SAY, LUNA?
YOU REALLY ARE LIKE *HIM*...
HE WOULD TAKE IN WEIRDOS AND ODDBALLS AS HIS SERVANTS JUST BECAUSE IT WOULD BE "FUN."
LUNA, THIS IS YOUR BATTLE.
AS A KNIGHT, I WILL DEFER TO YOU.
...
I REALLY WAS A FAILURE AS A KNIGHT.
IN THE END, I COULDN'T PROTECT MY KID BROTHER... ARTHUR...
NOT WHEN HE DREW EXCALIBUR FROM THE STONE... AND NOT AT THE DEVASTATION THAT WAS CAMLANN HILL.
SO THIS TIME, I'LL PROTECT YOU... I ANSWERED YOUR CALL SOLELY FOR THAT REASON.
THOUGH, YOU MIGHT HAVE DRAWN THE SHORT STRAW.
LISTEN UP, RINTAROU MAGAMI.

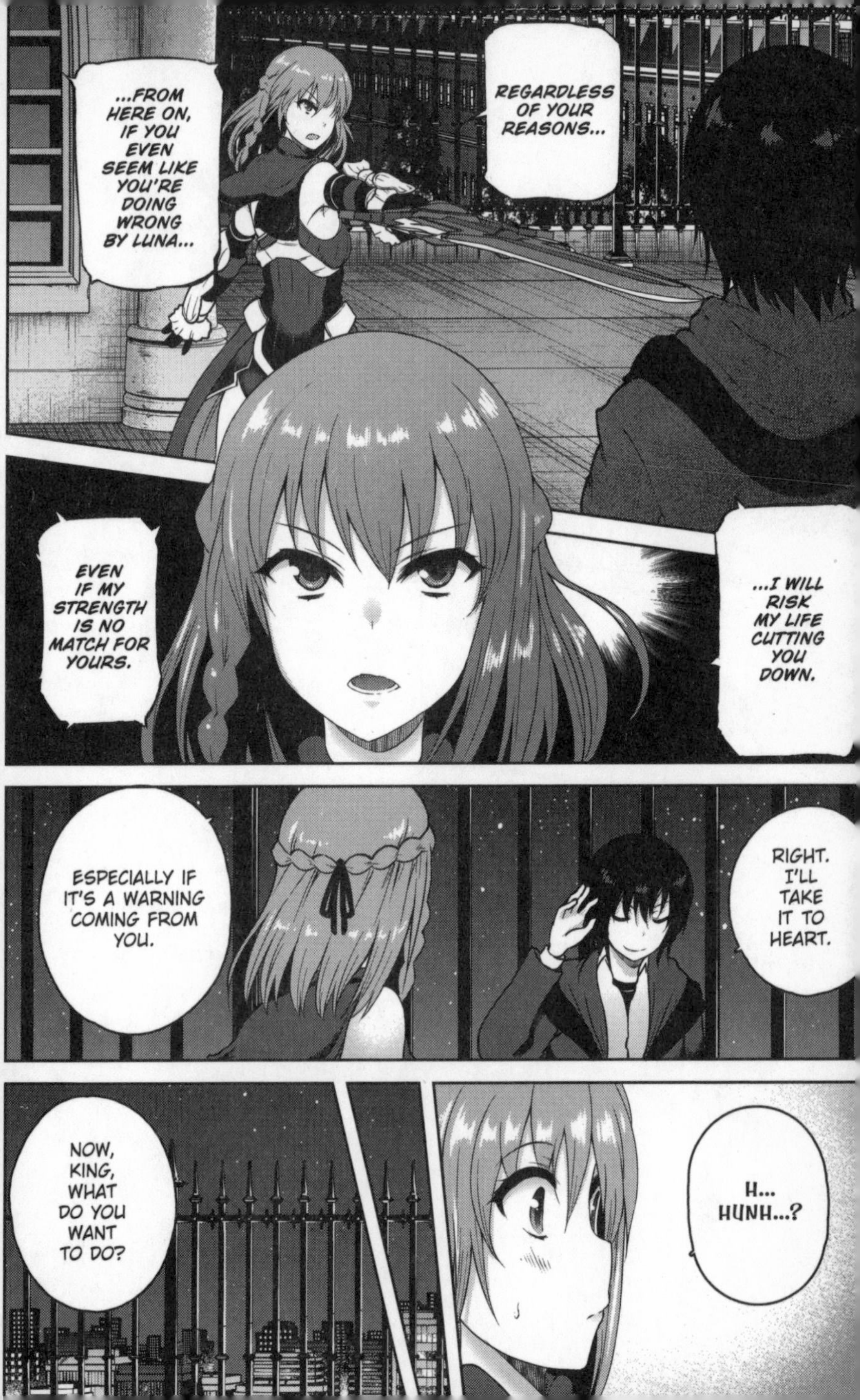
REGARDLESS OF YOUR REASONS...
...FROM HERE ON, IF YOU EVEN SEEM LIKE YOU'RE DOING WRONG BY LUNA...
...I WILL RISK MY LIFE CUTTING YOU DOWN.
EVEN IF MY STRENGTH IS NO MATCH FOR YOURS.
RIGHT. I'LL TAKE IT TO HEART.
ESPECIALLY IF IT'S A WARNING COMING FROM YOU.
H... HUNH...?
NOW, KING, WHAT DO YOU WANT TO DO?

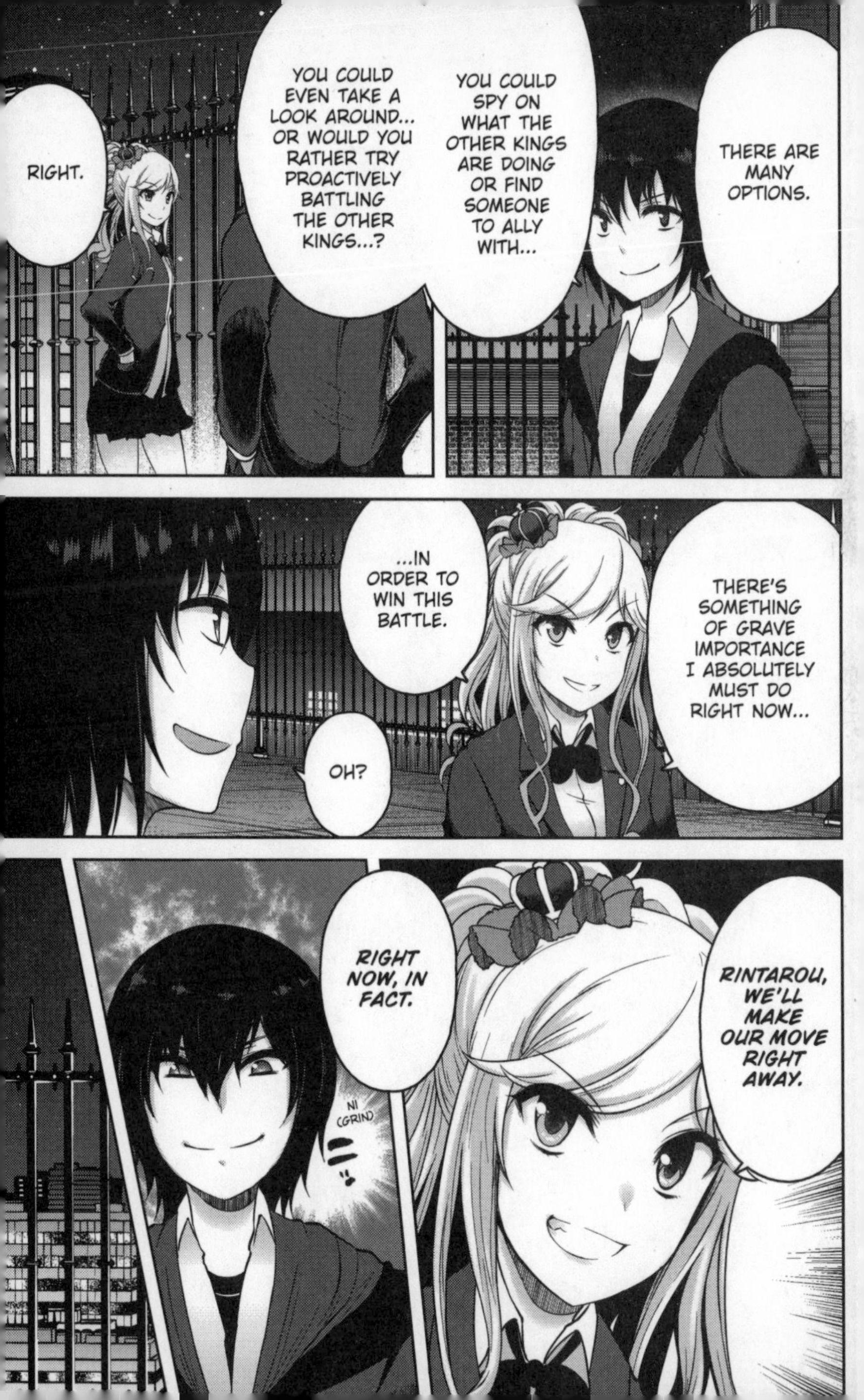
THERE ARE MANY OPTIONS.
YOU COULD SPY ON WHAT THE OTHER KINGS ARE DOING OR FIND SOMEONE TO ALLY WITH...
YOU COULD EVEN TAKE A LOOK AROUND... OR WOULD YOU RATHER TRY PROACTIVELY BATTLING THE OTHER KINGS...?
RIGHT.
THERE'S SOMETHING OF GRAVE IMPORTANCE I ABSOLUTELY MUST DO RIGHT NOW...
...IN ORDER TO WIN THIS BATTLE.
OH?
RINTAROU, WE'LL MAKE OUR MOVE RIGHT AWAY.
RIGHT NOW, IN FACT.
NI (GRIND)

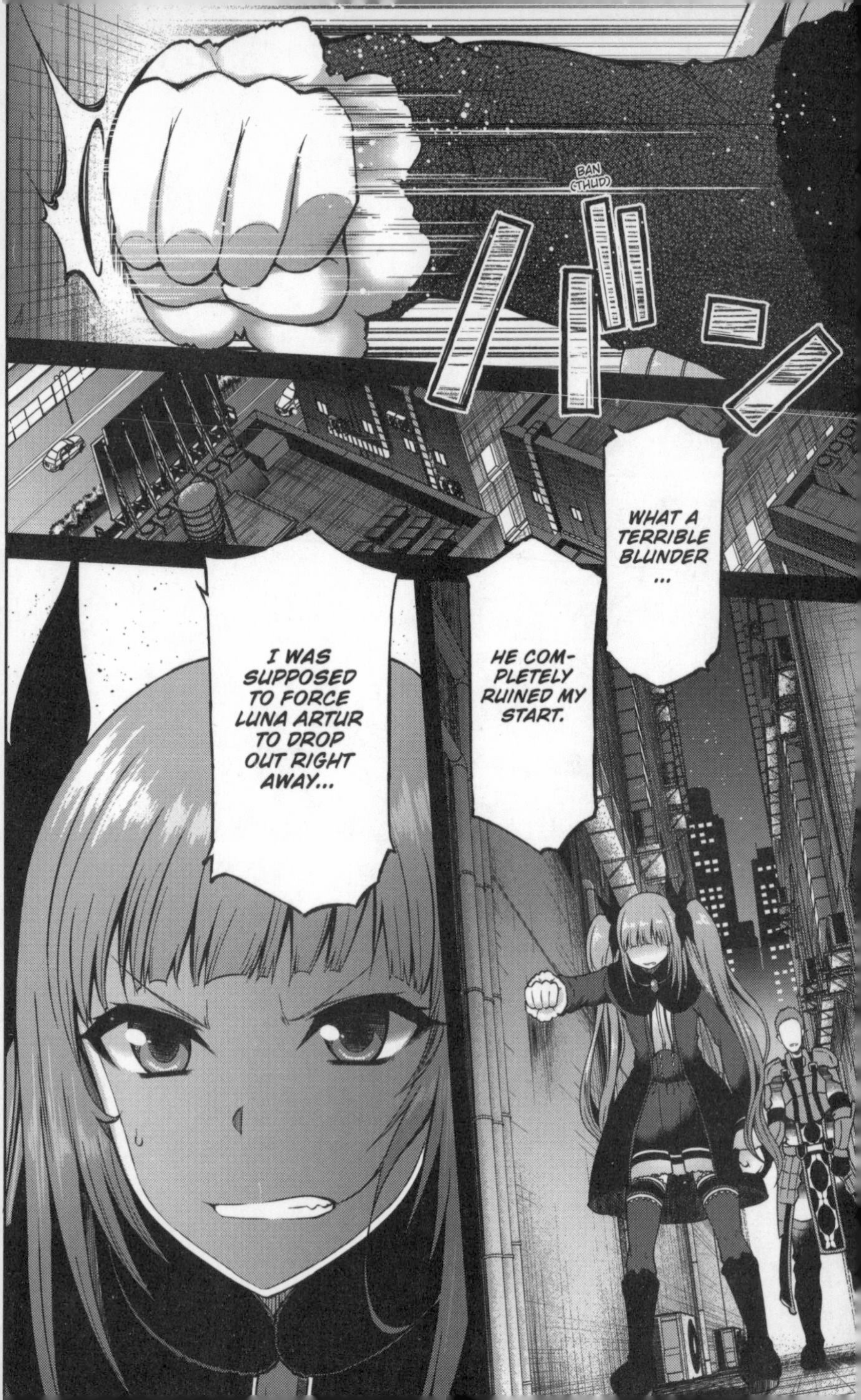
BAN (THUD)
WHAT A TERRIBLE BLUNDER ...
HE COM-PLETELY RUINED MY START.
I WAS SUPPOSED TO FORCE LUNA ARTUR TO DROP OUT RIGHT AWAY...

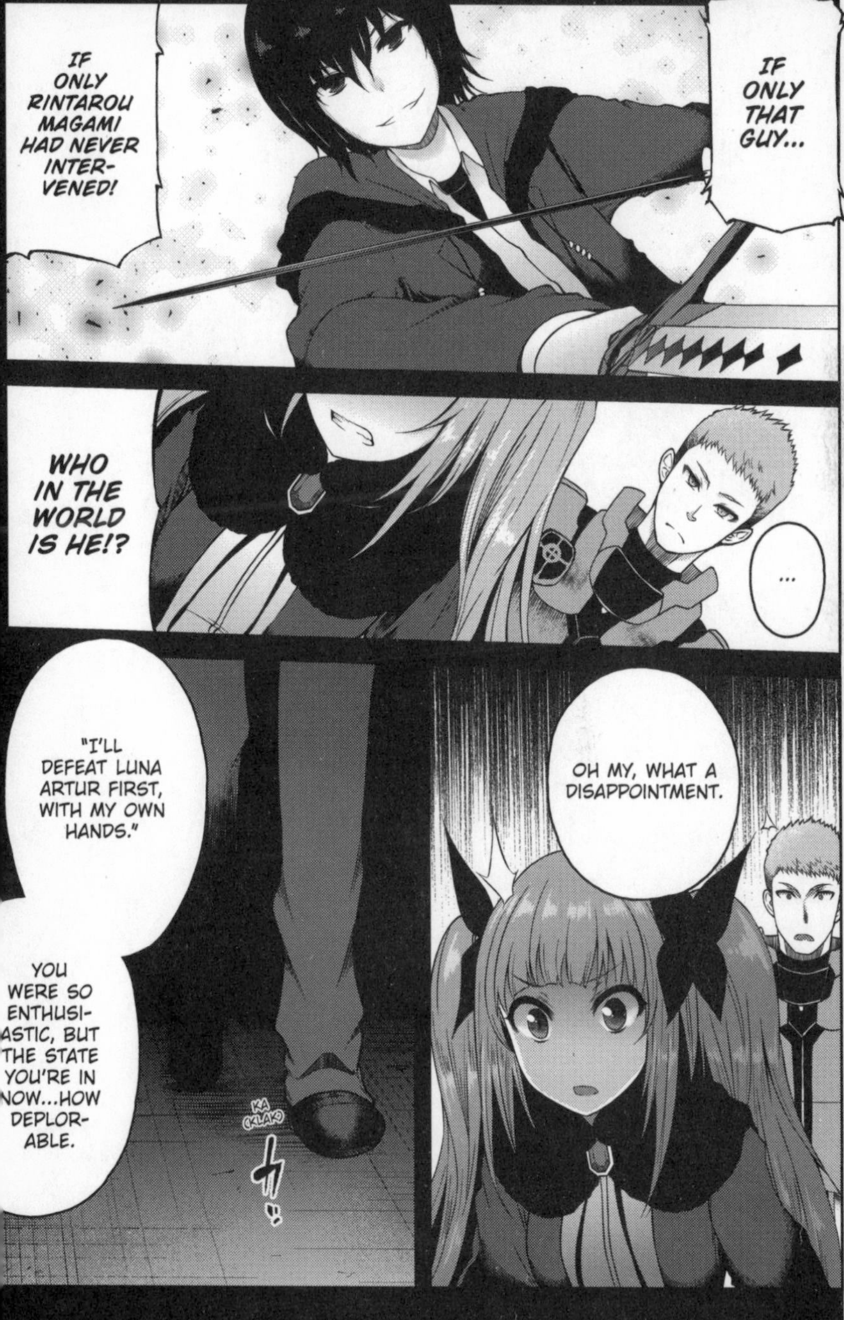
IF ONLY THAT GUY...
IF ONLY RINTAROU MAGAMI HAD NEVER INTER-VENED!
...
WHO IN THE WORLD IS HE!?
OH MY, WHAT A DISAPPOINTMENT.
"I'LL DEFEAT LUNA ARTUR FIRST, WITH MY OWN HANDS."
YOU WERE SO ENTHUSI-ASTIC, BUT THE STATE YOU'RE IN NOW...HOW DEPLOR-ABLE.
KA (KLAK)

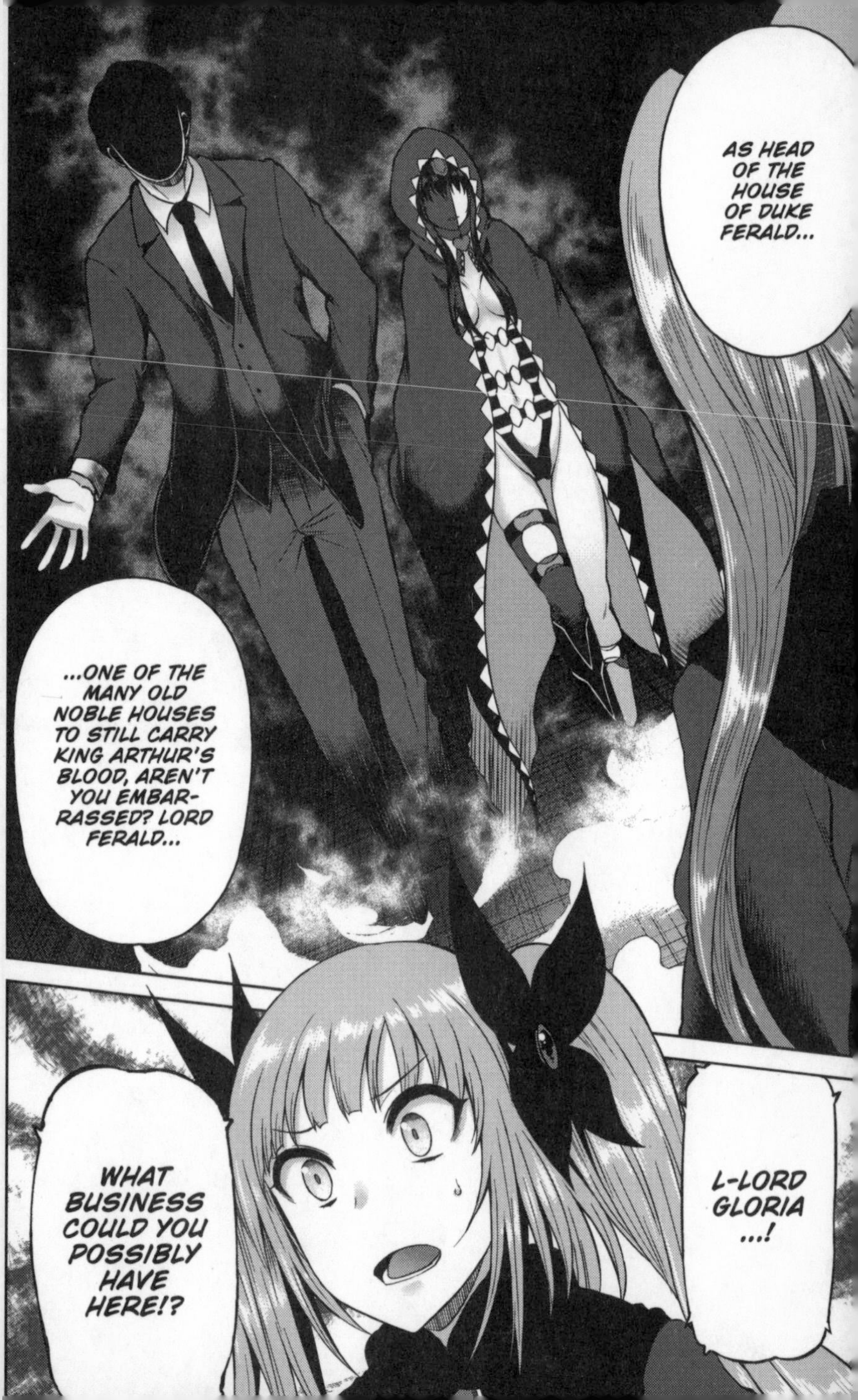
AS HEAD OF THE HOUSE OF DUKE FERALD...
...ONE OF THE MANY OLD NOBLE HOUSES TO STILL CARRY KING ARTHUR'S BLOOD, AREN'T YOU EMBARRASSED? LORD FERALD...
L-LORD GLORIA ...!
WHAT BUSINESS COULD YOU POSSIBLY HAVE HERE!?

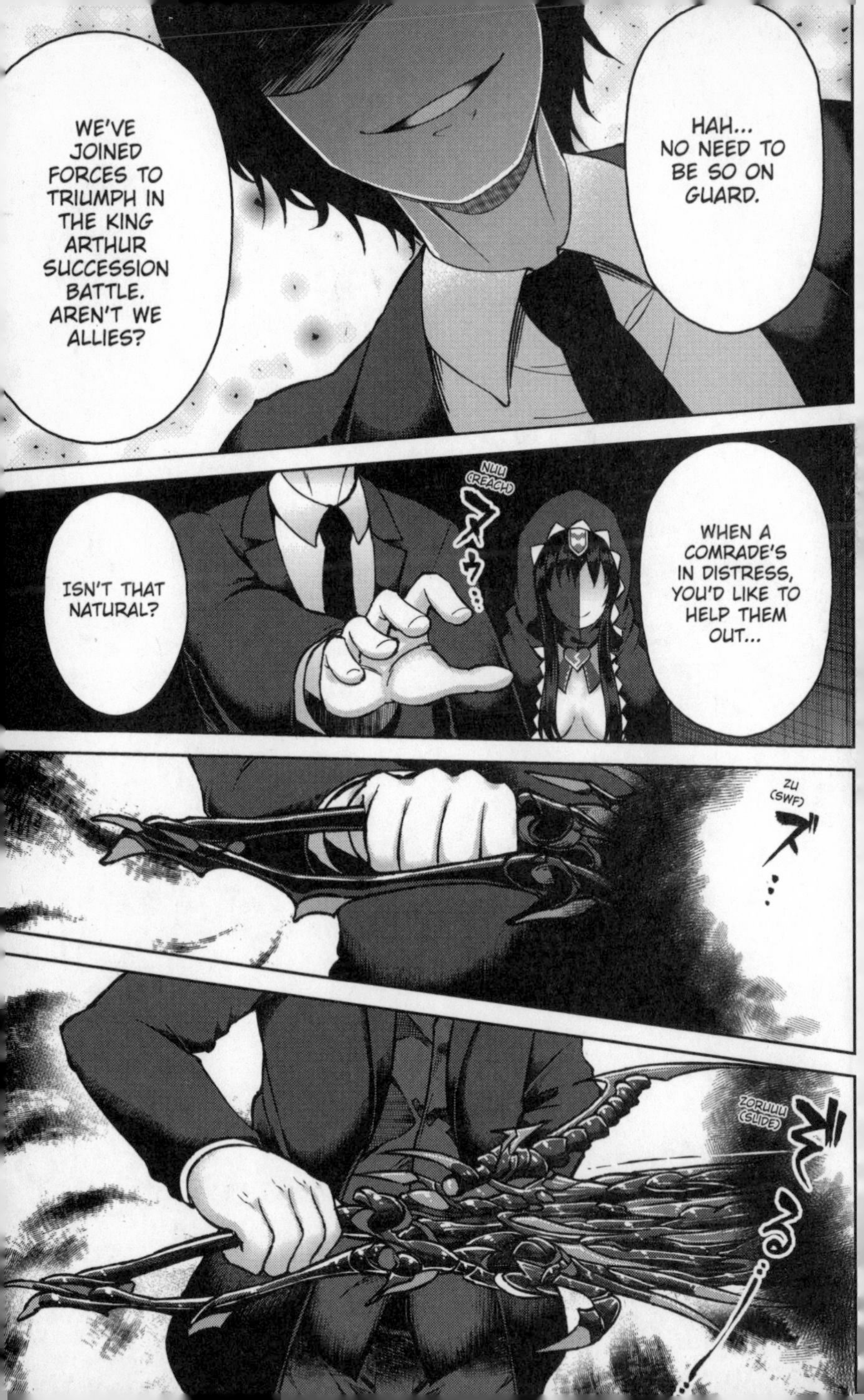
HAH... NO NEED TO BE SO ON GUARD.
WE'VE JOINED FORCES TO TRIUMPH IN THE KING ARTHUR SUCCESSION BATTLE. AREN'T WE ALLIES?
WHEN A COMRADE'S IN DISTRESS, YOU'D LIKE TO HELP THEM OUT...
NUU (REACH)
ISN'T THAT NATURAL?
ZU (SWF)
ZORUUU (SLIDE)

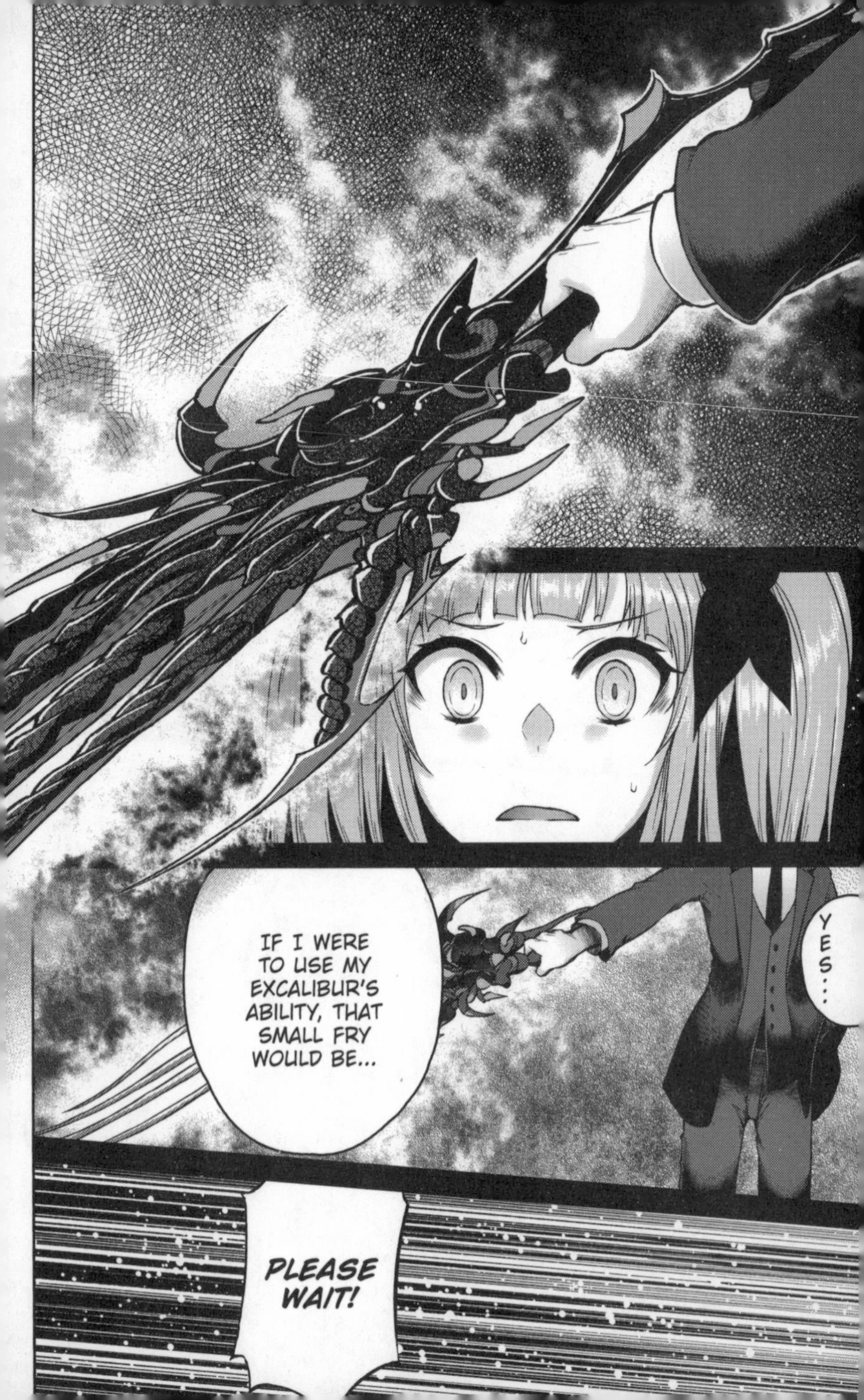
YES...
IF I WERE TO USE MY EXCALIBUR'S ABILITY, THAT SMALL FRY WOULD BE...
PLEASE WAIT!

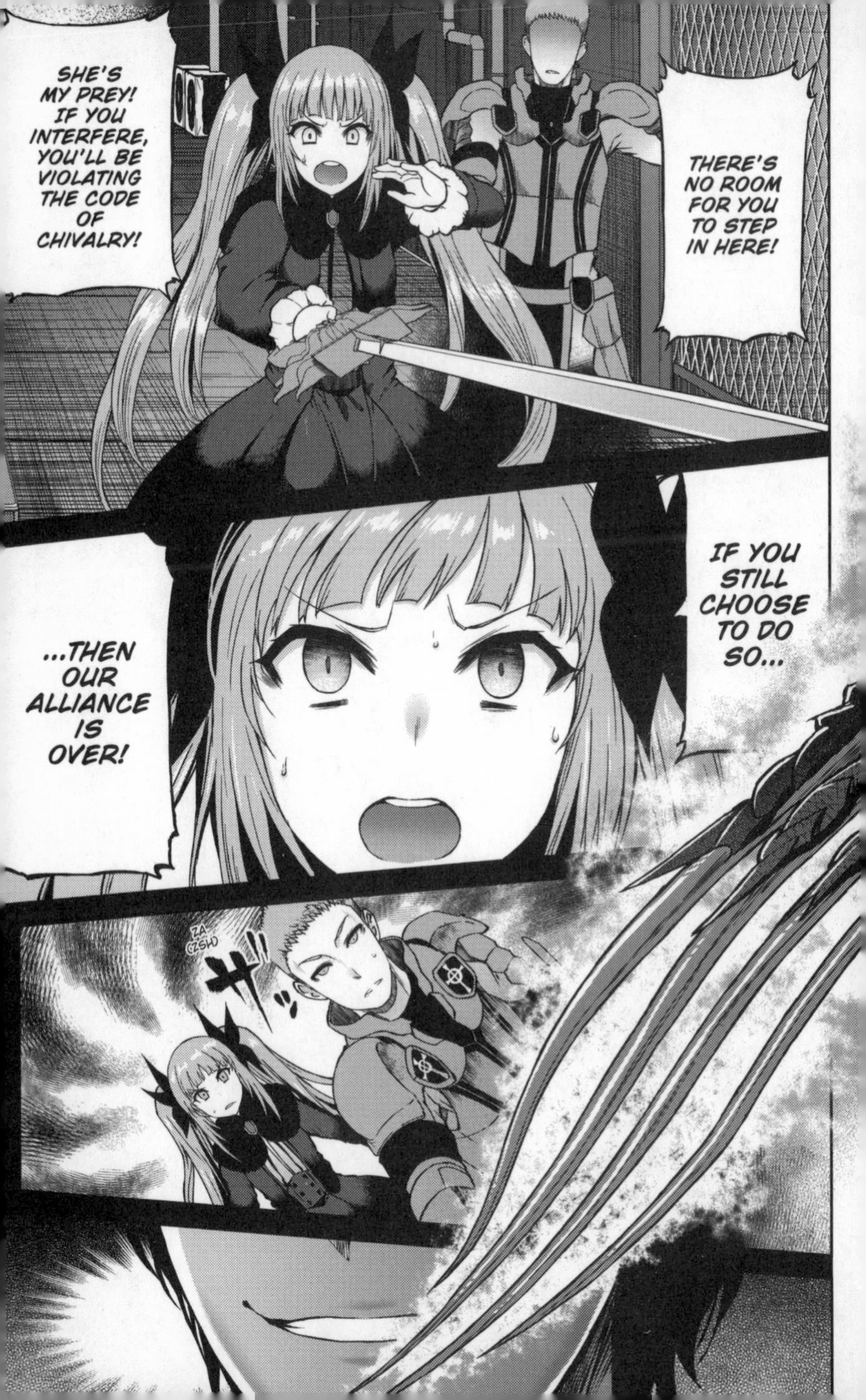
THERE'S NO ROOM FOR YOU TO STEP IN HERE!
SHE'S MY PREY! IF YOU INTERFERE, YOU'LL BE VIOLATING THE CODE OF CHIVALRY!
IF YOU STILL CHOOSE TO DO SO...
...THEN OUR ALLIANCE IS OVER!
ZA CZSH

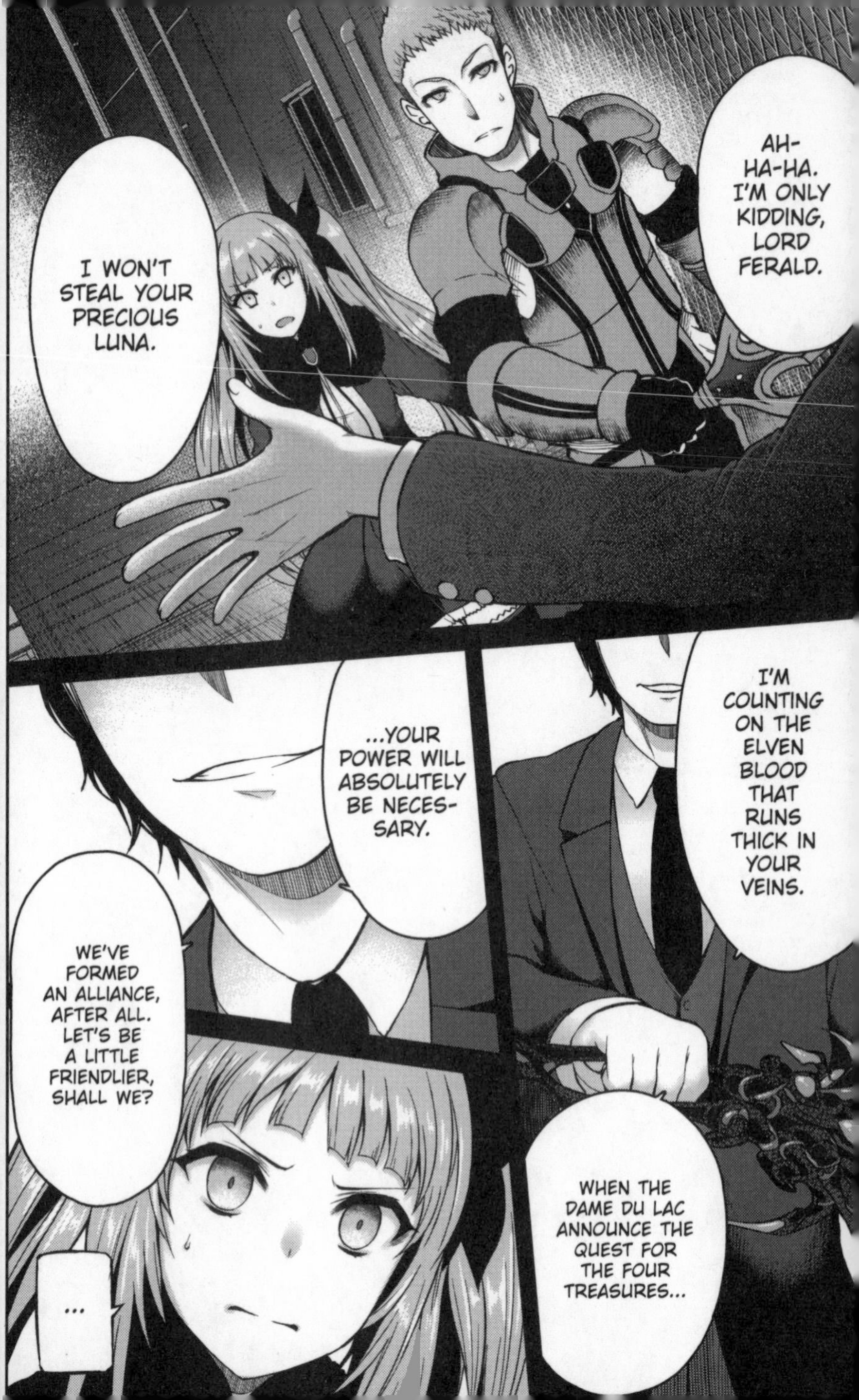
AH-HA-HA. I'M ONLY KIDDING, LORD FERALD.
I WON'T STEAL YOUR PRECIOUS LUNA.
I'M COUNTING ON THE ELVEN BLOOD THAT RUNS THICK IN YOUR VEINS.
WHEN THE DAME DU LAC ANNOUNCE THE QUEST FOR THE FOUR TREASURES...
...YOUR POWER WILL ABSOLUTELY BE NECES-SARY.
WE'VE FORMED AN ALLIANCE, AFTER ALL. LET'S BE A LITTLE FRIENDLIER, SHALL WE?
...

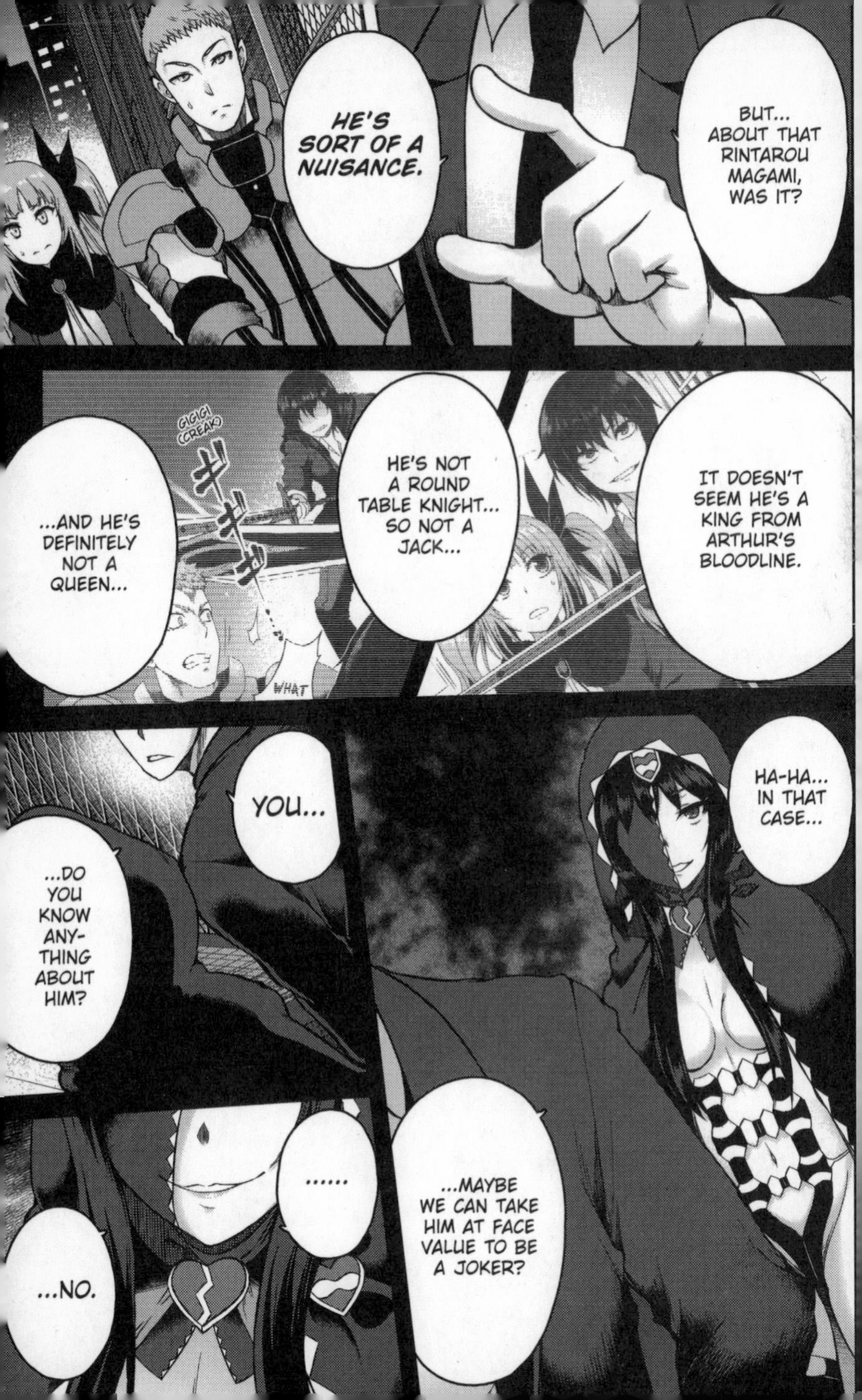
BUT... ABOUT THAT RINTAROU MAGAMI, WAS IT?
HE'S SORT OF A NUISANCE.
IT DOESN'T SEEM HE'S A KING FROM ARTHUR'S BLOODLINE.
HE'S NOT A ROUND TABLE KNIGHT... SO NOT A JACK...
GIGIGI (CREAK)
...AND HE'S DEFINITELY NOT A QUEEN...
WHAT
HA-HA... IN THAT CASE...
...MAYBE WE CAN TAKE HIM AT FACE VALUE TO BE A JOKER?
YOU...
...DO YOU KNOW ANY-THING ABOUT HIM?
......
...NO.

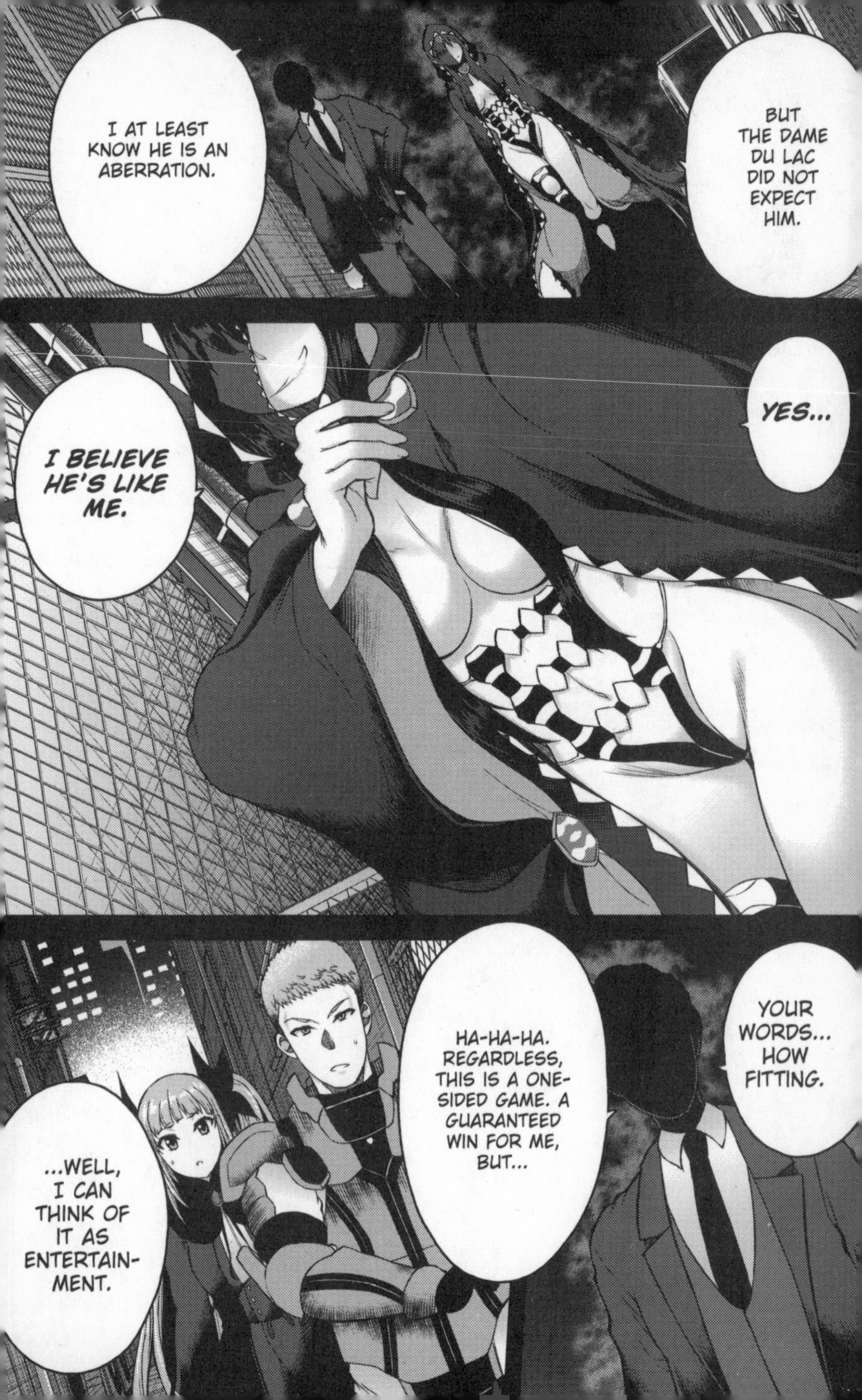
BUT THE DAME DU LAC DID NOT EXPECT HIM.
I AT LEAST KNOW HE IS AN ABERRATION.
YES...
I BELIEVE HE'S LIKE ME.
YOUR WORDS... HOW FITTING.
HA-HA-HA. REGARDLESS, THIS IS A ONE-SIDED GAME. A GUARANTEED WIN FOR ME, BUT...
...WELL, I CAN THINK OF IT AS ENTERTAINMENT.

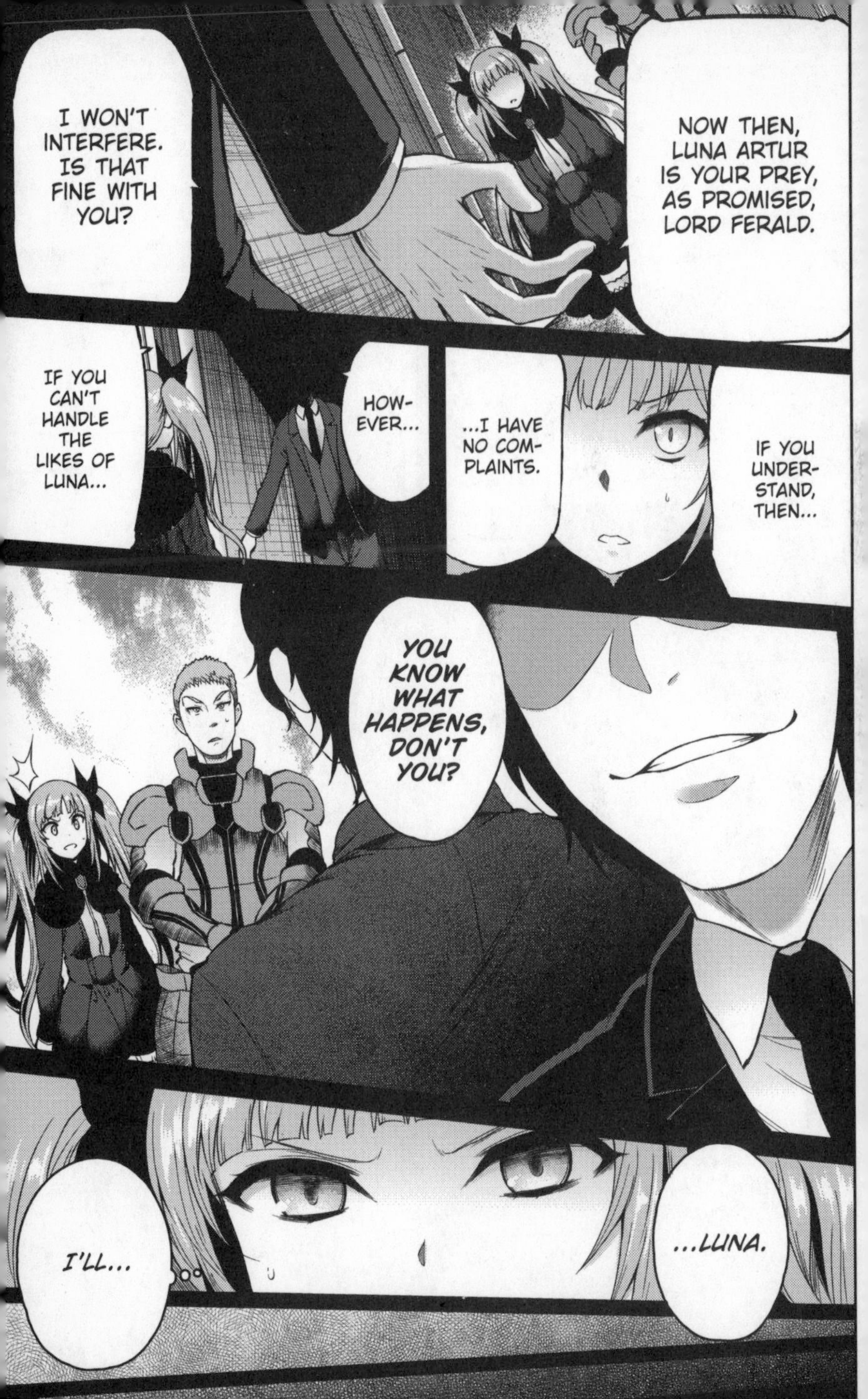
NOW THEN, LUNA ARTUR IS YOUR PREY, AS PROMISED, LORD FERALD.
I WON'T INTERFERE. IS THAT FINE WITH YOU?
IF YOU UNDER-STAND, THEN...
...I HAVE NO COM-PLAINTS.
HOW-EVER...
IF YOU CAN'T HANDLE THE LIKES OF LUNA...
YOU KNOW WHAT HAPPENS, DON'T YOU?
...LUNA.
I'LL...

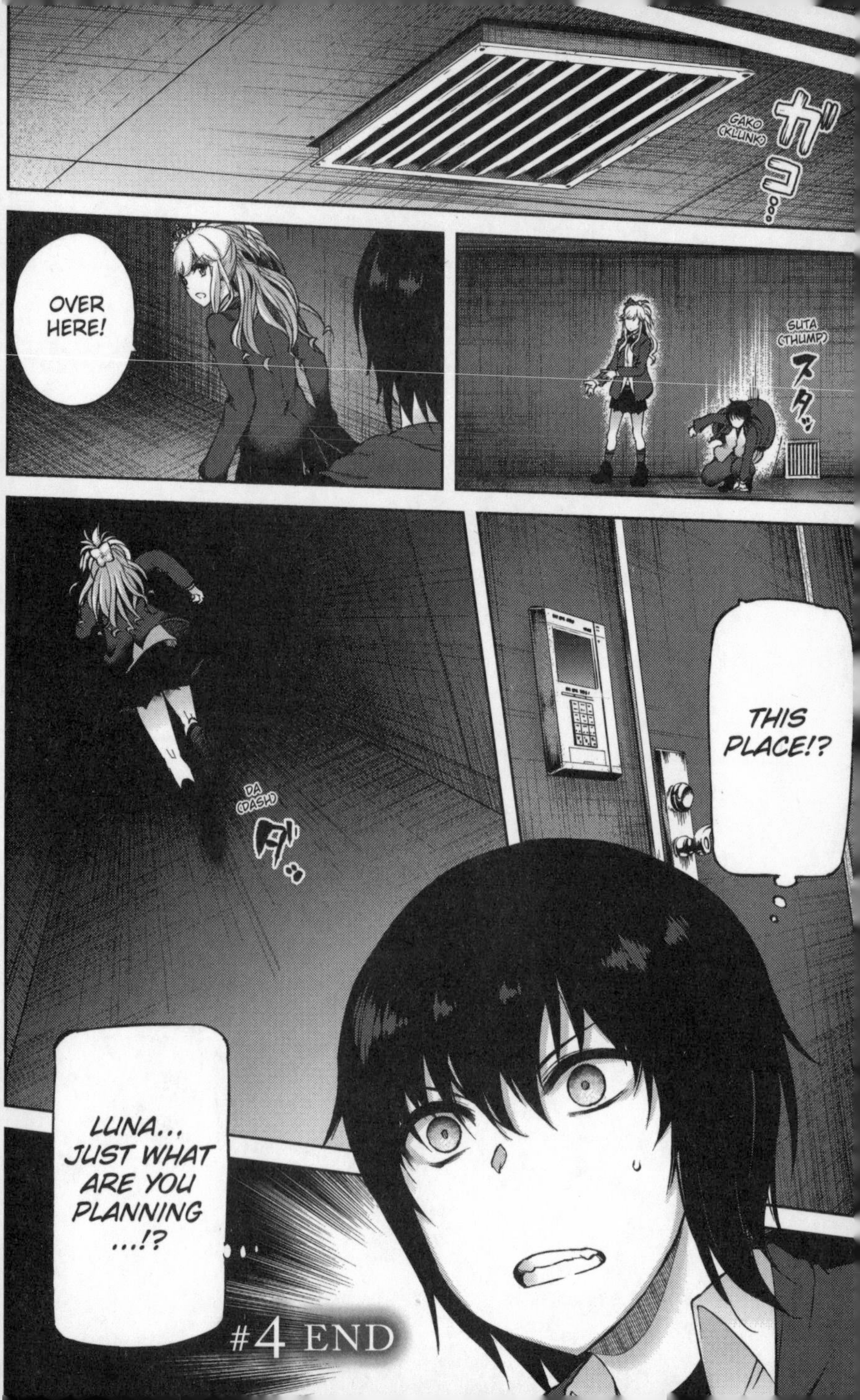
GAKO (KLUNK)
ガコ
SUTA (THUMP)
スタッ
OVER HERE!
THIS PLACE!?
DA (DASH)
ダッ
LUNA... JUST WHAT ARE YOU PLANNING ...!?
#4 END

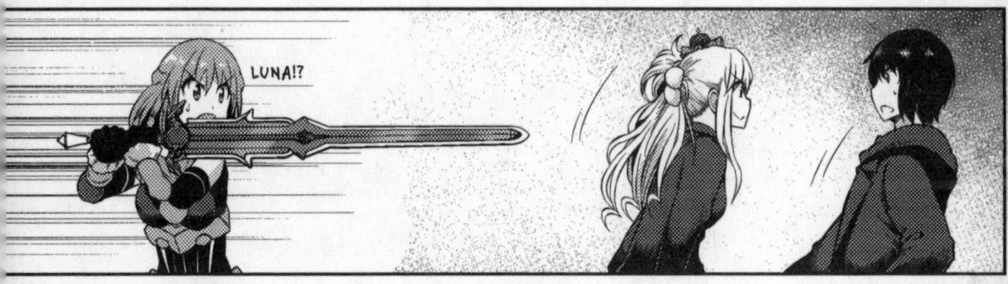
LUNA!?

LAST

ROUND

ARTHURS

5 CHAPTER THREE
The Lonely Demon and the Midnight Sun

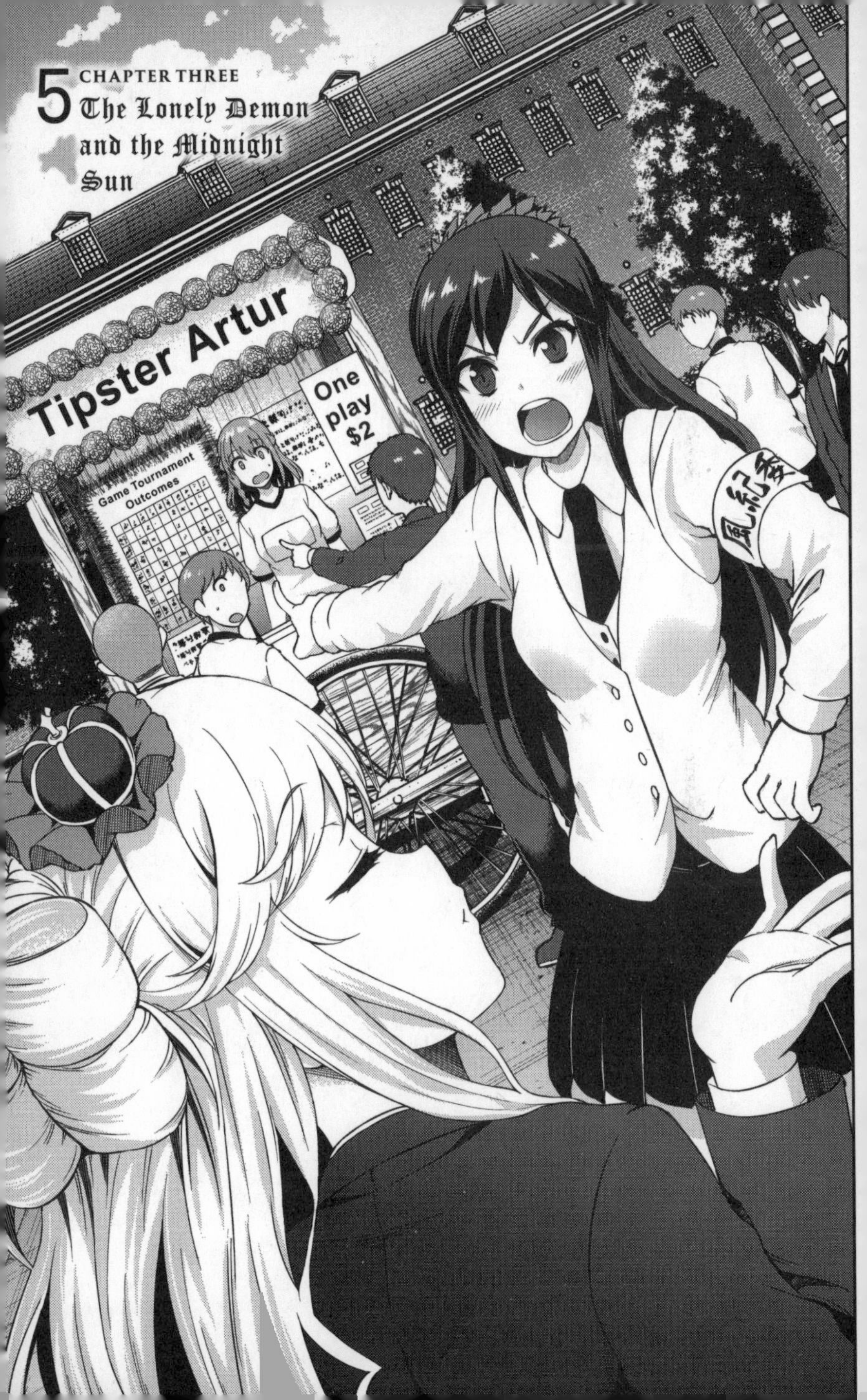
Tipster Artur
One play $2
Game Tournament Outcomes
風紀委

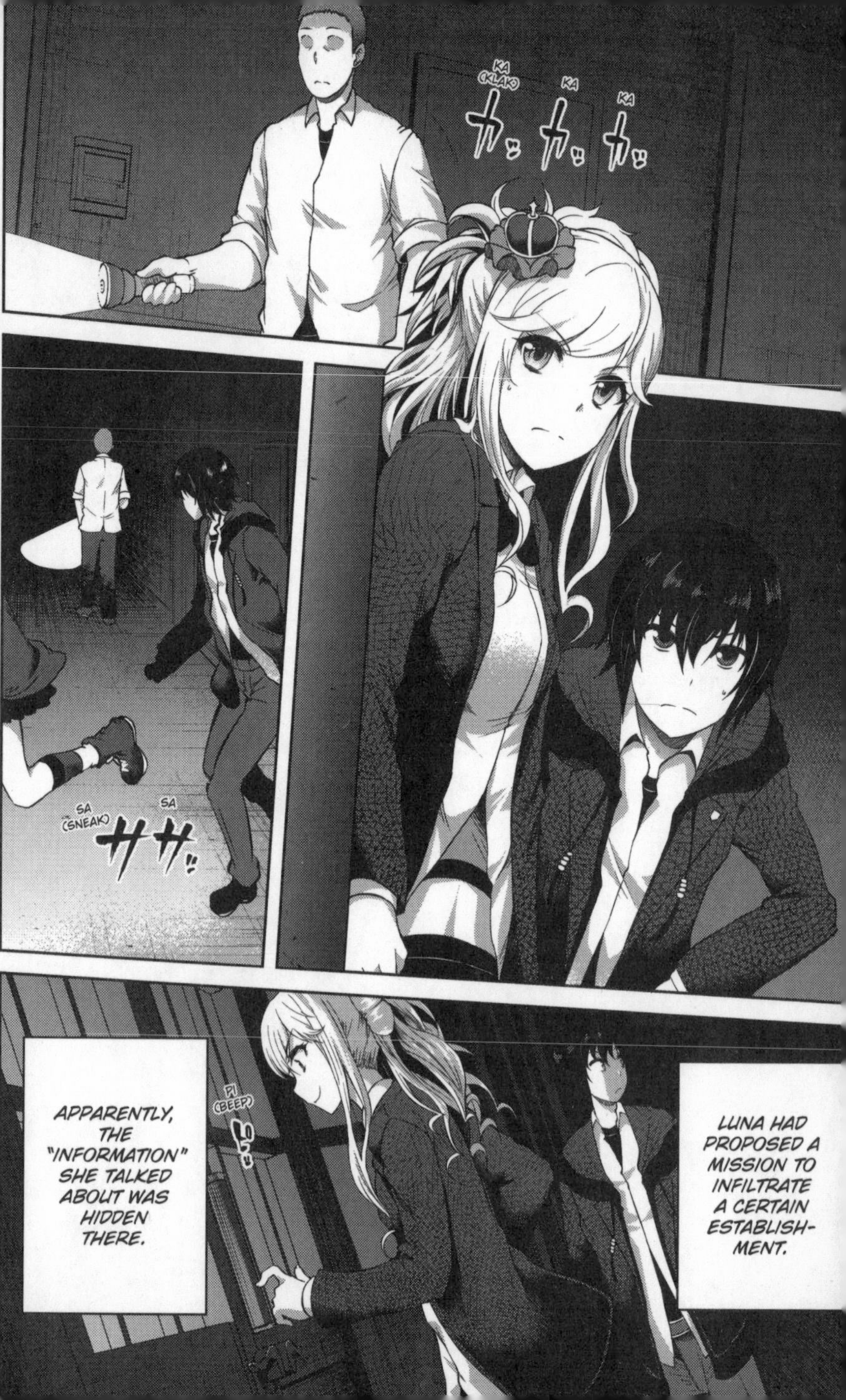

KA (KLAK)
KA
KA
SA (SNEAK)
SA
LUNA HAD PROPOSED A MISSION TO INFILTRATE A CERTAIN ESTABLISH-MENT.
PI (BEEP)
APPARENTLY, THE "INFORMATION" SHE TALKED ABOUT WAS HIDDEN THERE.

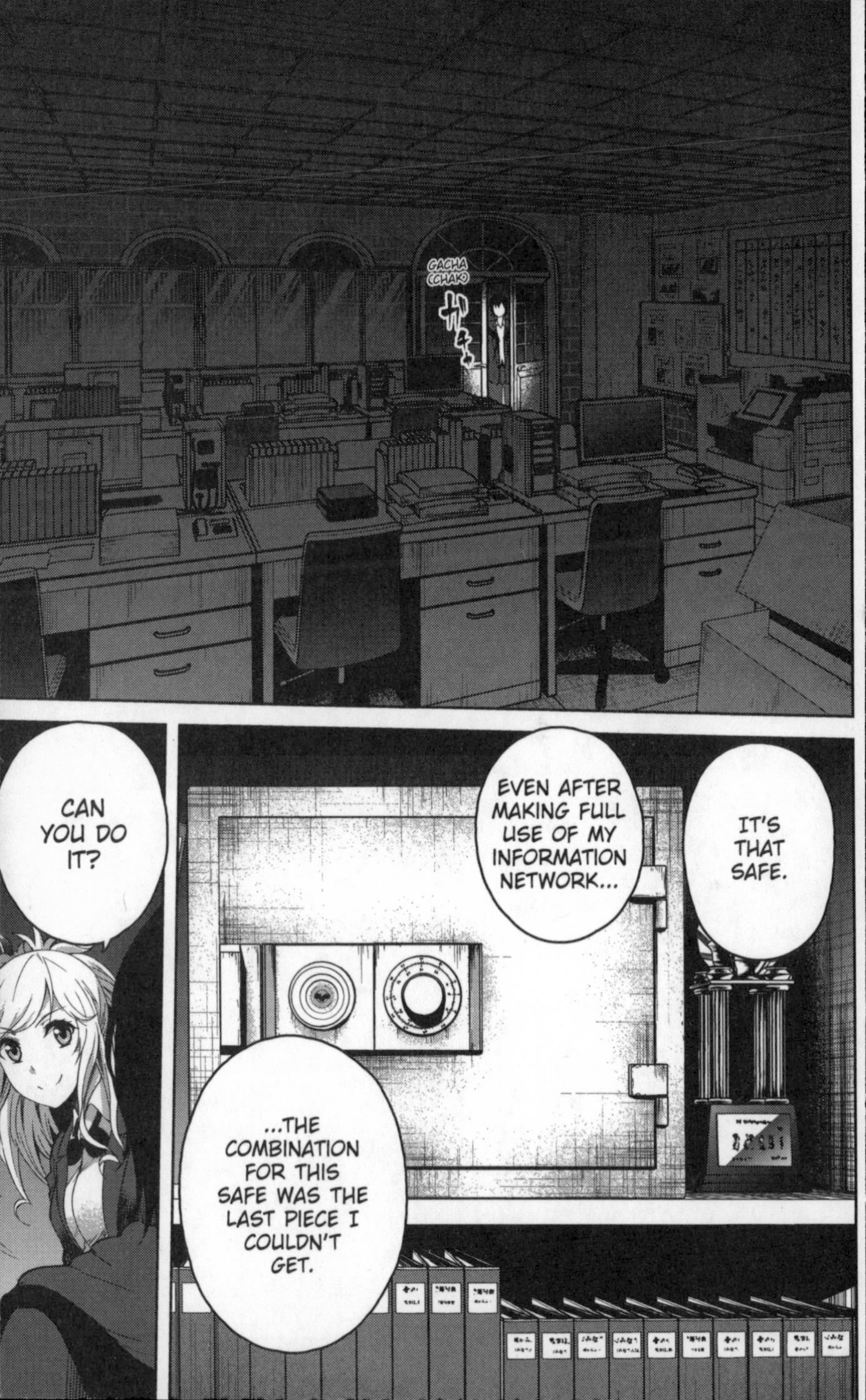
GACHA (CHAK)
IT'S THAT SAFE.
EVEN AFTER MAKING FULL USE OF MY INFORMATION NETWORK...
...THE COMBINATION FOR THIS SAFE WAS THE LAST PIECE I COULDN'T GET.
CAN YOU DO IT?

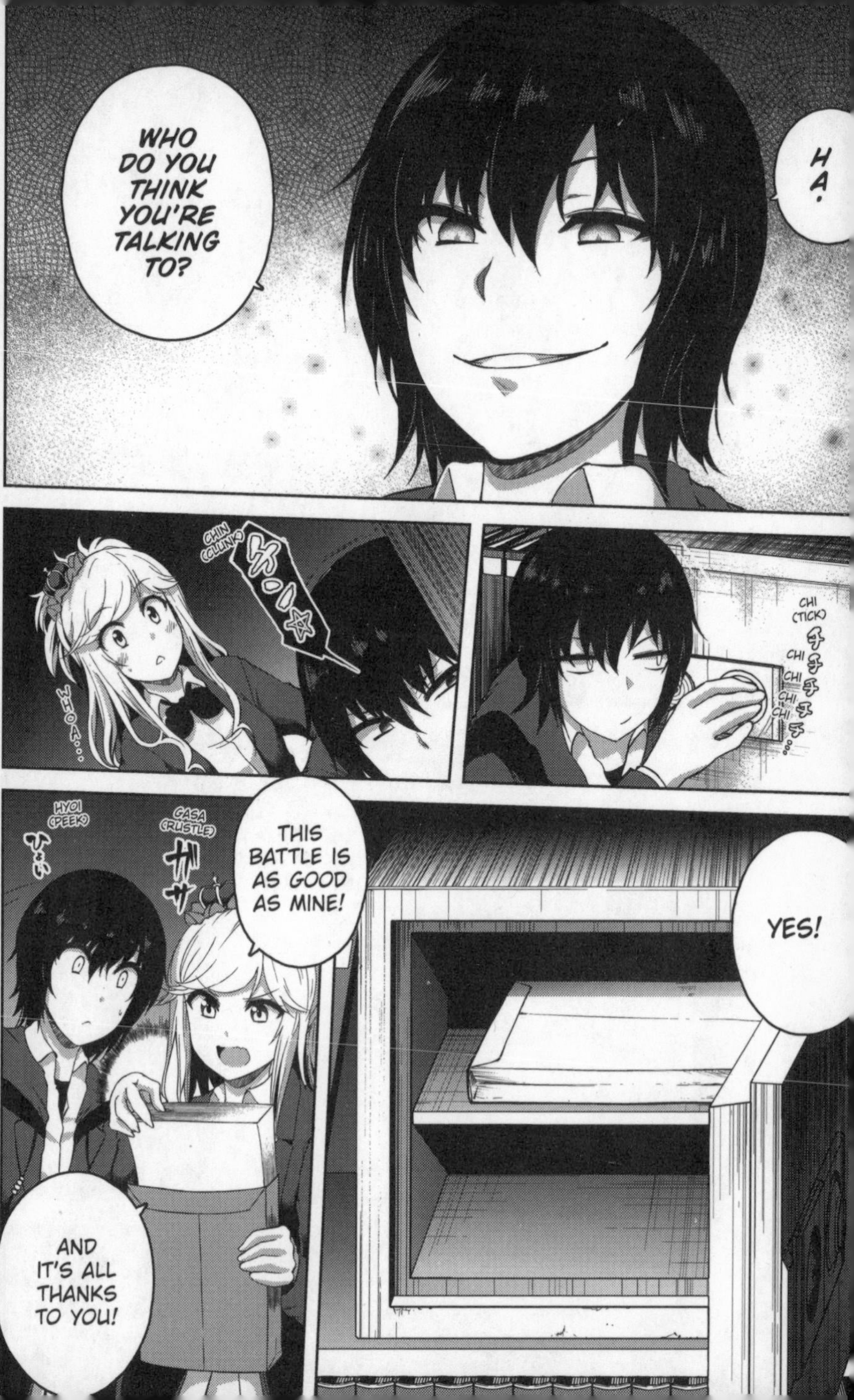
HA.
WHO DO YOU THINK YOU'RE TALKING TO?
CHI (TICK)
CHI
CHI
CHI
CHI...
CHIN (CLUNK)
WHOA...
YES!
THIS BATTLE IS AS GOOD AS MINE!
GASA (RUSTLE)
HYOI (PEEK)
AND IT'S ALL THANKS TO YOU!

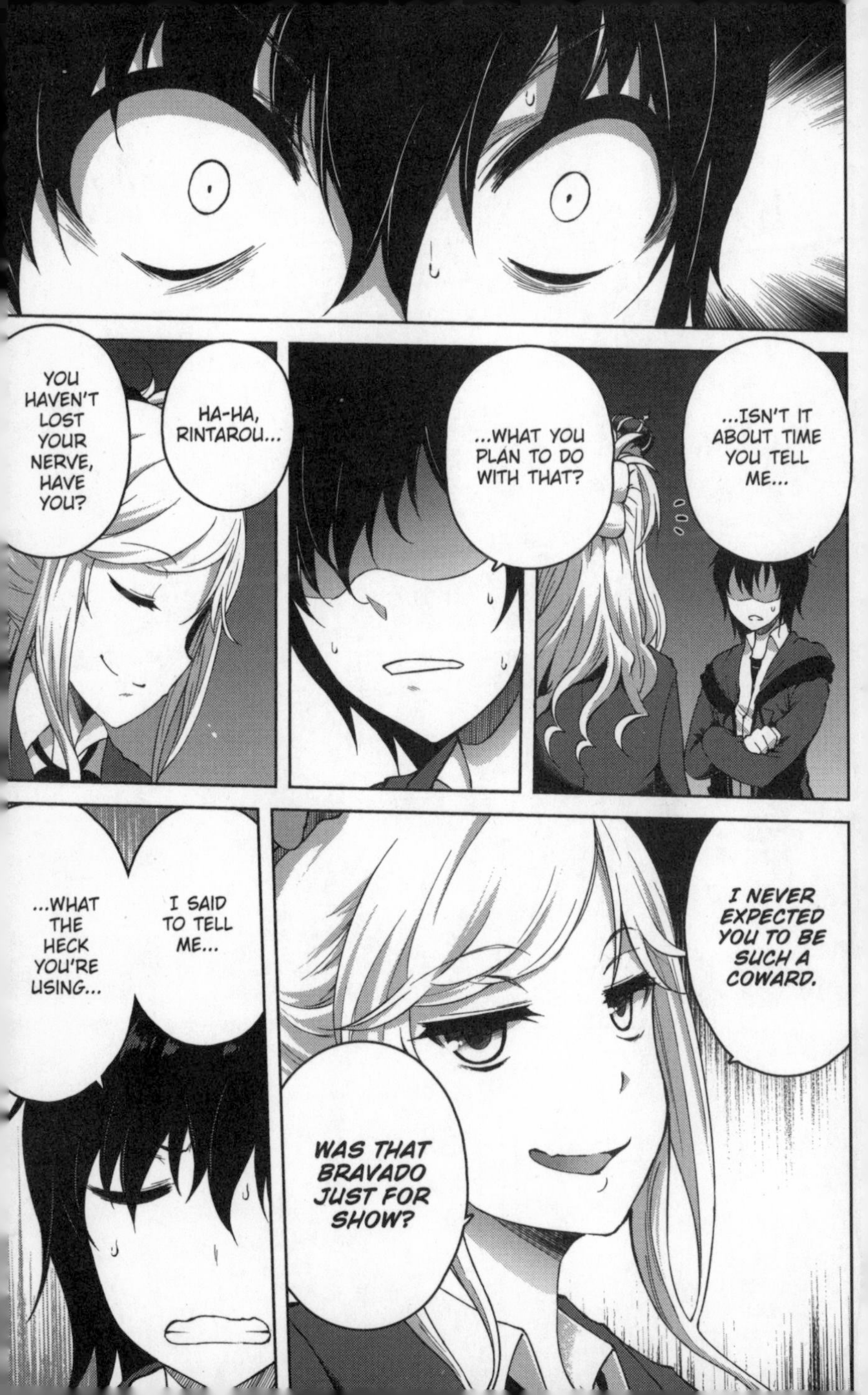
...ISN'T IT ABOUT TIME YOU TELL ME...
...WHAT YOU PLAN TO DO WITH THAT?
HA-HA, RINTAROU...
YOU HAVEN'T LOST YOUR NERVE, HAVE YOU?
I NEVER EXPECTED YOU TO BE SUCH A COWARD.
WAS THAT BRAVADO JUST FOR SHOW?
I SAID TO TELL ME...
...WHAT THE HECK YOU'RE USING...

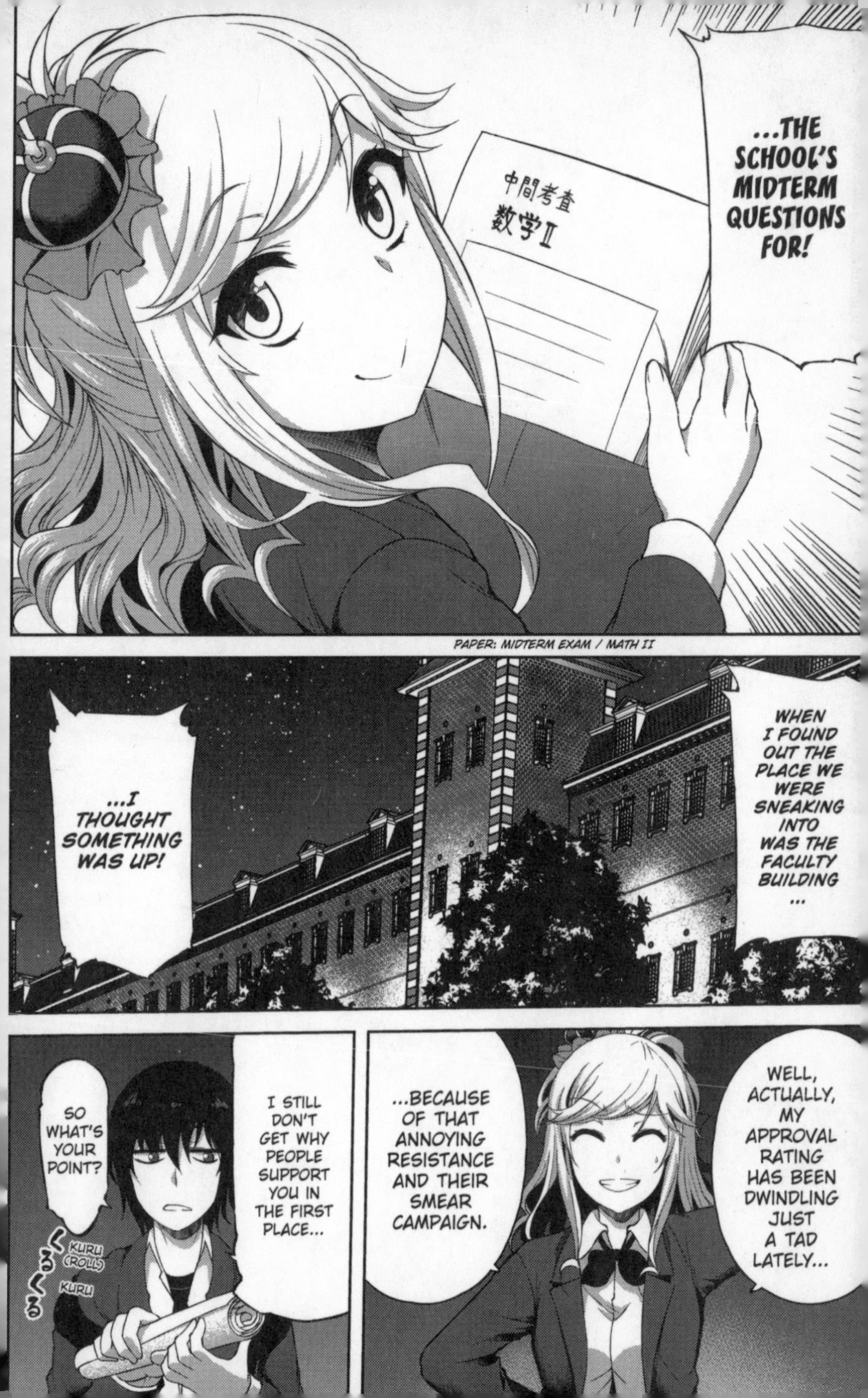
...THE SCHOOL'S MIDTERM QUESTIONS FOR!
中間考査
数学II
PAPER: MIDTERM EXAM / MATH II
WHEN I FOUND OUT THE PLACE WE WERE SNEAKING INTO WAS THE FACULTY BUILDING...
...I THOUGHT SOMETHING WAS UP!
WELL, ACTUALLY, MY APPROVAL RATING HAS BEEN DWINDLING JUST A TAD LATELY...
...BECAUSE OF THAT ANNOYING RESISTANCE AND THEIR SMEAR CAMPAIGN.
I STILL DON'T GET WHY PEOPLE SUPPORT YOU IN THE FIRST PLACE...
SO WHAT'S YOUR POINT?
くるくる
KURU (ROLL) KURU

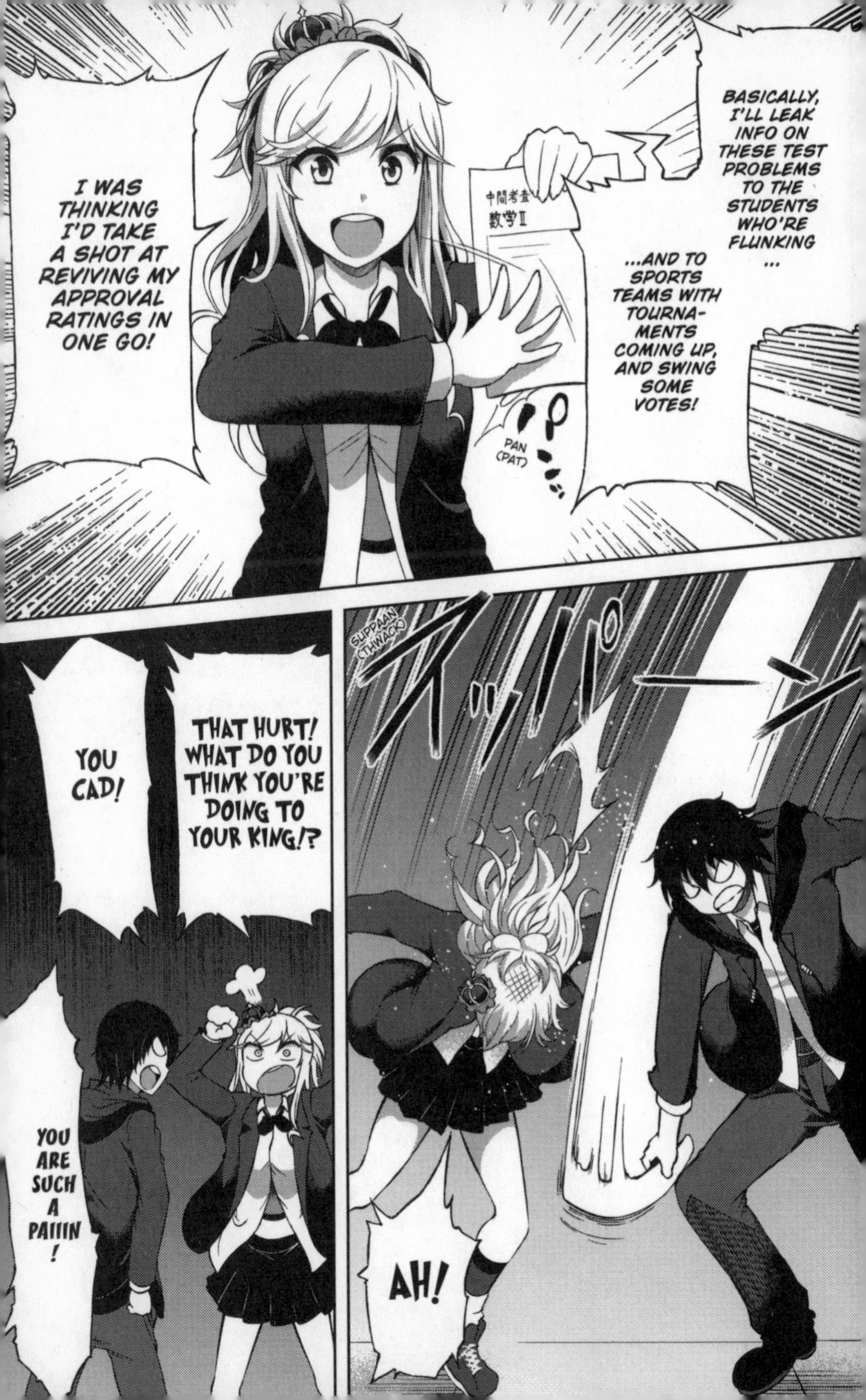
BASICALLY, I'LL LEAK INFO ON THESE TEST PROBLEMS TO THE STUDENTS WHO'RE FLUNKING ...
...AND TO SPORTS TEAMS WITH TOURNAMENTS COMING UP, AND SWING SOME VOTES!
中間考査
数学Ⅱ
PAN (PAT)
I WAS THINKING I'D TAKE A SHOT AT REVIVING MY APPROVAL RATINGS IN ONE GO!
SUPPAAN (THWACK)
AH!
THAT HURT! WHAT DO YOU THINK YOU'RE DOING TO YOUR KING!?
YOU CAD!
YOU ARE SUCH A PAIIIN!

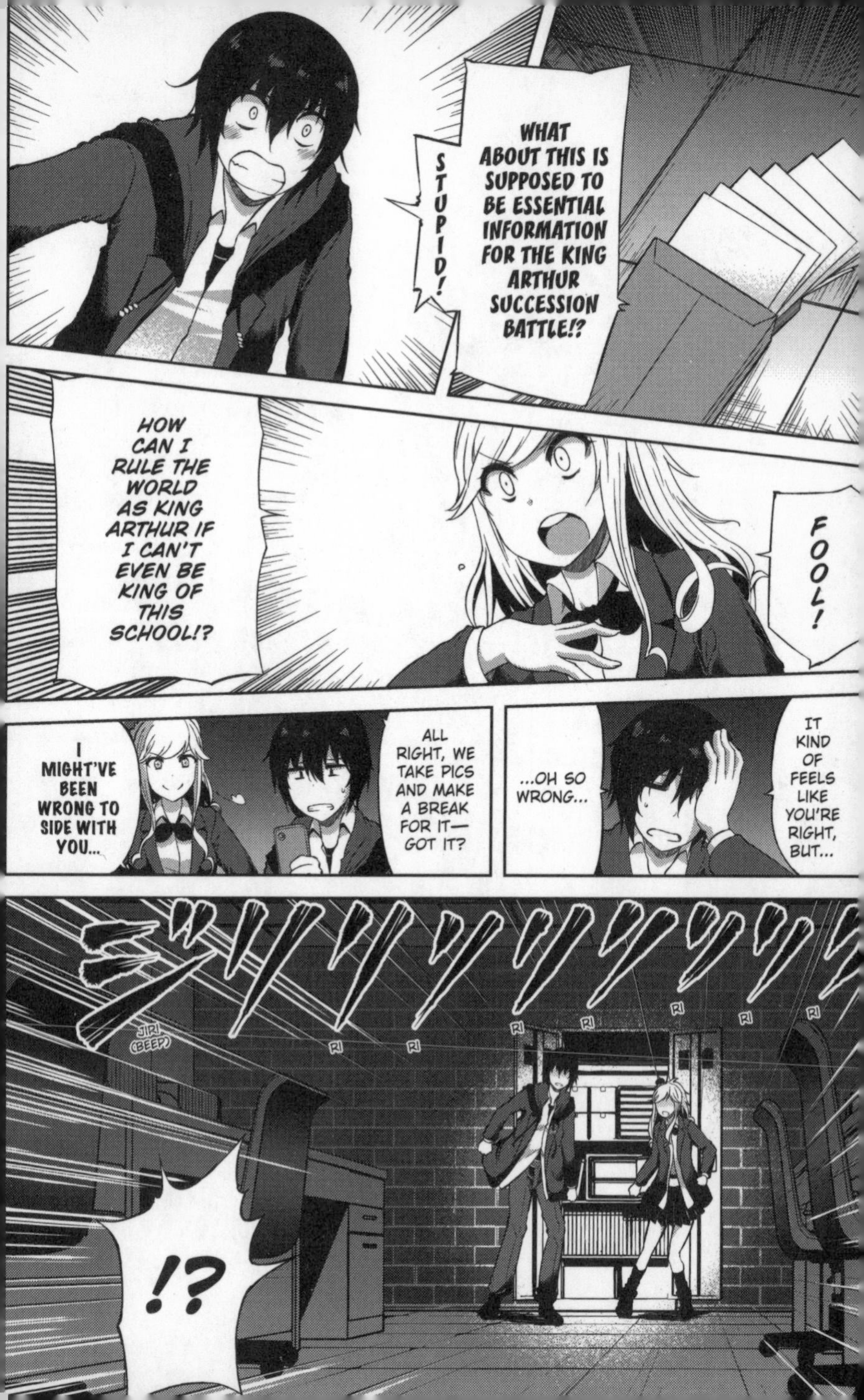
WHAT ABOUT THIS IS SUPPOSED TO BE ESSENTIAL INFORMATION FOR THE KING ARTHUR SUCCESSION BATTLE!?
STUPID!
FOOL!
HOW CAN I RULE THE WORLD AS KING ARTHUR IF I CAN'T EVEN BE KING OF THIS SCHOOL!?
IT KIND OF FEELS LIKE YOU'RE RIGHT, BUT...
...OH SO WRONG...
ALL RIGHT, WE TAKE PICS AND MAKE A BREAK FOR IT—GOT IT?
I MIGHT'VE BEEN WRONG TO SIDE WITH YOU...
RI RI RI RI RI RI RI
JIRI (BEEP)
!?

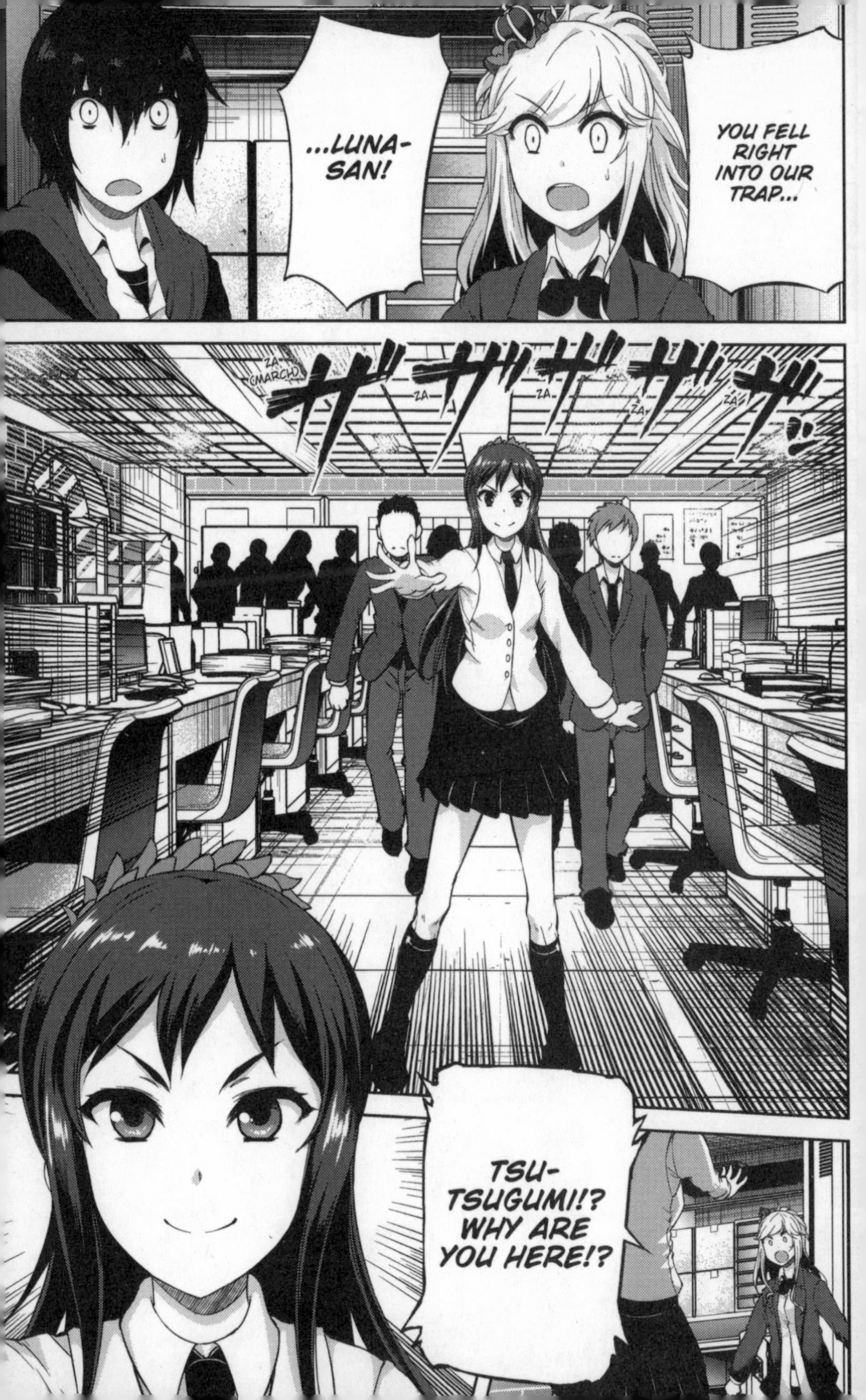
YOU FELL RIGHT INTO OUR TRAP...
...LUNA-SAN!
ZA (MARCH)
ZA
ZA
ZA
ZA
TSU-TSUGUMI!? WHY ARE YOU HERE!?

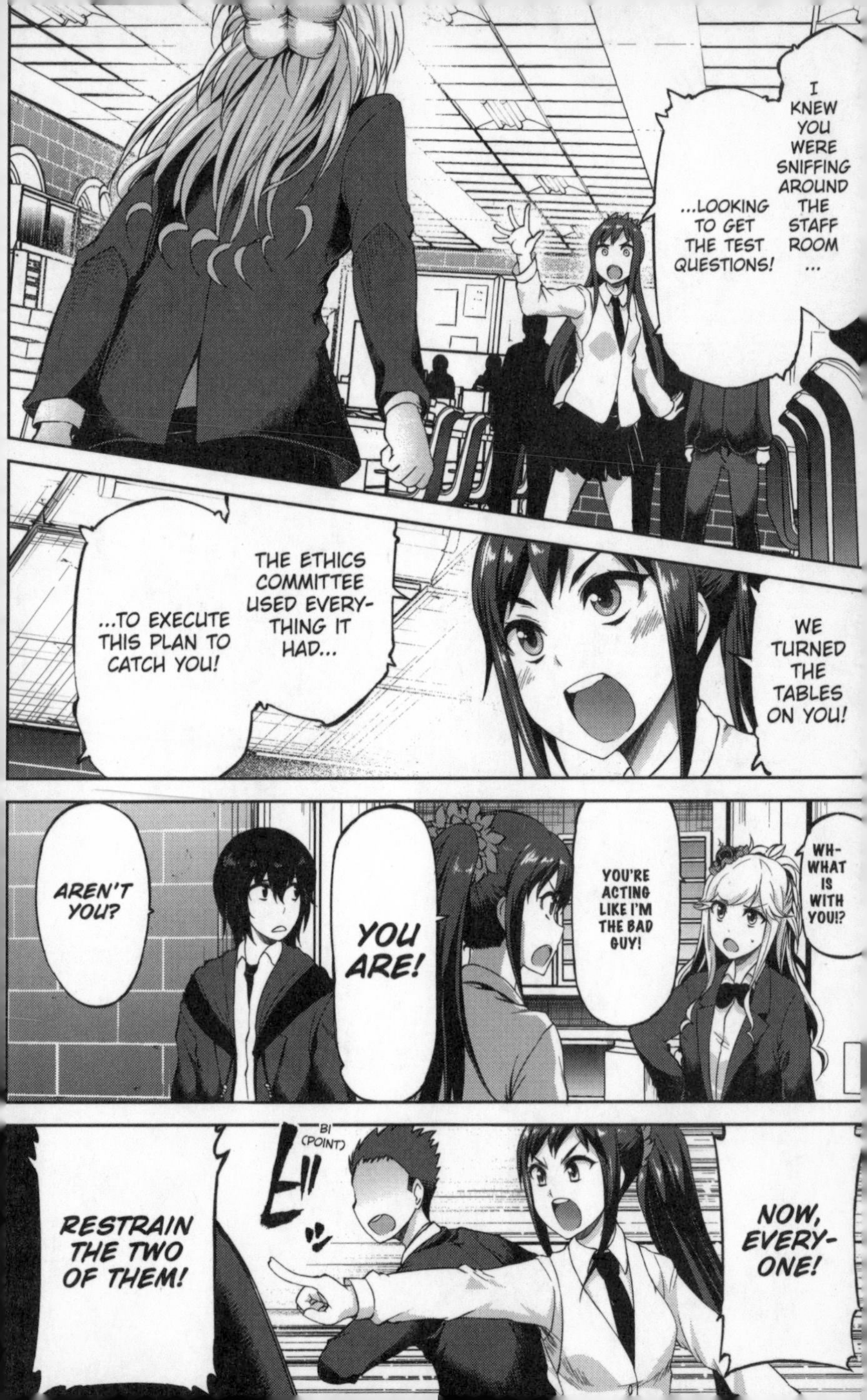
I KNEW YOU WERE SNIFFING AROUND THE STAFF ROOM...
...LOOKING TO GET THE TEST QUESTIONS!
WE TURNED THE TABLES ON YOU!
THE ETHICS COMMITTEE USED EVERY-THING IT HAD...
...TO EXECUTE THIS PLAN TO CATCH YOU!
WH-WHAT IS WITH YOU!?
YOU'RE ACTING LIKE I'M THE BAD GUY!
YOU ARE!
AREN'T YOU?
NOW, EVERY-ONE!
BI (POINT)
RESTRAIN THE TWO OF THEM!

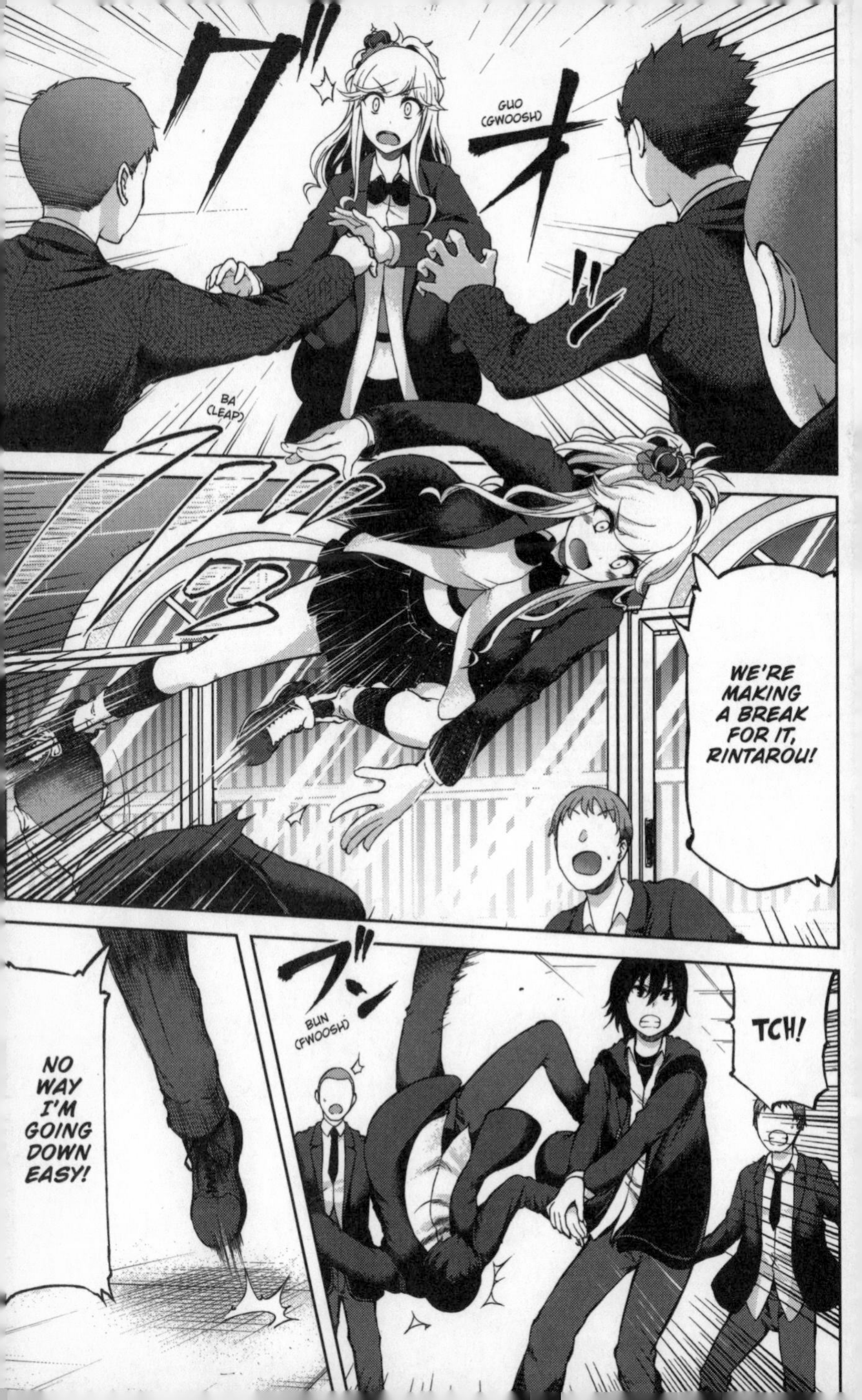
GUO (GWOOSH)
BA (LEAP)
WE'RE MAKING A BREAK FOR IT, RINTAROU!
TCH!
BUN (FWOOSH)
NO WAY I'M GOING DOWN EASY!

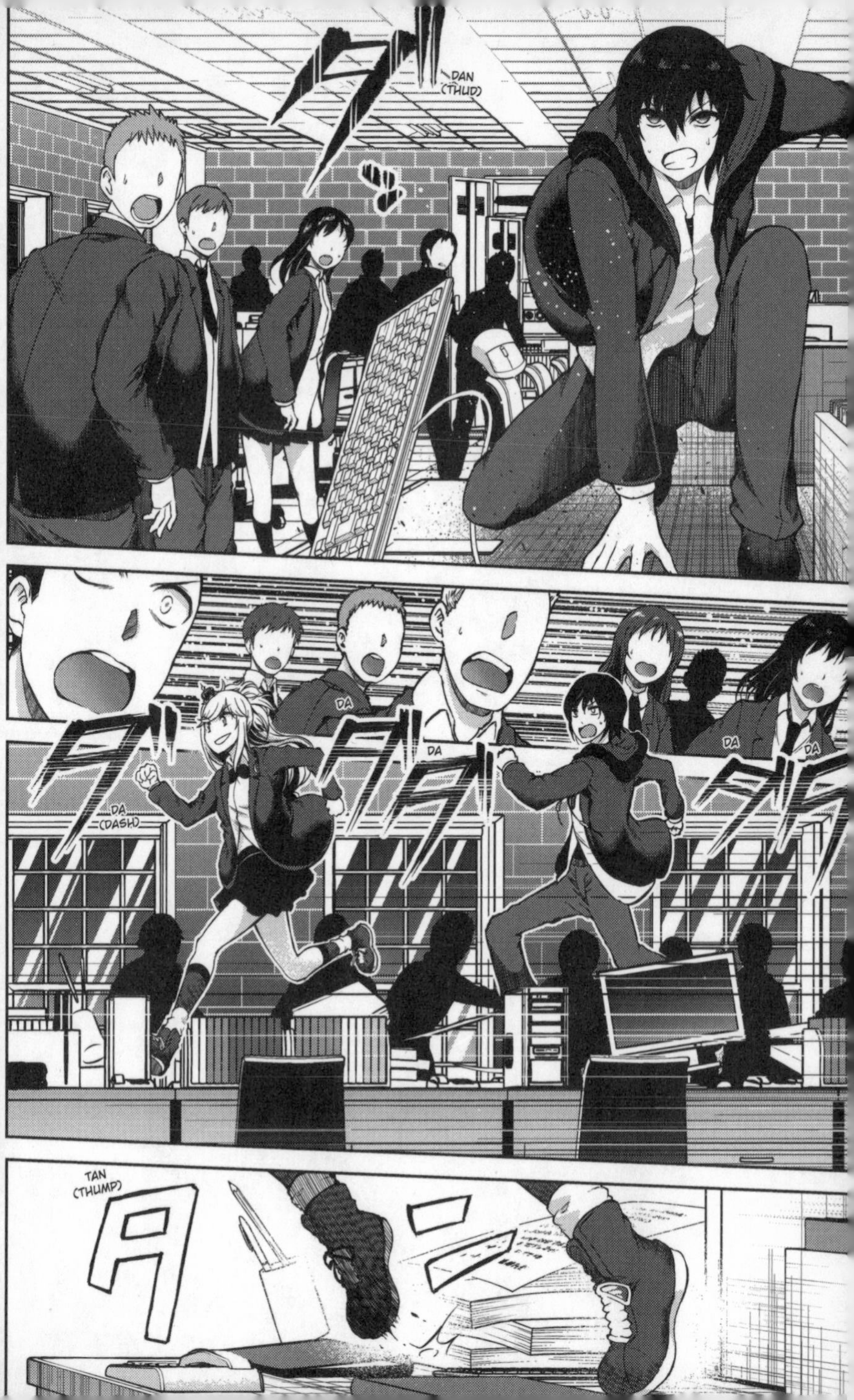
DAN
(THUD)
DA
DA
DA
DA
DA
(DASH)
TAN
(THUMP)

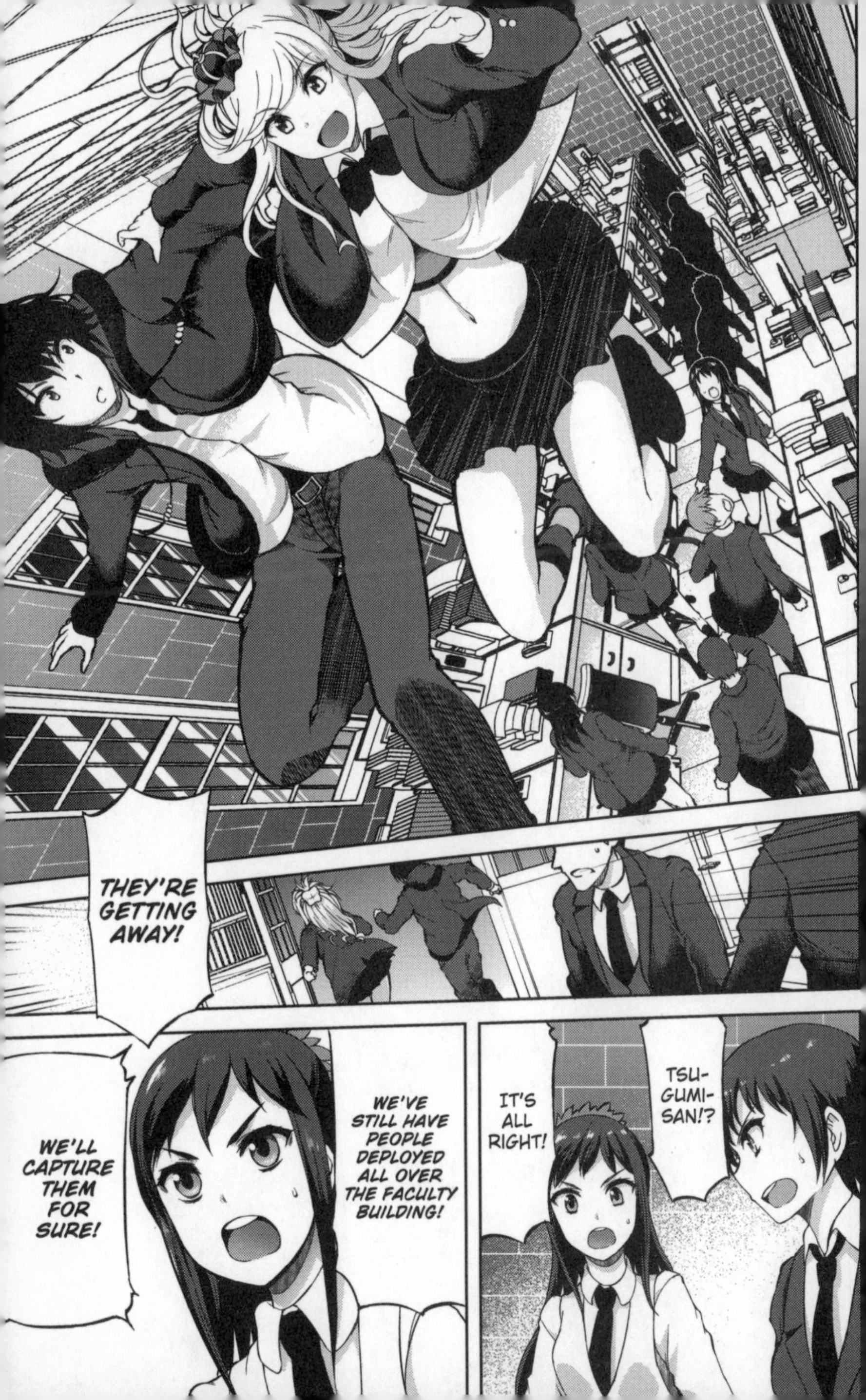
THEY'RE GETTING AWAY!
TSU-GUMI-SAN!?
IT'S ALL RIGHT!
WE'VE STILL HAVE PEOPLE DEPLOYED ALL OVER THE FACULTY BUILDING!
WE'LL CAPTURE THEM FOR SURE!

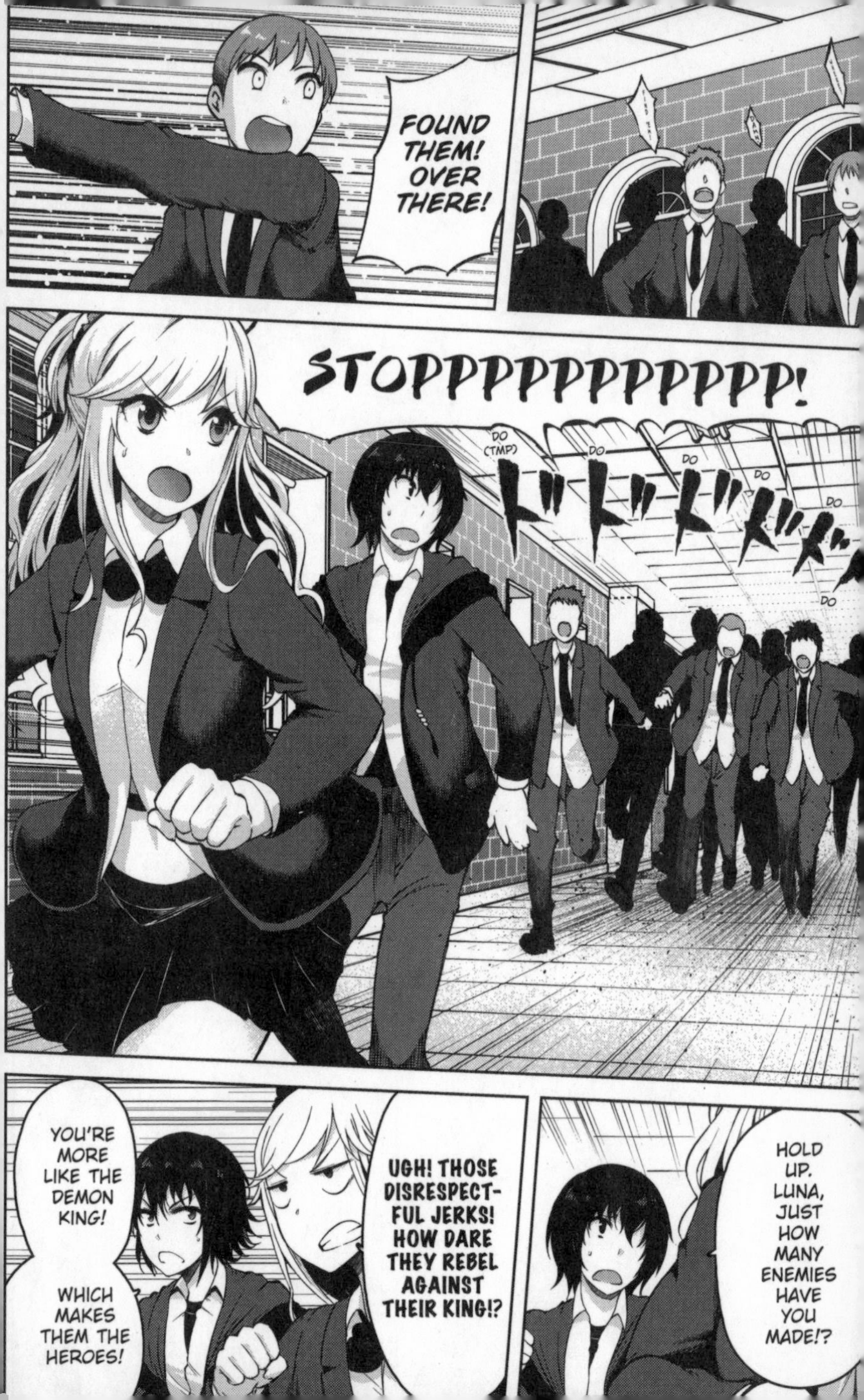
DAMN!
FIND 'EM!
FOUND THEM! OVER THERE!
STOPPPPPPPPPPPPP!
DO (TMP) DO DO DO DO DO
ドドドドドド
HOLD UP. LUNA, JUST HOW MANY ENEMIES HAVE YOU MADE!?
UGH! THOSE DISRESPECT-FUL JERKS! HOW DARE THEY REBEL AGAINST THEIR KING!?
YOU'RE MORE LIKE THE DEMON KING!
WHICH MAKES THEM THE HEROES!

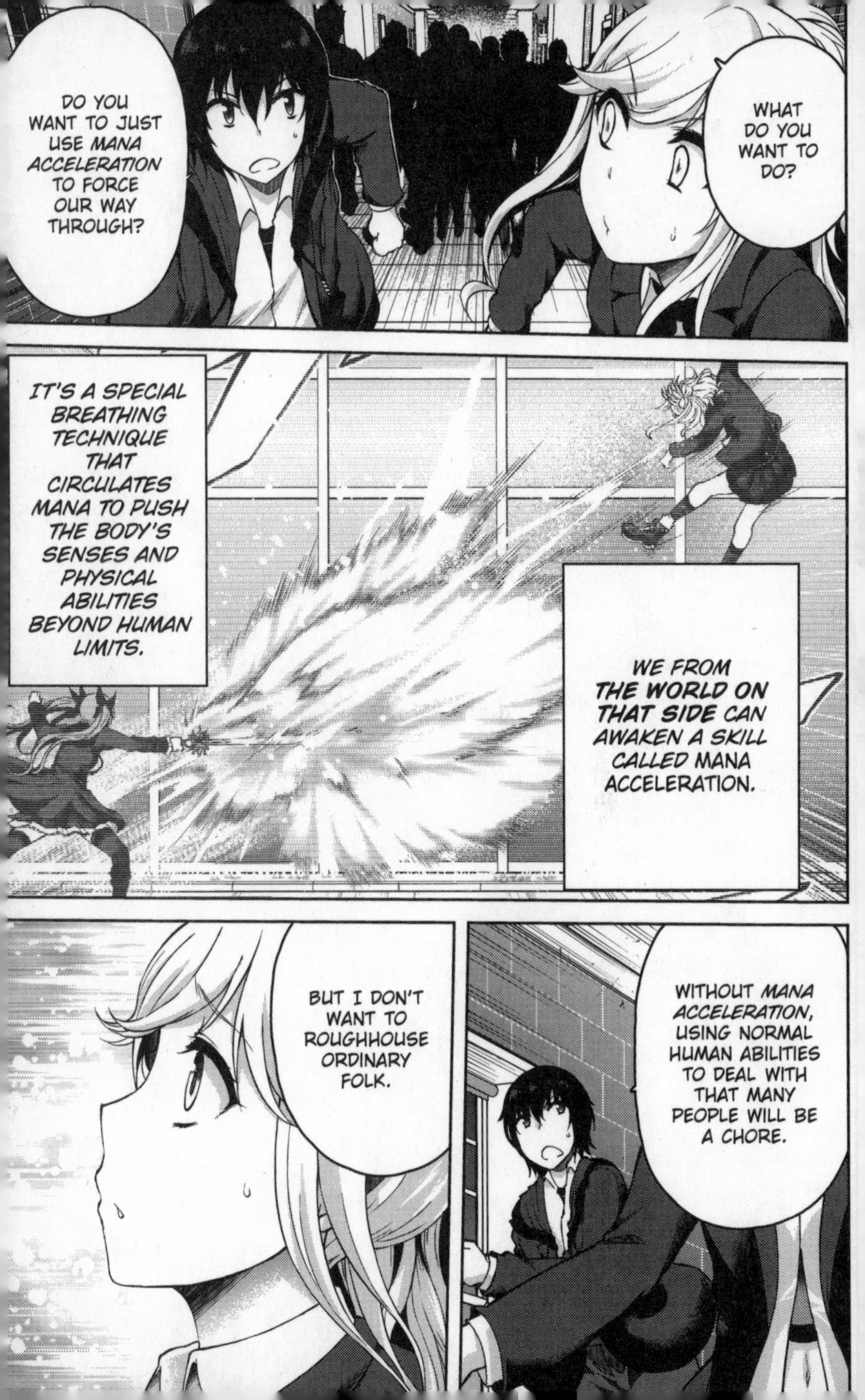
WHAT DO YOU WANT TO DO?
DO YOU WANT TO JUST USE MANA ACCELERATION TO FORCE OUR WAY THROUGH?
WE FROM THE WORLD ON THAT SIDE CAN AWAKEN A SKILL CALLED MANA ACCELERATION.
IT'S A SPECIAL BREATHING TECHNIQUE THAT CIRCULATES MANA TO PUSH THE BODY'S SENSES AND PHYSICAL ABILITIES BEYOND HUMAN LIMITS.
WITHOUT MANA ACCELERATION, USING NORMAL HUMAN ABILITIES TO DEAL WITH THAT MANY PEOPLE WILL BE A CHORE.
BUT I DON'T WANT TO ROUGHHOUSE ORDINARY FOLK.

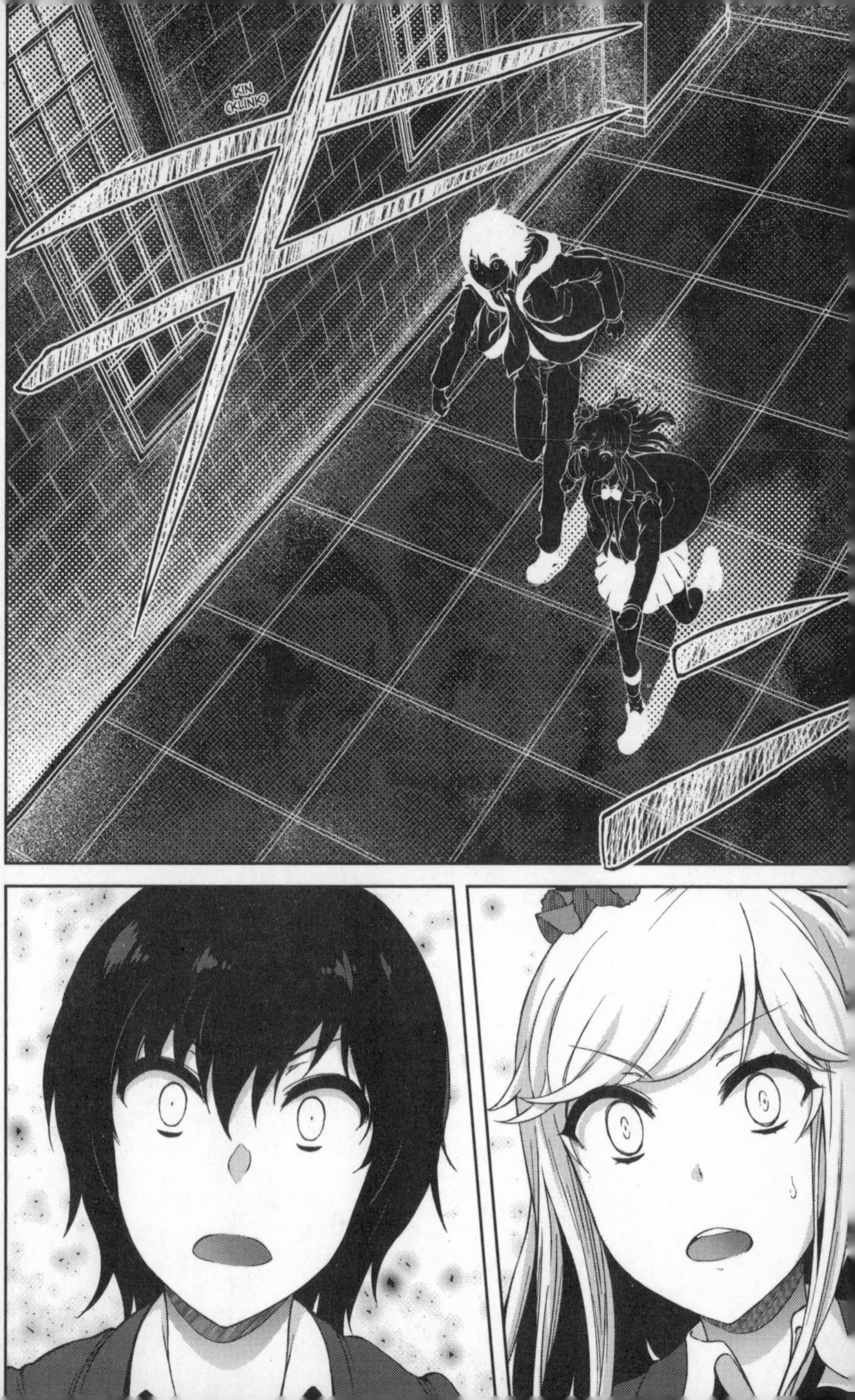
KIN
(KLINK)

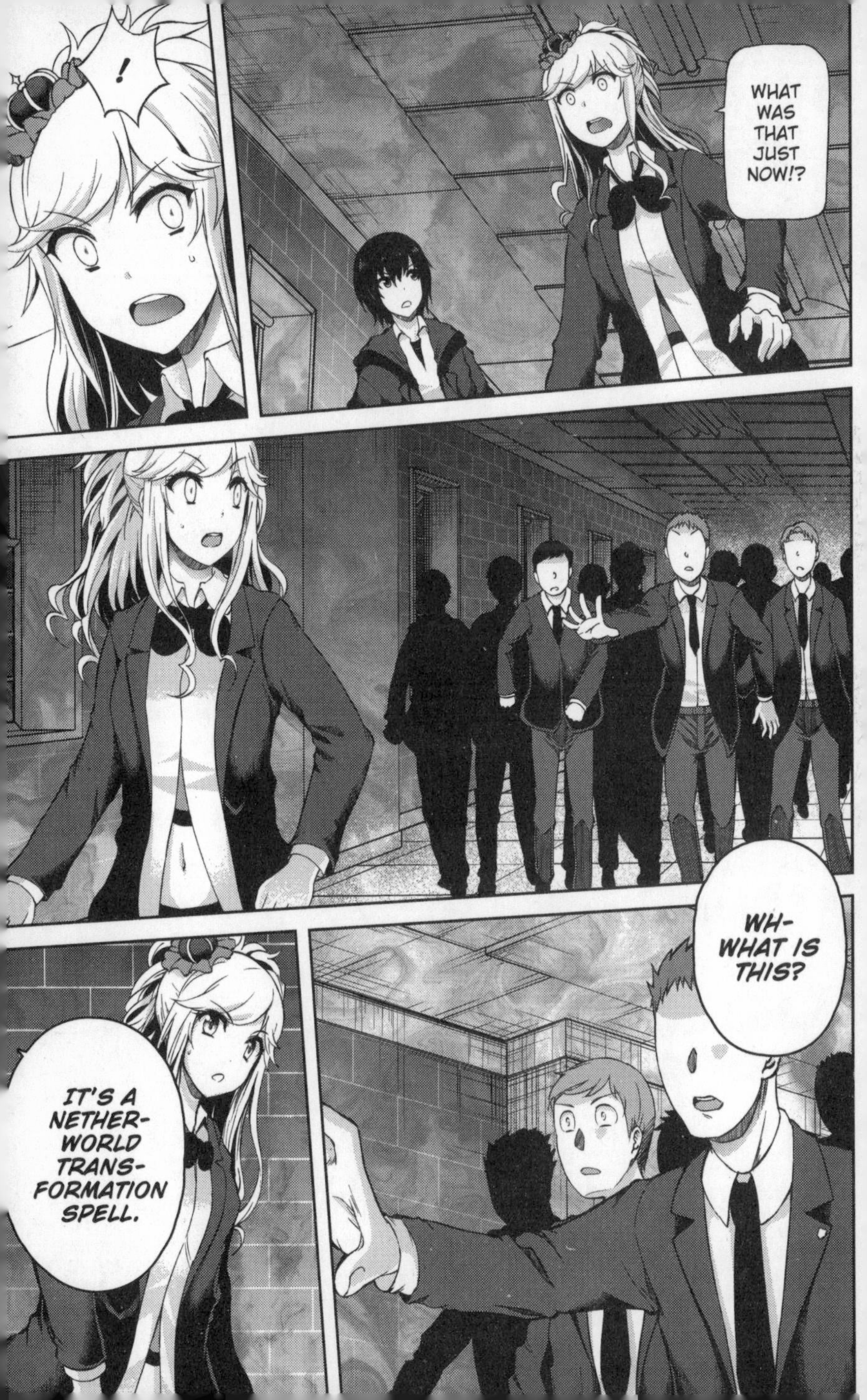
WHAT WAS THAT JUST NOW!?
!
WH- WHAT IS THIS?
IT'S A NETHER-WORLD TRANS-FORMATION SPELL.

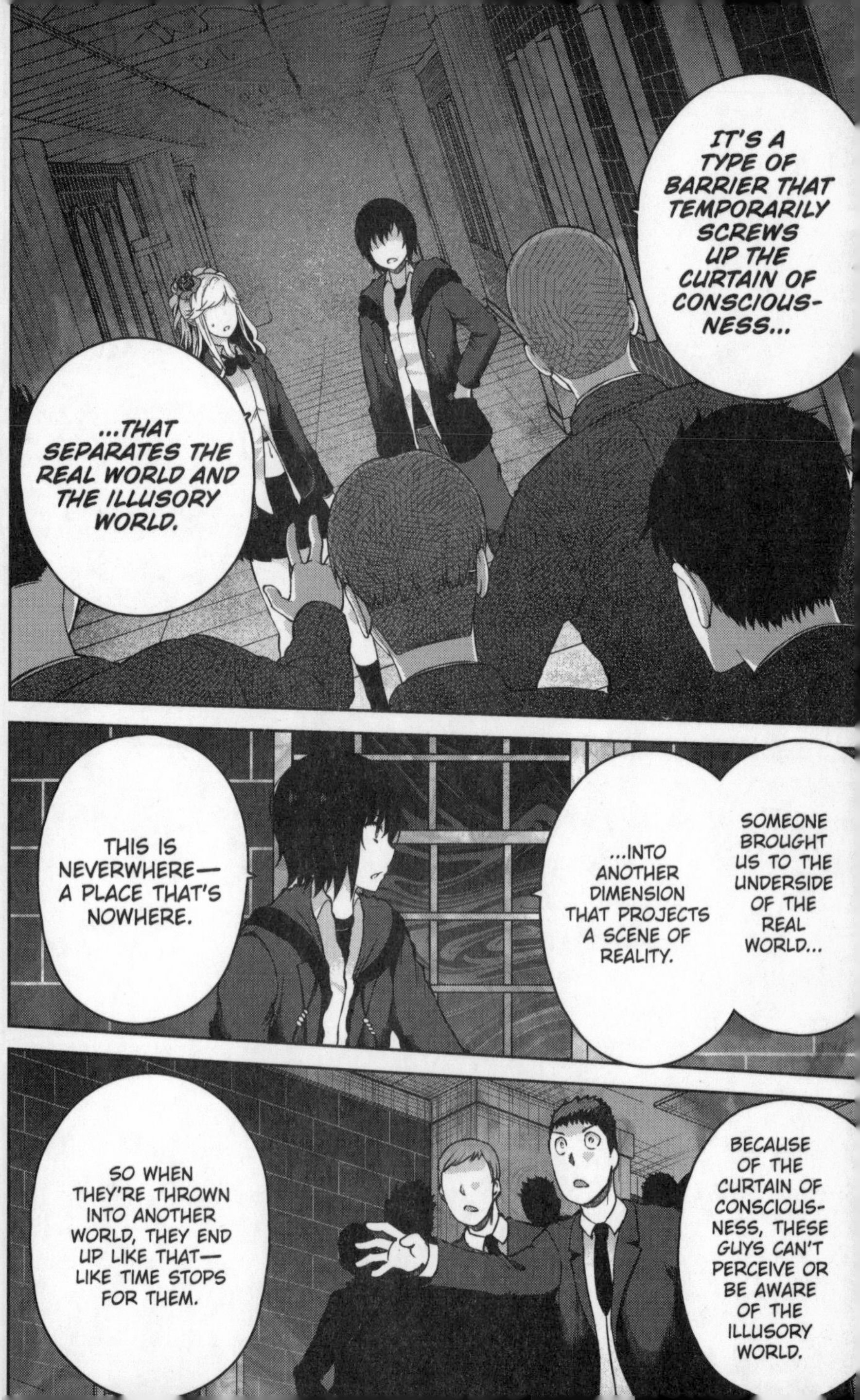
IT'S A TYPE OF BARRIER THAT TEMPORARILY SCREWS UP THE CURTAIN OF CONSCIOUS-NESS...
...THAT SEPARATES THE REAL WORLD AND THE ILLUSORY WORLD.
SOMEONE BROUGHT US TO THE UNDERSIDE OF THE REAL WORLD...
...INTO ANOTHER DIMENSION THAT PROJECTS A SCENE OF REALITY.
THIS IS NEVERWHERE— A PLACE THAT'S NOWHERE.
BECAUSE OF THE CURTAIN OF CONSCIOUS-NESS, THESE GUYS CAN'T PERCEIVE OR BE AWARE OF THE ILLUSORY WORLD.
SO WHEN THEY'RE THROWN INTO ANOTHER WORLD, THEY END UP LIKE THAT— LIKE TIME STOPS FOR THEM.

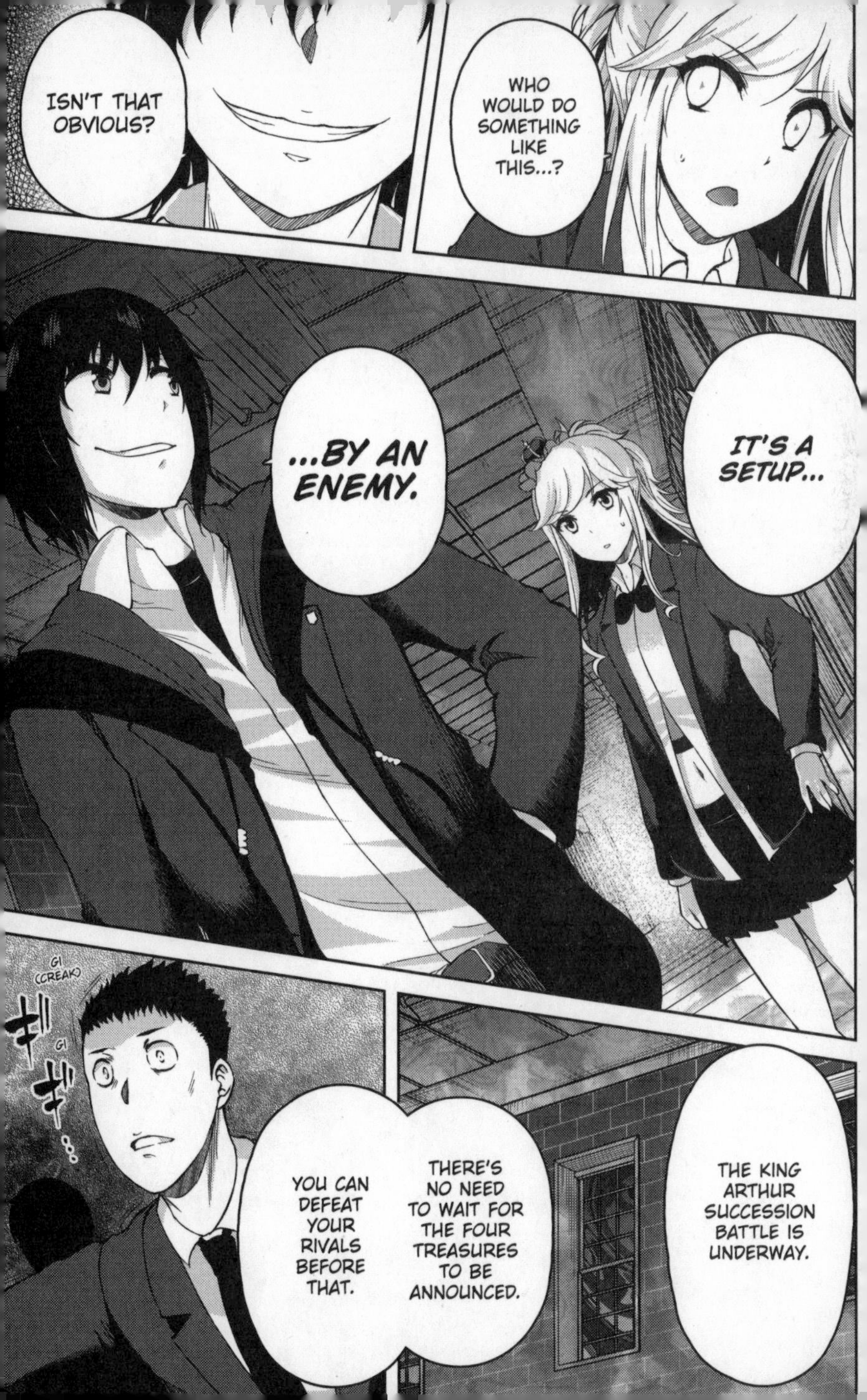
WHO WOULD DO SOMETHING LIKE THIS...?
ISN'T THAT OBVIOUS?
IT'S A SETUP...
...BY AN ENEMY.
THE KING ARTHUR SUCCESSION BATTLE IS UNDERWAY.
THERE'S NO NEED TO WAIT FOR THE FOUR TREASURES TO BE ANNOUNCED.
YOU CAN DEFEAT YOUR RIVALS BEFORE THAT.
GI (CREAK)
GI

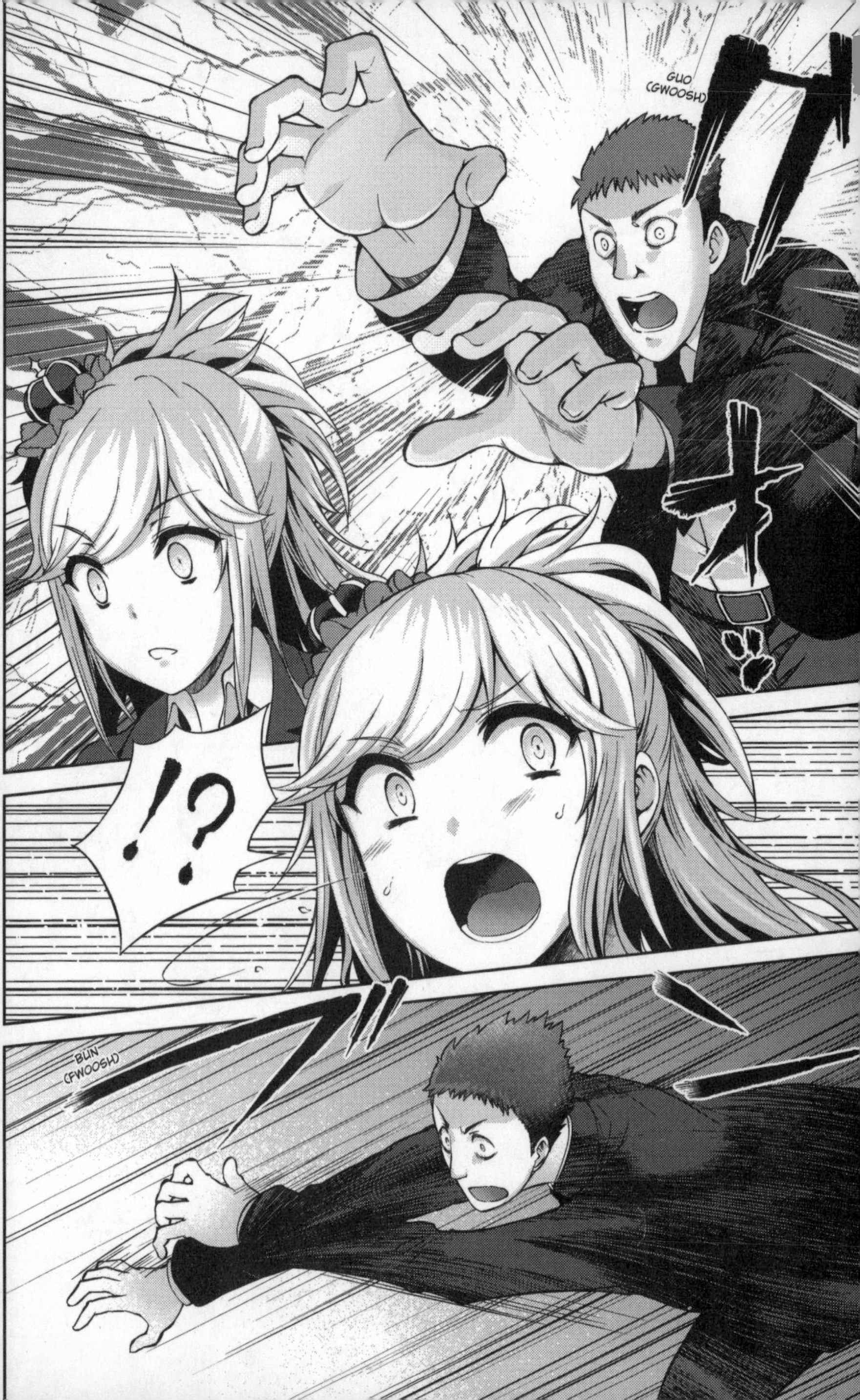
GUO (GWOOSH)
!?
BUN (FWOOSH)

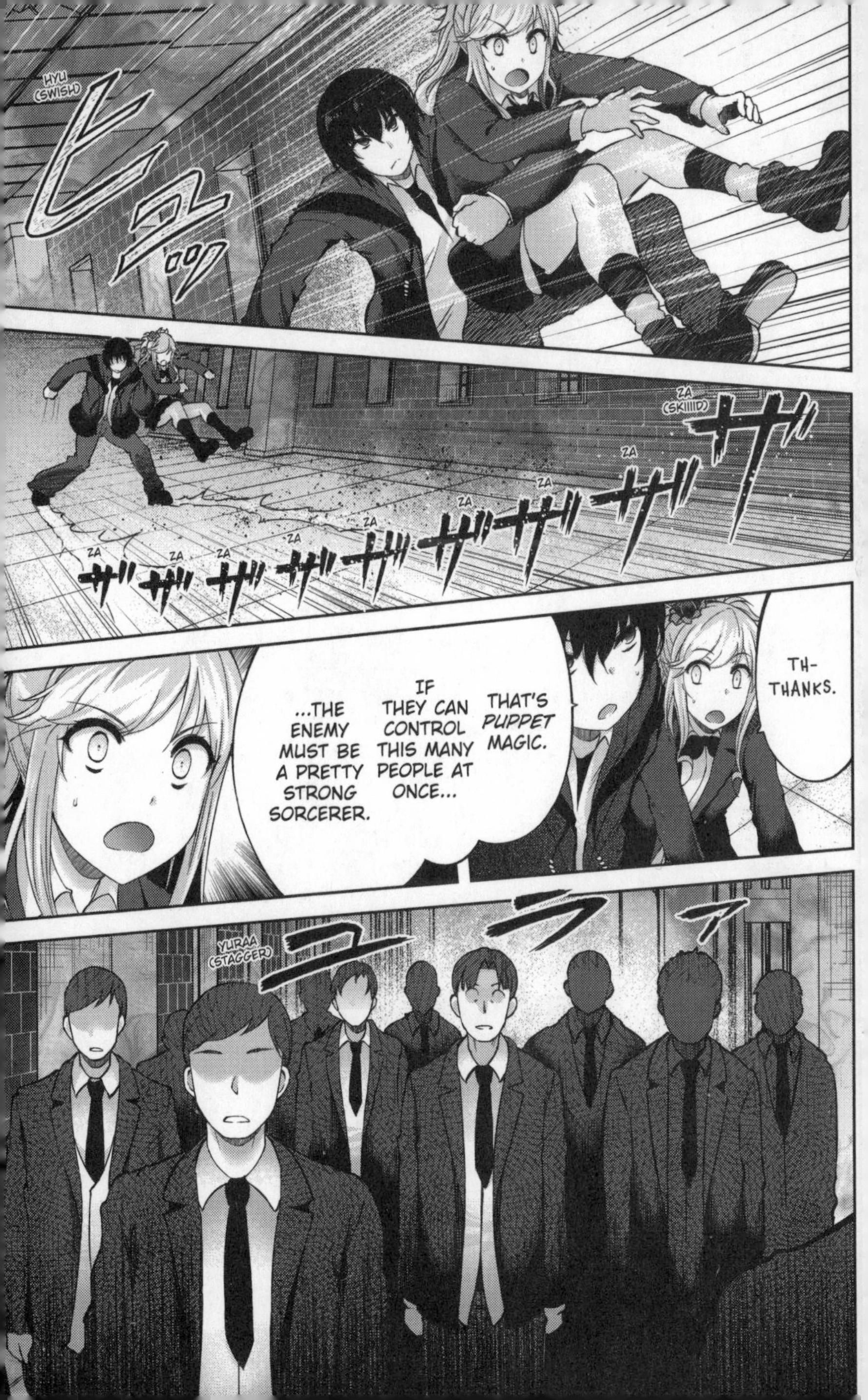
HYU (SWISH)
ZA (SKIIIID)
ZA
ZA
ZA
ZA
ZA
ZA
ZA
ZA
TH-THANKS.
THAT'S PUPPET MAGIC.
IF THEY CAN CONTROL THIS MANY PEOPLE AT ONCE...
...THE ENEMY MUST BE A PRETTY STRONG SORCERER.
YURAA (STAGGER)

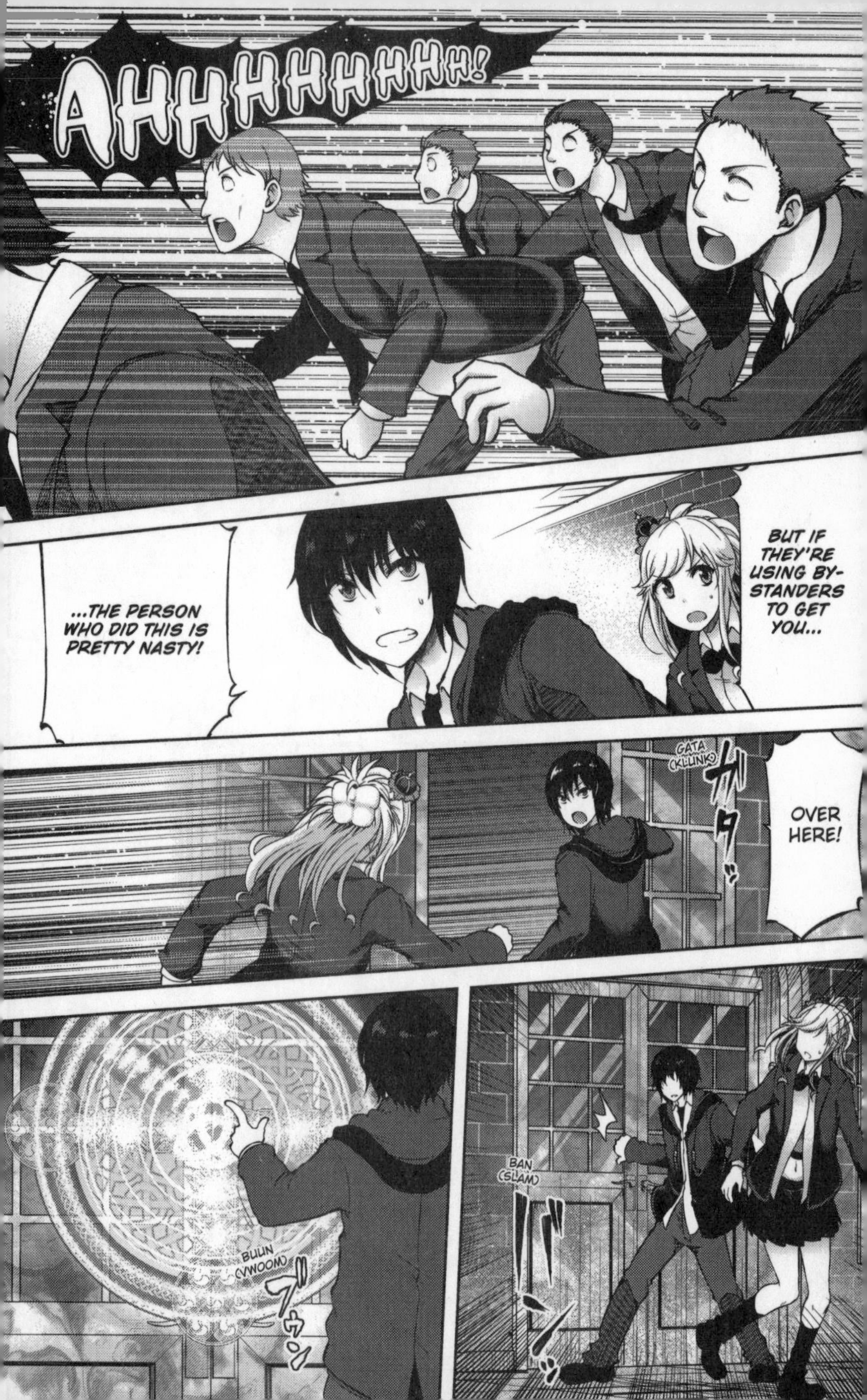
AHHHHHHHHH!
BUT IF THEY'RE USING BY-STANDERS TO GET YOU...
...THE PERSON WHO DID THIS IS PRETTY NASTY!
GATA (KLUNK)
OVER HERE!
BAN (SLAM)
BUUN (VWOOM)

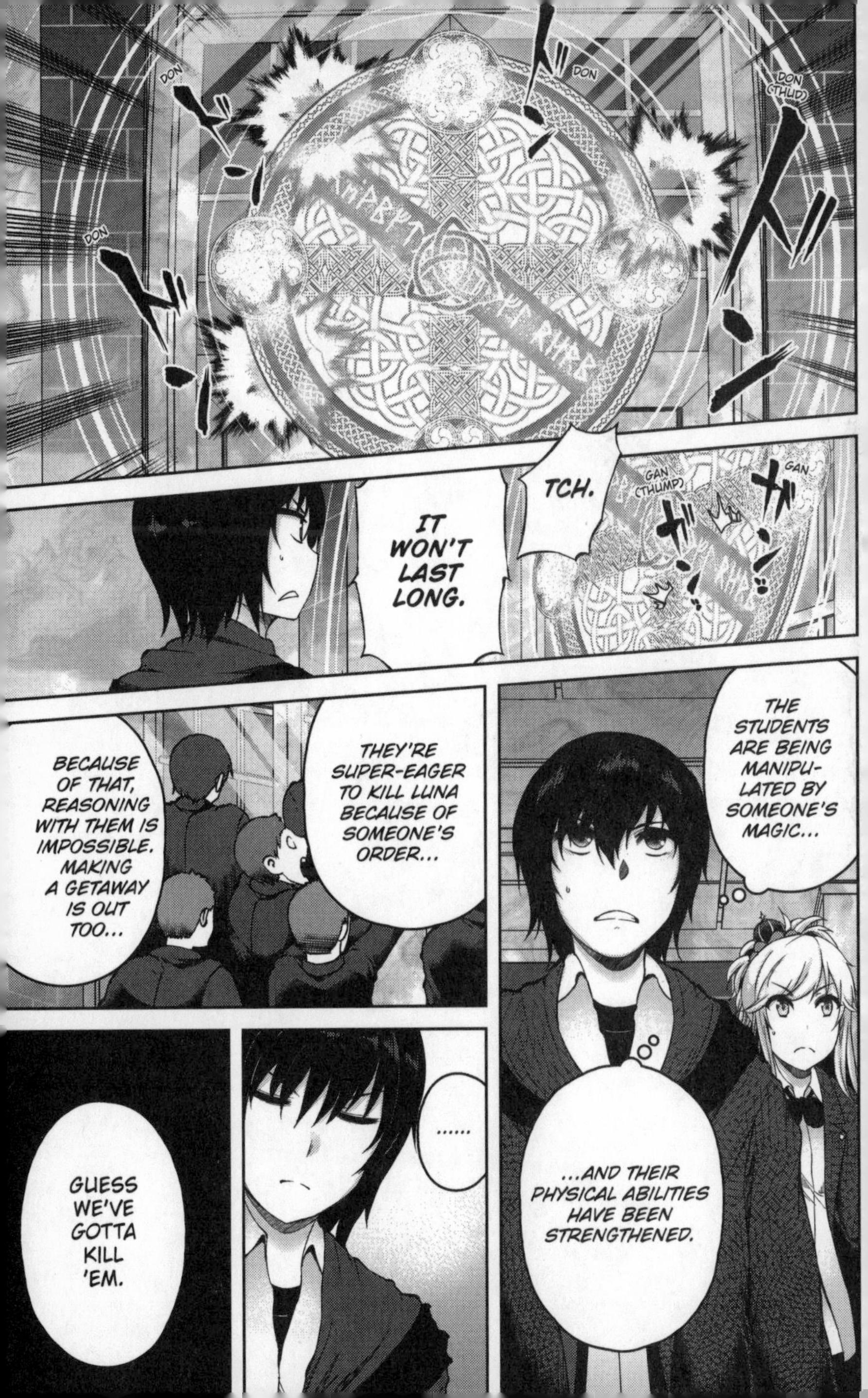
DON (THUD)
DON
DON
DON
GAN
GAN (THUMP)
TCH.
IT WON'T LAST LONG.
THE STUDENTS ARE BEING MANIPU-LATED BY SOMEONE'S MAGIC...
...AND THEIR PHYSICAL ABILITIES HAVE BEEN STRENGTHENED.
THEY'RE SUPER-EAGER TO KILL LUNA BECAUSE OF SOMEONE'S ORDER...
BECAUSE OF THAT, REASONING WITH THEM IS IMPOSSIBLE. MAKING A GETAWAY IS OUT TOO...
......
GUESS WE'VE GOTTA KILL 'EM.

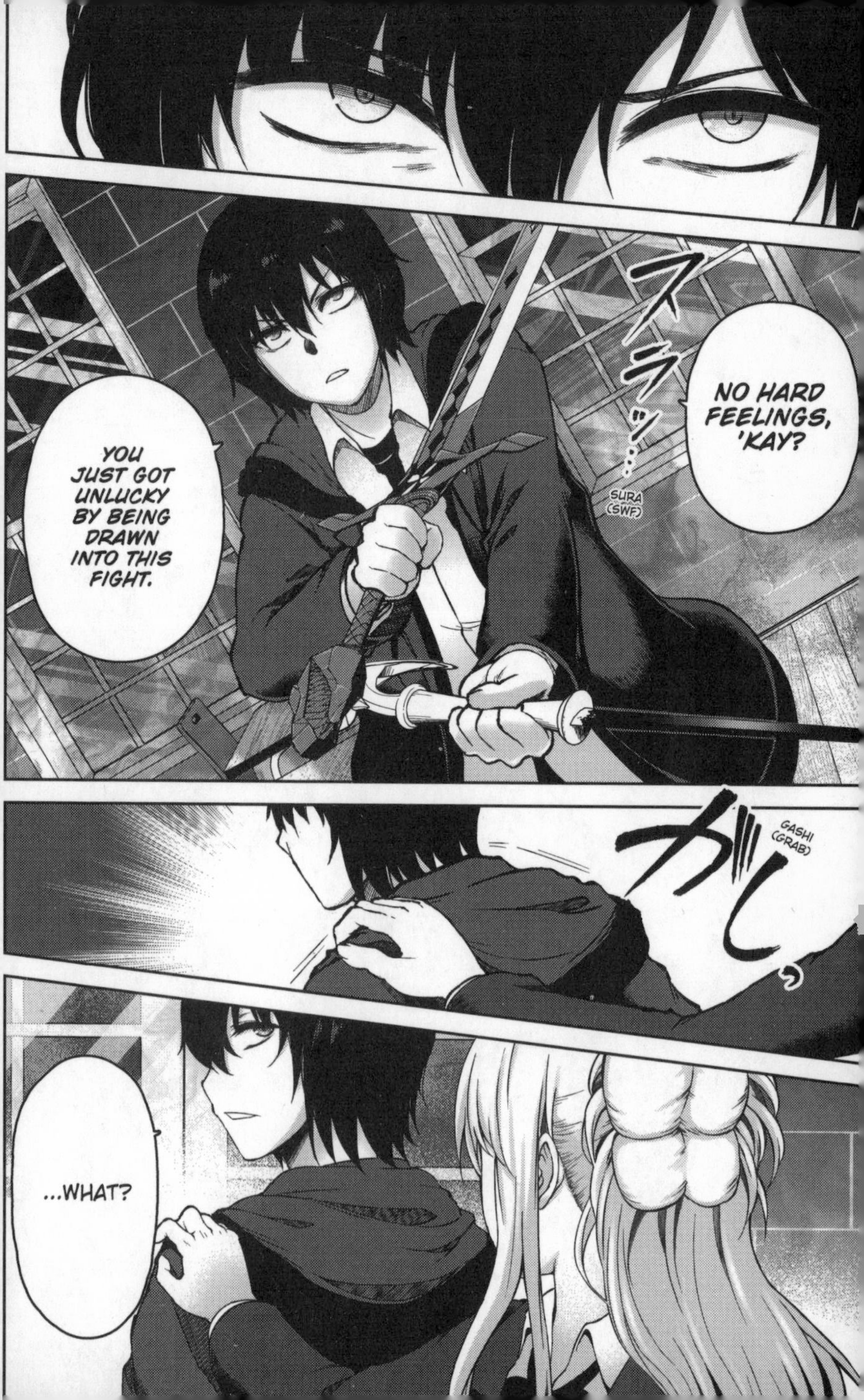
NO HARD FEELINGS, 'KAY?
スラッ…
SURA (SWF)
YOU JUST GOT UNLUCKY BY BEING DRAWN INTO THIS FIGHT.
ガシ、
GASHI (GRAB)
...WHAT?

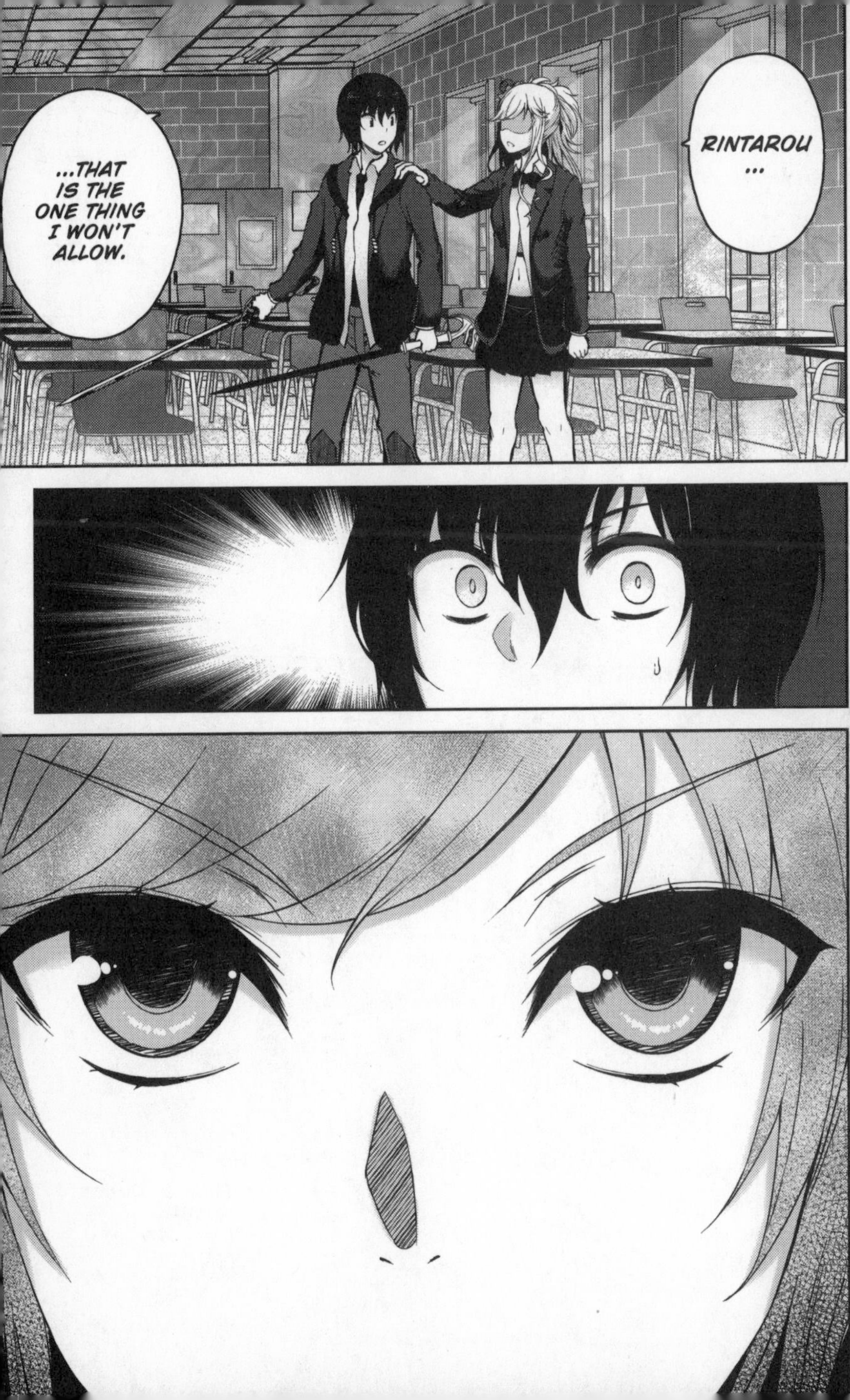
RINTAROU ...
...THAT IS THE ONE THING I WON'T ALLOW.

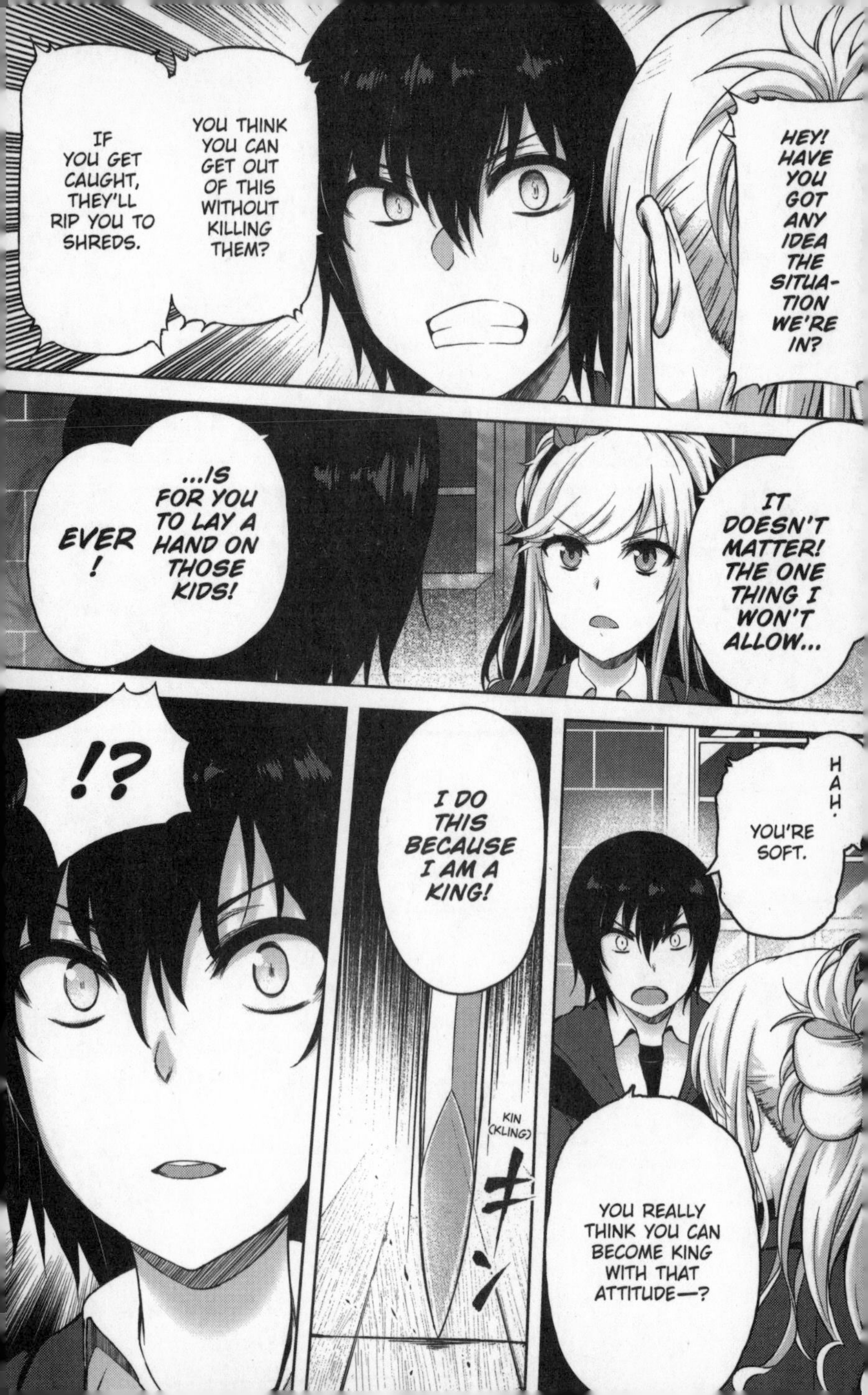
HEY! HAVE YOU GOT ANY IDEA THE SITUATION WE'RE IN?
YOU THINK YOU CAN GET OUT OF THIS WITHOUT KILLING THEM?
IF YOU GET CAUGHT, THEY'LL RIP YOU TO SHREDS.
IT DOESN'T MATTER! THE ONE THING I WON'T ALLOW...
...IS FOR YOU TO LAY A HAND ON THOSE KIDS!
EVER!
HAH.
YOU'RE SOFT.
YOU REALLY THINK YOU CAN BECOME KING WITH THAT ATTITUDE—?
I DO THIS BECAUSE I AM A KING!
KIN (KLING)
!?

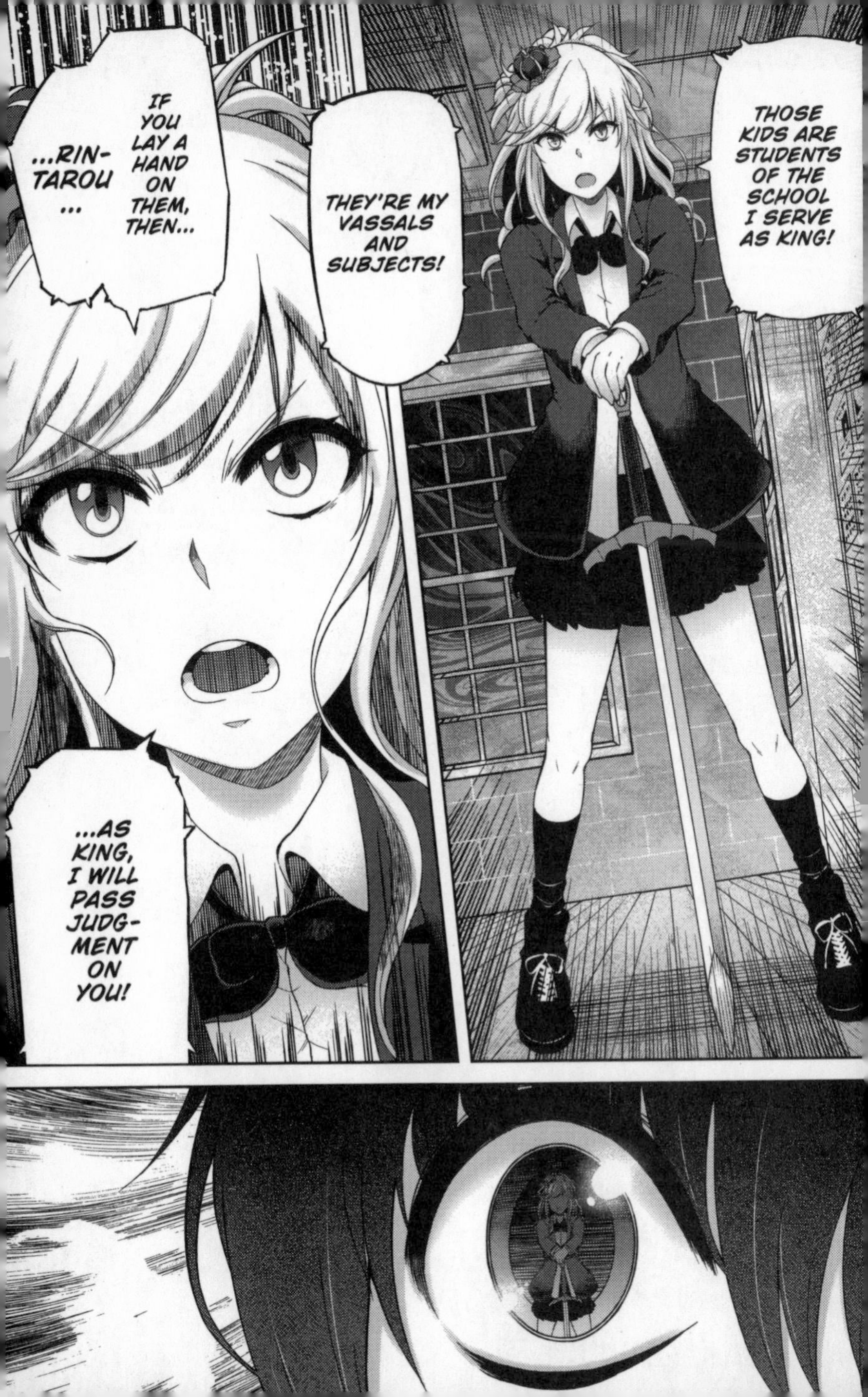
THOSE KIDS ARE STUDENTS OF THE SCHOOL I SERVE AS KING!
THEY'RE MY VASSALS AND SUBJECTS!
IF YOU LAY A HAND ON THEM, THEN...
...RIN-TAROU...
...AS KING, I WILL PASS JUDG-MENT ON YOU!

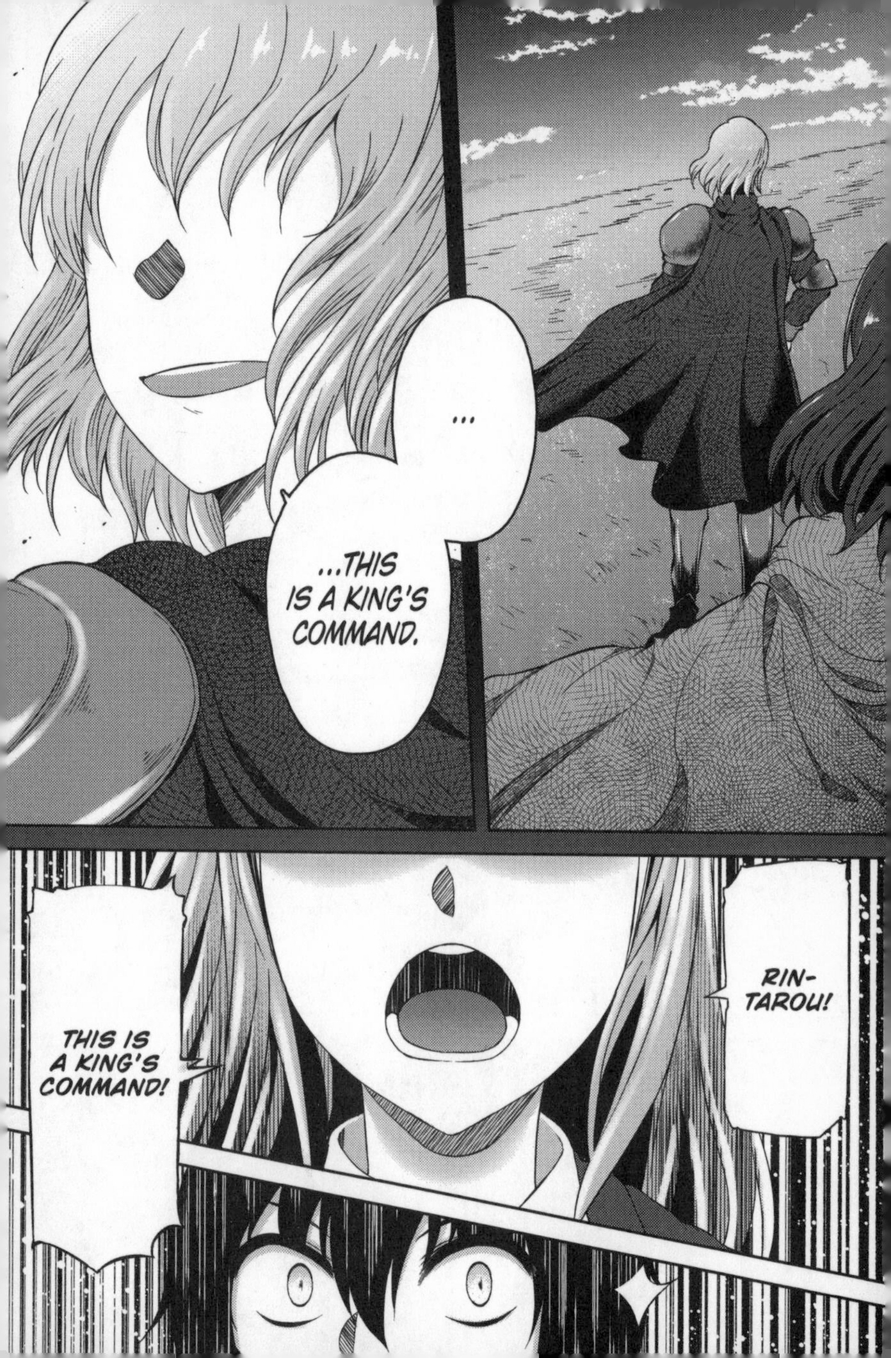
...
...THIS IS A KING'S COMMAND.
RIN-TAROU!
THIS IS A KING'S COMMAND!

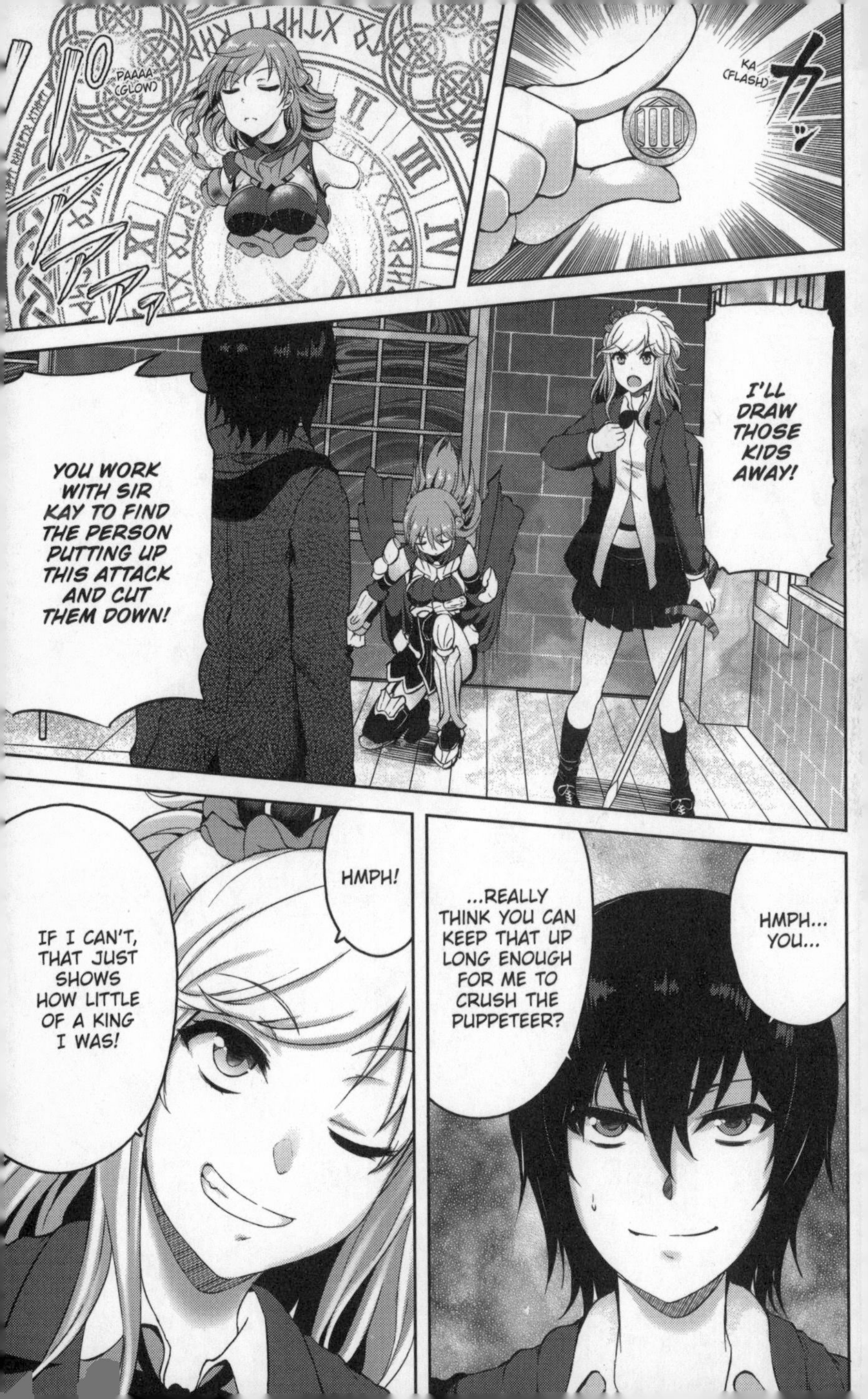
KA (FLASH)
PAAAA (GLOW)
I'LL DRAW THOSE KIDS AWAY!
YOU WORK WITH SIR KAY TO FIND THE PERSON PUTTING UP THIS ATTACK AND CUT THEM DOWN!
HMPH... YOU...
...REALLY THINK YOU CAN KEEP THAT UP LONG ENOUGH FOR ME TO CRUSH THE PUPPETEER?
HMPH!
IF I CAN'T, THAT JUST SHOWS HOW LITTLE OF A KING I WAS!

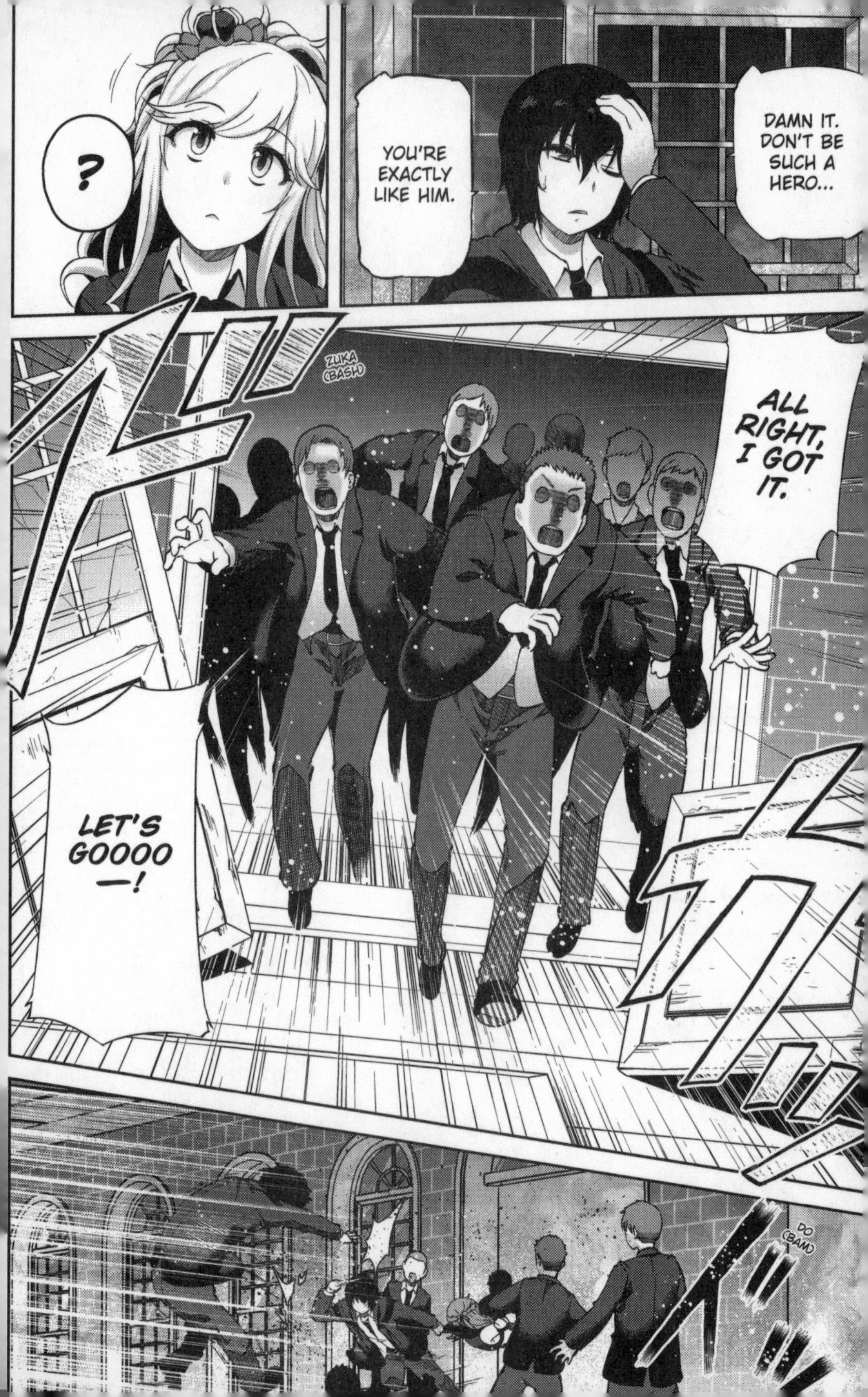
DAMN IT. DON'T BE SUCH A HERO...
YOU'RE EXACTLY LIKE HIM.
?
ALL RIGHT, I GOT IT.
ZUKA (BASH)
LET'S GOOOO—!
DO (BAM)

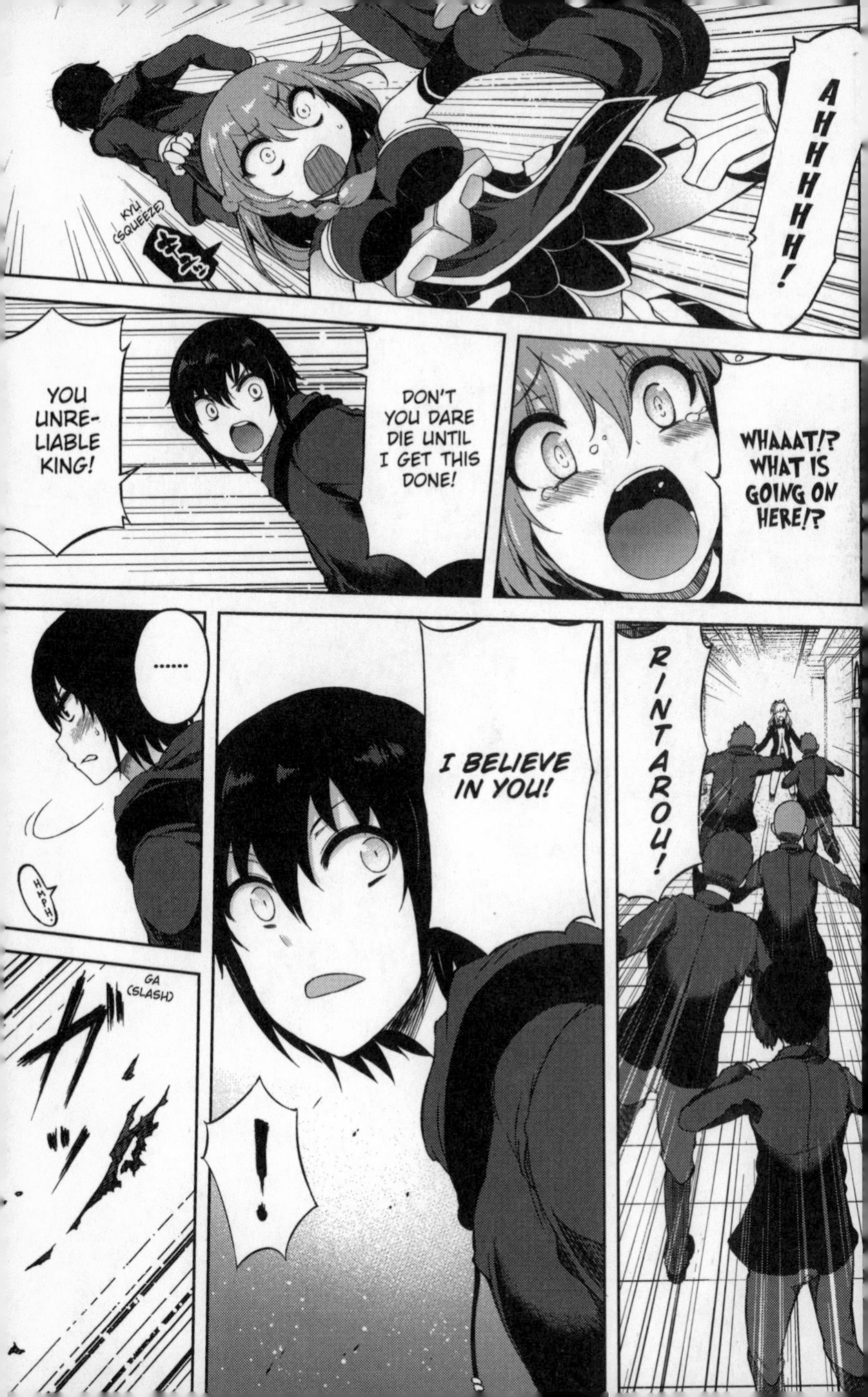
AHHHHHH!
KYU (SQUEEZE)
WHAAAT!? WHAT IS GOING ON HERE!?
DON'T YOU DARE DIE UNTIL I GET THIS DONE!
YOU UNRE-LIABLE KING!
RINTAROU!
I BELIEVE IN YOU!
!
......
HMPH.
GA (SLASH)

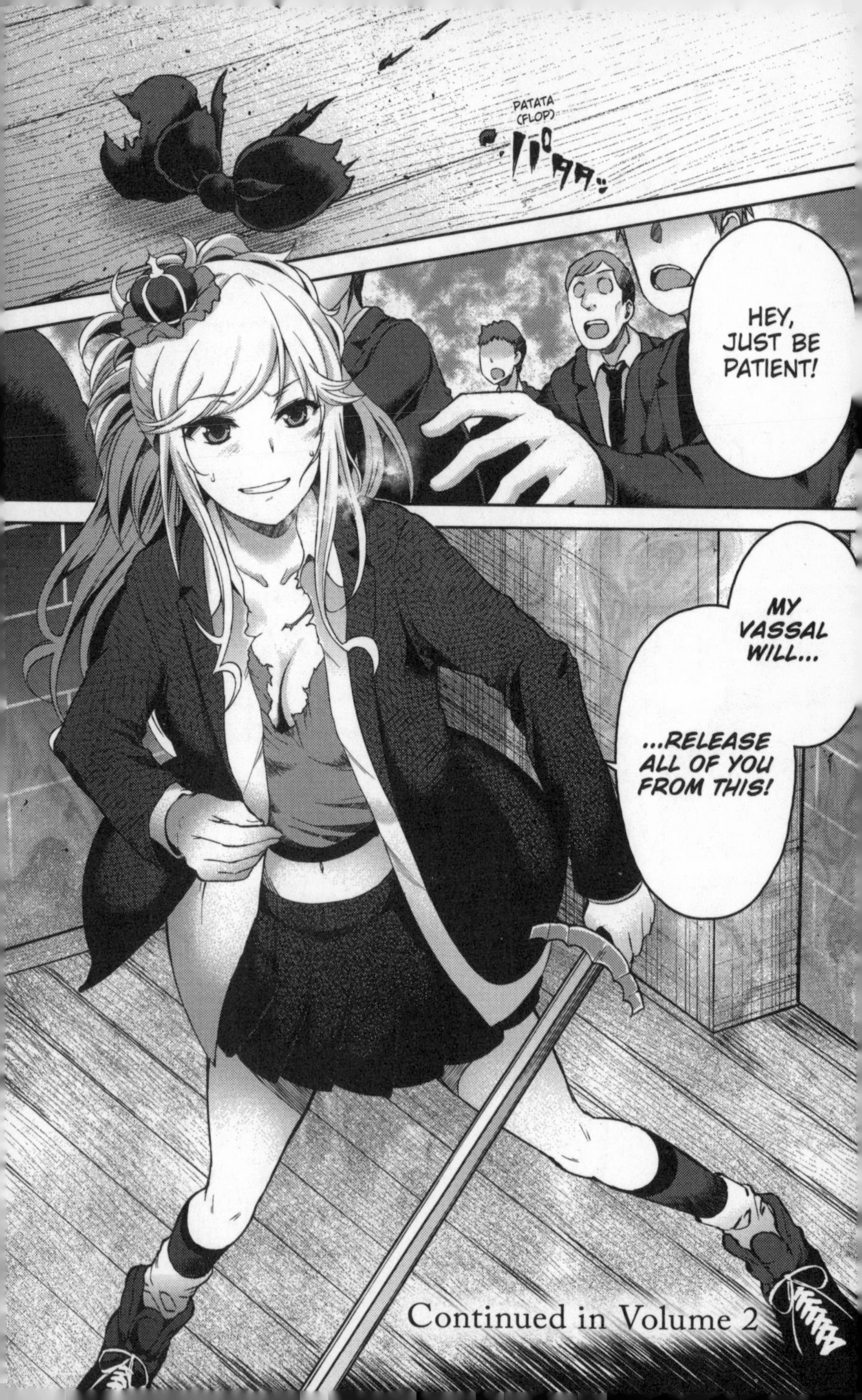
PATATA (FLOP)
HEY, JUST BE PATIENT!
MY VASSAL WILL...
...RELEASE ALL OF YOU FROM THIS!

Continued in Volume 2

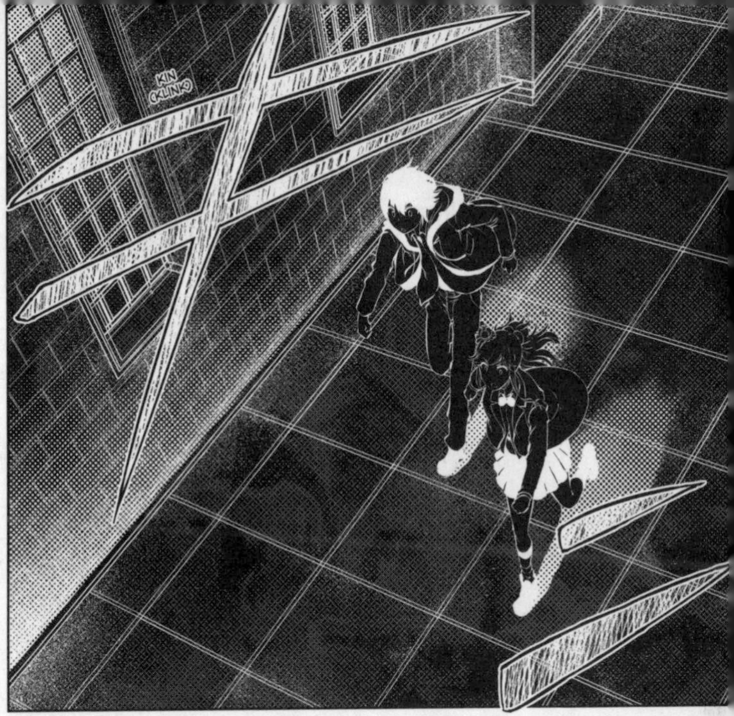
KIN
(KLINK)

LAST
ROUND ARTHURS

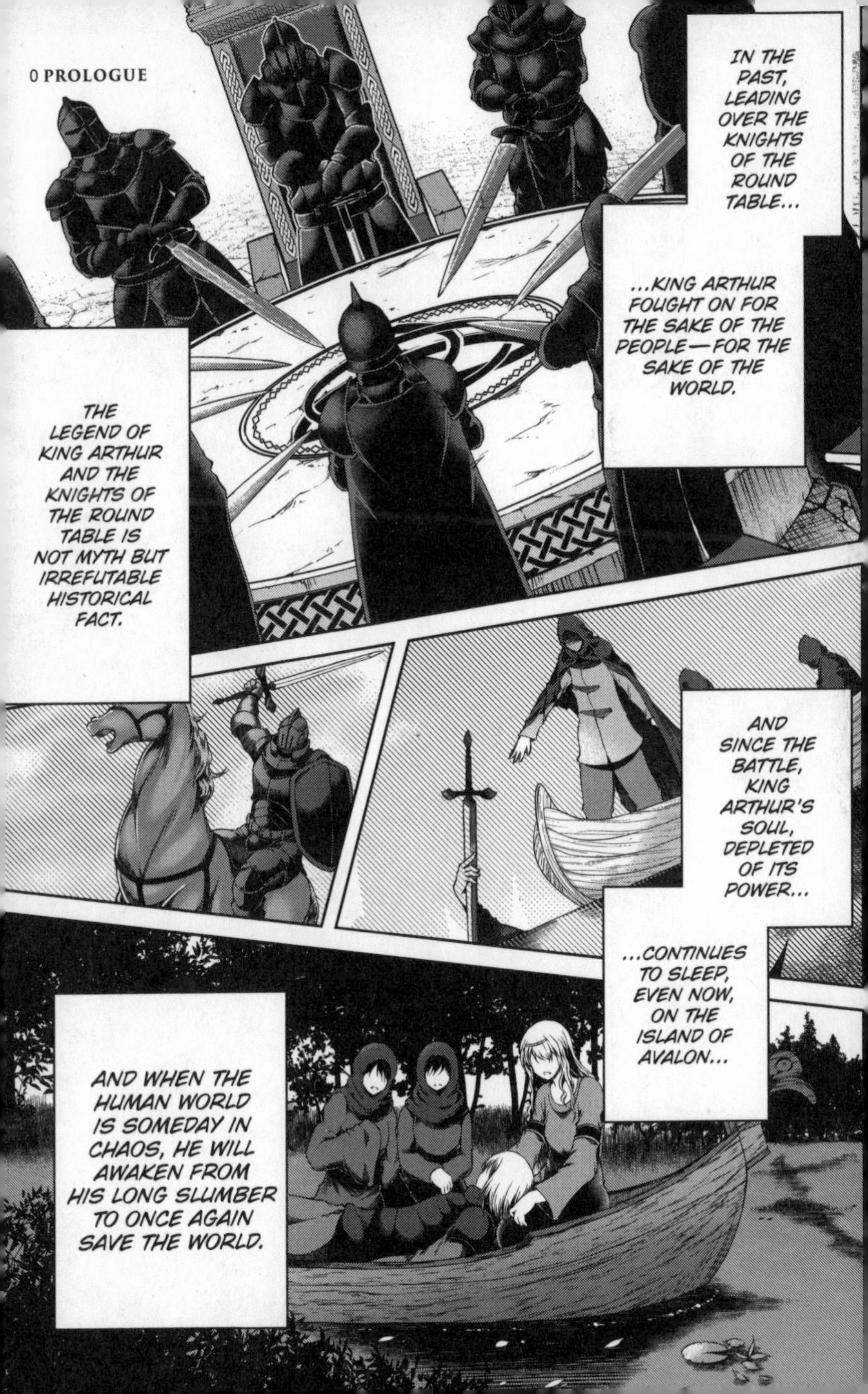
0 PROLOGUE
IN THE PAST, LEADING OVER THE KNIGHTS OF THE ROUND TABLE...
...KING ARTHUR FOUGHT ON FOR THE SAKE OF THE PEOPLE—FOR THE SAKE OF THE WORLD.
THE LEGEND OF KING ARTHUR AND THE KNIGHTS OF THE ROUND TABLE IS NOT MYTH BUT IRREFUTABLE HISTORICAL FACT.
AND SINCE THE BATTLE, KING ARTHUR'S SOUL, DEPLETED OF ITS POWER...
...CONTINUES TO SLEEP, EVEN NOW, ON THE ISLAND OF AVALON...
AND WHEN THE HUMAN WORLD IS SOMEDAY IN CHAOS, HE WILL AWAKEN FROM HIS LONG SLUMBER TO ONCE AGAIN SAVE THE WORLD.

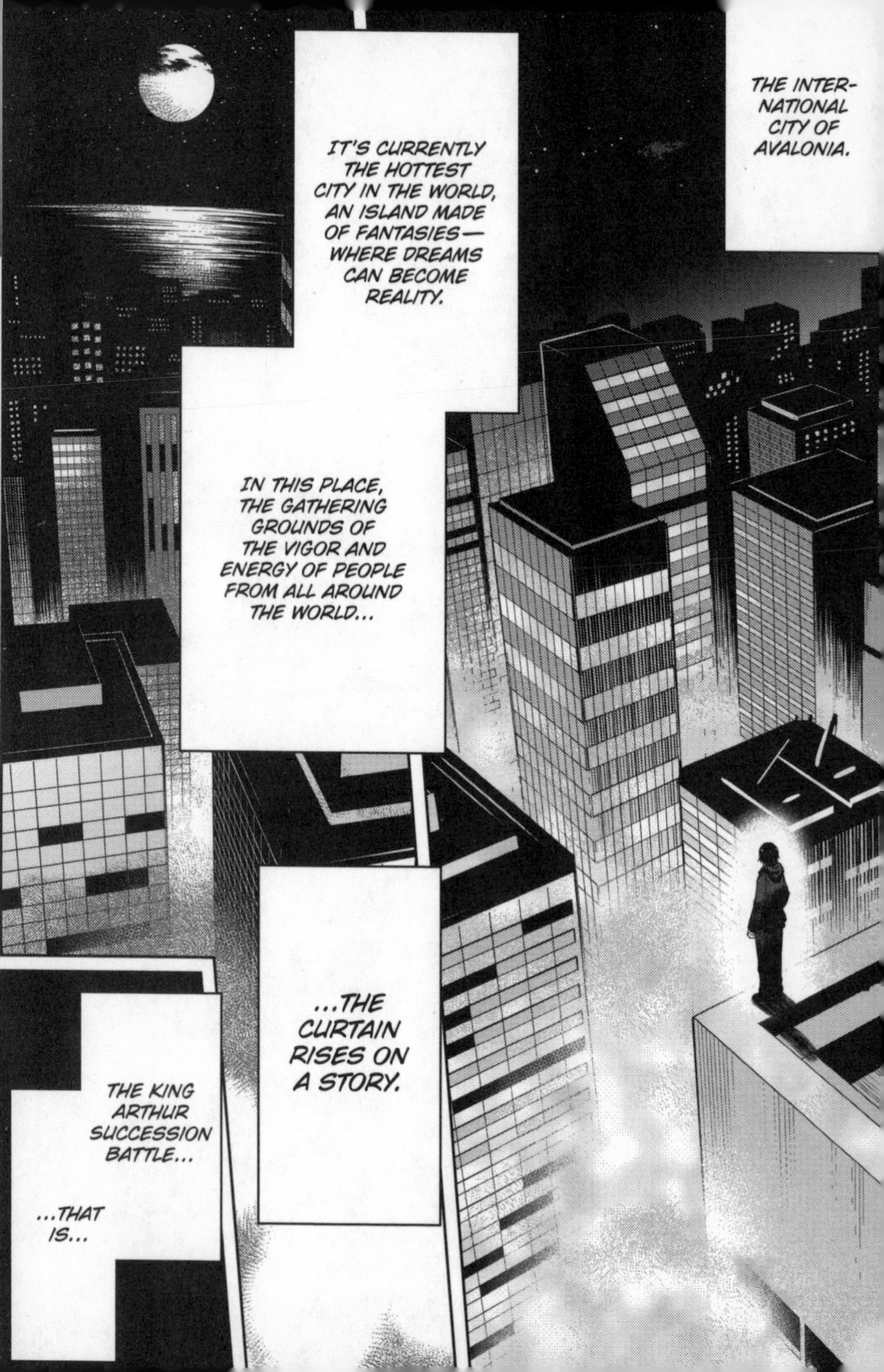
THE INTER-NATIONAL CITY OF AVALONIA.
IT'S CURRENTLY THE HOTTEST CITY IN THE WORLD, AN ISLAND MADE OF FANTASIES—WHERE DREAMS CAN BECOME REALITY.
IN THIS PLACE, THE GATHERING GROUNDS OF THE VIGOR AND ENERGY OF PEOPLE FROM ALL AROUND THE WORLD...
...THE CURTAIN RISES ON A STORY.
THE KING ARTHUR SUCCESSION BATTLE...
...THAT IS...

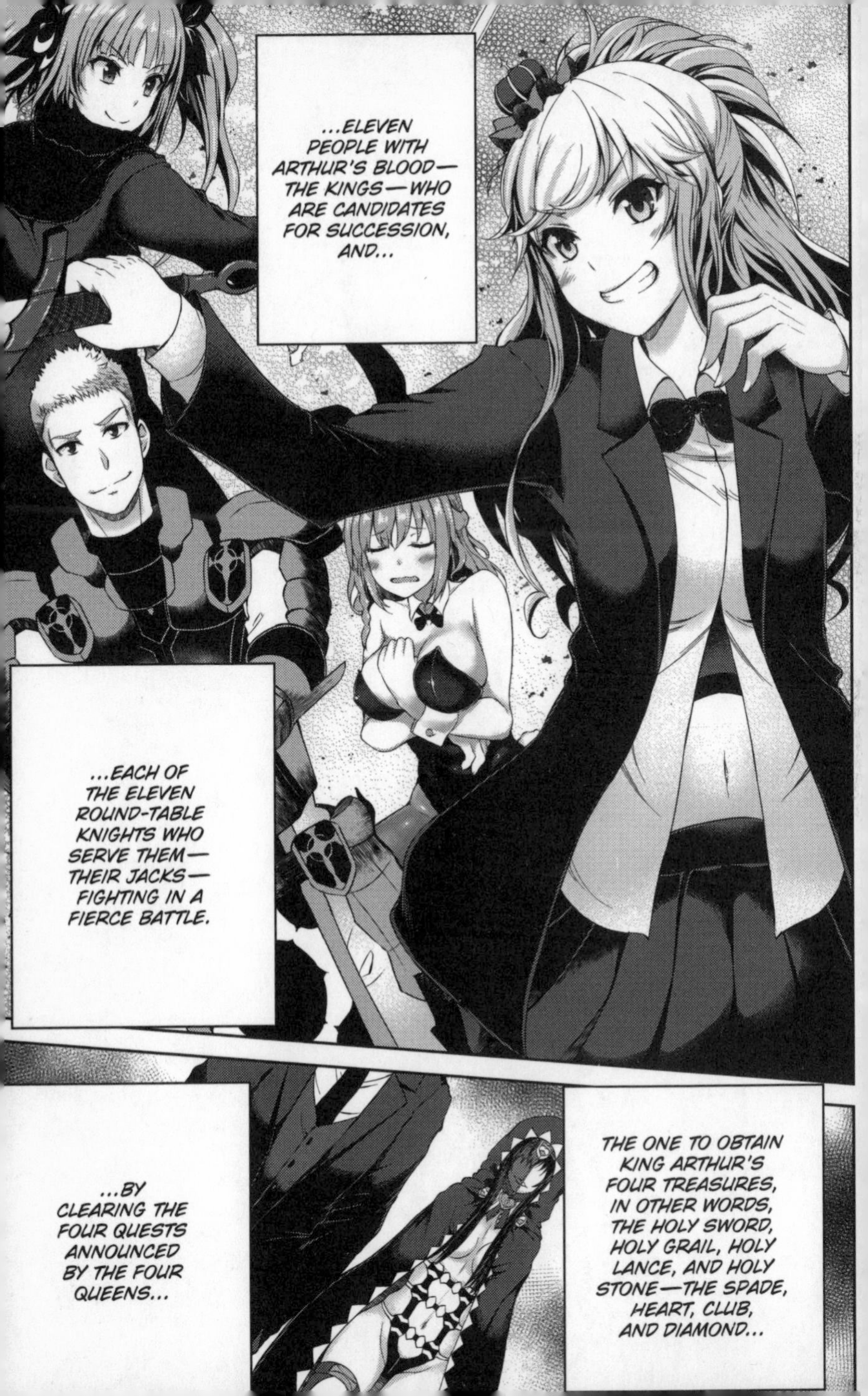
...ELEVEN PEOPLE WITH ARTHUR'S BLOOD—THE KINGS—WHO ARE CANDIDATES FOR SUCCESSION, AND...
...EACH OF THE ELEVEN ROUND-TABLE KNIGHTS WHO SERVE THEM—THEIR JACKS—FIGHTING IN A FIERCE BATTLE.
THE ONE TO OBTAIN KING ARTHUR'S FOUR TREASURES, IN OTHER WORDS, THE HOLY SWORD, HOLY GRAIL, HOLY LANCE, AND HOLY STONE—THE SPADE, HEART, CLUB, AND DIAMOND...
...BY CLEARING THE FOUR QUESTS ANNOUNCED BY THE FOUR QUEENS...

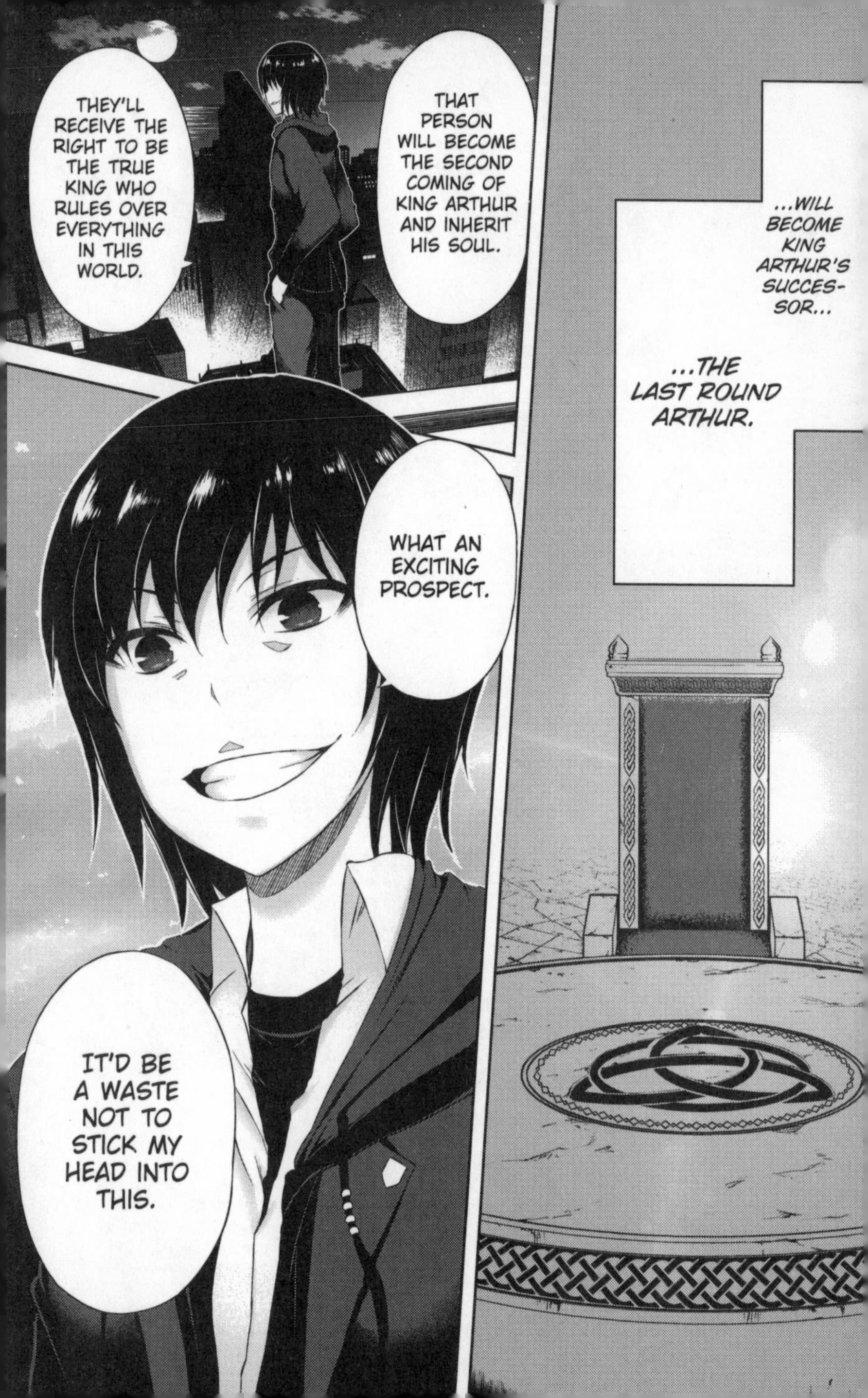
...WILL BECOME KING ARTHUR'S SUCCES-SOR...
...THE LAST ROUND ARTHUR.
THAT PERSON WILL BECOME THE SECOND COMING OF KING ARTHUR AND INHERIT HIS SOUL.
THEY'LL RECEIVE THE RIGHT TO BE THE TRUE KING WHO RULES OVER EVERYTHING IN THIS WORLD.
WHAT AN EXCITING PROSPECT.
IT'D BE A WASTE NOT TO STICK MY HEAD INTO THIS.

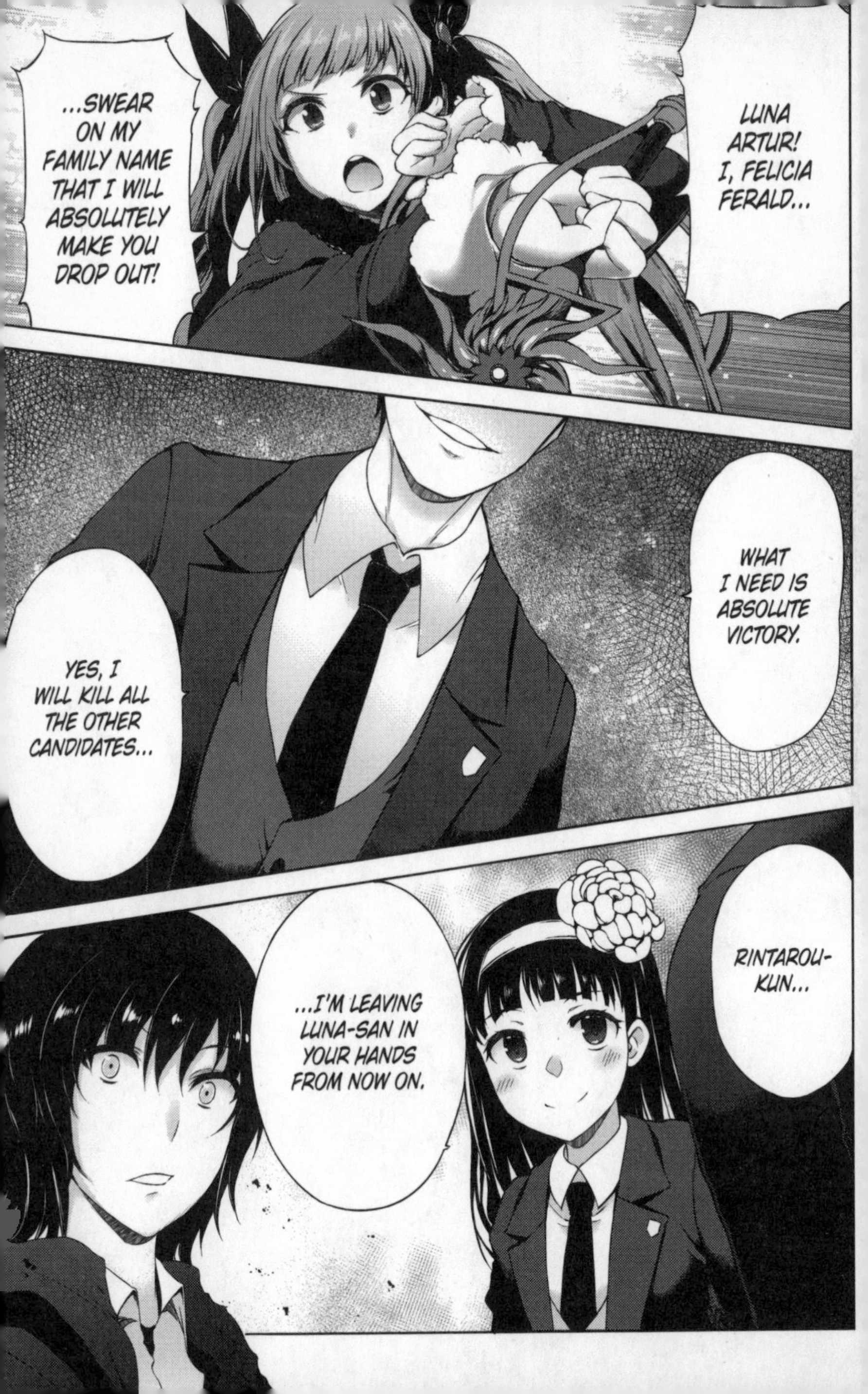
LUNA ARTUR! I, FELICIA FERALD...
...SWEAR ON MY FAMILY NAME THAT I WILL ABSOLUTELY MAKE YOU DROP OUT!
WHAT I NEED IS ABSOLUTE VICTORY.
YES, I WILL KILL ALL THE OTHER CANDIDATES...
RINTAROU-KUN...
...I'M LEAVING LUNA-SAN IN YOUR HANDS FROM NOW ON.

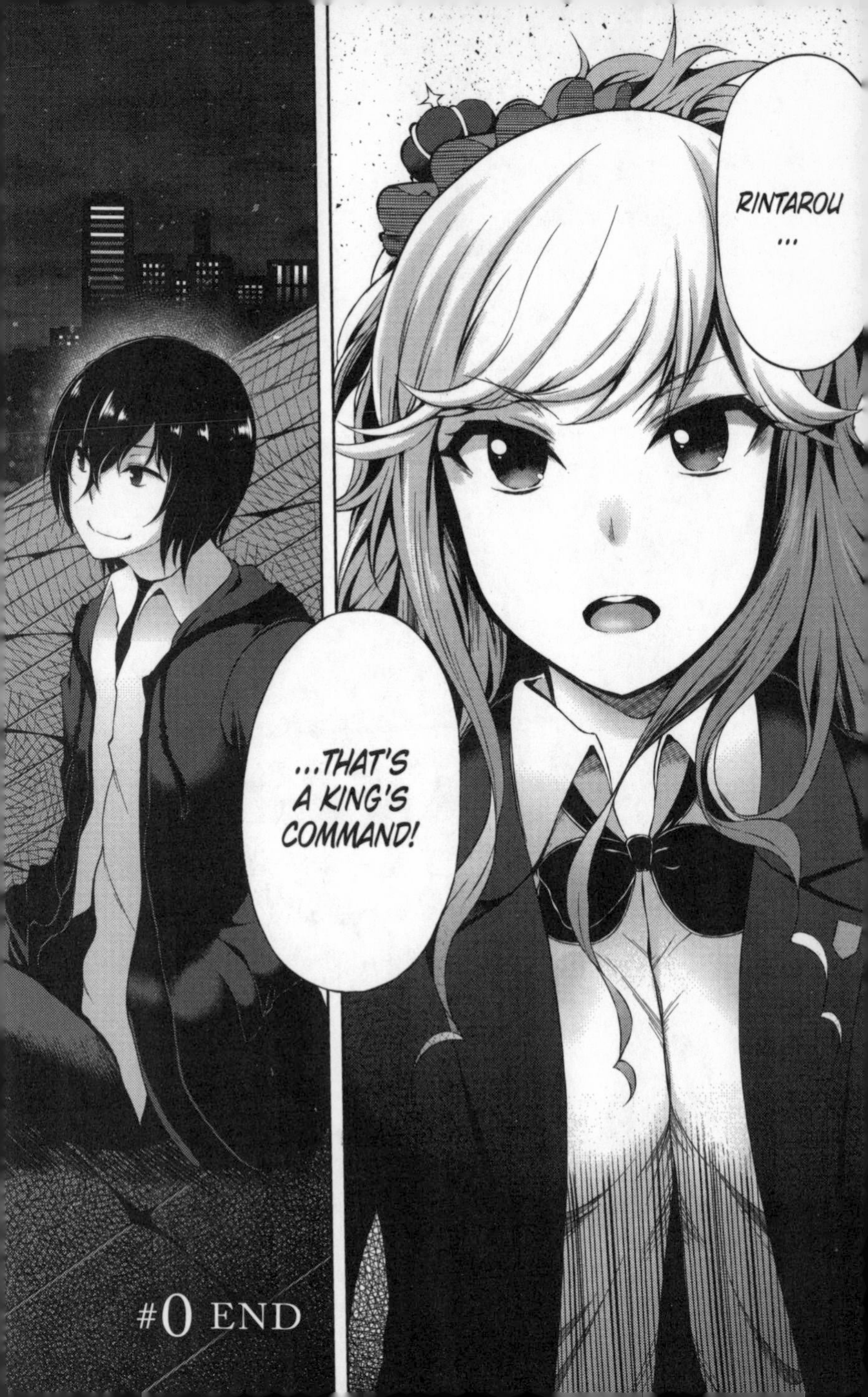
RINTAROU ...
...THAT'S A KING'S COMMAND!
#0 END

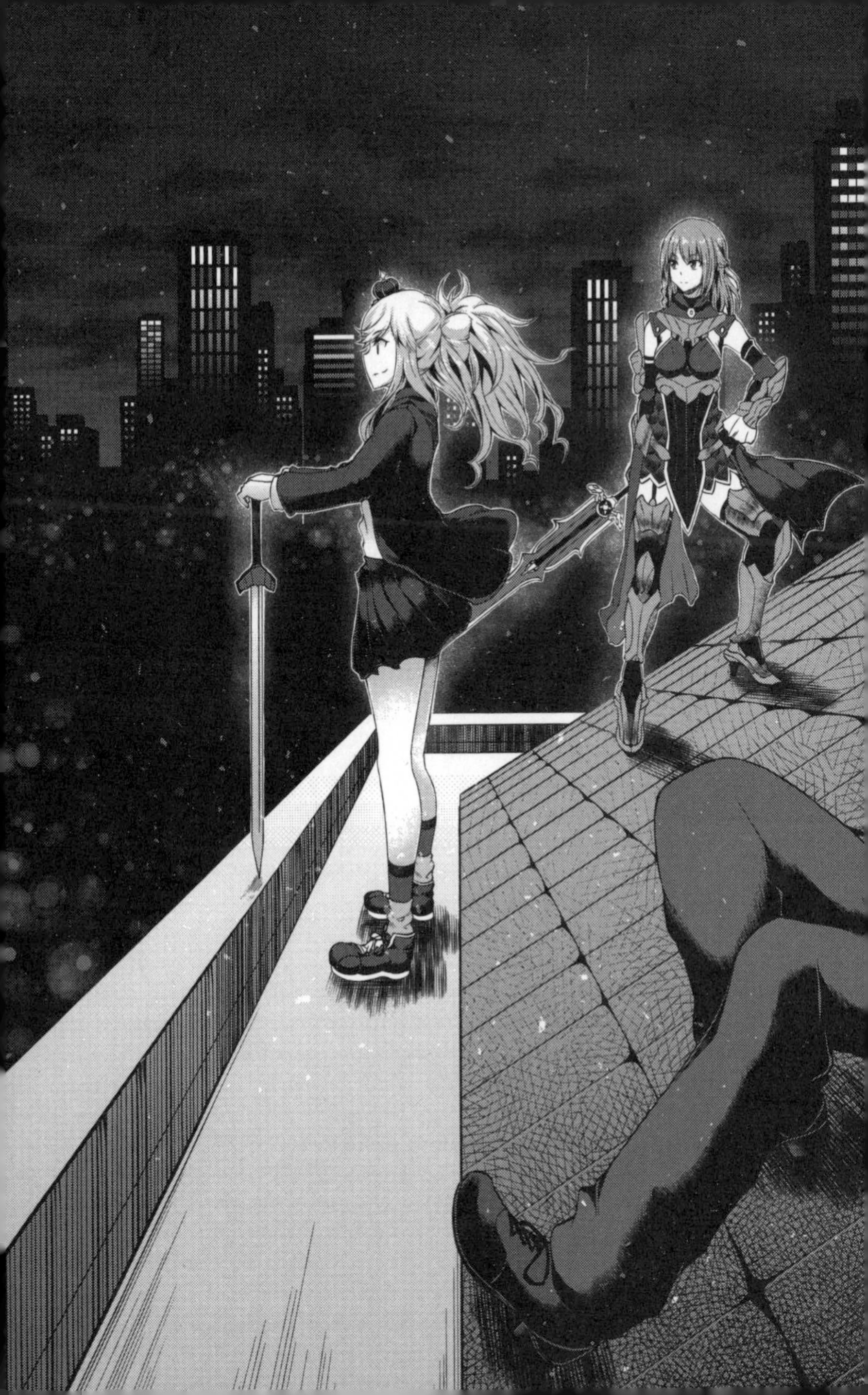

LAST ROUND
ARTHURS

Hello, everyone! I'm Taro Hitsuji, the original author of *Last Round Arthurs*.

This time around, I'd like to sincerely thank those who bought this comic adaptation of the story!

You see, the same happened for my previous work, *Akashic Records of Bastard Magic Instructor*, and I'm genuinely so happy to see the prose I've written rendered like this again in drawn form.

This all happened because of the editing department at Fantasia Bunko, as well as the editorial department at *Young Ace*, those who drew such beautiful drawings— Yuzuriha-sama and Taisuke Umeki-sama—and, most important, you readers who supported *Last Round Arthurs*! Thank you so very much!

The protagonist and heroine of this story are a lot more assertive and idiosyncratic than the ones from my previous work, *Akashic Records*, which makes this one a trying story to write. I hope you'll be able to enjoy both the original novels and the manga version. Thank you very much!

Afterword
Original author: Taro Hitsuji

Nice to meet you. I'm Taisuke Umeki. I'm in charge of the storyboards and composition of the comic version of *Last Round Arthurs.*

Though it's my first time being involved in a work of this format, and I had many anxieties about it, I've somehow powered through it with the help of the original author's lively characters and Yuzuriha-sensei's charming drawings.

I'll work hard to assist in creating a work that properly conveys the charming characters such as Luna and the appearance of the world!

Taisuke Umeki

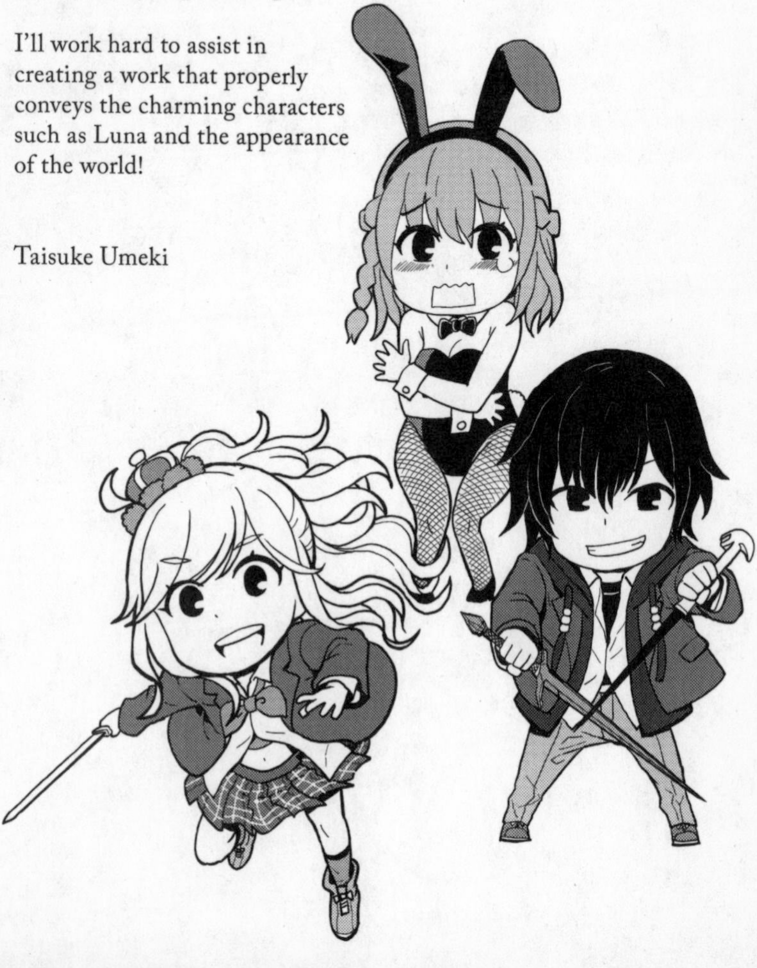

My name is Yuzuriha, and I've been tasked with turning *Last Round Arthurs* into a comic.

Thank you so much for reading the first volume.

Through the help of so many people, this has somehow taken shape. Starting with the managing editor, who set up many of the arrangements before serialization, I have learned so much every day from many amazing people such as my assistants, who have been steadfastly working with me, Umeki-sensei, who supplied genius storyboards every time, Hitsuji-sensei, who wrote such a fiery story, and Haimura-sensei, who drew such charming designs.

Thank you so very, very much.

I hope I grow along with the characters so I can draw cooler and cuter illustrations for the story, which is going to heat up even more from here on out.

Finally, once again, thank you to those who read this book!

Art: Yuzuriha

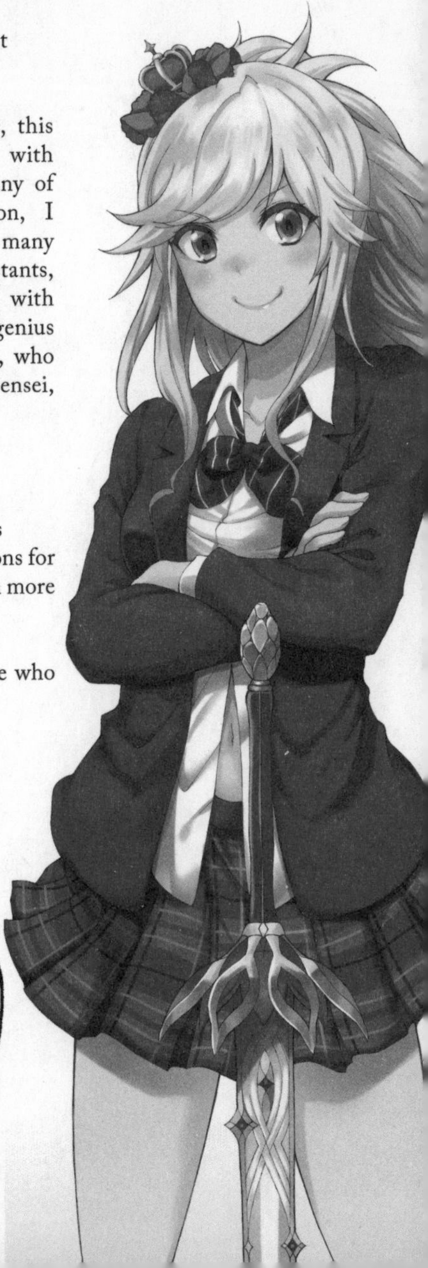

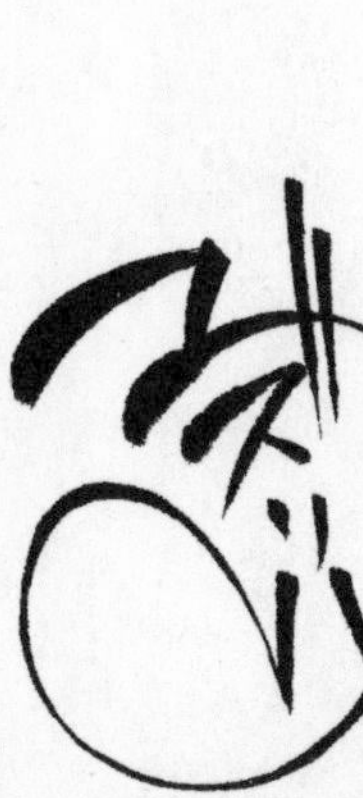

YUZURIHA

STAFF LIST

Art
Yuzuriha

Assistants
Minoru Suto
KOIZUMI

3D & Special Thanks
Kyoujyu Issei

Cover Design
Tsuyoshi Kusano Design Office

LAST ROUND ARTHURS

LAST
ROUND ARTHURS

LAST ROUND ARTHURS

1

ORIGINAL STORY
Taro Hitsuji

ART
Yuzuriha

CHARACTER DESIGN
Kiyotaka Haimura

STORYBOARDS
Taisuke Umeki

Translation: JAN MITSUKO CASH ◆ Lettering: PHIL CHRISTIE

LAST ROUND ARTHURS
©Taro Hitsuji 2019
©Yuzuriha 2019
©Kiyotaka Haimura 2019
©Taisuke Umeki 2019
First published in Japan in 2019 by KADOKAWA CORPORATION, Tokyo. English translation right arranged with KADOKAWA CORPORATION, Tokyo through Tuttle-Mori Agency, Inc.

English translation © 2020 by Yen Press, LLC

Yen Press
150 West 30th Street, 19th Floor
New York, NY 10001

Visit us at yenpress.com ◆ facebook.com/yenpress ◆ twitter.com/yenpress ◆ yenpress.tumblr.com ◆ instagram.com/yenpress

First Yen Press Edition: September 2020

Yen Press is an imprint of Yen Press, LLC.
The Yen Press name and logo are trademarks of Yen Press, LLC.

The publisher is not responsible for websites (or their content) that are not owned by the publisher.

Library of Congress Control Number: 2020938734

ISBN: 978-1-9753-1628-0 (paperback)
978-1-9753-1629-7 (ebook)

10 9 8 7 6 5 4 3 2 1

WOR

Printed in the United States of America